Lidia's Italian-American Kitchen

by Lidia Matticchio Bastianich

Photographs by
Christopher Hirsheimer

Alfred A. Knopf   New York   2001

Lidia's Italian-American Kitchen

THIS IS A BORZOI BOOK
PUBLISHED BY ALFRED A. KNOPF

Copyright © 2001 by A La Carte Communications and Tutti a Tavola, LLC
Photographs © 2001 by Christopher Hirsheimer

All rights reserved under International and Pan-American Copyright
Conventions. Published in the United States by Alfred A. Knopf, a division of
Random House, Inc., New York, and simultaneously in Canada by Random House
of Canada Limited, Toronto. Distributed by Random House, Inc., New York.

www.aaknopf.com

Knopf, Borzoi Books, and the colophon are registered trademarks
of Random House, Inc.

Library of Congress Cataloging-in-Publication Data
Bastianich, Lidia Matticchio.
  [Italian-American kitchen]
  Lidia's Italian-American kitchen / by Lidia Matticchio Bastianich ; photographs by
Christopher Hirsheimer.
    p. cm.
  Includes index.
  ISBN 0-375-41150-X
  1. Cookery, Italian. 2. Cookery, American. I. Title: Italian-American kitchen.
II. Title.
  TX723 .B319 2001
  641.5945—dc21   2001045009

Manufactured in the United States of America
Published November 2, 2001
Second Printing, December 2001

A few years have passed since my last book and the dedication to my angel Olivia. I now have two new angels, Lorenzo Francesco Manuali and Miles Maxwell Bastianich. To you two, my gentlemen angels, I dedicate this book with most profound and unconditional love. Noni has written this book for you, for you truly are the new generation of American Italians.

Contents

Acknowledgments

For me, each stage of writing a cookbook is like capturing a cross-section of my life's history. Every recipe has a story, and every story is a piece of my personal memoir. Along the way to creating and presenting this collection of America's favorite Italian-American recipes, I was deeply touched by the recollections of family, friends, restaurant customers, and members of our television audience who immigrated to America during the last century, bringing their tables with them. They laid the groundwork for America's great love affair with Italian food and culture.

In the process of writing this book and making the television series, I was supported by an enthusiastic, knowledgeable, and caring collection of family, friends, talented professionals, and organizations—their efforts and generosity made it possible for all of us to gather in my kitchen to enjoy the fruits of the collaboration and share *Lidia's Italian-American Kitchen* with you.

First and foremost, this book would not have been possible without the indefatigable support and assistance of four individuals. Chris Styler, my culinary editor and part-time recipe muse (and tester), was the expeditor of any and all food that needed to get into the book and in front of the camera. Shelly Burgess, my public relations director and incredibly able right hand, managed my time and projects with efficiency and ease. Geof Drummond, president of A La Carte Communications, a friend, producer, and writer (when I let him), was the person who saw the possibilities for this book and the series and then made it happen. And made it fun. And my mother, Erminia Matticchio, is not only my constant and unconditional mamma (and nonna to my children and grandchildren), but also a totally available reservoir of memories and inspiration, insight, advice, and direction.

The A La Carte production team, as comfortable and knowledgeable in the kitchen as in a studio, once again captured the essentials of my cooking — not just the preparation and presentation, but the texture and feeling behind it. Director Bruce Franchini and director of photography Dean Gaskill managed to present the food in just the way I would want to serve it. Kimberly Nolan, line producer, was everywhere, bringing order with a smile, without letting a crumb slip through the cracks. Our production team is the best in the business, including Gilles Morin, Eliat Goldman, Tommy Hamilton, Mark Britt, Jerry Cancel, Bob Haggerty, and Aaron Frutman on the technical side; Daisy Martinez and Angela Spensieri in the kitchen; Cathryn McVeigh with makeup; and editor Paul Swensen. Far from the kitchen, in body if not in spirit, Natan Katzman kept logistics on track, Alexandra Yperifanos handled sponsor relations with aplomb, and Hope Reed was the best maitre d' we could ever wish for in serving the series to our PBS stations and their viewers. Kim Yorio handled publicity like a Formula I driver: high performance in good style. At American Public Television, our distributors, Judy Barlow and Chris Funkhauser, provided invaluable help in getting the series out to you, our viewers.

Special thanks go to my son, Joe, and his wife, Deanna, and to my daughter, Tanya, and her husband, Corrado, for their support and participation, and to Giovanni, our de facto master craftsman on set and keeper of the international soccer standings. My dog, Cicia, was present throughout the series and kept a watchful eye on all that passed in and out of the house, particularly on and off the table. She will be remembered warmly every time this book is opened or an episode with her gentle bark in the background is broadcast.

I was thrilled with the opportunity to work with the renowned editor Judith Jones, who has published the best in the culinary field for many years. Judith "got" me — and with patience and prodding encouraged me to write the book I hoped I would write. The talented Christopher Hirsheimer produced all the beautiful and evocative photographs, capturing the simplicity as well as the sensuality and richness of the dishes in this book. Knopf's Paul Bogaards's enthusiasm and energy was and remains contagious and exciting, as he orchestrates my forays into bookstores, media interviews, and luncheons with other people cooking. I am also grateful to Ralph Fowler of Knopf for the beautiful design of the book, to Carol Devine Carson for her creative vision of the jacket, and to Ken Schneider, Judith's assistant, for his thoughtfulness and attention to detail. My agent, Jane Dystel, was always within a call's reach for support—before, during, and after publication.

Fortunato Nicotra, chef at Felidia, and my supportive staff at Felidia and Becco researched and supplied my home kitchen and the set with the best ingredients. They carried the torch at the restaurants in my absence while we were taping, giving me comfort and the time to focus on this book and the shoot. Also, very special thanks to my assistant Miguelina Polanco for juggling my time and schedule so that all this could happen with ease.

All of us owe a special debt of gratitude to our public television series underwriters and the supporters of this book: Colavita olive oil, Monari Federzoni balsamic vinegar of Modena, Cuisinart kitchen appliances and cookware, and Palm Bay Imports, international wine importers. Authentic quality cooking deserves—and requires—quality ingredients and tools. We are proud to have them in our kitchen. Our thanks to John Profaci of Colavita, Sabrina Federzoni and Fabrizio Baraldi of Monari Federzoni, Holly Arnold and Suzanne Sylte of Arnold Media, Paul Ackels, Mary Rodgers and Fabrizio Bottero of Cuisinart, and Marcy Whitman of Palm Bay Imports for their enthusiasm and support of *Lidia's Italian-American Kitchen*. We would also like to acknowledge and give special thanks to Connie Pfander of Ceramica for all of the beautiful plates and platters; Nancy Radke and Ciao Unlimited for the imported Parmigiano-Reggiano; Pam Geren of Crooked Brook for making my aprons; Ronald Keil of Keil Brothers for all of the wonderful plants, flowers, and greenery; Alex Lee and Bea Yang of Oxo for always being there with great kitchen tools; Lauren Peck and Amelia Barrett of Le Creuset for the gorgeous cookware; Julia Stanbulis of Waterford Wedgwood for platters and glassware; and Neil Crumley of Wüsthof-Trident for supplying chef-quality knives to our kitchen.

Introduction

Italian-American food—what cuisine is it? Is it Italian, American, or a piece of Americana with Italian roots? Like a beautiful hybrid flower that takes its genetic makeup from its seeds but derives its colors and aroma from the particular patch of earth in which it grows, it is unquestionably some of each.

I emigrated from Italy to America in 1958. We were considered political refugees, since we came from Istria, the part of Italy that was given to Yugoslavia after World War II. My parents didn't want to raise their children—my brother, Franco, and me—under communism, so we all became political refugees, escaping from Yugoslavia back to Italy. We were housed in San Saba, a refugee camp in Trieste, where we awaited our chance to cross over to the United States, the land of freedom and opportunity.

We spent two years in San Saba with other exiles whose lives had been as torn apart as ours. Although we had family in Trieste, the aftermath of war left everyone in Italy scrambling for survival. Our relatives could offer us only temporary shelter, so my parents decided to search for a new life on a new continent and new opportunities for their still-young children.

There were thousands of Istrians who made a new home in the States during that period, but Italians from all over the peninsula have been putting down roots for years in the United States. The biggest influx of Italian immigrants to the States took place at the turn of the last century, and by 1920 more than 4.5 million Italians had entered the country—most of them from the southern-Italian regions of Sicily, Campania, and Apulia. It is with these first immigrants that Italian-American cuisine and Italian-American culture were born.

As a young immigrant, I was most fascinated by this cuisine, which, although it was called Italian, I did not recognize. True, Italian cuisine is very regional and diversified, but I knew there was something distinctly different about this version of Italian cooking. It was years later that my fascination with food and culture turned into a profession, then into a quest to understand better this particular cuisine. Clearly, it had been developed by a people who came with a rich collection of memories of intense flavors and aromas and a patrimony of recipes and cooking techniques that in this new land had to be executed with different ingredients from those with which the immigrants were familiar.

I guess my fascination with cooking comes from growing up with grandparents who ran a *trattoria,* grew most of the food they sold and ate, produced their own olive oil and wine, distilled their own grappa, and cured their own meats—prosciutto, pancetta, guanciale, and *salsicce.* My grandma dried beans, figs, and raisins, as well as herbs and all members of the onion family, for the winter. I still remember going with her to the communal mill to grind the wheat into flour for pasta and bread. This "from-the-earth" understanding and respect for food has given me a definite advantage as a cook. Those pristine, unadulterated flavors remain with me and have become my reference library throughout my professional life.

My mother, Erminia, was an elementary school teacher in Italy and was very concerned about her children's education. She anticipated great opportunities for us in the States and felt that education for her children was the greatest gift America had to offer. But for her, life in the new country was not easy. She worked hard and long hours as a piece-worker, tailoring men's clothing at the Evan-Picone factory in North Bergen, New Jersey, so we could go to school.

Throughout high school, I worked part time at Walken's Bakery on Broadway in Astoria, right across the street from our apartment. I loved it. I began as a salesgirl but slowly gravitated toward the "back of the house," assisting the bakers in their baking, decorating, and really getting into the production of breads and desserts. It soon became evident to me that this was what I loved doing.

By no means was I a chef then, but I loved cooking. Throughout my younger years I used to prepare dinner for the family almost every night, when my mother commuted from New Jersey to Astoria, Queens, where we lived at the time. It was then that I first began exploring the world of new foods. I had never tasted a grapefruit before, or coconut, mango, or peanut butter. Tapioca was a novelty, and so were all those prepackaged goodies such as Jell-O, instant puddings, and cake mixes. Every one of these alien foods was exciting to try. I especially remember baking blueberry muffins from a mix. We all loved them, and they were so easy to make. I thought they were the ultimate until I discovered Wonder Bread. To me it was a true wonder that one slice of bread could be rolled into a lump the size of a glass marble, or that two slices of this wonder bread could, with a little pressure, take the shape and color of whatever they were sandwiching. What a marvel of food technology, I thought then.

My brother earned his Ph.D. in electronics engineering, and I received scholarships and attended Hunter College in New York City to finish my major in biology. But I fell in love and married without finishing out my years at college, much to my mother's dismay.

Courtship with my then husband led me to restaurants, and I began working in Italian-American restaurants, first as a hostess or waitress, then, inevitably, in the kitchen. I enjoyed working in the Italian-American restaurants of that time, but I was still puzzled at how different the food was from what we prepared and served at home. I can't say that I did not recognize everything. Most of the ingredients—tomatoes, cheeses, dry pasta, and fresh pasta—were familiar, but finished dishes like veal *parmigiana*, for example, was a dish I did not recall eating in Italy. *Vitello alla parmigiana* as served in Parma was a breaded veal cutlet or chop, topped with grated Parmigiano-Reggiano cheese. Spaghetti and meatballs was another dish that I had not encountered. We may have had *spaghetti al sugo*, or *spaghetti bolognese,* and we ate *polpette,* flat meatballs fried and served as a main dish with vegetables, but we never had the two served together.

In 1971, when I was twenty-four, my husband and I decided to open our own restaurant. A good opportunity came about when a small, thirty-seat restaurant went up for sale on Queens Boulevard, a busy, well-populated neighborhood in Forest Hills, Queens. With a little money we had saved and a loan from Mom and Dad, we were in business. We named the new restaurant Buonavia, "on the good road," and began planning and building. Looking over the many menus we had collected from the most popular and successful Italian restaurants of the time, we realized that what our clientele knew and wanted was Italian-American food. But we had a plan: We hired the best Italian-American chef we could find, and I went to work as his sous-chef. I learned as much as I could from him while cooking some of my traditional dishes, such as gnocchi, polenta, and risotto, and adding them slowly to the menu. We became wildly popular, and for the next ten years we ran two of the most popular Italian restaurants in Queens, adding Villa Secondo, in Fresh Meadows, about six years after we opened Buonavia.

I received many accolades for bringing traditional Italian cooking to my customers. But what I did not realize then was that in those ten years I had learned a new cuisine, the Italian-American cuisine.

In 1981, we were ready to move to Manhattan and sold both restaurants to open Felidia, a restaurant that went on to receive three stars from the *New York Times* and nationwide recognition for serving "true" Italian fare. Felidia is still the epicenter of my activities, although our reach has extended to several restaurants—Becco and Esca in New York City, and Lidia's in Kansas City and Pittsburgh. Several years ago, we started Esperienze Italiane, a travel company that specializes in the food, wine, culture, and art of Italy.

My infectious passion has touched both of my children. Joseph, besides being a great businessman and restaurateur, is passionate about wine and produces wonderful wines in Friuli, Italy. He is married to Deanna, and together they have blessed me with two grandchildren, Olivia and Miles. My daughter, Tanya, an art historian with a tremendous passion for Italian culture and art, received her Ph.D. in Italian Renaissance art from Oxford. Tanya and her husband, Corrado Manuali, a Roman attorney, have blessed me with another grandson, Lorenzo.

But there is an irony in all this success. While I, along with many of my contemporary colleagues, preached and practiced "*la vera cucina italiana*," and set out to bring the True Italian Culinary Culture to America, Italian-American cooking was being dismissed as an impostor by journalists and professionals alike. Still, the experience of those ten years in Queens, and the popularity of the dishes I served there, haunted me. I felt there was something real in that cuisine, a feeling that was reinforced by my frequent travels across America, where Italians—by now third- and fourth-generation—are still cooking this food, and their customers are still in love with it.

I just needed to get to the bottom of this phenomenon. Some of the answers became apparent when I read *La Storia: Five Centuries of the Italian American Experience* by Jerre Mangione and Ben Morreale (HarperPerennial Library, 1993).

Five hundred years ago, what did my *compatrioti* (countrymen) find in this new land? Did they find basilico, oregano, or rosemary? Did they find sweet and ripe San Marzano tomatoes, *broccoli di rabe,* or radicchio? I doubt if they found virgin olive oil, Parmigiano-Reggiano, fresh mozzarella, or ricotta. How sad and unaromatic their cupboard must have seemed to those early immigrants. They had to cook with the ingredients that were available, led by the memory of the flavors they recalled. And therein lies the beginning of the answer to "What is Italian-American cuisine?"

In Italy, the herbs are so aromatic, the San Marzano tomatoes are so sweet and intense, that with a touch of virgin olive oil and a sliced garlic clove you have the best marinara sauce in the world. How did the immigrants, who had no access to such ingredients, capture those flavor memories? I assume they tried to re-create the intense flavors of their homeland by adding a lot of what they did have—garlic, oregano, and other dried herbs, herbs that they most likely brought with them. On the other hand, meat was abundant in this new land. It was a symbol of well-being for the immigrants—a sign of the good life—and so the Sunday ragù, which back in Campania would have been flavored with a piece of pork, was enriched with sausages, *braciole,* and meatballs. This new cuisine devised by the early Italian immigrants was one of adaptation—one that went beyond cooking. It was a way for them to retain their culture proudly by using the ingredients they found in their new home. I would call this a venerable cuisine indeed.

Among the diversified ethnic immigrants who came to the United States, most Italians intended eventually to return home, after making enough money to build a new house for their families, according to *La Storia.* This led to the immigration of many single men, who in most cases lived in boarding houses where food was provided along with lodging. It is there that the Italian-American restaurant most likely had its birth. Not only were the residents fed, the public at large enjoyed the food, and the families that ran the boarding houses saw an opportunity to make additional money. With the increase in business from restaurant guests came the need for authentic ingredients, so Italians became the first ethnic group to set up import companies to provide the products they craved.

Americans love Italy and the Italians, their style, cars, wine, and food. So much so that, according to a poll taken by the Restaurant Association in 1998, the number-one ethnic cuisine is Italian. Americans fell in love with Italian-American cuisine first, then with regional Italian cooking. There is an old Italian saying *"Il primo amore non si scorda mai"* (the first love you never forget). And so it is with Americans and Italian-American food.

Here I offer you not only the classic Italian-American recipes—your "first love"—but some of my own creations and some classic Italian dishes that have become part of the American culinary culture. After all, cuisine, like other aspects of our lives, is not static but constantly evolving. Every time I return from Italy, I bring with me another piece of my homeland, sometimes traditional and sometimes contemporary. Culinary culture is not just what has happened in the past; it is what is happening today and what will be tomorrow. Today's innovation is tomorrow's tradition.

My life has been a commitment to carrying on the authenticity and tradition of the Italian cuisine in the United States. I recall the excitement created over the years by the arrival of authentic Italian products and how those products introduced my guests—who had been enjoying the pleasures of Italian-American cooking—to regional Italian cooking.

By the early seventies, I could get Arborio rice here, and that meant I could finally offer my clients a true risotto—not one made with long-grain rice. When Gorgonzola *dolce latte* became available, I served it drizzled with honey alongside ripe pears, or just melted over gnocchi. These simple flavors said "Italy" with every bite. In the beginning of the eighties (when I was running Felidia and Becco in Manhattan), fresh porcini mushrooms and white truffles caused a sensation. That was my first opportunity since I opened my own restaurant to sense the excitement, which still exists today, of inquisitive guests experiencing the pungent aroma of truffles floating throughout the restaurant and their delight when this potatolike tuber is shaved on top of a steaming plate of fresh egg pasta, right under their noses. When the import ban was lifted in the late eighties, traditional Prosciutto di Parma and Prosciutto di San Daniele began coming into the States to join the other newly discovered pleasures of the Italian table. These breakthrough products were imported and brought to the restaurants mostly by Italian merchants who, along with chefs, sensed that America was ready for these delicacies.

Italian-American food is a cuisine unto itself. It has become a part of us—a slice of Americana. And that is what makes America, the piecing together of a slice of every culture, which in total makes a great whole.

With this book I'll humbly try to pay homage to all of those Italians who came before me and laid the foundation so that we could all have a better life, immigrants and natives alike.

To you Italian-Americans I raise a glass of wine—a glass of Italian wine—as I salute you.

P.S. Running restaurants in New York, Pittsburgh, and Kansas City and hosting a cooking program that airs nationally on PBS give me an advantage that most cookbook authors don't have. I am accessible to my readers, both in person at the restaurants and via our website (lidiasitaly.com), through which I receive many letters and e-mails from you, my readers, viewers, and fellow cooks.

I appreciate this connection with you very much. It gives me a sense of what you like, what new things you'd like to see, and how I can improve. But most of all, I love when you share with me your sentiments and feelings. The first *Italian-American Kitchen* television shows that aired evoked many special sentiments among you. I would like to thank you for conveying them to me and, as you will see, I have selected some excerpts from them and scattered them throughout this book. I am sorry that there wasn't space enough to include all. But keep those e-mails coming. I read every one of them.

Lidia's Italian-American Kitchen

Television Series

In Order of Broadcast

Antipasti Caldi

Vongole Oreganate
Clams Casino
Stuffed Mushrooms
Roasted Pepper Halves with Bread
    Crumb Topping
Scampi alla Buonavia

The Lasagna Show

Caesar Salad
Italian-American Meat Sauce
Italian-American Lasagna

Welcome to My Seaside Kitchen

Bass Fillets with Olive-Caper
    Tomato Sauce
Swiss Chard Braised with Oil
    and Garlic
Scampi
Rice Timbales

The Mother of All Sauces

"Italian-American Sunday Sauce"
    with Rigatoni
Meatballs
Braciola di Manzo
Broccoli Rabe with Oil and Garlic

A Light Dinner

Tri-Color Salad
Sole Meunière
Fillet of Sole with a Light Bread
  Crumb Stuffing
Sole Oreganata
Spinach Sautéed with Bread
  Crumbs

Quick-Fix Dinners

Chicken Stock
Roman "Egg Drop" Soup
"Reinforced" Soup
Polpette
Wild Greens and Hard-Boiled
  Egg Salad

The Real Veal: Scallopine

Veal Scallopine in Lemon-
  Caper Sauce
Steamed Broccoli with Oil
  and Garlic
Veal Scallopine with Eggplant
  and Fontina Cheese
Veal Pizzaiola

Antipasti Freddi

Cherry Peppers Stuffed with
  Prosciutto and Provolone
Poached Seafood Salad
Striped Bass Salad
Prosciutto-Stuffed Mozzarella
Pickled Mushrooms
Seasoned Olives

Most Requested
Pasta Dishes

Penne alla Vodka
Rigatoni Woodsman-Style
Linguine with Mussels,
  Saffron, and Zucchini

Lobster Extravaganza

Lobster fra Diavolo with
  Spaghettini
San Martino Pear and
  Chocolate Tart

The Wrap and Roll Show

Manicotti
Meat and Spinach Cannelloni
Béchamel Sauce

The Big Buffet:
Do-Ahead Entertaining,
Italian-American Style

Ziti with Roasted Eggplant and
  Ricotta Cheese
Sausage and Peppers
Zucchini and Cherry Tomato
  Salad

Our Friend, the Cod

Salt Cod in the Style of
  Marechiara
Salt Cod, Potato, and
  String Bean Salad
Fillet of Fresh Cod with
  Lemon-Parsley Sauce

Welcome, Mangiafagioli

Arugula and White-Bean
  Salad
Pasta and Beans
Roasted Pears and Grapes

The Incredible Edible Eggplant

Eggplant Parmigiana
Eggplant Rollatini
Eggplant Fans

The Royal Family of Milanese Dishes

Pan-Fried Parmigiano-
  Reggiano–Coated Veal
  Scallopine
Chicken Parmigiana,
  New-Style
Pork Chops Capricciosa
Warm Potato, Onion, and
  Caper Salad

A Midsummer Meal

Marinated Artichokes
Rice Salad Caprese
Coffee Granita

A Sicilian Menu

Caponata
Spaghetti with Capers
  and Anchovies
Swordfish Skewers Glazed
  with Sweet and
  Sour Sauce

Fresh Pasta Bolognese, Two Ways

Fresh Egg Pasta
Tagliolini/Pasta
  Sheets/Pappardelle
Meat Sauce Bolognese
Fazzoletti

Dinner in Minutes

Spinach Salad
Stuffed Rolls of Veal
Pignoli Cookies

A Winter Dinner

Lentil and Broccoli Soup
Rustic-Cut Roasted Lamb
  Shoulder

Top Chops

Stuffed Veal Chop Valdostana
  and Broccoli-Taleggio
  Variation
Potato Croquettes

Dinner in Rome

Pot-Roasted Herb-Scented
  Pork Loin (Porchetta)
Braised Fennel
Braised Whole Radishes
  or Turnips

A Lesson in Risotto

Mushroom Risotto

Seaside Kitchen III

Capellini with Crabmeat
Stuffed Calamari Braised
with Fresh Peas

Give It a Fry

Fritto Misto
Tri-Color Salad

Light and Quick

Fried Banana Peppers
Shrimp in a Chunky Marinara
Sauce over Pasta and
over Fregola

Something Old, Something New

Risi e Bisi
Short Ribs of Beef Braised
in Barolo, with Carrots
and Onions

A Pasta Chronology

Baked Stuffed Shells
Whole-Wheat Linguine
Primavera
Capellini Cooked in
Red-Mullet Stew

Gnocchi Fest

Gnocchi
Gnocchi alla Bava
Gnocchi with Pesto, Potatoes,
and String Beans

Snack Time

Fried Potatoes and Eggs
Broccoli Rabe and Sausage
Ricotta Frittata
Pickled Vegetables

Cooking with Bread

Swiss Chard (or String Bean)
and Bread Soup
Broccoli Rabe with
Day-Old Bread
Pasta with Garlic, Anchovies,
and Bread Crumbs

Seafood Masterpiece

Mackerel in Saor
Savory Seafood Stew

An Informal Seaside Dinner

Clams in a Savory Tomato-
Vegetable Broth
Monkfish Meatballs in
Tomato Sauce

A Visit to the Butcher

Oxtail "Butcher-Style"
Braised Oxtail with
Rigatoni
Brussels Sprouts or Savoy
Cabbage Braised with
Vinegar

Two Italian-American Classics

Seared Filet Mignon with
Braised Chunky Vegetables
(Bistecca Giambotta)
Chocolate Tartufo

Half-Hour Chicken Dinners

Chicken Scallopine Marsala
with Garlic Mashed
Potatoes
Chicken Francese
Chicken Paillard with Sage
Leaves
Tuna and Chickpea Salad

Sunday Chicken Dinner

Shells with Fennel and Shrimp
Chicken Bites with Potatoes,
Sausages, and Vinegar

Sausage Making

Homemade Italian Sausage
Gemelli (Twins) with Sausage-
Tomato Sauce
Whole-Wheat Pasta with
Sausages, Leeks, and
Shredded Fontina

Ribs, Italian-American Style

Spare Ribs Roasted with
Vinegar and Red Pepper
Braised Kale with Bacon

Rustic Dinner

Beef-and-Rice Stuffed Peppers
Olive Oil Mashed Potatoes
Struffoli

Pasta Time

Buccatini with Chanterelles,
Spring Peas, and Prosciutto
Ricotta Gnocchi with Contessa
Sauce
Spaghetti with Mushrooms,
Garlic, and Parsley

Lidia's Italian-American Kitchen

Antipasti

Among the many things Italians brought with them to this country is their love for antipasti—those little bites to nibble on before the meal. An antipasto can be as simple as *prosciutto e melone, affetati* (an assortment of sliced, cured meats), or a lemony seafood salad. Or it can take up the better part of a table with a display of vegetables that are grilled, pickled, tossed in vinaigrette, broiled to golden brown, or fried; fish that has been cured, preserved in oil or salt, tossed in a salad, or made into a terrine; as well as all kinds of cured meats, cheeses, legumes, salads, and *crostate* (savory pastries). Whether simple or elaborate, an antipasto is meant to stimulate the taste buds and start the gastric juices flowing with an assortment of flavors, textures, colors, and aromas.

At home antipasti were usually made up of foods that could be found in the cupboard—cured, marinated, smoked, dried, or otherwise preserved foods and meats, and an assortment of dried or aged cheeses. In Italian-American restaurants of the 1970s and '80s, "antipasto" meant a plate of prosciutto, salami, cacciatorini, cheese, roasted peppers and all kinds of vegetables—artichokes, *giardiniera,* pickled mushrooms, assorted olives, beans—tuna in oil, anchovies, and hard-boiled eggs. All this would be dressed with some virgin olive oil and wine vinegar. Today, antipasti include a whole repertoire of hot preparations and salads in addition to these traditional favorites.

It is easier than ever to present an authentic family-style antipasto at home, because it is easier to get traditional products imported from Italy. Prosciutto, whether from Parma or the type of prosciutto known as San Daniele, from Friuli—is the king of any antipasto assortment and can now be found across the United States, as can many imported Italian cheeses, cured fish, and vegetables. The surest way to capture the flavors, colors, and textures of a culture is by using authentic products. If you take a bite of Parmigiano-Reggiano cheese or taste a drop of *aceto balsamico tradizionale,* there is no doubt in your mind, or on your palate, that you are eating Italian. Use that to your advantage and search out these authentic products, which will bring your table that much closer to Italy. And remember that cooking techniques are also important to the authenticity of a dish. In this chapter I share with you some of the antipasti that have become my favorites.

This appetizer was very popular at my first restaurant, Buonavia, which opened in 1971. It was a time when lots and lots of chopped garlic was used in Italian-American cooking. If you like a milder garlic flavor, use crushed or sliced garlic cloves instead, and remove them from the dish before you serve it.

Scampi Appetizer "Alla Buonavia"

Scampi alla Buonavia

3 tablespoons extra-virgin olive oil, plus more for finishing dish

3 cloves garlic, chopped fine

1 pound extra-large (about 25 to the pound) shrimp, completely shelled, deveined, and cut crosswise into 3 pieces

1 tablespoon chopped fresh chives

½ cup dry white wine

4 tablespoons unsalted butter, cut into 4 pieces

1 tablespoon lemon juice

1 tablespoon chopped fresh Italian parsley

½ teaspoon crushed hot red pepper

Salt

6 slices Italian bread (about ¼ inch thick and 2½ inches wide), toasted and kept warm

1 lemon, cut into slices

Whole chives and/or parsley sprigs, optional

Makes 6 servings

In this dish, high heat and speed are essential. Make sure the pan is good and hot when you add the shrimp and that it is wide enough to hold all the shrimp pieces in a single layer (so the pan doesn't cool down as the shrimp go in). And be sure to have all your ingredients right by the stove—once the shrimp go into the pan, it's "full speed ahead."

Heat 3 tablespoons olive oil in a large skillet, over medium heat. Add the garlic and cook, shaking the pan, until light golden, about 2 minutes. Raise the heat to high, add the shrimp, and toss until they are bright pink and seared on all sides, about 2 minutes. Stir in the chopped chives, then add the wine, butter, and lemon juice. Bring to a boil, and boil until the shrimp are barely opaque in the center and the sauce is reduced by half, about 2 minutes. Stir in the chopped parsley and crushed red pepper. Season with salt.

Place a piece of warm toast in the center of each of six warm plates. Spoon the shrimp and sauce over the toast, drizzling some of the sauce around the toast. Decorate the plates with lemon slices, and with the parsley sprigs and/or whole chives, if using.

The restaurant business is tough on family life. Joseph, my son, was only four years old when we opened our first restaurant, Buonavia, in Forest Hills, Queens. He would spend many days playing on tomato boxes, and when he got a little older, he would make pocket money by standing on a milk crate and helping with the dishes or the preparation of the day's vegetables. But he did have his rewards, and a plate of clams casino was one of his favorites.

Clams Casino

36 littleneck clams

4 tablespoons finely chopped fresh Italian parsley

2 red or yellow bell peppers, roasted and peeled as described on next page, cut into 1-inch squares

12 slices bacon, cut into 1-inch squares

6 tablespoons unsalted butter

1 cup dry white wine

Makes 6 servings

You can prepare the clams right in their baking dish up to several hours in advance and bake them just before you serve them.

Preheat the oven to 450° F.

Shuck the clams as described on page 7, reserving the clam juice and arranging the clams on the half shell side by side in a 13 × 11–inch baking dish. Strain the juice through cheesecloth or a very fine sieve into the baking dish. Sprinkle some of the parsley over the clams. Top each clam with a square of roasted pepper. Cover the pepper with two squares of bacon. Using about 3 tablespoons of the butter, dot the top of each clam with about $1/4$ teaspoon butter. Cut the remaining butter into several pieces and tuck them in and around the clams in the baking dish. Add the wine and remaining parsley to the baking dish.

Bake until the bacon is crisp and the pan juices are bubbling, about 12 minutes. Arrange clams on a warmed serving platter, or divide them among warmed plates. Pour the pan juices into a small saucepan and bring to a boil on top of the stove. Boil until lightly thickened, 1 to 2 minutes. Spoon the juices over the clams and serve immediately.

To Shuck Hard-Shell Clams

To OPEN CLAMS, you will need a clam knife—a thick-handled, round-tipped, and blunt-edged knife designed specifically for this purpose. Don't use a paring knife, or you will do damage to the blade and can cut yourself.

Place the clams in a large bowl of cold water and swish them to clean the shells. With a stiff brush, scrub the shells, including the joints. Dump the cleaned clams into a colander and, when all are scrubbed, rinse them under cold water. Drain thoroughly. Spread the clams out in a baking pan and put them in the freezer for 20 minutes.

Take a look at a clam and you'll notice one side is evenly rounded and one side has a pronounced protrusion. With your hands over a bowl to catch the juices, place a clam in the palm of your non-knife-wielding hand so the hinge and smooth side of the shell rest against the fleshy part of your palm, at the base of your thumb. Insert the blade of the knife between the two shells against the little protrusion and, while applying firm pressure, wiggle the blade between the shells. Once the shells are pried apart, work the blade of the knife along the top shell, freeing the clam and cutting through the two muscles that hold the shells together. Twist off and discard the top shell. Run the knife along the bottom shell, cutting through the two muscles and completely freeing the clam.

Flick any bits of shell out of the clam with the tip of the clam knife. You can rinse the clams to remove all traces of shell, but you'll lose a lot of flavor. Drain the reserved liquid through cheesecloth.

Two Ways to Roast a Bell Pepper

ROASTING PEPPERS imparts a subtle flavor to them, softens the texture, and removes the skin—which some people find hard to digest. Here are two ways to roast a pepper. Whether roasting green, red, or yellow peppers, choose thick-fleshed peppers that are boxy in shape—they will char more evenly and be easier to peel.

Turn the gas burners on high and, working with a pair of long-handled tongs, place the peppers on the grates, directly over the flames. Roast the peppers, turning them as necessary, until evenly blackened on all sides, about 8 minutes. Remove the peppers, place them in a bowl, and cover tightly with plastic wrap. Let stand until cool enough to handle, about 40 minutes.

Or place a rack in the uppermost position and preheat the oven to 475° F. Put the peppers on a baking sheet and roast them, turning as necessary, until all sides are evenly blackened, about 12 minutes. Remove the peppers to a bowl and cover tightly with plastic wrap. Let stand until cool enough to handle, about 40 minutes.

To peel the peppers: Pull out the stems and hold the peppers upside down, letting the seeds and juices flow out. Cut the peppers in half lengthwise and, using a short knife, scrape away the blackened skin, ribs, and remaining seeds.

This is a tasty dish adored by many people. Shucking the clams is easy, if you follow the directions on page 7. And it beats steaming them open, which toughens the clams.

Baked Clams Oreganata

Vongole Oreganate

½ cup extra-virgin olive oil

3 cloves garlic, sliced

36 littleneck clams

½ cup dry white wine

3 tablespoons chopped fresh Italian parsley

2 tablespoons unsalted butter, cut into small pieces

½ teaspoon crushed hot red pepper, chopped fine

2 cups coarse, dry bread crumbs

¼ cup grated Parmigiano-Reggiano cheese

¼ cup cubed (¼-inch) peeled and seeded tomatoes (see Note below)

1 teaspoon dried oregano, preferably the Sicilian or Greek type dried on the branch, crumbled

1 lemon, cut into thin slices

Makes 6 servings

I always add diced fresh tomato to this dish, because I think it contributes a little freshness. Now is the time to try to find the Greek or Sicilian oregano dried right on the branch—it makes a difference. Many Greek and Italian groceries will have it. You can buy powdered hot red pepper, but I like to chop up the flakes myself.

Let the oil and garlic steep in a small bowl 30 minutes to 2 hours.

Preheat oven to 475° F. Shuck the clams as described on page 7, reserving the clam juice. Strain the juice through cheesecloth or a very fine sieve into a 13 × 11–inch baking dish. Add the white wine, 1½ tablespoons of the parsley, the butter, and half of the crushed red pepper.

In a deep bowl, toss the bread crumbs, grated cheese, tomatoes, 3 tablespoons of the garlic-infused oil, the remaining 1½ tablespoons chopped parsley, the oregano, and the remaining ¼ teaspoon crushed red pepper until thoroughly blended.

Top each clam with about 1½ tablespoons of the bread-crumb topping, packing it down tight. Set clams in the prepared baking pan and drizzle the remaining infused oil over them. Bake until the pan juices are bubbling and the bread crumbs are golden brown, 12 to 15 minutes. Transfer the clams to a warm platter or divide among serving plates.

To keep the bread-crumb topping crunchy, spoon the sauce from the baking dish onto the plates—not over the clams. Serve immediately, garnished with the lemon slices.

USE THIS METHOD WITH EITHER plum or round tomatoes. Bring a large pot of water to a boil and set a bowl of ice water near the stove. Cut the cores out of the tomatoes and cut a small x in the opposite end. Slip a few tomatoes into the boiling water and cook just until the skin loosens, 1 to 2 minutes depending on the tomatoes. (Overcooking will make them soggy.) Fish the tomatoes out of the water with a wire skimmer or slotted spoon and drop them into the ice water. If necessary, let the water return to the boil and repeat with any remaining tomatoes. Slip the skins off the blanched tomatoes and cut the tomatoes in half—lengthwise for plum tomatoes, crosswise for round tomatoes. Gently squeeze out the seeds with your hands. The tomatoes are now ready to dice or cut as described in the recipe.

To Peel and Seed Tomatoes

Sweet and Sour Marinated Vegetables (page 52)

Baked Clams Oreganata (page 8)

Sardinian Old Bread and Tomato Casserole (page 360)

Stuffed Rolls of Veal (page 224)

Tripe in Tomato, Carrot, and Celery Sauce, Roman-Style (page 228)

Pan-Seared Steak with Pizzaiola Sauce (page 214)

Mostaccioli with Fresh Basil and Mozzarella (page 110)

Bucatini with Chanterelles, Spring Peas, and Prosciutto (page 113)

Garden-Style Whole-Wheat Pasta (page 118)

Capellini Cooked in Red-Mullet Stew (page 132)

Marinara Sauce (page 150)

Tomato Sauce (page 151)

Agnolotti with Crabmeat and Shrimp in Clam Sauce (page 192)

Chicken Parmigiana, New-Style (page 266)

It's funny, but in American cooking dishes aren't often named after places the way Italian dishes are. Think of *risotto alla milanese* and *pesto alla genovese*. I think some of the most familiar dishes in Italian-American cooking were given place names by immigrants who came from Italian neighborhoods with colorful names like Marechiara and Posillipo. Maybe the first time they made this dish on these shores, they said, "Ah, mussels like we used to eat in Posillipo."

Mussels in Spicy Tomato Sauce

Cozze alla Posillipo

¼ cup cornmeal

2 pounds large mussels, preferably cultivated

¼ cup extra-virgin olive oil, plus more for finishing the dish if you like

8 cloves garlic, sliced

One 1-pint basket ripe cherry tomatoes, cut in half, or 2 cups canned Italian plum tomatoes, crushed

½ teaspoon dried oregano, preferably the Sicilian or Greek type dried on the branch, crumbled

½ teaspoon crushed hot red pepper

1 cup dry white wine

10 large fresh basil leaves, shredded

Salt to taste

Makes 6 servings

This dish can wear many hats. As is, it makes a light appetizer. Served with a zoccolo (fried bread "clog"—see the recipe that follows), it becomes a more substantial main course. Or you can prepare the mussels as described and toss them with freshly cooked linguine. This recipe will make enough sauce for a pound of linguine—six generous servings.

To purge mussels of their grit, stir the cornmeal into 3 quarts of water, add the mussels, and let them soak, shaking them up once or twice, for 1 hour. Drain completely, scrub the shells well, and, if necessary, remove the wiry "beard" protruding from the shell by tugging firmly with your fingers.

Heat ¼ cup of the olive oil in a large skillet. Add the garlic and cook, shaking the pan, until golden, about 3 minutes. Slide the tomatoes into the skillet and stir in the oregano and red pepper. Cook, stirring, until the tomatoes have cooked down, about 5 minutes. Stir the mussels into the skillet, then pour in the wine. Bring to a boil, cover the pot, and cook just until the mussels are opened, about 3 minutes for cultivated mussels, slightly longer for thicker-shelled noncultivated mussels. Stir in the basil and, if you like, a generous drizzle of olive oil. Check the seasoning and add a little salt if necessary.

Discard any mussels with unopened shells. Divide the mussels among warmed serving bowls, topping each serving with a *zoccolo*, if you like.

☞ Make sure, whenever you buy mussels, they feel heavy in the palm of your hands and the shells are shut tight.

This oversize crouton looks like a chunky clog—hence the odd name. The texture of the bread you use for *zoccoli* should be firm, but not too dense. Whether you will need more than one loaf depends on the size and shape of the bread you are using.

Fried Bread "Clog"

Zoccolo

Day-old country-style bread from a loaf or loaves large enough to yield six pieces of bread cut as described below.

Vegetable oil as needed

Makes 6 servings

You know how I feel about "recycling" food—making sure we don't waste anything. This is the perfect place to use a big piece of day-old or 2-day-old bread. Even the trimmings from the bread can be turned into bread crumbs. Why buy them when you can make them yourself? The zoccolo *will be crispy on the outside, tender inside. The longer it sits in the juice from the mussels, the more it will absorb.*

Cut the crust off the bread and trim the bread into six pieces, each approximately $3^{1}/_{2} \times 2^{1}/_{2} \times 1^{1}/_{2}$ inches.

Pour enough oil into a large, deep skillet to fill $1^{1}/_{2}$ inches. Heat over medium heat to 350° F, or until a corner of one of the bread pieces gives off a lively sizzle when dipped into the oil. Add half the bread pieces and fry, turning as necessary, until golden brown on all sides, about 5 minutes. As they fry, adjust the heat under the pan to maintain a steady temperature. Drain on paper towels and repeat with the remaining bread. The *zoccoli* may be prepared several hours in advance. If so, you can rewarm them in a low oven while preparing the mussels.

Artichokes are very Italian and very delicious. Spring artichokes coincide with the first fresh mint of the season, and the arrival of the two is cause for excitement, particularly in and around Rome. Artichokes turn brown quickly when you are cleaning them, so be sure to have some water acidulated with lemon juice handy to soak them in once they are trimmed.

Stuffed Artichokes

Carciofi Imbottiti

6 tablespoons Garlic-Infused Oil (page 17) or extra-virgin olive oil

3 lemons

6 large artichokes

1 cup coarse bread crumbs

2 hard-boiled eggs (see page 17), chopped fine

4 tablespoons chopped fresh Italian parsley

2 tablespoons chopped fresh mint

2 anchovy fillets, chopped fine

2 tablespoons grated Parmigiano-Reggiano cheese

1 teaspoon crushed hot red pepper, chopped fine

Salt

2 tablespoons unsalted butter, cut into small pieces

Makes 6 servings

The flavorings in this dish are zesty — a combination of the traditional and a few touches of my own. The anchovies add a lot of flavor, but if you don't like them, don't use them. Lemon zest lightens the flavor of this hearty dish a little. (You might find that adding just a little bit of zest to other robust dishes will do the same for them.) It may seem strange to chop the crushed red pepper — especially as they fly around the chopping board a bit while you're trying to do so — but it prevents you from biting down on a big flake of pepper in the stuffing. If you have vegetable stock or chicken stock, you may use it in place of the water called for in the recipe. It will surely add flavor.

Put the olive oil and garlic in a small bowl and let steep 30 minutes to 2 hours. If you plan to hold the infused garlic oil longer than a few hours, strain out the garlic and reserve the flavored oil.

Preheat oven to 400° F.

Grate 1 teaspoon of zest from one of the lemons and set the zest aside. Squeeze the juice from the lemons and pour about half the juice into a large bowl of cool water. Reserve the remaining lemon juice and two of the lemon halves. Prepare the artichokes for stuffing as described on page 14, plunging them and the peeled stems into the acidulated water as you go.

Mix the bread crumbs, eggs, 2 tablespoons of the parsley, the mint, anchovies, Parmigiano-Reggiano, half the red pepper, the reserved lemon zest, and 3

Stuffing an
artichoke

tablespoons of garlic-infused olive oil together in a bowl. Taste and season with salt, if necessary. Mix well.

Remove the artichokes from the water and drain them a few minutes on a kitchen towel, rapping them once or twice to remove as much of the liquid as possible. Gently spread leaves open from the center to make sure as much stuffing as possible ends up between the leaves. Dividing the stuffing evenly among the artichokes and using the palm of one hand, work the stuffing between the artichoke leaves and into the center (see ill. 4, page 15) where the choke was. You may not need all the stuffing to fill the artichokes. If you have any left over, you may use it as described below to make a thicker sauce. (Or, if you prefer a thicker sauce, be sure to reserve about 3 tablespoons of the stuffing for that purpose.)

Nestle the artichokes into an oval 12-inch ceramic baking dish, or other dish into which they fit comfortably. Tuck the reserved stems in between the artichokes. Pour enough fresh water into the dish to cover the bottom third of the artichokes. Season water with salt, and add the remaining crushed red pepper, the remaining 3 tablespoons infused olive oil, the remaining 2 tablespoons parsley, and the remaining lemon juice and lemon halves to the water. Dot the tops of the artichokes with the butter. For a denser sauce, spoon any remaining or reserved stuffing into the liquid in the dish. Cover the dish tightly with aluminum foil, poke the foil a few times with a fork, and bake until the leaves are tender when pierced with a paring knife, 30 to 45 minutes.

Uncover the artichokes and bake until the top of the stuffing is browned and crusty and an outer leaf is easy to pluck from the artichoke, about 10 minutes. Serve the artichokes hot in shallow soup plates, spooning some of the cooking liquid around each.

☞ Artichokes should be firm, with a healthy green color—brownish streaks in the leaves indicate age. Hold an artichoke in your palm and make sure it is compact, not soft and loose. Two artichokes should squeak a little when rubbed together. Artichokes—for that matter, any vegetables that have a stem: eggplant, peppers, tomatoes, carrots—should have the stems left on when shipped to market. The stem acts as a reserve food supply for the vegetable while it is on display to be sold at market. Look for and ask for vegetables with stems.

How to Prepare Artichokes for Cooking

To serve the artichokes whole: Cut the stem flush with the bottom of the artichoke so the cooked artichoke will rest steadily on the plate. Cut a lemon in half, squeeze the juice into a large bowl of cool water, and keep the halves close by so you can rub them over the cut surfaces of the artichokes to prevent them from darkening.

1. Cut or pluck off the smaller leaves around the base of the artichoke.

2. Cut off the top third of the artichoke with a serrated knife. If you'd like, snip off the pointy tips of the outermost large leaves. Bring a large pot of salted water to a boil, and slip in the lemon halves and the prepared artichokes. Weight the artichokes down with a heatproof plate to keep them submerged as they cook. Boil until the bottom of the artichoke is tender

when poked with the tip of a paring knife, 20 to 30 minutes depending on size. To serve and eat the artichoke, remove the artichokes from the boiling water with a slotted spoon and drain them upside down in a colander. Stand them leaf-side up on a serving plate. Eat the artichoke by pulling off one leaf at a time and scraping off the pulp between your teeth. You can dip them in melted butter or olive oil first, if you like. When all the leaves have been eaten, enjoy the tender artichoke hearts, scraping off the fuzzy choke that completely covers the heart before you do so.

To prepare artichokes for stuffing: Trim the artichokes as described above.

3. Gently pull and spread the leaves outward to expose the purple-tipped leaves at the very center. Pull out the purple-tipped leaves to expose the fuzzy choke below.

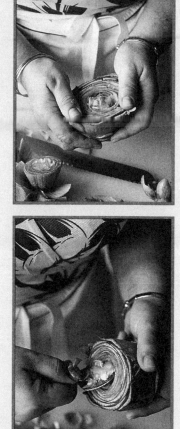

4. With a small teaspoon or espresso spoon, scrape away the choke all the way down to the artichoke heart—the smooth, firm flesh below the choke. Be sure to scrape the choke from the entire surface of the artichoke heart. The artichoke is now ready for stuffing. Use for Stuffed Artichokes (page 12).

For fully edible artichokes: Artichokes can be trimmed to make the pieces completely edible as they are in Orecchiette with Braised Artichokes (page 120) and Artichoke and Bread Frittata (page 36). The larger the artichoke, the more it needs to be trimmed to make it completely edible. Cut a lemon in half, squeeze the juice into a bowl of cool water, and keep the halves close by to rub over the cut surfaces of the artichokes to prevent them from darkening. With a paring knife, trim the base of the leaves flush with the artichoke bottom. Snip or pluck off the outer layers of leaves to expose the leaves that are pale yellow almost all the way to the tip. (In small artichokes, this will be one to two rows; in larger artichokes you may have to remove several layers of leaves.) Cut off the top third of the artichoke leaves with a sturdy serrated knife. With a vegetable peeler or a paring knife, trim the dark outer layer of the artichoke stem. Dip the artichoke in the lemon water as you go to prevent it from darkening. Cut the artichoke in half through the stem. Scrape out the fuzzy choke with a small teaspoon or espresso spoon. Pull out the inedible purple-tipped leaves, if there are any, that surround the choke. Place the trimmed artichoke halves in the lemon water as you go. These completely edible artichoke halves may be cooked as is or sliced or cut into wedges as described in a recipe.

Use completely edible artichokes in:

Marinated Artichokes (page 49)

Orecchiette with Braised Artichokes (page 120)

Everybody thinks of crispy vegetables as the way to go nowadays. But I remember my grandmother cooking green vegetables a long time, until they turned olive green. They were wonderful. These peppers, too, are a delicious example of how flavors develop when vegetables are cooked until tender.

Roasted Pepper Halves with Bread Crumb Topping

Peperoni Arrostiti

5 tablespoons Garlic-Infused Oil (see below) or extra-virgin olive oil

3 red or yellow bell peppers

Salt

½ cup fine, dry bread crumbs

3 tablespoons grated Parmigiano-Reggiano cheese

3 tablespoons chopped fresh Italian parsley

1½ teaspoons chopped fresh thyme, or 1 teaspoon dried thyme

½ teaspoon crushed hot red pepper, chopped coarsely

½ cup Chicken Stock (page 74) or Vegetable Stock (page 76) or canned reduced-sodium chicken broth or water

Makes 6 servings

I've updated these classics of Italian-American cuisine a little by using fresh thyme. If you like, you can substitute (or add) dried oregano. Chopped anchovies make a nice addition, too.

Preheat the oven to 375° F. Drizzle the bottom of a 13 × 9–inch baking dish with 1 tablespoon of the olive oil. (If you're using the infused oil, spoon a few of the garlic pieces into the dish as well.) Cut the peppers in half through the stems. Pull out the cores, stems, and seeds and, using a paring knife, cut out the ribs. Arrange the peppers side by side in the prepared dish. Drizzle 1 tablespoon of the olive oil over the peppers and season them with salt.

Stir the bread crumbs, the remaining 3 tablespoons of the oil, the grated cheese, 2 tablespoons of the parsley, the thyme, and the crushed red pepper together in a small bowl. Divide the crumb mixture among the peppers, making an even coating over the pepper halves. Pour in the stock and cover the dish tightly with aluminum foil. Bake until the peppers are tender, about 20 minutes.

Remove the foil and continue baking until the crumbs are lightly browned, about 10 minutes. Transfer the peppers to a serving platter, stir the remaining 1 tablespoon parsley into the juices in the baking pan, then spoon the juices over the peppers. Serve the peppers hot or at room temperature.

Garlic-Infused Oil

OLIVE OIL PERFUMED WITH GARLIC is a very handy thing to have in the kitchen. But it must be handled carefully: there is a slight chance that uncooked garlic that is steeped for too long in olive oil could be a breeding ground for the organism that causes botulism. *However, if you handle the garlic and oil carefully—and don't let it steep too long—the risk is virtually nonexistent.* If you are concerned about botulism, make the infusion with blanched or roasted garlic. It might not be as pronounced, but you will still have the flavor of garlic-infused olive oil.

To make garlic-infused oil, add 3 thickly sliced cloves of garlic to each cup of extra-virgin olive oil. Let steep at room temperature 2 to 3 hours. Strain the oil and discard the garlic if you're not using the garlic immediately. Keep the strained oil in a sealed container in the refrigerator.

Use garlic-infused oil to make:

Stuffed Artichokes (page 12)

Roasted Pepper Halves with Bread Crumb Topping (page 16)

And to drizzle over crostini and bruschetta, sauté vegetables, and make salad dressings

Hard-Boiled Eggs

THESE EGGS AREN'T REALLY BOILED, but slow-cooked in hot water, giving you a tender white and an evenly cooked creamy yolk without a trace of green. Put as many eggs as you'd like to cook in a roomy saucepan. Pour in enough cold water to cover the eggs by at least three fingers. Bring the eggs to a boil over high heat, then immediately remove the pan from the heat. Let the eggs stand in the water until cooled to room temperature.

To peel the eggs: Remove the eggs from the water, and roll them on a hard surface to crack the shells. Return the eggs to the water for a few minutes before peeling.

Use these hard-boiled eggs in:

Stuffed Artichokes (page 12)

Caesar Salad (page 58)

Stuffed Mushrooms

Funghi Ripieni

24 white or cremini mushrooms with caps about 1 ½ inches in diameter

2 tablespoons extra-virgin olive oil, plus more for the tops of the mushrooms if you like

½ cup finely chopped scallions

½ cup finely chopped red bell peppers

½ cup coarse bread crumbs (see below)

½ cup grated Parmigiano-Reggiano cheese

¼ cup finely chopped fresh Italian parsley

Salt

Freshly ground black pepper

4 tablespoons unsalted butter

½ cup Chicken Stock (page 74), Vegetable Stock (page 76) or canned reduced-sodium chicken broth

¼ cup dry white wine, optional

Makes 6 servings

Serve these nice and hot, or let them cool to room temperature. If you'd like to make this a little more contemporary, you can add a dash of balsamic vinegar to the red peppers and scallions as they cook. In true Italian-American style, these are topped with butter, but in Italy, we would use olive oil. Best yet, top them with butter, then "bless" them all with a little olive oil.

This wonderful stuffing is delicious in celery stalks baked with a light tomato sauce. You can also line up blanched asparagus on a baking sheet, sprinkle the bread crumbs over them, and bake them until the crumbs are crispy. I'm sure you can come up with a lot of uses for the bread crumbs. Remember, I give you the basics, but I want you to go and play.

Preheat oven to 425° F. Remove the stems from the mushrooms and chop the stems fine.

Heat 2 tablespoons olive oil in a medium skillet over medium heat. Add the scallions and cook until wilted, about 1 minute. Stir in the red peppers and chopped mushroom stems and cook, stirring, until tender, about 3 minutes. Remove and cool.

Toss the bread crumbs, grated cheese, 2 tablespoons of the parsley, and the sautéed vegetables until thoroughly blended. Season to taste with salt and pepper. Stuff the cavity of each mushroom with the filling, pressing it in with a teaspoon until even with the sides of the mushrooms.

Using 2 tablespoons of the butter, grease a 12 × 18–inch low-sided baking pan. Arrange the mushrooms side by side in the pan and, using the remaining 2 tablespoons butter, dot the top of each mushroom with about ¼ teaspoon butter. Add the stock, wine, if using, and remaining 2 tablespoons parsley to the pan. If you like, drizzle the tops of the mushrooms with olive oil. Bake until the mushrooms are cooked through and the bread crumbs are golden brown, about 20 minutes.

Serve the mushrooms on a warmed platter or divide them among warmed plates. Pour the pan juices into a small saucepan and bring to a boil on top of the stove. Boil until lightly thickened, 1 to 2 minutes. Spoon the juices over the mushrooms and serve immediately.

Bread Crumbs

BREAD CRUMBS TURN UP A LOT IN MY COOKING—they are a truly essential ingredient in the Italian culinary culture and a good way to recycle old bread. I use bread crumbs to coat foods before frying or baking them; to toss into pasta dishes as the "poor man's cheese"; to firm up ravioli fillings; to thicken sauces; and to add a crust to baked and gratinéed food. I even use them in desserts: to make a crust for cheesecakes; as a topping for baked fruit; and to absorb juices in strudels and tarts that would otherwise seep out and make for a soggy crust.

Italian or any kind of hearty white bread is best for making your own crumbs. Before you make bread crumbs, let the bread dry in an airy place, so mold doesn't have a chance to form. (Or set the bread overnight in an oven with the pilot light on.) Once it is dry, grate the bread on a box grater or break the bread into chunks and process them in a food processor. Sift crumbs through a medium-size sieve and grind or crush the larger pieces that remain in the sieve. Store bread crumbs in a tightly sealed container. They will keep for up to 2 weeks in the refrigerator and up to 2 months in the freezer. Bread crumbs can be made out of all types of bread: whole wheat, garlic bread, and sourdough, to name a few. Keep in mind that each bread will have its own characteristics. For example, whole-wheat and garlic bread crumbs will give you a much darker and toasted effect, and sourdough bread crumbs will have a pronounced sour flavor.

If you buy bread crumbs, I recommend the unflavored ones. Starting from scratch like that, you can flavor them as you need, or as I call for in the recipes. Most of the seasoned-bread-crumb recipes here call for fresh herbs. You might not have fresh herbs available, so use dry herbs. Just be sure not to overseason the crumbs. If you like the bulky, crunchy effect of foods coated with large bread crumbs, save some of the larger crumbs when you sieve them, or buy the very coarse Japanese bread crumbs called *panko*. Next time you thicken a sauce, like pan juices from a roast or braising liquid, I'd like you to try bread crumbs instead of flour or vegetable starch. Just stir the bread crumbs into the sauce and let them cook a few minutes so they release their starches. Strain the sauce, pressing all the liquid out of the crumbs. Bread crumbs will not leave a raw-floury feeling on your tongue. Until you get the feel of thickening sauces with bread crumbs, add them a little bit at a time, and remember it takes a few minutes before you can see the thickening effect.

continued on next page

Bread Crumbs

continued from previous page

Seasoned Bread Crumbs 1

To top baked fish fillets, scallops, shrimp, or chicken breasts

2 cups bread crumbs
4 tablespoons extra-virgin olive oil
3 tablespoons chopped fresh Italian parsley
2 tablespoons chopped fresh thyme
Grated zest of 1 lemon
Pinch salt

Mix all ingredients in a small bowl until the crumbs are evenly moistened with the oil.

Seasoned Bread Crumbs 2

To top baked vegetables, like asparagus, broccoli, zucchini, cauliflower, carrots, and parsnips

2 cups bread crumbs
1 cup grated Parmigiano-Reggiano cheese
4 tablespoons extra-virgin olive oil
2 tablespoons chopped fresh Italian parsley
Pinch salt

If the vegetables you are preparing can cook in 10 minutes or so—thin asparagus or thinly sliced zucchini, for example—there is no need to precook them. Boil vegetables that take longer—sliced carrots or parsnips—in salted water until al dente, *then proceed.*

Mix the bread crumbs, grated cheese, olive oil, parsley, and salt together in a small bowl until the crumbs are evenly moistened with the oil. Arrange the vegetables in an even layer in a baking dish, sprinkle them with enough crumbs to make an even but not thick coating, and bake in a 400° F oven until the bread crumbs are browned and crispy and the vegetables are heated through, about 12 minutes.

Seasoned Bread Crumbs 3

To use in desserts—strudels, crusts, tarts, etc.

4 tablespoons butter
1 cup bread crumbs
$\frac{1}{2}$ cup sugar
$\frac{1}{2}$ tablespoon ground cinnamon

Melt the butter in a wide skillet over medium heat. Stir in the bread crumbs and toast, stirring often, until golden. Remove from the heat and stir in the sugar and cinnamon.

Seasoned Bread Crumbs 4

For a pasta dressing

2 tablespoons extra-virgin olive oil
1 cup bread crumbs
½ cup pine nuts

Heat the oil in a wide skillet over medium heat. Stir in the bread crumbs and pine nuts and toast them, stirring often, until golden brown. Use the toasted crumbs to dress pastas made with oil and garlic, like the Spaghettini with Oil and Garlic on page 103, or a vegetable sauce, like the Cavatelli with Bread Crumbs, Pancetta, and Cauliflower on page 114. I don't suggest using them with tomato sauce or any very saucy pasta.

Bread Crumbs

continued from previous page

Fried Mozzarella Sandwich Skewers

Spiedini alla Romana

For the Spiedini

16 slices whole-wheat bread, toasted lightly
1 ½ pounds *mozzarella di bufala,* or any freshly made mozzarella, sliced ¼ inch thick
1 quart vegetable oil, or as needed
4 large eggs
¼ cup milk
1 teaspoon salt
Pinch ground black pepper
1 cup all-purpose flour

For the Sauce

5 tablespoons extra-virgin olive oil

ingredients continued on next page

We made this dish at Ristorante Buonavia in the early 1970s with white bread. Now I find I like the flavor and texture of wheat bread, and I like it even more if the bread is lightly toasted before you put the sandwiches together. Vegetable stock is nice here — it cuts the acidity of the white wine without adding a definitive flavor. If you don't have vegetable stock, use water or, if you want to add a richer flavor, chicken stock.

Preheat oven to 200° F or lowest setting. Using eight slices of bread for each, make two layered sandwiches alternating bread and mozzarella. Cut and fit the mozzarella slices as necessary to cover the bread more or less evenly. The cheese shouldn't overhang the bread slices, as the crusts will be trimmed off before cooking. Imagine each sandwich cut into four squares, and place a sturdy wooden skewer through the center of each imaginary square. With a serrated knife, cut off the crust on all four sides, then cut the sandwich into

continued on next page

Fried Mozzarella Sandwich Skewers *(continued)*

4 cloves garlic, crushed

8 anchovy fillets, chopped coarsely

3 tablespoons small capers in brine, drained

3 tablespoons fresh lemon juice

⅓ cup dry white wine

¼ cup Vegetable Stock (page 76) or water

2 tablespoons chopped fresh Italian parsley

Makes 8 appetizer servings

four squares, with a skewer at the center of each square. Press gently as you cut, to make nice, compact sandwiches. Repeat with the other sandwich. You now have eight multilayered sandwiches, each on a skewer.

Pour enough vegetable oil into a wide, deep skillet—cast iron is perfect—to fill it by 1½ inches. Heat over medium heat until the oil registers 350° F on a deep-frying thermometer. Line a baking sheet with a double thickness of paper towels and set aside. Meanwhile, in a shallow wide bowl, whisk the eggs, milk, salt, and pepper until thoroughly blended.

When the oil comes to temperature, dredge each skewered square in the flour, being sure to coat all sides lightly but well. Working with half the floured skewers at a time, dip them in the egg mixture to coat on all sides. Don't soak the bread in the egg, just coat it thoroughly. Let some of the excess egg drip back into the bowl, and gently slip the squares into the oil. Fry, turning as necessary with a pair of long tongs, until golden brown on all sides, about 4 minutes. Drain the sandwiches on the paper-towel-lined pan and place in the warm oven. Repeat with the remaining sandwiches.

Make the sauce: Heat the olive oil and garlic in a small skillet over medium heat. Cook, shaking the pan occasionally, until the garlic is golden. Stir in the anchovies and cook until they dissolve. Stir in the capers and cook till they sizzle. Pour in the lemon juice, then the white wine. Bring the ingredients to a vigorous boil, add the vegetable stock, and boil until the sauce is lightly thickened, about 3 minutes. Stir in the parsley and remove from the heat.

Arrange the hot mozzarella sandwiches on a warm platter or plates and pull the skewers from them. Spoon the sauce over and around the sandwiches and serve immediately.

Fried Mozzarella "in a Carriage"

Mozzarella Fritta in Carrozza

1 pound *mozzarella di bufala* or any freshly made mozzarella, sliced ¼ inch thick

12 slices whole-wheat bread

2 eggs

1 teaspoon salt

¼ teaspoon freshly ground black pepper

All-purpose flour

2 cups vegetable oil for frying

Caper-anchovy sauce from preceding recipe

2 tablespoons chopped fresh Italian parsley, optional

Makes 6 servings

The carriage in the title refers to the bread that the mozzarella rides in. Like the preceding recipe, this dish was originally made with white bread. Whole-wheat bread adds texture and complexity. You can see in the directions below that everything is laid out before the oil is heated. Once the oil comes to temperature, you should be ready to start frying right away.

Divide the mozzarella among six of the bread slices, making even layers that go right up to the edges. Cover with the remaining slices of bread. Trim the crusts from the bread, making neat sandwiches. Insert a toothpick in each sandwich to hold it together.

Heat the oven to 200° F or to the lowest setting. Line a baking sheet with a double thickness of paper towels. Whisk the eggs with the salt and pepper in a wide, shallow bowl. Spread the flour out in an even layer on a flat plate. Dredge each sandwich in flour, making sure to coat the sides. That will help keep the cheese from leaking during frying.

Pour the oil into a heavy, deep skillet at least 12 inches wide. Heat the oil to 350° F. Dip three of the sandwiches, one at a time, in the egg mixture, turning them as necessary to coat them on all sides. Carefully slip each sandwich into the oil as soon as it has been coated, and fry, turning them once, until they are golden brown on both sides, about 4 minutes. Keep an eye on the temperature of the oil. It should be hot enough so the sandwiches give off a lively sizzle, but not hot enough to smoke or turn the bits of egg that fall off the sandwiches dark brown. Remove the sandwiches from the oil with a slotted spatula, draining them briefly over the oil, before placing them on the lined baking sheet. Keep the sandwiches warm in the oven and repeat with the remaining sandwiches.

Prepare the caper-anchovy sauce as directed in the preceding recipe.

Cut each sandwich into four triangles and arrange on a plate so the slices resemble a flower. Spoon the sauce over the sandwiches and sprinkle with chopped parsley if you like.

These frittelle are wonderful as hors d'oeuvres or, served with a tossed salad, as a summer meal. It is a perfect way also to use trimmings from baccalà you might be serving as a main course.

Salt Cod Fritters

Frittelle di Baccalà

For the Fritters

- 1 pound boneless salt cod (see note below), soaked as described on page 299
- 2 slices day-old white bread
- 1 small red bell pepper cut in half, or half a large pepper, core, seeds, and stem removed
- 2 large eggs
- 2 tablespoons chopped fresh Italian parsley
- 2 tablespoons small capers, rinsed and drained
- Freshly ground black pepper to taste
- Fine, dry bread crumbs, if needed

Just as you use trimmings from baccalà to make salt-cod fritters, you can use this same method to make fritters from other types of fish. Whether using baccalà or other fish, finely diced fresh tomatoes or sliced scallions would make a nice addition to the batter.

Place the cod in a 3-quart saucepan. Pour in enough water to cover by at least three fingers. Bring the water to a boil over high heat. Adjust the heat to simmering and cook just until the cod starts to flake, from 5 to 12 minutes, depending on the size and shape of the piece(s) you are cooking. Drain the salt cod thoroughly and let stand until cool enough to work with.

Meanwhile, put the bread in a small bowl and pour in enough cold water to cover. Let stand several minutes, until soaked through. While the bread is soaking, slip the pepper halves into the water with the cod. Simmer 2 minutes, fish them out, and let cool.

Squeeze the excess water from the bread and place the squeezed bread in a mixing bowl. Pat the pepper dry and cut it into fine dice and add to the bread along with the eggs, pepper, parsley, and capers. Beat with a fork until the eggs and bread are thoroughly mixed. Flake the cooled salt cod into 1-inch pieces and stir into the egg mixture. Refrigerate until thoroughly chilled, about 30 minutes. At this point, test the consistency of the cod mixture. Roll a heaping tablespoon into a ball; the cod mixture should be firm enough to hold its shape. If not, add bread crumbs, about 1 teaspoon at a time, until it is firm enough.

Make the batter: In a separate mixing bowl, whisk the beer, egg yolks, and lemon zest until smooth. Add $1\frac{3}{4}$ cups of flour and whisk just until smooth. Let the batter stand at room temperature at least 15 minutes or up to 1 hour.

For Battering/Frying

2 cups beer

2 large egg yolks

Grated zest of 1 lemon

1¾ cups unbleached flour, plus more for dredging the fritters

Vegetable oil as needed

2 lemons, sliced, optional

**Makes about 24 fritters
(6 appetizer servings)**

Pour enough vegetable oil into a deep 12-inch skillet to fill it by 1½ inches. Heat over medium heat until it registers 350° F on a deep-frying thermometer. Preheat the oven to "Warm" or to the lowest setting, and line a baking sheet with paper towels.

While the oil is coming to temperature, form the fritters: Roll 1 tablespoon of the salt-cod mixture between your palms into an egg shape. Repeat until you have used up all the mixture. You should have about twenty-four fritters. Dredge the fritters in the additional flour to coat lightly on all sides, and drop them into the batter.

With a wire skimmer, remove a few of the fritters at a time from the batter, allowing excess batter to drip back into the bowl. Slip the fritters into the oil. Add only as many fritters as will float freely in the oil. Don't overcrowd the pan or the oil temperature will drop significantly and the fritters will be soggy and oily. Fry, turning the fritters as necessary, until they are evenly golden brown on all sides, about 5 minutes. While the fritters are frying, adjust the heat as necessary to keep the temperature of the oil as close to 350° F as possible. Transfer the fritters with the skimmer to the prepared baking sheet. Keep them warm in the oven and repeat as necessary with the remaining fritters. Serve hot, with lemon slices, if you like.

☞ If you have trimmings from a whole boneless or bone-in side of baccalà, use them here. If you trim the baccalà before you soak it, save the unsoaked trimmings in the refrigerator until you're ready to make the fritters. Soaked trimming should be used within a day or two.

The name of this dish, *arancine*, means "small oranges," referring to the shape and size of these fried rice balls filled with a meat-and-pea ragù. The recipe comes from Sicily, although you can find *arancine* all around Rome and Naples. *Arancine* make an easy-to-eat and delicious snack or hors d'oeuvre, either passed or as part of a buffet. Or pile a platter high with them and serve with a saucy main course, like the Beef Short Ribs Braised in Red Wine on page 218.

Stuffed Rice Balls

Arancine

For the Ragù

1/4 cup extra-virgin olive oil

1 pound ground beef

1/2 cup chopped onion

Salt

1/4 cup grated carrots

1/4 cup finely diced celery

One 14-ounce can Italian plum tomatoes (preferably San Marzano) with juice, crushed

1 teaspoon tomato paste

1/2 teaspoon crushed hot red pepper

1 cup fresh or frozen peas

For the Rice

5 cups Chicken Stock (page 74), canned reduced-sodium chicken broth or water

2 tablespoons extra-virgin olive oil

Traditionally, this dish was made with short-grain rice, Arborio or Carnaroli, that's been boiled in salted water with a little oil, and that's how I make it here. If you have leftover risotto, you can use that instead of starting from scratch with the rice. On the other hand, if you have leftover Bolognese sauce, you can skip making the ragù; all you need do is to add some peas and a little water to the sauce and simmer until the peas are tender and the sauce is dense, not runny.

The recipe for the ragù below makes about 3 cups, approximately twice as much as you'll need. Either freeze the remaining ragù for your next batch of rice balls, or enjoy the sauce over pasta like rigatoni or penne.

Make the ragù (up to 3 days in advance): Heat 1/4 cup olive oil in a 3-quart saucepan over medium heat. Crumble in the meat and add the onion. Cook, stirring often, until the water given off by the meat is evaporated and the meat and onion begin to brown, about 10 minutes.

Season the beef and onion lightly with salt. Stir in the carrots and celery and continue cooking until the vegetables are tender, about 10 minutes. Stir in the tomatoes, tomato paste, red pepper, and salt to taste. Adjust the heat to

2 cups short-grain rice,
such as Carnaroli or
Arborio

4 large eggs

2 cups grated Pecorino
Romano cheese

**To Coat and Fry the
Rice Balls**

2 eggs

1 cup all-purpose flour

2 cups fine, dry bread
crumbs

$2/3$ cup vegetable oil

$1/3$ cup olive oil, plus extra
for frying

Makes about 20 rice balls

simmering and continue cooking, stirring occasionally, until the sauce is thickened, about 30 minutes. If the sauce starts sticking to the pan at any time during cooking, stir in a few tablespoons of water. Stir in the peas and cook until they are very tender, about 10 minutes for frozen peas and 20 minutes for fresh peas. The finished ragù should be dense and reduced. Remove and cool to room temperature.

While the ragù is cooling, make the rice: Bring the stock or water and 2 tablespoons olive oil to a boil in a 3-quart saucepan. Stir in the rice, return the water to boil, then adjust the heat to simmering. Cook the rice, uncovered, until *al dente*—tender but firm—about 12 minutes. Drain the rice and spread out on a tray to cool to room temperature. When the rice is cool, scrape it into a mixing bowl and beat in the 4 eggs and the grated cheese.

Take a handful (about $1/3$ cup) of the cooled rice mixture and shape it into a small ball in the palm of your hand. Make a well in the center of the ball and drop in 1 tablespoon of the ragù. Work the rice so that it completely encloses the ragù, and re-form the rice into a smooth ball. Continue forming *arancine* with the remaining rice and ragù.

Whisk the 2 eggs in a mixing bowl. Spread the flour on one plate and the bread crumbs on another, in an even layer.

Dredge a few of the rice balls in flour to coat all sides. Tap off excess flour. Roll the rice balls in the beaten egg to coat, allowing any excess egg to drip back into the bowl. Finally, roll the rice balls in the bread crumbs, pressing lightly to coat evenly with the crumbs. Remove to a clean baking sheet. Repeat with the remaining rice balls.

If you'd like to serve the rice balls hot, heat the oven to 200° F or to the lowest setting. Line a baking sheet with a double thickness of paper towels. Pour the vegetable oil and olive oil into a deep skillet. Insert a deep-frying thermometer in the oil and heat the oil over medium heat to 375° F. (If you are working without a thermometer, test the temperature as directed below.) Once the oil reaches temperature, adjust the heat under the pot to maintain a steady temperature.

If you're not working with a thermometer, test the temperature of the oil by dipping a rice ball in the oil. It should give off a lively but steady sizzle. If nothing happens, the oil isn't hot enough; if the oil around the bread-crumb coating boils and sputters, the oil is too hot. Adjust the heat accordingly.

continued on next page

Stuffed Rice Balls *(continued)*

When the oil comes to temperature, carefully slip about a third of the rice balls into the oil. Fry, turning as necessary with tongs or a slotted spoon, until golden brown and crisp on all sides, about 4 minutes. Remove to the paper-towel-lined baking sheet, keeping them hot in the oven if you like. Fry the remaining rice balls. The *arancine* can be served hot or at room temperature.

Deep-Frying

FRYING IS A WONDERFUL OPTION to have in the kitchen. The high temperature locks in flavor and keeps foods moist while giving them a delicious, crispy coating. Some people have a phobia or serious apprehension when it comes to frying. Maybe it's the fat content—but if you fry correctly (and don't do it all the time), you don't have to worry about that. Here are a few tips for successful frying.

Use a deep-frying thermometer. There are two types of deep-frying thermometers: one with a round dial on top of a long stem, and another with the temperature markings—usually in Fahrenheit and centigrade—running alongside a mercury-filled tube. Either is fine, as long as the end of the stem or bottom of the mercury tube is completely immersed in oil. Thermometers are inexpensive and are, really, the only way to judge the temperature of the oil accurately.

Heat source: You'll see that, once you add foods to hot oil, the temperature of the oil will drop. If the temperature of the oil doesn't start to climb again within a few seconds, give the heat under the oil a boost. But keep an eye on it and lower the heat again before the oil reaches the recommended temperature. Even after you lower the heat, the temperature will climb a bit.

Reusing oil: If oil becomes too hot or is kept heated for a long time, it "breaks down," becoming difficult to digest and taking on an unpleasant taste. As a rule of thumb, I suggest that you don't reuse oil for frying. By frying one recipe's worth of pizzette, for example, in several batches, you are in effect using the oil a few times. If, however, you have fried only one batch of food in the oil, and regulated the temperature during frying, the oil should remain clear and light in color when you are finished. In that case, you can reuse the oil once. After cooling the oil completely, strain it through a fine sieve and store it in a tightly sealed container. Store the strained oil in a cool place and use it within a few weeks.

To dispose of used oil: Wait until it is completely cool, then pour it into an empty milk container or coffee can. Freeze the fat until it is solid, then discard it.

This recipe will be a hit at your cocktail parties. The rolls can be prepared in advance, refrigerated for several hours, and fried when your guests arrive. They can even be fried and kept in a warm oven for 15 minutes or so before serving.

Fried Fontina and Prosciutto–Wrapped Asparagus

Asparagi Fritti Avrolti nel Prosciutto

18 thick asparagus spears

18 thin slices Fontina cheese (about 7 ounces)

18 slices imported Italian prosciutto (about 5 ounces)

18 fresh sage leaves

2 large eggs

½ teaspoon salt

¼ teaspoon freshly ground black pepper

1 cup all-purpose flour

2 cups fine, dry bread crumbs

1 cup vegetable oil

½ cup olive oil

Makes 18 pieces

Bring a large pot of salted water to a boil. Set a large bowl of cold water by the sink. Bend each stalk of asparagus until it snaps and discard the tough ends. Remove the tough outer skin of the asparagus spears with a vegetable peeler. Slide the spears into the boiling water and cook until the asparagus is tender but still firm, about 4 minutes. Drain in a colander and plunge into the cold water. Let stand until cooled through. Drain thoroughly and pat the spears dry.

On a clean and dry work surface, lay out a slice of Fontina cheese with one of the corners facing you. Lay an asparagus spear over the cheese so the corner of the cheese closest to you is about halfway down the stalk. Roll the cheese tightly around the asparagus, covering the entire stalk with Fontina. Lay out a slice of prosciutto as you did the Fontina. Place a sage leaf over one end of the prosciutto and roll the cheese-coated asparagus spears up to enclose them completely. Tuck any overhanging cheese and prosciutto underneath the asparagus to make a neat bundle. Repeat with the remaining asparagus.

Whisk the eggs, salt, and pepper in a mixing bowl. Spread the flour and bread crumbs in an even layer on two separate plates.

Dredge the asparagus bundles in flour to coat all sides. Tap off excess flour. Roll the asparagus in the beaten egg to coat. Remove the asparagus, allowing any excess egg to drip back into the bowl. Transfer the asparagus to the bread crumbs and roll, pressing lightly, to coat evenly with the crumbs. Remove to a clean baking sheet. Repeat with the remaining asparagus bundles.

Heat the oven to 200° F or lowest setting. Line a baking sheet with a double thickness of paper towels. Pour the vegetable oil and olive oil into a deep skillet. Heat the oil over medium heat until the oil registers 350° F on a deep-

continued on next page

frying thermometer. (If you're frying without a thermometer, the oil is ready when one end of an asparagus bundle gives off a lively but steady sizzle when dipped in the oil.) Once the oil reaches the desired temperature, adjust the heat under the pot to maintain a steady temperature, and continue adjusting the heat as necessary during frying. Carefully slip as many asparagus spears into the oil as will fit without touching. Fry the asparagus, turning as necessary with tongs or a slotted spoon, until golden brown and crisp on all sides, about 4 minutes. Remove to the paper-towel-lined baking sheet. Keep them warm in the oven while frying remaining asparagus bundles. Serve hot.

Me in curlers, when I first came to America, dusting my first TV set, c. 1963

Slices of fried zucchini between crusty Italian bread make a great sandwich. As children, we took it to school often for *merenda* (snack). Here, in the States, my mother would make it for my children, Joseph and Tanya, when *they* went to school. Only years later did we find out they threw their sandwiches away because none of the other children had strange lunches like that. Oh, they ate it at home—they just were embarrassed at school.

Breaded and Fried Zucchini

Zucchini Fritti

1½ pounds "fancy" zucchini
2 eggs
1 teaspoon salt
¼ teaspoon freshly ground black pepper
1 cup all-purpose flour
1 cup coarse cornmeal
2 cups bread crumbs
2 cups vegetable oil
½ cup extra-virgin olive oil

Makes 6 servings

When my mother made fried zucchini for us, she would slice the zucchini lengthwise into ¼-inch slices. Sometimes she would flour them, dip them in egg batter, cover them well with bread crumbs, and fry them, as I do here. But sometimes she would just dip them in flour and eggs and fry them. I liked them both ways. The ones without bread crumbs I make often for a vegetable buffet or antipasto. After they are fried and drained, I roll them like a jelly roll and serve them just like that.

The best zucchini to use for this—and most—recipes are small ones, about 6 inches long, with bright skins and a firm texture. Zucchini of this size are called "fancy" in the restaurant business. You'll see them labeled like that in some markets as well.

Fry the zucchini in batches for better results. Overcrowding the oil when frying zucchini, or for that matter anything, lowers the temperature of the oil drastically, and that causes a lot of problems. First, the food becomes poached and not fried, and absorbs much more oil. The zucchini pieces will stick to each other and cook unevenly, without the nice, crispy crust which is one of the reasons we fry in the first place.

continued on next page

Wash and dry the zucchini. Cut the stems and tips off, then cut the zucchini crosswise into 2-inch lengths. Cut the zucchini pieces lengthwise into $\frac{1}{4}$-inch slices, then cut the slices lengthwise into $\frac{1}{4}$-inch julienne strips.

Whisk the eggs, salt, and pepper in a mixing bowl. Stir the flour and cornmeal together in a second bowl, and pour the bread crumbs into a third bowl.

Heat the oven to 200° F or lowest setting. Line a baking sheet with a double thickness of paper towels. Pour the vegetable oil and olive oil into a deep skillet. Insert a deep-frying thermometer in the oil and heat the oil over medium heat to 375° F. (If you are working without a thermometer, test the temperature as directed below.) Once the oil reaches the desired temperature, adjust the heat under the pot to maintain a steady temperature.

Working with a handful of zucchini sticks at a time, toss the zucchini in flour, transfer them to a strainer, and shake them to remove excess flour. Toss the floured zucchini in the egg mixture, then transfer them to a second sieve, placed over a bowl, to drain off excess egg. Toss the coated zucchini in the bread crumbs, pressing them lightly so the bread crumbs stick, until coated well. Lift them from the crumbs, shaking them gently to remove excess crumbs.

To test the temperature of the oil without a thermometer, add one breaded zucchini stick. If the zucchini doesn't sizzle and bubble, the oil is not hot enough. When the oil comes to temperature (375° F), carefully slip a small handful of zucchini into the oil. Push the zucchini around in the oil with a wire skimmer or slotted spoon to keep them from sticking together, submerging them in the oil with the skimmer so the oil reaches all sides of the zucchini and they brown evenly. Fry until golden brown and crisp on all sides, 3 to 4 minutes. Using the skimmer or slotted spoon, carefully fish out the zucchini, setting them on paper towels to drain. Keep warm in the oven while frying the remaining zucchini. Sprinkle them evenly with salt and serve.

Rita de Rosa is an excellent cook who ran a restaurant with her son in New York City until her native Naples called her home. I watched Rita make these pizzette on a trip I made to Naples. After we went on a shopping excursion through the city, she welcomed me into her kitchen to spend the day cooking and talking.

Little Pizza Turnovers

Pizzette

For the Dough

1 package active dry yeast

½ cup warm water

8 tablespoons unsalted butter, softened

3 large eggs

3½ cups all-purpose flour, or as needed

½ teaspoon salt

For the Filling

1 large egg

1 cup fresh ricotta or store-bought whole-milk ricotta

½ cup grated Parmigiano-Reggiano cheese

½ cup diced (¼-inch) smoked mozzarella

¼ cup chopped cacciatorini or other salami

6 cups vegetable oil

Makes 36 pieces

If you haven't bought a deep-frying thermometer yet, this is a good time to do it. A few of the pizzette may "spring a leak" while they fry—you can minimize the risk by not overfilling the pizzette, and by wetting and sealing the edges well as you form them.

Make the dough: Sprinkle the yeast over the warm water in a small bowl. Let stand until dissolved. Process the butter and 3 eggs in the work bowl of a food processor until blended. Add the yeast mixture, 3 cups of the flour, and the salt and process until incorporated. With the motor running, continue mixing the dough, adding enough of the remaining flour in small additions to form a stiff dough. Turn the dough out onto a lightly floured surface and knead, adding flour as necessary to prevent sticking, until the dough is smooth and elastic. Cover the dough with a clean kitchen towel and let it rest at room temperature while preparing the filling.

Make the filling: In a large bowl, beat the egg until foamy. Add the ricotta and grated cheese and mix well. Stir in the smoked mozzarella and salami.

On a lightly floured surface, roll out the dough to ⅛ inch thick. Cut 3-inch circles from the dough and place 1 tablespoon filling in the center of each circle. Wet the edges of each circle with a pastry brush or the tip of your finger dipped in cool water. Fold half the circle over the filling to make half-moon-shaped turnovers, pressing the edges firmly to seal as you go. Place the pizzette on a kitchen-towel-lined baking sheet as you form them. Reroll the scraps of dough as necessary to use all the filling.

continued on next page

Cover the sheet with a kitchen towel and set the pizzette aside in a warm place until they have puffed slightly, about 20 minutes.

Meanwhile, heat the vegetable oil in a heavy, deep 4-quart pot until a deep-frying thermometer registers 350° F. Carefully slip as many of the pizzette as will float freely into the hot oil. Fry, turning with a wire skimmer as necessary, until golden brown on all sides, about 4 minutes. Remove and drain on paper towels. Repeat with the remaining pizzette, allowing the oil to return to temperature, if necessary, before adding more pizzette.

A cast-iron skillet is perfect for making the frittata, but it is a hot and heavy handful when filled with frittata and right out of the oven. Use two heavy oven mitts or pot holders to lift the frittata from the oven. And take a tip from restaurant kitchens: leave one of the pot holders or mitts draped over the skillet handle as a sign to all that the handle is very hot.

Potato and Pepper Frittata

Frittata di Patate e Peperoni

1 large (about 10 ounces) Idaho potato

12 large eggs

1/3 cup heavy cream

Salt

Freshly ground black pepper

1 1/3 cups cubed (1-inch) day-old bread, crusts removed

3 tablespoons extra-virgin olive oil

1 onion, cut into 1/2-inch strips

1 red and 1 green bell pepper, cored, seeded, and cut into 1/4-inch slices

1 tablespoon unsalted butter

Makes 6 servings

What makes this frittata different is the bread. It soaks up the egg and cream and gives the frittata a firm but still tender texture. It also makes it easier to slide onto a serving plate, if that's how you want to serve it.

Put the potato in a medium saucepan and pour in enough cold salted water to cover by at least four fingers. Bring to a boil, and boil until the potato is tender, about 40 minutes. Remove and let stand until cool enough to peel. Peel the potato and cut it into 1/2-inch slices.

Preheat the oven to 350° F. Beat the eggs, heavy cream, and salt and pepper to taste in a large bowl. Add the bread cubes and let soak until softened, about 15 minutes.

Heat 2 tablespoons of the olive oil in a 10-inch cast-iron or nonstick skillet with a heatproof handle over medium heat. Add the onion and cook until wilted, about 4 minutes. Add the peppers and cook, stirring until crisp-tender, about 5 minutes. Season well with salt and pepper. Stir the sliced potato into the skillet gently. Add the butter and the remaining 1 tablespoon oil to the skillet, and heat until the butter is foaming. Add the egg mixture to the pan and cook, still over medium heat, without stirring, just until the bottom is lightly browned, about 5 minutes. There should be a few bubbles at a time around the edges—any more than that means the frittata is cooking too quickly and the bottom will be too brown. In that case, remove the skillet from the heat, reduce the heat, and let the skillet sit a minute or two before returning it to the heat.

Transfer the skillet to the oven and cook just until the center is set—firm to the touch—about 25 minutes. If the edges are set and beginning to brown

continued on next page

before the center is set, remove the frittata from the oven and finish the frittata under a preheated broiler.

If you'd like to serve the frittata hot, let it stand at room temperature about 15 minutes. If you prefer it warm or at room temperature, let it stand a little longer. Run a rubber spatula around the edges of the frittata and shake the pan gently to free the bottom of the frittata. You can serve the frittata right out of the pan or slide it out onto a serving platter.

☞ This simple and satisfying dish can be made even simpler by using a leftover baked potato instead of starting from scratch by boiling a potato.

Variation

Ricotta Frittata

Omit the potato from the above recipe. After pouring the egg mixture into the pan, drop $1^{1}/_{3}$ cups fresh or whole-milk ricotta into the egg by the rounded tablespoonful, forming little pockets of ricotta throughout the frittata. Continue cooking as described above.

Artichoke and Bread Frittata

Frittata di Carciofi con Pane

1 pound baby artichokes

10 large eggs

$^{1}/_{4}$ cup milk

Salt

Freshly ground black pepper

1 $^{1}/_{2}$ cups cubed ($^{1}/_{2}$-inch) day-old bread, crusts removed

5 tablespoons extra-virgin olive oil

1 medium yellow onion, sliced thin (about 1 $^{1}/_{2}$ cups)

Makes 6 servings

Clean the artichokes as described in "for fully edible artichokes" on page 15. Leave them in the acidulated water until you're ready to slice them.

Drain the artichokes thoroughly and rap them, stem side up, on a kitchen towel to remove as much water as possible. Slice them $^{1}/_{4}$ inch thick.

Preheat the oven to 350° F. Beat the eggs, milk, 1 teaspoon salt, and $^{1}/_{4}$ teaspoon pepper in a large bowl. Add the bread cubes and let soak until softened, about 15 minutes.

While the bread is soaking, heat the olive oil in a 10-inch cast-iron or nonstick skillet with a heatproof handle over medium heat. Add the onion and artichokes and cook until softened, about 10 minutes. Season well with salt and pepper.

Add the egg mixture to the pan. Cook and serve as described in the preceding Potato and Pepper Frittata recipe.

Poached Seafood Salad

Insalata di Frutta di Mare

For the Court Bouillon

2 quarts water

½ cup dry white wine

2 celery stalks, trimmed and cut into 1-inch lengths

2 medium carrots, peeled and cut into 1-inch lengths

4 bay leaves

1 teaspoon black peppercorns

Salt

For the Salad

16 extra-large shrimp (about ¾ pound), shells and tails removed, deveined

1 pound small (with bodies from 4 to 6 inches long) calamari (squid), cleaned, bodies cut into ½-inch rings, tentacles reserved (page 40)

1½ pounds mussels, preferably cultivated

4 inner stalks celery with leaves, sliced thin (about 1½ cups)

2 tablespoons coarsely chopped fresh Italian parsley

1 teaspoon chopped garlic

½ cup extra-virgin olive oil

2 tablespoons wine vinegar

Salt

Crushed hot red pepper

Makes 6 servings

This is one of those dishes you can take in any direction you like. You can use whatever seafood is available — scungilli (sea conch), crabmeat, scallops, or any firm fish fillets. You can use lemon juice in place of part or all of the vinegar and dress the salad up with capers, black or green olives, roasted peppers, or diced tomatoes.

However you make it, it's best prepared about ½ hour before you serve it, to give the flavors a chance to develop. You can refrigerate the salad, but not for too long. And be sure to bring it to room temperature and check the seasonings before you serve it.

Make the court bouillon: Bring the water, wine, celery, carrots, bay leaves, peppercorns, and salt to a boil in a wide casserole or skillet. Adjust the heat to simmering, cover, and cook 10 minutes.

Add the shrimp to the court bouillon and cook them until they are barely opaque in the center, about 4 minutes. Fish the shrimp out with a wire skimmer and spread them out on a baking sheet. Don't worry if they aren't completely drained—you'll use some of the liquid to finish the salad. Add the calamari and poach just until they are firm and tender, about 3 minutes. If in doubt, bite into one ring—it should be springy but tender, not chewy or tough. Don't overcook the calamari or it will become tough. Fish out the calamari and add them to the shrimp.

Bring the court bouillon to a boil. Stir in the mussels, cover the pot, and cook until the shells open and the mussels are firm but not tough, about 4 minutes. Remove with a skimmer and add to the other poached seafood. (You can speed things up a little by ladling about ½ cup of the court bouillon into a 3-quart saucepan before you add the shrimp. Bring the liquid in the saucepan to a boil and cook the mussels in that.) When the mussels are cool enough, pluck the meat from the shells directly into a large serving bowl.

continued on next page

Poached Seafood Salad *(continued)*

☞ I like the crunch of celery here, but also the flavor the leaves give. Use some of the thinner, pale stalks from the heart of the celery and you'll get both.

Make the salad: Transfer the cooled shrimp and calamari to the bowl with the mussels, shaking off any peppercorns as you do. Add the celery, parsley, and garlic, then pour in the olive oil and vinegar. Toss until mixed, drizzling in some of the reserved cooking liquid to taste. Season the salad to taste with salt and crushed red pepper. The salad should be very moist and glisten with dressing. If not, add a dash of olive oil and vinegar and a little more of the cooking liquid. Let the salad stand at room temperature about 30 minutes, tossing once or twice. Check the seasoning and toss well just before serving.

Striped Bass Salad

Insalata di Branzino

Court bouillon (see preceding recipe)

1 large cucumber

1 medium red onion, sliced thin (about 1 cup)

2 to 3 tablespoons coarsely chopped fresh Italian parsley

1 pound striped-bass fillets or steaks or any other firm-fleshed fish, like sea bass or black bass, or head and trimmings from a 5-pound whole fish

½ cup extra-virgin olive oil, or as needed

3 tablespoons red-wine vinegar, or as needed

Crushed hot red pepper

Salt

Makes 6 servings

I love this salad—it's so fresh and clean-tasting. Sometimes I make a meal of it. Because I really want you to make this salad, I'm calling for store-bought fillets. But if you have a whole striped bass that you've filleted, this salad is a great way to use odds and ends from the fish. Poach the fish head and the belly parts you've trimmed from the fillets in the court bouillon. Remove the meat from the cheeks and along the top of the head, and trim the bellies of bones and skin.

I like the crushed red pepper to be conspicuous in this salad, so don't be afraid to use it. Start with about ½ teaspoon and go from there. And don't throw the cooking liquid out: save it to make the salad nice and juicy. You could use crabmeat or even chicken instead, I guess, but white fish, like the bass, is perfect prepared this way.

Prepare the court bouillon as described in preceding recipe, but use white-wine vinegar instead of white wine. While it is simmering, trim the ends from the cucumber, peel it, and cut it in half lengthwise. Scrape out the seeds—or leave them in if you like them—and cut the cucumber pieces into half-moons. Place the cucumber, red onion, and parsley in a mixing bowl.

Slide the bass into the boiling court bouillon and reduce the heat immediately to a simmer. Cook until the fish "opens up"—barely starts to flake—about 8 minutes. Remove the fillets and cool them to room temperature. Peel off the skin if necessary, and scrape or cut away the soft, darker meat from the skin side of the fillet. Flake the fish into big pieces, removing any bones and adding the fish pieces to the mixing bowl as you do.

Drizzle the olive oil and vinegar over the salad and toss to mix. Season generously with crushed red pepper and salt to taste. Spoon in enough of the reserved cooking liquid to make the salad nice and juicy. Taste the salad, adding more vinegar, salt, or crushed red pepper if you like. Mound the salad high on a deep serving platter and spoon the juices left in the bowl over it. If you like, drizzle olive oil onto the platter around the salad.

☞ In preparing the court bouillon, substitute white-wine vinegar for the dry white wine. The vinegar will help keep the fish fillets in this recipe intact, but it can toughen shrimp and other shellfish. That's why I use dry white wine in the court bouillon in the preceding recipe.

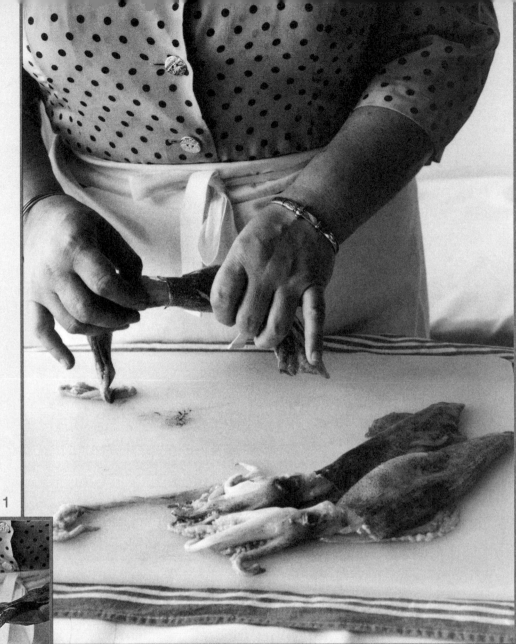

To Clean Calamari (Squid)

1. Holding the body of the squid firmly with one hand, grasp the tentacles firmly with the other. Wiggle and pull the tentacles to remove them and all the innards attached to them from the body cavity. If you pull slowly but surely, you'll remove all the insides in one shot. If not, reach in and pull out with your fingers what you missed.

2. With your thumb and forefinger, pull the transparent quill out of the body.

3. Cut off the tentacles just below the eyes.

4. Remove the "beak," the hard round object that acts as the squid's mouth, as well. Cut off the pointed tip of the body. Holding the body under cold running water, rinse the inside of the body, letting water flow through the body.

5. If the recipe calls for peeling, pull the skin off the body. Depending on the recipe, leave the bodies whole or cut them crosswise into rings in the size specified in the recipe.

Use cleaned calamari in:

> *Calamari in the "Luciana" Style (page 293)*
>
> *Poached Seafood Salad (page 37)*
>
> *Fried Squid (page 290)*
>
> *Grilled Calamari (page 292)*
>
> *Oven-Baked Squid (page 294)*
>
> *Stuffed Calamari Braised with Fresh Peas (page 295)*

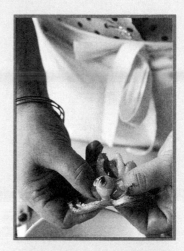

4

5

3

We eat a lot of seafood-and-potato salads on the Istrian Peninsula, where I come from. The potatoes act like pasta—a neutral carrier of the flavors of octopus, salt cod, or whatever seafood you are using, making a heartier and satisfying dish. When I opened my first restaurant in 1971, salt cod was a tough sell. It still is to some extent, but I keep trying, because I love it so much and it's such an important part of the Italian culinary culture. Any day now, I keep telling myself, it will catch on.

Salt Cod, Potato, and String Bean Salad

Insalata di Baccalà, Patate, e Fagiolini

1 pound salt cod, preferably trimmings from Baccalà Marechiara (page 298) soaked as described on page 299

2 medium Idaho or Yukon Gold potatoes (about 1¼ pounds)

½ pound haricots verts or young string beans, both ends trimmed

½ cup thinly sliced red onion

1 tablespoon chopped fresh Italian parsley

½ cup extra-virgin olive oil

Salt

Freshly ground black pepper

3 tablespoons red-wine vinegar

Fresh Italian parsley sprigs, optional

Makes 6 appetizer servings

Salt cod is expensive. This salad is a good way to use trimmings from a whole boneless or bone-in side of baccalà you bought to make the Marechiara on page 298. If you trim the baccalà before you soak it and save the unsoaked trimmings in the refrigerator, you can take your time making the salad. If you trim the baccalà after soaking it, you'll have to make the salad within a day or two.

I picture this dish as part of a beautiful buffet, but it would make a nice first course at dinner, or a lunch dish all by itself. The directions below will give you a warm salad—the way I like it. If you'd rather have a room-temperature salad, just let the potatoes and beans cool all the way. But please don't make this with chilled potatoes. Cooked potatoes should never see the inside of the refrigerator. They become waxy and tasteless.

Bring a large saucepan of water to the simmer and drop in the soaked salt cod. Cook until the salt cod starts to "open up" and flake, about 8 minutes. Remove the salt cod from the water with a slotted spoon or skimmer and let cool to room temperature. With your fingers, flake the cod into pieces of about 1½ inches, removing any bones and skin as you go.

Scrub the potatoes, place them in a large saucepan, and add enough cold, salted water to cover them by at least four fingers. Bring the water to a boil and cook the potatoes until tender but not mushy, about 35 minutes. Check them carefully toward the end of cooking and remove them before the jackets split. Once that happens, the potatoes can become waterlogged. Let the potatoes stand until they are cool enough to peel.

While the potatoes are boiling, cook the haricots verts or string beans in a large pot of boiling salted water until *al dente*, tender but firm, 6 to 8 minutes. Drain and rinse very briefly under cold running water. If using the string beans, split them in half by pinching one end of the beans and pulling the halves apart, reserving any of the little beans that pop out. Set aside.

Assemble the salad while the potatoes are still warm. Peel the potatoes, slice them about $1/2$ inch thick, and place in a large bowl. Add the string beans, red onion, chopped parsley, and salt cod. You may add all the salt cod at this point, or set aside some of the larger pieces to decorate the top of the finished salad. Drizzle all but 3 tablespoons of the oil over the salad and toss gently, to coat the ingredients with olive oil but keep the pieces of salt cod as large as possible. Season to taste with salt and pepper.

Beat the remaining 3 tablespoons olive oil with the vinegar and salt and pepper to taste. Arrange the salad in the center of a large platter or divide it among plates. Drizzle the vinaigrette around the salad and decorate with the reserved salt cod and parsley sprigs, if you like.

I love scungilli—those delicacies of the Mediterranean that look like little conchs. They have such wonderful texture and flavor that, even though you might be unfamiliar with them and have to search them out, I want to include them here for you to enjoy. More than just give you recipes, I want to lead you gently through my culinary culture, to take your hand and share with you what made me what I am. Also, scungilli are so much a part of the Italian-American table that to omit them would make this book truly incomplete.

Scungilli can be found fresh in their shells in Italian fish markets or, in many seafood stores, removed from the shells and frozen. They are good both ways, although I prefer the frozen ones, as the freezing process tenderizes them. This dish is a great appetizer, but it can be served as a main course on a hot summer day, or as part of a buffet table.

Scungilli Salad

Insalata di Scungilli

1 ½ pounds frozen scungilli, or 18 to 20 pieces fresh in the shell

3 bay leaves

1 ½ cups tender stalks of celery, sliced

1 cup pitted and sliced green olives, preferably Cerignola

3 cloves garlic, chopped

½ teaspoon crushed hot red pepper

6 tablespoons extra-virgin olive oil

4 tablespoons red-wine vinegar

I like this and other seafood salads served at room temperature as soon as they are made, but most people like this dish chilled. If you are one of them, refrigerate it just long enough to chill it, a half-hour or so. Longer will dull the fresh flavors of the salad. Toss well and check the seasonings just before you serve it.

For frozen scungilli: First defrost the scungilli for several hours in the refrigerator. Put the scungilli in a large saucepan and pour in enough water to cover them by two fingers. Drop in the bay leaves and bring the water to a boil over high heat. Adjust the heat to simmering and cook until a fork pierces the scungilli easily and slips right out, about 30 minutes.

For fresh scungilli: Place the scungilli, still in their shells, in a large pot. Pour in enough water to cover by two fingers. Drop in the bay leaves and

¼ cup chopped fresh
    Italian parsley, not too
    fine
Fine sea salt

Makes 6 servings

bring the water to a boil over high heat. Adjust the heat to simmering and cook 30 minutes. Remove one of the scungilli and, with a fork, try to pry the meat out of its shell. If it comes out easily and the fork slips out (as above), they are done. If not, continue cooking and check the scungilli for doneness every few minutes.

Drain the scungilli, reserving ½ cup of the cooking liquid, and let them stand until cool enough to handle. Clean the scungilli: Remove the hard, round cartilage from the fat end of the conch. Look for the brown digestive sac that curls along the outer curved side of the tail, and remove that by scraping it out. Slice the cleaned scungilli thin lengthwise.

Toss the sliced scungilli, celery, olives, garlic, hot pepper, and reserved cooking liquid in a large bowl. Add oil and vinegar, parsley, and salt, toss, and serve.

To: Lidia Bastianich
From: Suzanne Sciarretta
Subject:

>>>I love Lidia; she makes me happy because I'm Italian and she reminds me of my aunt and some of my family memories of good Italian meals, storytelling, and the warmth we Italians share with others. *Mille grazie!* What great cooks we are!<<<

As is, this salad is a delicious bruschetta topping that can be used as an appetizer or an hors d'oeuvre. Served over a bed of dressed arugula, it makes a great lunch.

Chickpea and Tuna Salad

Insalata di Tonno e Ceci

1½ cups dried chickpeas

1 teaspoon salt, or as needed

Three 6-ounce cans tuna packed in olive oil, drained (about 2 cups)

1 small red onion, sliced thin (about 1 cup)

¼ cup extra-virgin olive oil

2 tablespoons red-wine vinegar

2 tablespoons chopped fresh Italian parsley

Freshly ground black pepper

6 thick slices country bread, toasted or grilled lightly, optional

Makes 6 servings

In Tuscany, cannellini beans would be paired with tuna for a similar dish. I don't see why black-eyed peas or kidney beans couldn't be used as well. Just make sure the beans are tender— almost to the point of breaking—so that they absorb the tuna flavor and stay put on the toasted bread, if that's how you choose to serve them. Don't be afraid to crush them lightly!

Place the chickpeas in a small, deep bowl and pour in enough cold water to cover by at least 4 inches. Let the beans soak in a cool place or the refrigerator at least 12 hours or up to 1 day.

Drain the beans and transfer them to a 3-quart saucepan. Pour in enough water to cover by three fingers. Bring to a boil over high heat. Adjust the heat to simmering and cook until the beans are tender, 1½ to 2 hours. Check the level of the water, adding a little water from time to time to keep the beans completely covered. Remove the chickpeas from the heat, stir in the salt, and let stand until cooled.

Drain the beans and transfer them to a large serving bowl. Add the tuna, red onion, olive oil, vinegar, and parsley. Toss gently to keep the tuna in big pieces. Add salt if necessary, and pepper to taste. Toss gently and serve, with the bread if you like.

Italians eat a lot of *contorni* (side dishes) with their meals. Years ago, as the workforce turned from tending the fields, where they were able to gather at home for lunch, to working in factories, where they had to bring their lunch with them, pickled vegetables became welcome in the lunch box. They were, and are, a convenient and tasty vegetable side dish that travels well.

Pickled Vegetables

Giardiniera

2 cups distilled white vinegar

2 tablespoons salt, preferably coarse sea salt

2 medium carrots, peeled and cut into $\frac{1}{4} \times \frac{1}{4} \times$ 2–inch julienne strips (about 1 $\frac{1}{2}$ cups)

16 small pearl onions, peeled (about 1 cup)

2 cups cauliflower florets, cut into 1-inch pieces (about half a small head)

2 medium celery stalks, trimmed, peeled, and cut into 1-inch pieces (about 1 cup)

1 medium red bell pepper, cored, seeded, and sliced $\frac{1}{3}$ inch thick (1 generous cup)

$\frac{1}{2}$ cup pitted meaty green olives, such as Cerignola

3 tablespoons extra-virgin olive oil

Makes 3 quarts

There is not much to peel in celery, just the strings that run along the ribs that can be annoying to eat. To remove them, I take a peeler and lightly run it along the back of the celery rib. Another way to remove them is with a paring knife. When you are trimming the base or the top of the stalk, don't just chop away, but gently hold the stalk in your hands and cut from the inside of the stalk to the outside without cutting all the way through. Just before finishing the cut, pull the knife toward you and the strings should peel off down the length of the stalk.

Pour 3 quarts of water into a 5-quart pot, add the vinegar and salt, and bring to a boil. Add the carrots and onions; cook 2 minutes. Add the cauliflower and celery; cook 2 minutes. Stir in the red pepper and continue cooking until all the vegetables are softened but still quite firm, about 1 minute. Drain the vegetables well and transfer them to a bowl large enough to hold them comfortably. Cool to room temperature.

When all the vegetables are cool, season them with salt, toss in the olives, and drizzle the olive oil over everything. Toss well and let marinate at least 1 hour at room temperature, or 1 to 2 days in the refrigerator, before serving. (The *giardiniera* will keep refrigerated up to 7 days.) If refrigerated, bring the *giardiniera* to room temperature before serving.

Pickled Mushrooms

Funghi sott'Olio

1 pound small, firm white or cremini mushrooms, with caps about 1 inch in diameter

1¾ cups white-wine vinegar

1 cup water

4 cloves garlic, crushed

2 bay leaves

2 teaspoons black peppercorns

¼ cup extra-virgin olive oil

Salt

Makes 3 cups

☞ Choose firm, unblemished mushrooms without exposed gills for this preparation. They will look nicer after pickling.

If you like, trim the stems of the mushrooms even with the caps— they will look neater that way. Save the stems for vegetable stock or chop them for a vegetable soup. The mushrooms keep for a few days in the refrigerator. If you want to keep them longer, top them off with enough oil and vinegar to cover them completely. The oil will float to the top and seal out air. They'll keep a couple of weeks like this.

Wash the mushrooms in a sieve briefly under cold water. Dry them well. Bring ¾ cup of the vinegar, the water, garlic, bay leaves, and peppercorns to a boil in a 2-quart saucepan. Add the mushrooms, return the liquid to a boil, and cook 2 minutes. Let cool.

When cool, transfer the entire mixture to a clean 1-quart jar with a tight-fitting lid. Pour in the olive oil, add a couple healthy pinches of salt, then pour in enough of the remaining white-wine vinegar to come to the top of the mushrooms, about 1 cup. Shake the jar well and marinate the mushrooms in the refrigerator for 2 to 3 days. Bring to room temperature and pick out and discard the peppercorns before you serve the mushrooms.

The ultimate family food critic: Grandma Erminia giving her rating

These herby, lemony artichokes make a lovely dish for a buffet table or as part of an assorted antipasto. I serve it as a main course at Felidia, especially in summer, with dressed steamed shrimps or with *mozzarella di bufala.*

Marinated Artichokes

Carciofi Marinati

2 lemons

24 small artichokes (about 3 pounds)

¼ cup extra-virgin olive oil

8 cloves garlic, crushed and peeled

2 tablespoons chopped fresh Italian parsley

1 tablespoon chopped fresh mint

2 teaspoons salt

1 teaspoon crushed hot red pepper

Freshly ground black pepper

Makes 6 servings

Remove the peel from the lemons with a vegetable peeler. Squeeze the juice.

Clean the artichokes according to the directions for "fully edible artichokes" on page 15. Be sure to plunge them into the acidulated water as you work.

Drain the cleaned artichokes thoroughly. Choose a pot large enough to hold the artichokes snugly side by side. Arrange the artichokes cut side down in the pot. Pour the olive oil into the pot. Scatter the garlic, parsley, mint, and lemon peel over the artichokes. Pour in the lemon juice, then enough water to cover the artichokes up to but not over the base of the stems.

Add the salt and red and black pepper, cover the pot loosely with aluminum foil, and bring to a boil over high heat. Adjust the heat to simmering and cook until the artichoke hearts are tender and about a third of the liquid is left, about 30 minutes. Let the artichokes cool to room temperature in the cooking liquid. Serve at room temperature with some of the cooking liquid as a sauce.

Fried Banana Peppers

Peperoni in Padella

¼ cup extra-virgin olive oil

6 banana or cubanella peppers or other long, thin-fleshed mildly spicy pepper

12 cloves garlic, peeled

Salt

¼ cup plain bread crumbs or Seasoned Bread Crumbs 1 or 2 (page 20)

Makes 6 servings

Banana peppers are a long, thin-skinned mildly spicy variety of pepper that, because of their skin and fairly meaty texture, are perfect for frying. To serve them as a room-temperature salad, prepare them as described below. If you prefer to serve them hot, arrange the peeled peppers and their juices in a baking dish, sprinkle the bread crumbs over them, and bake in a hot oven until the crumbs are lightly browned.

Heat the olive oil in a large, heavy skillet over medium heat. Arrange the whole peppers in a single layer in the skillet. Whack the garlic cloves with the flat side of a knife and scatter them around the peppers. Place a smaller skillet over the peppers to weight them lightly. As the peppers soften, the weight of the skillet will help them cook and brown evenly. Fry the peppers and garlic, turning as necessary, until the peppers are evenly browned and blistered on all sides and the garlic is golden brown, about 10 minutes for the peppers, less for the garlic. Remove and reserve the garlic cloves as they brown.

Remove the skillet from the heat and transfer the peppers to a baking pan to cool. Reserve the oil in the pan and any juices from the pan.

Pull out and discard the core and seeds from the peppers, draining the juice from inside the pepper and adding it to the juices in the baking pan. Pull off as much of the skins from the peppers as possible and tear each pepper lengthwise into four strips. Arrange the pepper strips in a serving dish as you work. Add the oil from the skillet and the reserved garlic to the juices in the baking pan and season to taste with salt. Sprinkle the pepper strips with a light coat of bread crumbs and toss to mix. Let stand at room temperature 30 minutes to 1 hour before serving.

O LIVES, LIKE PROSCIUTTO, should be included in any antipasto, elaborate or simple. Here are a couple of ways to dress up olives for your own *antipasto di casa*. Both suggestions use citrus to brighten up the flavor, and both benefit from standing at room temperature about an hour before serving. To make thin strips of orange or lemon zest, use a special tool called a zester, or remove the zest with a vegetable peeler, then cut it into thin strips. In either case, be sure to remove just the orange or yellow part of the fruit, without the bitter white pith that lies underneath.

Toss large, meaty green olives like Cerignolas with strips of lemon zest, a little lemon juice, some dried oregano, and a generous drizzle of olive oil.

Toss thin strips of orange zest with oil-cured Gaeta olives and a little squeeze of juice from the orange. Add some crushed hot red pepper if you like.

Seasoned Olives

To: Lidia Bastianich
From: Linda Haythorn
Subject:

> > > Most of all, you make me want to hug you after each show; your warmth comes through and the love for what you do shows clearly. You make me want to go back to my Italian roots, get back into the kitchen, and never buy fast food again.< < <

Sweet-and-sour dishes seem to be mostly tied to coastal Italy, where vinegar-preserved vegetables or fish were popular with the seafaring sailors on their long journeys. Caponata is one of these preparations—a traditional Sicilian mix of fried vegetables, eggplant being chief among them, dressed with a sweet-and-sour sauce.

This dish was ever-present on the menus of Italian-American restaurants. It's a good recipe for a home cook, too. It's simple to make and needs no imported ingredients—just good vegetables and the proper technique.

Sweet and Sour Marinated Vegetables

Caponata

1 medium red bell pepper, cored, seeded, and cut into 1-inch squares

½ cup vegetable oil

1 medium eggplant, stem removed, cut into 1-inch cubes

¼ cup olive oil

1 cup cubed (½-inch) zucchini

1 medium white onion, cut into large cubes (about 1½ cups)

½ cup diced celery

½ cup golden raisins

¼ cup pitted green olives

1 tablespoon pine nuts

1 tablespoon tiny capers, drained and rinsed

Salt and pepper to taste

2 fresh tomatoes, peeled, seeded, and diced (page 9)

Sometimes I peel eggplants completely, sometimes not at all. Leaving the peel on adds a slightly bitter taste—which I like— but also helps the eggplant hold its shape after you cut it into cubes or slices. If you want the best of both worlds, remove thick stripes of peel from the eggplant, leaving half the peel intact.

Caponata can last several days in the refrigerator and is even better after marinating for a day. It is best eaten at room temperature, so remove it from the refrigerator about 2 hours before serving. Caponata is usually served as part of an antipasto assortment, although it makes a wonderful summer contorno, or side dish, to grilled meats or fish.

Bring a medium saucepan of salted water to a boil. Stir in the red pepper and cook 1 minute. Drain thoroughly.

Heat the vegetable oil in a large skillet over medium heat until a cube of eggplant dipped in the oil gives off a lively sizzle. Add the eggplant cubes and fry, stirring and turning them so they cook evenly, until the eggplant is golden brown on all sides. Remove the eggplant with a slotted spoon and drain on a paper towel.

¼ cup white vinegar

2 tablespoons sugar

1 tablespoon chopped fresh mint leaves

Makes 6 servings

Heat the olive oil in a separate large skillet. Add the zucchini and cook, stirring occasionally, until golden, about 5 minutes. Remove with a slotted spoon and set aside. Add the onion to the oil remaining in pan and cook, stirring, 1 minute. Stir in the celery and cook until the vegetables are wilted, about 5 minutes. Stir in the raisins, green olives, pine nuts, capers, and blanched pepper. Season with salt and pepper to taste and continue cooking, stirring, until the vegetables are soft but not mushy, about 10 minutes. Add the diced tomatoes and cook until they are softened, about 5 minutes.

While the vegetables are cooking, make the sugar-mint syrup. Bring the vinegar to a boil in a small saucepan. Add the sugar and the mint, reduce the heat to low, and simmer until thick and syrupy, about 5 minutes.

Pour the syrup into the skillet of vegetables and cook until the vegetables are very soft and juicy but not broken up—you should be able to see the shape of each vegetable—3 to 4 minutes. Finally, stir in the eggplant and zucchini and cook 1 to 2 minutes. Cool completely before refrigerating.

Pan-Fried Garlic Bread

TRADITIONALLY, IN ITALIAN-AMERICAN RESTAURANTS, garlic bread entailed lots of chopped garlic mixed with butter and a little oil. This version, *struffinato*—or rubbed—with a smashed garlic clove, is more subtle, and is the right match for the Arugula and White-Bean Salad (page 60) or the Escarole and White-Bean Soup (page 86).

Choose a large, heavy skillet—cast iron is ideal—brush it lightly with olive oil, and set it over medium-low heat. Cut a loaf of Italian bread in half lengthwise, then cut it crosswise into 3- or 4-inch pieces. Rub the cut surfaces with a smashed garlic clove and brush them with Garlic-Infused Oil (page 17) or extra-virgin olive oil. Arrange as many of the pieces, cut side down, in the pan as fit without touching. Weight the bread down with a slightly smaller skillet and cook until the underside of the bread is golden brown and crispy, about 5 minutes. Remove and repeat as necessary with the remaining bread. You may keep the cooked garlic bread warm in an oven turned to the lowest setting.

Mozzarella

MOZZARELLA, A FRESH CHEESE, is made from *pasta filata* or pulled curds, a method that gives the cheese its chewy texture and fresh flavor. The process of mozzarella making starts as it does for other cheeses, by adding rennet, an enzyme, to warm milk. The rennet causes the milk to coagulate into curds (solids) that separate from the whey (liquid). To make mozzarella, these curds are then drained well and the mass of dried curd is added to a container of body-temperature milk, where it falls to the bottom and forms a smooth, soft mass. The cheesemaker lifts out the softened curds and gently pulls them, much like taffy and usually by hand, until they form a smooth, textured, and layered mass that is shaped by hand into mozzarella forms. All this needs to be done rather quickly, so the curds do not harden before the mozzarella is formed. In this process of pulling and forming the cheese, milk is captured between the layers, where it forms what in Italy is called *la lacrima* — the tear. When fresh mozzarella is cut, it releases some of the milk caught between the layers. The qualities of a good mozzarella are a resilient texture, a complex flavor from the milk, and juiciness from the *lacrime*.

Campania, the region of Italy that claims Naples for its capital, is the epicenter of Italian mozzarella making. Much of the mozzarella made in Campania starts with water-buffalo milk, which gives the cheese a special tang and complexity of flavor. According to the people of Campania, *mozzarella di bufala* should be eaten within 3 hours after it's made — a luxury not available to us here in the States. But we do have excellent *mozzarella di bufala* flown in on an almost daily basis. When you are buying imported *mozzarella di bufala*, a reputable producer and distributor are very important. Look for a mozzarella that has been packaged in its own whey, and is sealed tightly with plastic. When you open the package, the cheese should be firm and moist, not falling apart or very soft; it should be sweet with a pleasant tang, but not at all sour. It is best to use the mozzarella once the package is opened, but you can keep it for a day, drained and wrapped in plastic wrap. If you can't find *mozzarella di bufala*, track down a local maker of cow's-milk mozzarella — someone who makes the cheese fresh at least every day, if not several times a day.

Fresh mozzarella rolls with spirals of prosciutto running through them are staples at every Italian-American deli. They are made by stretching the still-warm fresh mozzarella into a rectangle, covering the cheese with prosciutto, and rolling the whole thing up into a neat loaf shape. As the mozzarella cools, it firms up and becomes compact and easy to slice. You can come close to this effect by following this procedure.

Prosciutto-Stuffed Mozzarella

One piece fresh mozzarella, about 1 pound

4 to 5 slices imported Italian prosciutto

Makes about 20 slices

If you can buy fresh mozzarella "hot off the press," before it's been refrigerated, it will be easier to cut and fill. There are a lot of different fillings you can use in place of the prosciutto — olives, salami, fresh basil leaves, or pesto.

Choose a thin-bladed knife with a blade long enough for you to see what the blade is doing as it cuts through the cheese.

Place the mozzarella on the work surface with one of the short ends facing you. Make a cut parallel to the work surface about $\frac{1}{2}$ inch from the top of the cheese but don't cut all the way through the cheese. Continue cutting, turning the cheese as you go to "unroll" the cheese and form a more or less even $\frac{1}{2}$-inch sheet. If you have cut through the cheese, it can be patched.

Take a look at the sheet of cheese. You'll notice that the two ends curl inward. Arrange the cheese on a large piece of plastic wrap with the two ends of the cheese that curl inward facing up — that will make the cheese easier to re-form. Cover the top of the cheese with an even layer of prosciutto. Roll the cheese more or less into its original shape. Wrap the cheese snugly in plastic wrap and refrigerate until it is firm, at least 12 hours or up to 1 full day.

Unwrap the cheese and cut into thin slices with a thin-bladed knife.

If you're preparing an antipasto that includes provolone and prosciutto—and every antipasto should include prosciutto—this is a good place to use odds and ends of both.

Cherry Peppers Stuffed with Prosciutto and Provolone

Bottled hot cherry peppers

Imported provolone, in
1 piece

Thinly sliced prosciutto

Cherry peppers are plump, round peppers that are usually sold pickled in vinegar. They range in color from bright red to dull green, and in spiciness from mild to hot. Good in salads and as part of an antipasto tray, they add a kick to cooked dishes, too, like the Chicken Scarpariello on page 262. These stuffed cherry peppers will look very nice and go a long way to dressing up an antipasto table if you use both red and green peppers. Sometimes you will see these already stuffed hot peppers marinating in oil and vinegar. You can do the same by packing the stuffed peppers into a clean jar and pouring the liquid from the jar of cherry peppers and some olive oil over them. Store them in the refrigerator for up to a few days like that, but be sure to drain them well before you serve them, or they will be messy to eat.

Cut out the stems and scrape out the seeds from the cherry peppers. Cut pieces of provolone that will fit comfortably into the cherry peppers. Wrap each piece of provolone in a single layer of prosciutto, then place the prosciutto-wrapped provolone pieces into the peppers. Either serve them as is, or place them in an empty jar and pour enough of the liquid from the jar of cherry peppers to come within an inch of the top of the jar. Pour in olive oil to fill. Cover the jar tightly and store in the refrigerator for up to 3 days.

Red radicchio—there is also the green *radicchio zuccherino* (see page 62)—takes its name from the town where it originated. The round radicchio that looks like a small head of red cabbage is *radicchio di Chioggia* and is named for Chioggia, a city on the Adriatic that is also known for its wonderful and bountiful wholesale fish market. The longer, more bitter, and deeper red *radicchio Trevisano* is from Treviso, a city in the Veneto where radicchio is king. When the Trevisano is in season in the fall and winter, it is celebrated and enjoyed in just about everything: pasta, risotto, soups, *contorni*, and, of course, in salads.

Tri-Color Salad

Insalata Tricolore

4 bunches arugula, stems trimmed and leaves cut in half

2 small heads of *radicchio di Chioggia* or *Trevisano*, cores removed, leaves cut in 1-inch pieces

4 heads of endive, cored, trimmed, and cut into 1-inch pieces

Salt

Freshly ground pepper

6 tablespoons extra-virgin olive oil, or as needed

3 tablespoons red-wine or balsamic vinegar, or as needed

Makes 6 servings

This was one of the first dishes that brought the taste of contemporary Italy to the Italian-American restaurant scene. It came into vogue in the early seventies when red radicchio and arugula became available in the States. While the Italians will toss any vegetable in their salads, I think the addition of endive was a play on the color of the red, green, and white Italian flag.

This salad is a great base for additions, from walnuts and pine nuts to different cheeses and cold cuts, such as salami or turkey, and even fish such as tuna, shrimp, or poached whitefish.

Wash and dry the arugula, radicchio, and endive according to the directions on page 67. Store loosely covered in the refrigerator for up to one day.

Tumble the greens into a serving bowl and season them lightly with salt and pepper. Drizzle enough olive oil over them, while tossing gently, to coat the leaves evenly and lightly. Drizzle the vinegar over the salad, while tossing gently, until the balance of oil and acidity is to your taste. Taste and season with additional salt and pepper if necessary.

This salad is not traditionally Italian—it was invented in Las Vegas—but it was very much a part of the Italian-American restaurant scene in the 1960s and '70s. Typically, the dressing was made in front of the guests, a process that started by rubbing the salad bowl with a clove of garlic. Anchovies were mashed in the bowl, condiments were added, and the dressing was finished with olive oil and lemon juice before the romaine and croutons were tossed in. The finishing touches were a hot 2-minute egg, cracked open, its yolk separated on a spoon, then, with a fork, broken and drizzled over the salad; a sprinkling of Parmigiano-Reggiano; and, of course, a grinding of black pepper from a yard-long wooden pepper mill!

Caesar Salad

Insalata Cesare

- 2 cups cubed (½-inch) firm-textured white bread
- 3 young, firm heads romaine lettuce, or one 18-ounce package hearts of romaine
- 2 tablespoons red-wine vinegar, plus more for dressing the salad
- 2 tablespoons fresh lemon juice
- 4 cloves garlic
- 4 anchovy fillets
- ⅓ cup extra-virgin olive oil, or as needed
- 1 tablespoon Dijon mustard
- 1 hard-boiled egg yolk (page 17)
- ½ teaspoon salt

Pick the youngest, crunchiest romaine heads you can find. Keep them crisp, before and after cleaning, in the vegetable drawer of the refrigerator. Even if you pick young, crispy lettuce, you should use only the pale-green and yellow inner leaves for this salad. But don't throw out the outer leaves. Shred them and stir them into soups, or into a panful of sautéed fresh peas.

The dressing shouldn't be too dense; it should be just thick enough to coat each leaf lightly. The cheese that is added at the end will thicken it a little. Oil and vinegar stirred in at the end is a little touch of mine. It's how we serve the salad at Lidia's Kansas City and Pittsburgh. Another little touch that looks nice on a plate is to set one or two whole romaine leaves on the plate and pile the cut leaves over it. Shaving Parmigiano-Reggiano over the finished salad looks nice and tastes nice, too. It's a good thing to keep in mind for other salads as well.

½ teaspoon Worcestershire
sauce

Freshly ground black pepper

1 cup grated Parmigiano
Reggiano cheese, plus a
block of Parmigiano-
Reggiano for shaving

Makes 6 servings

Traditionally, Caesar salad was made with a barely cooked egg. Here I use a hard-boiled egg, as I do in my restaurants, for safety reasons.

Heat the oven to 350° F. Spread the bread cubes out on a baking sheet and bake, tossing them once or twice so they cook evenly, until golden brown, about 12 minutes. Remove and cool. (The croutons may be prepared up to a day in advance. If necessary, recrisp them in a 350° F oven for a few minutes.)

If using whole heads of romaine lettuce, remove the darker outer leaves to expose the pale-green center. Reserve the outer leaves for another use, if you like. Cut out the core and separate the hearts of romaine into individual leaves. Wash the leaves in a sink of cool water and drain them well, preferably in a salad spinner. Place the leaves in a large bowl, cover them loosely with damp paper towels, and store in the refrigerator up to 8 hours.

Combine 2 tablespoons vinegar, the lemon juice, garlic, and anchovies in a blender or the work bowl of a food processor. Blend until smooth, adding some of the ⅓ cup olive oil if there isn't enough liquid to move the mixture around the blender jar. Add the mustard, hard-boiled egg yolk, salt, Worcestershire sauce, pepper, and remaining olive oil if any. Blend until smooth and creamy. Taste the dressing; if it's a little too tangy, pour in a splash or two of olive oil and blend until it's incorporated.

Stack the leaves in a large, preferably wooden serving bowl. Bring the bowl to the table and, using a salad fork and spoon, cut the leaves into 1-inch pieces, as used to be done tableside at Italian-American restaurants. (Of course, you can cut the leaves with a knife beforehand.) Pour the dressing over the salad, add a splash of vinegar and a healthy splash of olive oil, and toss until all the leaves are coated with dressing. Toss in the croutons and ground black pepper to taste. Lastly (so it doesn't clump), sprinkle the grated cheese over the salad, tossing as you add. Serve on chilled plates and, with a vegetable peeler, shave some of the block of Parmigiano-Reggiano over each serving.

Arugula and White-Bean Salad

Insalata di Rucola e Cannellini

¾ cup Braised Cannellini
(page 349)

2 large bunches arugula
(about 1 pound)

1 small red onion, sliced
thin

Salt

Freshly ground black pepper

¼ cup extra-virgin olive oil,
or to taste

1 ½ tablespoons red-wine
vinegar, or to taste

Makes 6 servings

You can make this salad with Braised Cannellini, and save the rest for a side dish, or you can soak and cook an extra ¹/₂ cup of beans when you make the Escarole and White-Bean Soup on page 86. In that case, remove the beans for this salad before you stir in the escarole and finish the soup. If you do make this salad when you're making escarole soup, substitute some of the tender, inner leaves of escarole for the arugula, and use the tougher, outer escarole leaves for the soup.

You don't have to use cannellini beans. Kidney beans, chickpeas, or just about any beans you like can go into this salad. Whichever beans you use, cut the onion thin and at the last minute so it stays crunchy.

Fish the right amount of beans out of the cooking liquid and let them cool completely on a baking pan.

Meanwhile, pluck off the protruding stem ends of the arugula and discard any wilted or yellow leaves. Wash the arugula in a large bowl or sinkful of water to remove all sand and grit. Dry the arugula well, preferably in a salad spinner, and transfer it to a large mixing bowl. Scatter the cooled beans and the onion over the greens, and season everything with salt and pepper. Pour enough of the olive oil over the salad to coat the leaves lightly, toss to coat, then repeat with the vinegar. Check the seasoning, adding more salt, pepper, oil, or vinegar as you like. Serve immediately.

Spinach Salad

Insalata di Spinaci

¾ pound baby spinach leaves or tender leaf spinach, cut into ½-inch strips

6 large white mushrooms, stem ends trimmed, wiped clean and sliced thin (about 2 cups)

6 strips thick-sliced bacon, cut crosswise into ½-inch strips

Salt

Freshly ground black pepper

3 tablespoons red-wine vinegar

2 tablespoons extra-virgin olive oil

Makes 6 servings

This is the way we first served spinach salad at Ristorante Buonavia — and the way it was served in a lot of other Italian-American restaurants at the time. I love it just as much with sliced roasted or boiled beets in place of the mushrooms. If you don't have bacon, or don't want to use it, make a spinach-and-mushroom salad with an oil-and-vinegar dressing (using about ¼ cup olive oil to 3 tablespoons of vinegar). With a vegetable peeler, shave 1 cup of Parmigiano-Reggiano cheese and toss it in at the end.

Wash the spinach and dry it according to the directions on page 67. Toss the spinach and mushrooms in a large serving bowl and set them aside (or refrigerate for up to 6 hours).

Just before you're ready to serve the salad, scatter the bacon over the bottom of a heavy, small skillet. Place the skillet over medium heat and cook, stirring once in a while, until the bacon just starts to get crisp, about 5 minutes. Don't let the bacon get too crisp or too brown. While the bacon is cooking, season the salad well with salt and pepper. Pour the vinegar into the skillet and bring the liquid in the skillet to a quick boil. Immediately pour the hot dressing over the spinach and toss well. Drizzle the olive oil over the salad and toss to mix. Taste, adding salt, pepper, vinegar, or oil if you like. Serve immediately.

All throughout Istria, the corner of Italy where I grew up, people grow *radicchio zuccherino,* a member of the chicory family with rounded green leaves, related to the red radicchios more common in this country. In the corner of New York City where I live now, Grandma Erminia—my mother—tends our garden, which includes its own little patch of *radicchio zuccherino.* Although *zucchero* means "sugar" in Italian, this green could only be considered sweet when compared with the other members of the chicory family. It is slightly bitter, with a unique flavor that I love. My favorite is *primo taglio,* or "first cut," the first tender leaves that appear in the spring. Each time the leaves grow back after that first cut, they are a little more assertive and a little more bitter. They make a great salad, too, but there is nothing like *primo taglio.* If you are lucky enough to find it, or can get hold of the seeds to grow it, treat the leaves gently and dress it simply, as I do. I serve this salad in season at Felidia and Becco in New York. Grandma has a fresh harvest for me every morning.

Radicchio Zuccherino Salad

Insalata di Radicchio Zuccherino

6 cups *radicchio zuccherino* or other young, mildly bitter greens, such as chicory, frisée, or mâche

2 cloves garlic, crushed and peeled

Salt

Freshly ground black pepper

3 tablespoons extra-virgin olive oil

2 tablespoons mild red-wine vinegar

Makes 4 servings

Pick over the greens, discarding any wilted or yellow leaves. Wash and dry the greens according to directions on page 67. Rub a salad bowl with the garlic. Either discard the garlic or, for a more pronounced garlic flavor, cut it in a few big pieces which can be spotted easily and fished out of the salad. Add the greens and the garlic, if using, to the bowl. Season with salt and pepper, then drizzle enough olive oil over the greens to barely coat them. Toss gently, but well. Sprinkle the vinegar very lightly over the salad, using about one-fourth the amount of olive oil you used. Taste and add another light sprinkle of vinegar if you like. Check the seasonings and serve immediately.

When I was young, our big meal of the day was eaten early in the afternoon. Our evening meal was light—often a salad like this, with fresh-picked greens, and eggs collected that morning from the hens. For a real treat, and one that has Italy written all over it, round out this light meal with chunks of Parmigiano-Reggiano drizzled with a *tradizionale* balsamic vinegar.

Wild Greens and Hard-Boiled Egg Salad

Insalata di Cicoria e Uova

10 cups (loosely packed) wild and/or bitter greens, such as young chicory, young dandelion greens, arugula, wild arugula, or a mix of any of these

2 cloves garlic, peeled and cut in half

Salt

Freshly ground black pepper

⅓ cup extra-virgin olive oil, or as needed

2 tablespoons red-wine vinegar, or more to taste

4 hard-boiled eggs (page 17), peeled and cut into quarters lengthwise

Makes 6 servings

Pick over the greens, discarding any wilted or yellow leaves. Wash and dry the greens, gently remove them to a salad spinner, and dry them. Rub the inside of a large salad bowl with a clove of garlic and transfer the greens to the bowl. Season the greens with salt and pepper, then drizzle with ⅓ cup olive oil. Toss gently, but well. Sprinkle 2 tablespoons vinegar over the salad and toss well. Taste, and add another light sprinkle of olive oil or vinegar if you like. Add the eggs, toss gently, and serve immediately.

As a little girl, I went with my grandmother to search the woods for mushrooms and greens. When it came to dandelions, my grandmother would look for the young plants that hadn't formed a bud or yellow flower yet, gather up their leaves, and cut these off without damaging the root, so the plant's leaves would grow again the next year.

Salad of Dandelion Greens with Almond Vinaigrette and Dried Ricotta

Insalata di Dente di Leone con Vinaigrette di Mandorle e Ricotta Salata

1 pound tender, young dandelion greens (about 10 loosely packed cups)

6 tablespoons extra-virgin olive oil

¼ cup sliced almonds, toasted

2 tablespoons red-wine vinegar

1 teaspoon honey

Salt

Freshly ground black pepper

¼ pound ricotta salata, cut into shards with a vegetable peeler

Makes 6 servings

We found the greens for this salad by foraging in the woods and fields. You can forage farmers' markets for tender young dandelion greens, purslane, wild fennel, and pea shoots to make a tasty salad. Even your refrigerator or kitchen garden might yield some goodies, like chives, tender young Italian parsley, thinly sliced red cabbage, or the yellow leaves from celery hearts.

Cut any tough stems from the greens and trim any wilted, yellow, or tough leaves. Wash and dry them according to directions on page 67. The greens can be prepared up to several hours in advance and kept, loosely covered with a clean towel, in the refrigerator.

To make the dressing, combine the olive oil, 2 tablespoons of the toasted almonds, vinegar, and honey in a blender and blend until smooth. Add salt and pepper to taste. Place the greens in a large bowl, season them with salt and pepper, and pour the dressing over them. Toss well and divide the dressed greens among six plates, mounding them in the center of the plate. Sprinkle with the remaining 2 tablespoons of toasted almonds and top with shavings of ricotta salata. Serve immediately.

As far as I'm concerned, pasta salads shouldn't exist. Most often they are bland, overcooked, sticky, oily, or, as is often the case, all of the above. As much as I detest pasta salads, I love rice salads. In most Italian households, rarely a day goes by without some kind of carbohydrate—polenta, rice, or pasta—on the menu. On a summer day, when it is too hot to cook a big pot of polenta or pasta, a rice salad is just the ticket. You can boil the rice hours before you need it but toss it together with the other ingredients 30 minutes before you sit down to eat, so the rice absorbs the flavors of the other ingredients.

Rice Salad Caprese

Insalata di Riso alla Caprese

Rice salad can be made with long- or short-grain rice. I prefer short-grain rice, like Arborio, because it cooks up fluffier and absorbs more of the flavors of the other ingredients in the salad. Long-grain rice, like Carolina and Uncle Ben's, stays firmer and has a more "staccato" effect—that is, it'll stand more separately and distinctly from the other ingredients.

The one good thing I can say about pasta salads is that people feel comfortable improvising with them. Feel free to treat rice salads the same way. Although there are some traditional combinations, like seafood rice salad or shrimp-and-asparagus rice salad, you can really be creative and make any combination. And they are a great way to use leftovers.

For this dish, I took the classic salad of mozzarella, tomato, and basil from Capri, added rice, and dressed it with virgin olive oil and lemon juice. Some of my other favorite combinations are shredded grilled chicken, tomatoes, and arugula; cubes of grilled fresh tuna,

continued on next page

2 cups Arborio or other short-grain Italian rice

2 large or 3 medium vine-ripened tomatoes, cored and cut into 1-inch chunks (about 3 cups)

8 ounces fresh mozzarella, preferably *mozzarella di bufala,* cut in ½-inch cubes (1 generous cup)

Salt

Freshly ground black pepper

¼ cup extra-virgin olive oil

¼ cup fresh lemon juice

½ cup shredded fresh basil leaves

Makes 6 servings

Gaeta olives, Cerignola olives, cherry tomatoes, sliced red onion, and basil; grilled vegetables like peppers, zucchini, eggplant, and mushrooms with shavings of Parmigiano-Reggiano; thinly sliced raw baby artichokes, diced celery, and shavings of Parmigiano-Reggiano; rice-salad "antipasto" with cubed prosciutto, mortadella, cacciatorino, provola, Pecorino, Gaeta olives, roasted peppers, pickled mushrooms, and pickled artichokes.

Bring 2 quarts of salted water to boil in a large saucepan. Stir in the rice and cook until the rice is *al dente,* tender but firm, 14 to 16 minutes. Drain the rice and spread it out on a clean tray to cool.

When the rice is cool and feels dry, toss it in a bowl along with the tomatoes, mozzarella, salt, and pepper. Whisk the oil and lemon juice together in a small separate bowl and pour over the salad, tossing gently until all the rice is coated and the ingredients are mixed well. Let stand at room temperature 30 minutes to an hour. Just before serving, toss in the basil, check the seasoning, and serve.

Variations

Rice Salad with Chicken and Vegetables

This is a delicious way to use up whatever is left of a roasted or grilled chicken. The following amounts are just suggestions. You can use whatever vegetables you like or have in the garden, keeping more or less to a ratio of two parts rice to one part each vegetable and chicken. Cook and cool the rice as described above. When it is cool, toss in a large bowl together with 2 cups of room-temperature shredded or diced chicken with the skin removed, 10 cherry tomatoes cut in half, and ½ cup each cooked string beans cut into 1-inch lengths, thinly sliced scallions, and finely diced cooked carrots. Either dress with the lemon dressing from the above recipe, or make a simple oil and vinegar dressing, seasoned with mustard and honey to taste. If you like, lighten the salad by tossing it together with the cleaned salad greens of your choice.

Rice Salad with Seafood and Capers

Cook and cool the rice as described above. When it is cool, toss together with 2 cups cooked shrimp or scallops or 1 cup crabmeat, 1 cup sliced celery, 1/2 cup thinly sliced scallions, and 1/4 cup each pitted, chopped green olives and drained tiny capers. In a separate small bowl, mash 2 hard-boiled egg yolks together with 3 tablespoons wine vinegar. Switch to a whisk and beat in 1/3 cup extra-virgin olive oil. Taste and season with salt and pepper. Toss the dressing with the salad and taste, adding, salt, pepper, oil, or vinegar as you like. The salad can be lightened by tossing together with cleaned arugula leaves, torn into pieces.

REGARDLESS OF WHICH TYPE OR TYPES of salad greens you choose for your salad, there are a few basics that apply to caring for them. First, buy the greens as close to when you plan to serve them as possible. Second, dry the greens as thoroughly as possible so the dressing clings to the leaves and the salad isn't soggy. (Inexpensive salad spinners are the best way to do this.) Lastly, dress the salad just before you serve it.

Pick over whatever greens you are using for the salad, removing any wilted, yellow, or dark leaves. If necessary, cut the heads of lettuce in half and remove the core. Cut the leaves into bite-size pieces. Fill a clean sink with cool water, dump in the greens, and swish them gently in the water. Wait a few minutes to give the dirt a chance to settle to the bottom of the sink, then lift the greens to a bowl with a wire skimmer or your hands, letting as much of the water as possible drain back into the sink. Refill the sink and repeat the swishing. Drain again. Remove as much water from the greens as possible by spinning them in a salad spinner or shaking as much water from them as possible. Store them in the refrigerator in a colander over a bowl, covered with a kitchen towel. If you don't use a salad spinner, toss the greens gently in a large kitchen towel just before you dress them.

The simplest dressing, and the one I suggest to highlight the flavors of really fresh greens, is made with virgin olive oil, vinegar, salt, and pepper. Use these proportions as a guideline for dressing any kind of salad: three parts of extra-virgin olive oil to two parts of red- or white-wine vinegar. (You'll need about 1/2 cup dressing for each 6 cups of greens.) The way I dress a salad is first to season the greens with salt and pepper, then drizzle the oil over the greens and toss them to coat with oil. Lastly, I pour the vinegar over the greens and toss again. If you prefer, you can whisk the oil, vinegar, salt, and pepper in a bowl and toss the dressing with the salad. In either case, taste the salad and add oil, vinegar, salt, or pepper as you see fit.

Salad Basics

Soups

Soup is one of my favorite courses. You can create a soup out of just about anything, or out of almost nothing. As a child, I loved a two-ingredient soup my mother made by cooking flour in olive oil until golden, then adding water. She would season the soup with salt and pepper, let it simmer for 20 minutes, and it was done. With a thick slice of her homemade bread, it was delicious and heartwarming on cold winter nights. Sometimes she would add a sprig of rosemary as the soup simmered; sometimes she would whisk an egg or two and stir it into the soup. It was called *brodo brustula,* or "toasted soup."

Soup is a mellow, gentle food. Through simmering, all the characters become equally important—there is no sole protagonist. If food could have a political inclination, soups would surely be of the democratic persuasion, because every component is of equal importance; there is one harmonious and homogenized flavor, spoonful after spoonful.

When cooking soups, the work is mostly in the preparation of the ingredients. Once the vegetables are chopped and the other ingredients are prepared, the bulk of the work is behind you. After a quick sautéing of ingredients, the soup just perks away, needing only an occasional stir or a sprinkle of salt.

In Italy, soups are a very important course. The large repertoire of soup preparations can be divided into three basic categories, each with specific characteristics. *Brodo* is a clear soup made with meats, fish, or vegetables to which a little pasta, rice, eggs, vegetables, or cheese is added at the end of cooking. *Zuppa* is the name given to clear legume or vegetable soups thickened with bread, added toward the end of cooking and simmered until the bread breaks down, thickening the soup. A *minestra* is a soup made with legumes, vegetables, or meat, alone or in any combination, to which pasta or rice is added at the end of cooking.

Some traditional Italian soups have turned into classics of the Italian-American table. Bean-and-escarole soup (*escarola e fagioli*) came to the States with immigrants from the south of Italy. Three or four generations later, it is still being cooked and enjoyed in Italian-American households and restaurants. *Stracciatella alla romana*— spinach egg-drop soup—was a staple of Italian-American restaurant menus. Easy to make at home, once you have the stock, it is quick and nourishing—a light meal in minutes. In Italy it is used often as a meal for babies and children.

Lentil soup, whether simmered with broccoli or potato, or turned into *minestra di lenticchie* with the addition of rice, is still a favorite soup at my restaurants. Nutritious and delicious, lentils have been part of the Italian culture forever, and are resurging as a *contorno* (side dish) to complement simple and elegant main courses.

More often than not while I was growing up, *pasta e fagioli*— bean-and-pasta soup—or minestrone would be turned into a one-pot meal in our household. A piece of cured or fresh pork or a string of sausages added to the soup gave it flavor and did double duty as a second course. Although the *pasta e fagioli* stayed fairly constant year-round, the minestrone always took on the vestiges of the season. In spring, the aroma of wild fennel would waft through the kitchen while the pot of minestrone simmered; in summer, sweet kernels of corn from ears picked minutes before adding them to the soup would crackle under my teeth. Squash and mushrooms mellowed the minestrone in fall and turned its texture velvety. On the coldest days of winter, hearty root vegetables and cabbages were a welcome addition to the pot.

A holiday meal at our house always had a soup course. In most cases it was a *brodo* made from a freshly killed chicken or capon. "*Gallina veccia fa bon brodo,*" we used to say in dialect—"The old hen makes the best soup"—an old proverb that is still used today, although mostly in a different context: the statement of a maturing woman claiming her worth.

When my family traveled, soup was always a must. Till this day, when I come home from a trip there is always a pot of steaming chicken-and-rice soup awaiting me, put on for me by my mother,

Erminia, who has lived with me ever since my children, Joseph and Tanya, were born. She did this in order to allow me to pursue my passion and career as a chef. We shared the task of raising my children—the only way I could, or would, do it. But, then, it is in our culture for a family to stay close, to give each other support and unconditional love, and to pass on the wisdom of generations.

I know that the self-assurance and strength that I have are due in large part to the close, loving relationships I had with my family, especially my grandparents. As we moved on and immigrated to the United States in 1958, I felt the need for family even more, and made every effort to have my children grow up surrounded by the love and wisdom of their grandparents. And so my grandchildren, Olivia, Lorenzo, and Miles, are blessed with the love of three generations before them. There's always a special little pot on the stove for them when they come over—Olivia loves her grilled fish, which she dunks in olive oil; Lorenzo, a true Roman like his father, has to have his *pasta e sugo;* Miles, the smallest one, is just beginning to explore the world of flavors.

Stracciatelle are "little rags," and that is what the strands of beaten eggs cooked in the broth resemble. Eggs, so fresh they were still warm from the chicken or duck, were a cherished food as well as a good source of nourishment when I was growing up. We enjoyed them all ways, even raw. (My grandfather Giovanni would sip them still warm, puncturing a little hole in the egg and sipping the egg right from the shell.) One of my favorite breakfast treats was a whipped *zabaglione* folded into black coffee. Our *merende*— morning snacks—were often a frittata of some type, or eggs whisked into a simple soup, like this one. Eggs were used in making pasta dough or dropped in the pasta as a condiment.

Roman "Egg Drop" Soup

Stracciatella alla Romana

6 cups strained and defatted Chicken Stock (recipe follows)

Salt

Freshly ground black pepper

3 cups fresh spinach, stemmed, washed, and cut into ½-inch strips

3 eggs

⅓ cup freshly grated Parmigiano-Reggiano cheese, plus more for sprinkling over the soup

Makes 6 servings

When I make a brodo—*clear soup with a little something in it—I think of my father. He loved all kinds of soup, but especially these simple and elegant ones. My father was a very proper man who insisted on beautiful place settings and crisp linens. When we were young, my grandmother made this soup with duck eggs, chicken eggs, or even goose eggs—whichever type was freshest. Prepared without the spinach, this is a perfect soup for infants.*

Bring the chicken stock to a boil and season lightly with salt and pepper. Stir in the spinach and cook until wilted, about 1 minute. Meanwhile, beat the eggs with a good grinding of black pepper until thoroughly blended. Beat in the grated cheese. Pour the egg mixture into the soup while stirring constantly to break it into "little rags." Check the seasoning and serve immediately.

"STOCK" IS A PROFESSIONAL COOK'S WORD for a clear broth made by simmering poultry, meat, or fish bones along with herbs and aromatic vegetables. (It is possible to make an all-vegetable stock, too; see the recipe on page 76.) Homemade stocks make a big difference in the flavor of soups, sauces, and braised foods.

Making a stock is not a lot of work, and although it simmers for hours, you need only skim it a few times during that period. Mostly it perks away unattended until it is ready to be strained. There is one main thing to keep in mind when you make stocks and soups: If you start a stock by combining bones and meat with cold water, then bringing them to a simmer, you will extract more of the flavor from the bones into the stock. If, on the other hand, you add bones or meat to simmering water, you will lock in more of the flavor in the meat—which is good if you want to use the meat in the finished soup—and have a slightly less flavorful stock. If I add meat or poultry to a stock with the intention of serving some of the meat in the soup, as I do in the "Reinforced" Soup on page 78 or the Chicken and Rice Soup on page 75, I'll start the bones in cold water and add the meat once the bones have begun to simmer. This way, I get a good, rich stock *and* flavorful meat to add to the finished soup.

To end up with a nice clear broth, bring the stock ingredients to a vigorous boil and let them boil for a minute or so. Skim off the foam and fat that rise to the surface. Adjust the heat to a gentle simmer—one or two bubbles should rise to the top at a time—and let the broth simmer for about an hour before adding the vegetables and seasonings and any meat you plan to serve in the finished soup. Continue cooking for 2 to 3 hours, maintaining the heat at a gentle simmer and skimming any foam and fat from the surface occasionally.

To help keep your clear stock clear, strain it as follows: Place a colander lined with a double thickness of cheesecloth over a large bowl. Ladle the stock through the colander, making sure to get every drop. Cool the stock to room temperature, if time allows, then refrigerate it. Any fat in the stock will rise to the surface and solidify, making it easy to remove.

Once chilled and defatted, store the stock in small (1- to 2-cup) containers in the refrigerator or freezer. Refrigerated, the stock will last up to 5 days. Frozen, the stock will keep 3 or 4 months. In either case, bring the stock to a boil before using.

Stock Basics

Chicken stock is a necessity in my restaurants. It is simple enough to make so that it should become one in your kitchen as well. If you have one large pot—about 16 quarts or so—or two 8-quart pots, you can easily double this recipe. Use what you need for today's soup and freeze the rest.

Chicken Stock

Brodo di Pollo

3 pounds chicken and/or capon wings, backs, necks, and giblets (not including the liver)

1 pound turkey wings

5 quarts water

1 large onion (about $\frac{1}{2}$ pound), cut in half

3 medium carrots, trimmed, peeled, and cut into 3-inch lengths

2 large ripe tomatoes, quartered, or 1 tablespoon tomato paste

8 cloves garlic, unpeeled

10 sprigs fresh Italian parsley

12 black peppercorns

Salt

Makes about 4 quarts

Capon soup is an Italian holiday tradition, but I like to use at least a little capon every time I make stock. I buy a capon, cut it in pieces, and freeze the pieces separately. When I make chicken stock, I add a piece or two of the frozen capon. I also add some turkey wings when I make chicken stock—I think it adds richness of flavor. The tomato (or paste) adds a little color and balances the sweetness of the carrot.

Rinse the poultry pieces in a colander under cold running water and drain them well. Place them in an 8- to 10-quart stockpot. Pour in the cold water and bring to a boil over high heat. Boil for a minute or two and you will see foam rising to the surface. Skim off and discard the foam, lower the heat to a strong simmer, and cook 1 hour, occasionally skimming the foam and fat from the surface.

Add the remaining ingredients except the salt to the pot. Bring to a boil, then adjust the heat to simmering. Cook, partially covered, 2 to 3 hours, skimming the foam and fat from the surface occasionally.

Strain the broth through a very fine sieve, or a colander lined with a double thickness of cheesecloth or a clean kitchen towel. Season lightly with salt. To use the stock right away, wait a minute or two and spoon off the fat that rises to the surface. The last little traces of fat can be "swept" off the surface with a folded piece of paper towel. It is much easier, however, to remove the fat from chilled stock—the fat will rise to the top and solidify, where it can be easily removed.

Mixed Meat Stock

For a rich meat stock, simply substitute 3 pounds meaty veal and beef bones—like beef shin, veal shank bones, and/or short ribs—for 2 pounds of the chicken/capon bones and all the turkey bones. Continue as described above.

Chicken and Rice Soup

THIS IS A SIMPLE SOUP TO MAKE on the day you're making chicken stock. This will yield eight servings, but the recipe can easily be cut in half to make four servings and yield more stock for the freezer. Make the Chicken Stock (see page 74), adding two bone-in chicken legs or chicken breasts to the stock along with the vegetables. Remove the chicken breasts or legs from the stock after 1 hour of cooking and let them stand at room temperature until cool enough to handle. Discard the skin and pick the meat off the bone, shredding it coarsely and discarding little bones and cartilage as you do.

Bring 8 cups of the stock to a boil in a large saucepan. (Cool the remaining stock and refrigerate or freeze it for future use.) Add 2 cups long-grain rice and cook until *al dente*—tender but firm—about 10 minutes. (If you like very tender rice, cook a few minutes more.) Stir the shredded chicken meat and ¼ cup chopped fresh Italian parsley into the soup, check the seasonings, and serve the soup in warm bowls, passing grated Parmigiano-Reggiano cheese separately at the table.

You can make this soup even easier to serve by cooking the rice separately and adding it to the stock at the last minute. That will give you a clearer soup, as the starch from the rice won't cloud the stock, but the flavor is better if the rice is cooked right in the broth. And that is how we made the soup traditionally.

The extra chicken pieces added to the stock enrich the stock and furnish the meat for the finished soup. If you'd rather, use the shredded chicken meat to make this simple salad to accompany the soup or serve on its own: Pour enough of the hot stock over ½ cup raisins to cover them and steep until the raisins are softened. Drain them and toss with the shredded chicken meat and sea salt, freshly ground black pepper, chopped fresh Italian parsley, and extra-virgin olive oil to taste.

Vegetable Stock

Brodo di Verdure

4 quarts cold water

4 celery stalks with leaves, cut into large dice

4 carrots, peeled and cut into 3-inch lengths

2 medium onions, cut into quarters

2 leeks, white and green parts, trimmed, sliced, and washed (page 80)

½ pound mushrooms or mushroom stems, chopped coarse

2 large ripe tomatoes, quartered, or 1 tablespoon tomato paste

6 sprigs fresh Italian parsley

4 sprigs fresh thyme

2 bay leaves

12 black peppercorns

Salt

Makes about 2 quarts

Put all ingredients except the salt in a large (about 8-quart) stockpot. Bring to a boil over medium heat, skimming any foam that rises to the surface. Adjust the heat to a strong simmer and cook, partially covered, 1 hour. Skim the foam that rises to the surface once or twice as the stock cooks.

Strain the stock through a fine sieve and cool to room temperature. The stock can be refrigerated up to 4 days or frozen up to 3 months.

Risi e bisi is a spring soup best and sweetest when the peas are young and fresh. It is a typical soup of the Veneto Region, of which Venice is the capital. The Venetians ruled that area, including Friuli Venezia-Giulia, Istria (where I was born), and the Dalmatian coast for over 700 years. The empire was called La Serenissima, and its vibrant economy was driven by the spice trade. The cuisine still reflects that, with its extensive use of pepper, cinnamon, cloves, and even ginger. But this soup is simpler, one most likely cooked by everyday citizens, since spices were a luxury. It probably became part of the Italian-American table after World War I, when many immigrants from the Friuli-Venezia-Giulia area came over.

Rice and Spring Pea Soup

Risi e Bisi

2 tablespoons extra-virgin olive oil

2 tablespoons unsalted butter

1 medium onion, finely diced (about 1 ½ cups)

2 cloves garlic, chopped fine

1 pound fresh peas, shelled (about 1 ½ cups shelled peas), or one 10-ounce box frozen peas, defrosted and drained

½ cup finely chopped celery, including leaves

Salt

Freshly ground black pepper

8 cups Chicken Stock (page 74) or canned reduced-sodium chicken broth

1 cup Arborio or other Italian short-grain rice

½ cup grated Parmigiano-Reggiano cheese

Makes 6 servings

Heat the olive oil and butter in a 4- to 5-quart pot over medium heat until the butter is foaming. Stir in the onion and cook, stirring, until light golden, about 8 minutes. Add the garlic and cook until golden, 1 to 2 minutes. Stir in the peas and celery, season the vegetables lightly with salt and pepper, and cook, stirring occasionally, until the peas are softened, about 5 minutes. Add the chicken stock and bring to a boil over high heat. Adjust the heat to simmering and cook until the peas and other vegetables are very tender, about 20 minutes.

Stir in the rice and cook until tender, 12 to 14 minutes, stirring occasionally. (For a firmer texture, cook the rice a few minutes less.)

Remove the soup from the heat and check the seasonings, remembering the cheese will add a little saltiness. Stir in the grated cheese and serve immediately.

This interesting soup starts with a rich broth that is then "reinforced" with greens, savory little meatballs, shredded chicken from the stock, and, just at the end, an addition of diced provola cheese. In spite of all the different elements, it maintains a clean, fresh flavor.

I understand that you might not have homemade stock on hand, and that is why I offer canned broth as an alternative in most recipes in this book. This, however, is one soup I wouldn't make from canned broth. You need the rich flavor of homemade stock to make this soup as it should be made. By adding the chicken pieces to the basic stock as it simmers, you make an even richer stock and end up with shredded chicken meat to "reinforce" the soup further. And because the finished soup calls for only half a recipe of stock, you'll have the added benefit of leftover stock to refrigerate or freeze for another soup.

"Reinforced" Soup

Zuppa di Rinforzamento

8 cups Chicken Stock (page 74)

2 bone-in chicken-breast halves or chicken legs

1 pound ground beef

⅓ cup fine, dry bread crumbs

¼ cup chopped fresh Italian parsley

3 tablespoons grated Parmigiano-Reggiano

1 large egg

¾ teaspoon salt, plus more for seasoning the soup

¼ teaspoon freshly ground black pepper, plus more for seasoning the soup

You have all seen those large, wax-coated provolone cheeses hanging like oversized pears in Italian groceries. When the same cheese is made into smaller shapes, which are hung to dry only briefly, they are sold as a softer, milder cheese known as provola. The wonderful soft texture of the cheese is perfect for this reinforced soup. If you cannot find provola, substitute a young soft cheese like Fontina or fresh Pecorino. You can use fresh mozzarella, but it will be very stringy when ladling and eating the soup.

Boiling the meatballs before adding them to the soup may seem a little odd, but it removes some of the raw-meat flavor and helps keep the clear flavors of the soup intact.

Prepare the Chicken Stock as described on page 74, adding the chicken breasts or legs along with the vegetables. Remove the chicken breasts or legs

3 cups shredded ($\frac{1}{2}$-inch) escarole leaves

3 cups shredded ($\frac{1}{2}$-inch) curly chicory leaves

4 cups shredded ($\frac{1}{2}$-inch) fresh spinach leaves

$\frac{1}{2}$ pound provola or other soft cheese, rind removed if necessary, cut into $\frac{1}{2}$-inch cubes (about 1 generous cup)

Makes 6 servings

from the stock after 1 hour of cooking and let them stand at room temperature until cool enough to handle. Discard the skin and pick the meat off the bone, shredding it coarsely and discarding little bones and cartilage as you do. Return the bones to the stock.

Bring a large saucepan of salted water to the boil. Crumble the ground beef into a large mixing bowl and sprinkle the bread crumbs, parsley, and grated cheese over it. Beat the egg with $\frac{3}{4}$ teaspoon salt and $\frac{1}{4}$ teaspoon pepper until blended, and pour over the beef. Mix thoroughly with clean hands until evenly blended. Roll a heaping tablespoon of the meat mixture between your palms to form a 1-inch ball. Repeat with the remaining meatball mix. Carefully slip the meatballs into the boiling water and cook 2 minutes. Remove the meatballs with a wire skimmer or slotted spoon and drain thoroughly. (The meatball mixture can be prepared and the meatballs formed up to several hours in advance, but keep them refrigerated, and don't poach them until just before serving the soup.)

Ladle 8 cups of the chicken stock through a fine sieve into a 4-quart pot. Bring to a simmer. Stir in the escarole and chicory and simmer 5 minutes.

Stir the reserved shredded chicken into the pot. Stir in the poached meatballs and spinach, return to the simmer, and cook until the meatballs are cooked through and all the greens are tender, about 5 minutes. Season to taste with salt and pepper, remove from the heat, and stir in the provola. Ladle immediately into warmed soup bowls.

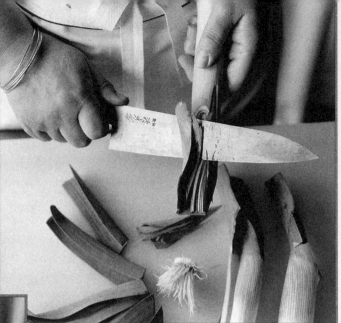

Leeks

Leeks, a member of the onion family with a flavor sweeter and mellower than yellow or Spanish onions, are at the base of many good soups, pasta sauces, meat and fish preparations. They are available in just about every supermarket and are quite delicious. If you have never cooked with leeks, I make this suggestion: take a favorite recipe that calls for onions and try the same recipe substituting a more or less equal amount of leeks.

Leeks grow best in sandy soil, so you will find grit between the leaves. Make sure you wash them well, or that grit will end up in whatever you are cooking. To clean leeks, I pull off and discard the tough outer leaves.

1. Hold the leek by the root end and shave away the tough outer green leaves with a knife.

2. Continue until you are down to the pale-green center leaves. Don't throw away the dark-green leaves; use them to flavor chicken or meat stock, or to form the base for a vegetable stock.

3. Trim off the roots, then cut the white, yellow, and light-green parts in half lengthwise. Cut the leek as described in the recipe—chopped or sliced into thin or thick semicircles. (Thin semicircles will dissipate into the sauce, thicker ones will remain visible.)

Wash the sliced leeks in abundant water, changing the water once. Give the grit a minute or two to settle to the bottom, then fish the leeks out of the water with your fingers or a wire skimmer. Drain the leeks thoroughly in a colander before cooking with them.

Zucchini and Potato Minestra

Minestra di Zucchini e Patate

10 cups hot Chicken Stock (page 74) or canned reduced-sodium chicken broth

½ ounce (about ⅔ cup) dried porcini mushrooms

3 tablespoons extra-virgin olive oil

2 large Yukon Gold or Idaho potatoes, peeled and cut into ½-inch cubes (about 3 cups)

2 small leeks, white parts only, trimmed, cleaned, and chopped (about 2 cups)

2 medium carrots, trimmed, peeled, and coarsely shredded (about 1 cup)

Salt

2 fresh or dried bay leaves

Freshly ground black pepper

1 pound small ("fancy") zucchini, washed and cut into ½-inch cubes (about 3 cups)

1 cup Arborio or other short-grain Italian rice

½ cup chopped fresh Italian parsley leaves

¼ cup freshly grated Parmigiano-Reggiano cheese

Makes 8 servings

Stock will make a much more flavorful soup, but if you do not have any handy, use canned broth or even water—the soup will still be quite good. When using canned stock for this soup, I always dilute it by half with water. In most cases, the flavor of canned broth is too pronounced when taken straight and masks the fresh vegetal flavor of the other ingredients.

Pour 1 cup of the hot stock over the dried porcini mushrooms in a small bowl. Let stand until the porcini are softened, about 20 minutes. Drain the porcini, straining the soaking liquid through a coffee filter or a sieve lined with a double thickness of cheesecloth. Pour the strained soaking liquid into the remaining stock. Rinse the soaked mushrooms thoroughly to remove any sand and grit. Drain the mushrooms well and chop them fine.

Heat the olive oil in a deep, heavy 4- to 5-quart pot over medium heat. Add the potatoes and cook, stirring occasionally, until they begin to stick and are lightly browned, about 5 minutes. If necessary, adjust the level of heat to prevent the bits of potato that stick from getting too dark. Stir in the leeks and carrots, season the vegetables lightly with salt, and cook, stirring, until the leeks are softened, 2 to 3 minutes. Pour in the hot stock and bay leaves. Bring to a boil, scraping up the bits of potato that stick to the pot. Adjust the level of heat to a simmer and season the soup lightly with salt and pepper. Cover the pot and simmer 15 minutes. Stir in the zucchini, cover the pot, and continue cooking until the potatoes and zucchini are very tender, about 15 minutes.

Stir in the rice. Cook, stirring well, until the rice is *al dente*—tender but still firm, about 14 minutes. Remove the bay leaves. Stir the parsley into the soup and check the seasoning, adding salt and pepper if necessary. Ladle the soup into warm bowls and sprinkle each serving with some of the grated cheese.

Potato, Swiss Chard, and Bread Soup

Zuppa di Patate, Bietole, e Pane

¾ pound Yukon Gold or Idaho potatoes, peeled, rinsed, and cut into ½-inch slices

Salt

1 small bunch Swiss chard (about 1½ pounds)

½ cup diced (½-inch) day-old Italian bread without crusts

¼ cup extra-virgin olive oil

6 cloves garlic, peeled

½ teaspoon crushed hot red pepper

½ cup freshly grated Pecorino Romano cheese

Makes 6 servings

Pour enough cold water over the potatoes in a deep, heavy 4-quart pot to cover by three fingers. Salt the water lightly and bring to a boil. Adjust the heat so the water is at a gentle boil and cook the potatoes, covered, until they are tender but still hold their shape, about 15 minutes.

Meanwhile, strip the chard leaves from the stems. (Reserve the stems for another use; see page 322.) Wash the chard in a sinkful of cool water, swishing it well and waiting for the dirt to settle to the bottom of the sink. Scoop the chard out with a wire skimmer or your hands; drain well in a colander. Cut the chard leaves into 1½-inch strips and stir them into the water after the potatoes have been cooking about 5 minutes.

Stir the bread into the pot after the chard has been cooking about 5 minutes. Season the soup with salt and cook until the potatoes and chard are tender and the bread is falling apart, about 10 minutes.

Meanwhile, heat the olive oil in a small skillet over low heat. Whack the garlic cloves with the side of a knife and stir them into the oil. Sprinkle the crushed red pepper over the oil and cook until the garlic is golden, about 3 minutes. Scrape the contents of the skillet into the pot. Stir well. Taste the soup and season with additional salt if you like. Ladle the soup into warm bowls, and sprinkle some of the grated cheese over the top of each, or pass a bowl of cheese separately.

To SOME PEOPLE, SOUP ISN'T SOUP unless it's piping hot. I suggest that, rather than serve a bean or vegetable soup hot off the burner, you let it rest 10 to 15 minutes first. (There are some exceptions: it's not necessary to rest clear soups, like the "Reinforced" Soup on page 78, and you shouldn't rest soups that contain starches like pasta or rice for more than 5 minutes—the starch will turn mushy while the soup rests. I do, however, suggest resting the soups before you add the starch. See the recipes for details.) Even this brief time will make a big difference, resulting in a mellow harmony of all the soup's flavors.

At home I enjoy foods served warm or at room temperature, but in my restaurants everything from soups to fish to meats must be served piping hot and on heated plates. This preference in serving temperature is a big difference between the way in which Italians and Americans eat. In Italy, food is not usually served at boiling-hot temperatures just off the stove or out of the oven—with the exception of pasta or risotto. Roasts are allowed to rest for 20 to 30 minutes before carving to make them even juicier; braised meats are taken from the fire and covered, to sit and soak in even more of the flavorful liquid in which they've been cooking. Aside from improving the taste of the food, this practice makes life a little easier: when you are entertaining or even serving your family dinner, there is no need for last-minute reheating to get that piping-hot effect.

I like serving food at this gentler temperature. It seems that taste buds respond with more sensitivity. I experience more of the flavors. The same theory holds true for cold drinks and food: Italians need very little ice in their drinks and eat their fruit and salads at room temperature. Intense cold, like intense heat, numbs our tasting capabilities to some extent.

The first time you make a soup from this chapter, I suggest letting it rest a bit before serving. As difficult as that might be when faced with a full pot of aromatic soup, I am sure that once you've tried it you'll come around to my way of thinking.

Resting
Soup

Beans

SOME OF THE BEAN VARIETIES used in Italy today, like cannellini, borlotti, and *fagioli di Spagna* (also called Corona), were introduced to the Mediterranean from the New World. But beans of the species *fagioli del occhio,* commonly known as broad beans, have been cooked and enjoyed on the Italian peninsula since antiquity.

The cannellini family of beans are medium in size and, usually, white in color. The quality that makes this bean so mellow and tasty is its thin skin. The Sorana white bean, a variety of cannellini from Tuscany that is costly and scarce, is the ultimate in white beans. When a recipe calls for cannellini, start with a search for Sorana beans. But if that fails, any bean labeled "cannellini" or "white kidney bean" will do. On the other hand, the borlotti bean—a member of the kidney-bean family similar to cranberry beans and recognizable by its patterned pink skin—can be substituted for any other member of the kidney-bean family.

Fresh shell beans, like fresh limas or fresh cranberry beans, can be substituted in all recipes where I call for dried beans. The resulting soup will be more velvety in texture and more vegetal in flavor. Fresh beans, of course, don't have to be soaked, and the cooking time is much less, usually about 30 minutes to 1 hour.

It's always a good idea to pick over dried beans to remove any dirt or tiny stones. Then soak them in one of these two ways: Dump the beans into a 2- to 3-quart container and pour in enough cold water to cover them by at least 4 inches. Let soak in a cool place at least 8 hours or up to 24 hours. Drain thoroughly. Alternatively, you may quick-soak the beans by placing them in a large saucepan, covering them generously with cold water, and bringing them to a boil. Boil 1 minute before removing from the heat. Let stand uncovered 1 hour, then drain and continue with the recipe.

Using either method, keep in mind that all dried beans are not the same. Older dried beans will need longer to soak—and to cook—than fresher dried beans. Let your senses be your guide: thoroughly soaked beans should be plump and not at all wrinkled; cooked beans should be evenly tender after cooking, not at all hard or mealy.

Start soaked beans in cold water and bring them up to a boil before adjusting the heat to simmering. Do not add salt to the cooking water—it will toughen the beans. Do flavor the cooking water with herbs or spices of your liking—for example, bay leaves, rosemary sprigs, garlic cloves, onions, and carrots. Adding a few tablespoons of olive oil to flavor the beans as they cook is traditional in Italy. When the beans are tender, do not drain them immediately, but, rather, add salt to the water in the pot (and olive oil, if you haven't already done so), and let the beans steep and take in the flavors.

As a child, I remember the ritual of bean drying in preparation for the long winter months. The whole bean plant, with pods still attached, was uprooted when the pods and plant were already fairly dry. The plants were hung upside down, tied in clusters by their roots outside, to dry in the sun. After a week or so, the dry pods were plucked from the bush. At this point the children were given the chore of shelling the beans. We would all sit in a circle with a long apron spread over our laps, gathering the beans as we removed them from their pods. We'd listen, bored, to the older women chatting away. Once in a while, when they were not looking, we kids would take aim at each other with the beans. When we got caught, as we always did, we were lectured by the elders on how much work it took to grow these beans, and how many children were not as lucky as we were, to have a pot of *pasta e fagioli* on their dinner tables.

But my favorite bean moment was the final cleaning of the shelled beans. We'd wait for the wind to rise, and then we'd stand, one of us holding each side of an apron taut, and toss the shelled beans in the air so the wind would blow off any small particles of the shell that had collected while we were shelling them. We'd huff and puff along with the wind, making a game of it.

In the ideal world, you'll think about making this soup the day before, or at least several hours in advance—time enough to soak and cook the beans. In the real world, however, you may not have that kind of time. In that case, it's OK to blaspheme and use canned beans. (Two 15-ounce cans of white beans will give you about the right amount.) Just promise me you'll make it the ideal way when you have the time.

Escarole and White-Bean Soup

Zuppa di Scarola e Cannellini

1 ½ cups cannellini, Great Northern, baby lima, or other small dried white beans

2 quarts water

2 bay leaves

½ cup extra-virgin olive oil, plus more for drizzling over the finished soup

Salt

6 cups coarsely shredded escarole leaves (preferably the tough outer leaves), washed and drained

8 cloves garlic, peeled and cut in half

4 to 6 whole dried peperoncini (hot red peppers)

Pan-Fried Garlic Bread (page 53), optional

Makes 6 servings

If you're making salad with the tender, inner leaves of a head of escarole, this is a good place to use the tough outer leaves. In fact, they're even better for this soup. Just remove any bruised or yellow parts of the leaf and shred the rest.

If you like, double the amount of beans in this recipe, fish half of them out of the pot after cooking, and save them for the Arugula and White-Bean Salad on page 60. Spoon off all but enough of the cooking liquid barely to cover the remaining beans before adding the escarole and finishing the soup.

Whole dried peperoncino or diavolillo peppers are the type of chili peppers that are used, seeds and all, to make the crushed red pepper that you are familiar with. Toasting the whole peppers along with garlic cloves in olive oil brings out their nuttiness and spice. I like to serve them whole right in the soup, where they can be easily spotted and removed.

Cold-soak or quick-soak the beans according to the directions on page 84. Drain and transfer to a 5- or 6-quart pot. Pour in 2 quarts of water, toss in the bay leaves, and bring to a boil. Adjust the heat to simmering, pour in ¼ cup of the olive oil, and cook until the beans are tender, 1 to 1½ hours. By the time the beans are tender, they should be covered by about 1 inch of cooking liquid. Season the beans to taste with salt. Stir in the escarole and cook, stirring occasionally, until the escarole is quite tender, about 15 minutes. Remove the pot from the heat.

Heat the remaining $\frac{1}{4}$ cup oil in a small skillet over medium heat. Add the garlic and cook, shaking the pan, until lightly browned. Add the whole peperoncini and cook, shaking the pan, just until the peppers change color, about 1 minute or less. Remove from the heat, and carefully—it will sputter quite a bit—pour one ladleful of soup into the skillet. Swirl the pan to blend the two, then stir the panful of seasoned soup back into the large pot. Check the seasoning and let the soup rest off the heat, covered, 10 to 15 minutes. Serve, with the garlic bread if you like.

Me at my restaurant Buonavia in Queens, in 1974, three years after it opened, chatting with a customer across the bar

Soups are often thought of as a first course, but hearty soups like this one can easily make a meal when accompanied by a salad or followed by bread and cheese.

Chickpea and White-Bean Soup

Minestra di Ceci e Cannellini

2 cups dried chickpeas

1 cup dried cannellini (white kidney) beans

3 tablespoons extra-virgin olive oil

1 cup chopped onions

2 cloves garlic, chopped fine

1 Idaho potato, peeled and diced ($\frac{1}{2}$-inch) (about 1 cup)

2 medium carrots, peeled and coarsely shredded (about 1 cup)

1 cup canned Italian tomatoes with their liquid, crushed

5 quarts hot water

2 sprigs fresh rosemary

2 bay leaves

1 teaspoon crushed hot red pepper

Salt, preferably sea salt

Cold-soak or quick-soak the chickpeas and cannellini in the same container or pot.

Heat the 3 tablespoons olive oil in a large (at least 6-quart), heavy pot over medium heat. Stir in the onions and garlic and cook, stirring, until golden, about 10 minutes. Add the potato and stir until the pieces begin to stick to the pot, about 3 minutes. Stir in the carrots; cook until they wilt, about 2 minutes. Pour the crushed tomatoes and their liquid into the pot and bring to a boil.

Pour in the hot water; add the rosemary, bay leaves, and crushed red pepper. Add salt to taste. Drain the chickpeas and cannellini and add to the pot. Bring to a boil, then adjust the heat to a gentle boil. Cook, semi-covered, until the chickpeas are tender, about 2 hours. (At this point the cannellini will be very tender.) While the soup cooks, check the level of the liquid. There should always be enough liquid to cover the beans generously. If not, add hot water as necessary.

Make the pesto dressing: Combine the basil and olive oil in the work bowl of a food processor or the blender jar. Process until the leaves are chopped fine. Add the grated cheese and continue processing until the mixture forms a rough paste.

If you'd like a very dense soup, stir the broken fettuccine into the soup once the beans are tender and cook, stirring often, until the pasta is *al dente*—tender but firm. Add water as necessary, if the soup becomes too

For the Pesto Dressing

- 1 cup fresh basil leaves, washed and dried well
- ¼ cup extra-virgin olive oil
- ½ cup grated Parmigiano-Reggiano cheese
- ½ pound dry fettuccine pasta broken into 1-inch pieces (about 2 cups), optional

Makes 8 main-course servings (quantities can easily be divided in half to yield 4 servings)

thick while cooking the pasta. (If you are cooking the soup in advance, do not add the pasta until you reheat the soup.) If you are serving the soup without fettuccine, let it rest, covered, off the heat 10 to 15 minutes before serving. If you have added the fettuccine, serve the soup immediately.

Either stir a dollop of the basil paste into the soup pot or spoon a little into each warm soup bowl before ladling in the soup.

Leftovers

MANY OF THE SOUPS IN THIS CHAPTER make much more than the four or six servings you'll find throughout the rest of the book. I have a few good reasons for offering these soups in larger quantities:

Most hearty soups cook better in large quantities—where they have a chance to perk and the flavors have time to mellow.

When you make a big batch of *pasta e fagioli*—or any soup, for that matter—it is nice to have some left over for another day, or for much later, if you decide to freeze it. Just remember, don't add pasta or rice to a soup until you're ready to serve it.

Most soups taste better when they have rested and are reheated. That goes for soups that have been frozen, too.

Pasta e fagioli is a soup that reaches into every corner of Italy. Each region—and every locality within that region—has its own version. The only common denominators are a base of simmered beans and a finishing touch of cooked pasta. To these two ingredients layers of flavor and texture can be added by using a variety of vegetables, tubers, squashes, or corn. If you'd like to take the soup in some other delicious directions, add barley, rice, or bread in place of the pasta.

As a finishing condiment, I suggest thin strips of browned cured pork—either bacon, pancetta, or guanciale—or simply a drizzle of olive oil. Here, I have pureed a portion of the beans, but for a chunkier soup, leave all the beans whole. For meals when a lighter soup course is warranted, puree all the beans and strain out the bits of shell before finishing the soup. This *vellutata* (meaning "velvety") is also a favorite with children and is a very nice alternative indeed when serving your next *pasta e fagioli*.

Pasta e fagioli was cooked once a week and served twice in our house. It keeps well for a few days, and as a matter of fact tastes better a day or two after being made, provided, of course, you don't add the pasta until just before you serve it.

Pasta and Beans

Pasta e Fagioli

1 pound cannellini (white kidney) beans

6 quarts water

3 large Idaho potatoes (about 1¾ pounds), peeled

3 sprigs fresh rosemary

2 bay leaves

12 slices bacon, cut crosswise into ½-inch strips (about 1 cup)

Cold-soak or quick-soak the beans according to the directions on page 84.

Pour 6 quarts water into a tall, large (at least 10-quart) pot. Add the drained beans, potatoes, rosemary, and bay leaves. Bring to a rolling boil over high heat, then adjust the heat to a gentle boil. Let boil while preparing the sautéed vegetables, about 25 minutes.

Process the bacon and garlic to a paste in a food processor, stopping once or twice to scrape down the sides of the work bowl. Heat the oil in a large skillet over medium heat. Scrape in the bacon-garlic paste and cook, stirring, until golden, about 5 minutes. Stir in the onion and cook, stirring, until translu-

4 cloves garlic, peeled

¼ cup extra-virgin olive oil, plus more for drizzling over the soup

1 medium onion, chopped (about 1 cup)

2 medium carrots, peeled and coarsely shredded (about 1 cup)

2 cups canned Italian plum tomatoes (preferably San Marzano) with their liquid, crushed

Salt

Freshly ground black pepper

1 pound ditalini, or 3 cups elbow pasta

Freshly grated Parmigiano-Reggiano cheese

Makes about 5½ quarts (12 servings; quantities can easily be divided in half to yield 6 servings)

cent, about 4 minutes. Stir in the carrots and cook until the onion begins to brown, about 5 minutes. Add the crushed tomatoes, bring to a boil, then lower the heat and simmer for 5 minutes.

Pour two ladlefuls of the bean-cooking water into the skillet and bring to a boil, then pour the contents of the skillet into the soup pot. Season lightly with salt and pepper and bring to a slow boil. Cook until the beans are tender, 45 minutes to 1 hour after adding the vegetables from the skillet.

Ladle about one-third of the beans, along with enough cooking liquid to cover them, into a baking dish or other shallow container where they will cool quickly. Cool the beans until no longer steaming. (Blending or processing hot beans can cause splatters. Stirring will speed up the cooling process.) Process the beans and liquid in a food processor or blender until creamy. Return the pureed beans to the pot.

Fish out the potatoes onto a plate. Mash them coarsely with a fork and return them to the pot. Cook 10 minutes to give the flavors a chance to blend. (If you're setting some of the soup aside to serve at another time, ladle it off now, before adding the pasta.) Let the soup rest off the heat, covered, 10 to 15 minutes.

While the soup is resting, cook the ditalini or elbow pasta in salted water until very *al dente*. (Cook all the pasta if serving the full recipe of soup, or a proportionate amount if you're setting some of the soup aside for later.) Drain thoroughly and stir into the soup. Let all rest for 5 minutes, then serve in warm soup bowls, with a drizzle of extra-virgin olive oil and a sprinkle of Parmigiano-Reggiano.

Minestrone—Vegetarian or with Pork

Minestrone—Vegetariano o con Maiale

1 cup dried cannellini, kidney, or Great Northern beans, or chickpeas

1 piece (about 1 ½ pounds) smoked pork shoulder butt, optional

3 tablespoons extra-virgin olive oil

1 medium onion, chopped (about 1 cup)

Salt, preferably sea salt

2 cloves garlic, chopped fine

One 14-ounce can Italian plum tomatoes (preferably San Marzano)

1 teaspoon crushed hot red pepper

2 bay leaves

1 cup peeled and chopped (¼-inch) carrots

½ cup peeled and chopped (¼-inch) celery, with leaves

1 large Idaho potato, peeled and diced (½-inch) (about 1 ½ cups)

4 cups shredded green cabbage

5 quarts hot water

2 small ("fancy") zucchini, trimmed and diced (½-inch) (about 1 ½ cups)

Sprinkling the onions with salt as they cook not only seasons them, but extracts some of the water and intensifies their flavor. Keep the water hot before adding it to the soup, as described below, and you won't interrupt the cooking—it will flow smoothly from start to end. Remember this when braising meats like the short ribs on page 218, or when making risotto.

You can use the method outlined below—bringing the beans to a boil, then soaking them in hot water for an hour—anytime you want to cook beans without soaking them overnight, or anytime you've forgotten to soak them a day in advance. It works especially well here because, by soaking the pork along with the beans, you kill two birds with one stone. (I soak the dried or cured pork to remove some of the intense curing-and-smoking flavor. If you like it intense, just rinse the pork under cold water before adding it to the soup.)

Place the beans in a large saucepan of cold water. Bring to a boil, add the smoked pork if using, cover the pot, and remove it from the heat. Let stand 1 hour.

In a large (8- to 10-quart), heavy pot, heat 3 tablespoons olive oil over medium heat. Add the onion, season lightly with salt, and cook, stirring occasionally, until wilted, about 4 minutes. Add the garlic and continue cooking until the onion is golden, about 5 minutes. With your hands, remove the seeds from the tomatoes and crush the tomatoes coarsely. Add the crushed tomatoes and their liquid, crushed red pepper, and bay leaves to the pot and bring to a boil. Add the carrots, celery, and potato, bring to a boil, and cook 5 minutes. Season lightly with salt. Stir in the cabbage, adjust the heat to simmering, and cook 5 minutes.

Pour the hot water into the pot and bring to a boil. Adjust the heat to a gentle boil and cook 20 minutes. Drain the beans and pork and add them to the pot,

¾ cup ditalini or other small pasta shape, such as tubettini

For the Basil Dressing

½ cup (lightly packed) fresh basil leaves

½ cup grated Parmigiano-Reggiano cheese

3 tablespoons extra-virgin olive oil, or as needed

Salt

Makes 8 full-meal servings

tucking the pork into the vegetables so it is completely submerged. Bring the soup to a rolling boil, adjust the heat to simmering, and cook, covered, until the beans are tender, about 1½ hours.

Add zucchini and cook until softened, about 4 minutes. (The soup can be prepared to this point up to 2 days in advance. Cool to room temperature, then chill completely. Bring to a boil, stirring occasionally, before continuing.)

Remove the pork from the soup and let stand on a cutting board. Stir the pasta into the soup and cook, stirring occasionally, until *al dente*—tender but firm—about 8 minutes. (If you plan to set aside some of the soup to serve in the future, ladle it from the pot before you add the pasta. Add the proportionate amount of pasta to the remaining soup. Cool the reserved soup, refrigerate or freeze it, and add the pasta when you bring it back to a boil.)

While the pasta is cooking, combine the basil, grated cheese, and oil in a small food processor or blender. Process until you have a rough paste, adding a little more oil if necessary. Season to taste with salt.

Taste the soup, seasoning with salt and pepper if necessary. Let rest off the heat for 5 minutes. While the soup is resting, cut the pork into ½-inch slices and tent them with aluminum foil to keep them warm.

If you like, stir a dollop of the basil paste into the soup. (Otherwise, place a small dollop in each warm soup bowl before ladling in the soup, or pass the basil paste at the table, letting guests help themselves.) Lay a slice of smoked pork in the bottom of each warm soup bowl and ladle the soup over it.

☞ This recipe makes quite a bit of soup. If you plan to refrigerate or freeze some for future use, do so before you add the pasta—the pasta will continue to absorb liquid and swell after cooking, making for overcooked pasta and a too-thick soup. Reduce the amount of pasta called for in the recipe according to how much of the soup you plan to serve immediately.

Ribollita means "reboiled." A traditional *ribollita*, rich with vegetables and legumes, is slowly simmered, then allowed to rest. Chunks of day-old bread are stirred into the soup and it is *ribollita*, or reboiled. I have been preaching throughout this chapter about the virtues of mellow, rested *minestre* and *zuppe;* this is the epitome of a well-rested soup.

Tuscan Twice-Boiled Soup

Ribollita

3 cups dried cannellini (white kidney) beans

8 cups cold water

½ cup extra-virgin olive oil, plus more for drizzling over the soup

2 medium onions, chopped (about 2 cups)

1 tablespoon tomato paste

1 pound kale, washed and cut into ½-inch strips (about 8 cups)

4 cups savoy cabbage, cored and cut into ½-inch strips (about 8 ounces)

½ pound Swiss chard leaves washed and cut into ½-inch strips (about 4 cups)

2 large Yukon Gold or Idaho potatoes, peeled and cut into ½-inch pieces (about 3 cups)

4 medium carrots, peeled and grated (about 2 cups)

Dump the beans into a 2- to 3-quart container and pour in enough cold water to cover them by at least 4 inches. Let soak in a cool place at least 8 hours or up to 24 hours. Drain thoroughly. (Alternatively, you may quick-soak the beans as follows: Place the beans in a large saucepan of cold water. Bring to a boil, boil 1 minute, and remove from the heat. Let stand 1 hour, then drain and continue with the recipe.)

Pour 8 cups of cold water into a 4- to 5-quart pot and add the beans. Bring to a boil, adjust the heat to simmering, and cook until the beans are tender, 45 minutes to 1 hour.

Fish out the tender beans from the cooking liquid with a wire skimmer or slotted spoon, and cool them as described on page 91. Put about three-quarters of them into a food-processor bowl or blender. Add a ladle or two of the cooking liquid and process the beans until smooth. Stir the bean puree into the cooking liquid. Set aside the remaining whole beans.

Heat the oil in an 8- to 10-quart stockpot. Stir in the onions and cook, stirring, until wilted, about 4 minutes. Stir the tomato paste and ½ cup water together in a small bowl, and stir into the wilted onions. Pour in the bean puree, then add the kale, cabbage, Swiss chard, potatoes, carrots, and celery. Pour in the beans and their cooking liquid. Bring to a boil, then adjust the heat to simmering. Season lightly with salt and pepper and cook 45 minutes. Let rest at least 30 minutes, or cool completely and refrigerate until the next day.

2 medium stalks celery,
with leaves, chopped
(about 1 cup)

Salt

Freshly ground black pepper

2 cups ½-inch pieces
day-old country bread,
crusts removed

1 medium red onion,
chopped

Makes 12 servings

Stir the bread into the soup. Taste, adding salt and pepper if necessary. Cook until thickened and dense, about 30 minutes, or longer if the soup has been refrigerated. Remove from the heat, stir well, and let stand about 15 minutes before serving.

Ladle the soup into warm bowls. Sprinkle some of the chopped red onion over each serving and drizzle a little olive oil on top.

To reheat leftover *ribollita* in the oven: Preheat the oven to 400° F. Ladle the soup into individual 10- to 12-ounce ovenproof crocks (French onion-soup crocks work well). Scatter some of the chopped onion over each serving. Drizzle a little olive oil over each, set the crocks on a sturdy baking sheet, and bake until the soup is bubbling around the edges and the onions are golden, about 20 minutes. Let the crocks of soup rest about 5 minutes before serving.

To: Lidia Bastianich
From: Jill and Luca Razza
Subject:

> > > We just saw the show where your son Joseph was with you. It reminded me of my own mother cooking in her kitchen and I can still remember the wonderful aromas wafting through the whole house. It smelled like love: the feeling you present on your shows. Please never stop.< < <

Lentils

LENTILS SEEM TO BE ONE OF the oldest legumes consumed by man, with origins in Asia (around present-day Syria) dating to about 7000 B.C. The plant quickly spread throughout the Mediterranean region and became one of the staple foods of the Greeks and the Romans. In present-day Italy, some of the best lentils— like wine—grow in specific geographical locations such as Castelluccio, Mormanno, and Villalba. Lentils are dried seeds, which range in size and color from tiny and nearly black to large and yellow, green, or reddish brown. Though they are usually sold in their shell, there are some types that are shelled. Shelled lentils, which you can spot by their bright orange-pink color, will take much less time to cook. If you do not time them accordingly, you'll end up with mashed lentils.

Some people believe in presoaking lentils before cooking them. I don't. First I pick over them to remove any rocks or dirt, and then I wash them. To cook lentils, I just plunk them into boiling water or soup, where they should take 30 to 40 minutes to cook, depending on the size and how tender or *al dente* you like them. If you'd like to serve lentils as a side dish, cook them with aromatic herbs and vegetables such as carrots, celery, onions, and bay leaves. (Leave the vegetables in large pieces that can be fished out easily after cooking, or cut them fine and serve them along with the lentils.) Pour off any excess liquid. "Bless" the lentils with olive oil and season them with salt and pepper, and you're in business. Keep in mind that, when cooking lentils, like beans, salt should be added at the end of the cooking process to prevent them from toughening.

Lentils keep quite well, sealed tightly in a glass container, plastic bag, or canister. They do not need to be refrigerated and can keep for long periods of time— even a year. Keep in mind, though, that lentils will continue drying as you keep them. (Older lentils will take longer to cook.) Try to use newly bought lentils in these and other recipes.

Lentil and Broccoli Soup

Zuppa di Lenticchie e Broccoli

1 pound (about 2 medium heads) broccoli

⅓ cup extra-virgin olive oil, plus more for serving the soup

2 medium Idaho potatoes (about 1 pound), peeled and cut into ⅓-inch cubes

6 cloves garlic, peeled

10 cups hot water

3 bay leaves

1 pound brown or green lentils

Salt

Freshly ground black pepper

½ cup freshly grated Pecorino Romano cheese

Makes 8 generous servings

This, like bean- and potato-based soups, can be made ahead, but will thicken a lot. The best bet, if you plan to make the soup in advance, is to reheat it slowly, adding water or stock as needed to restore the soup to its original thickness. And always check the seasoning of reheated soups before you serve them.

Cut the florets from the broccoli stalks. Cut the florets into pieces of about ½ inch. Trim the rough bottoms from the stalks, peel the stalks, and cut them into ½-inch dice.

Heat the oil in a deep, heavy 4- to 5-quart pot over medium heat. Add the potatoes and cook, stirring, until they are golden and begin to stick to the bottom of the pot. Don't worry if they stick; the little brown bits will add lots of flavor to the soup. Whack the garlic with the flat side of a knife, stir it into the pot and cook a few minutes, stirring occasionally, until you can smell the garlic. Pour in the hot water and bring to a vigorous boil, stirring as you do to scrape up the browned bits of potato. Toss in the bay leaves and cook for 15 minutes. Stir in the lentils, reduce the heat to simmering, and let simmer 15 minutes.

Stir in the broccoli, season the soup with salt and pepper, and cook until the broccoli and lentils are very tender, about 15 minutes. Skim any foam that rises to the surface as the soup simmers.

Remove the soup from the heat, pluck out the bay leaves, and let the soup rest off the heat, covered, 10 to 15 minutes. Ladle the soup into warm bowls and drizzle with olive oil. Pass the grated Pecorino separately.

"Clam Soup" was always one of the biggest sellers on my Italian-American menu at Buonavia. In its simplicity, this dish comes out as well in the States as it would in Italy. (Littleneck clams are an excellent alternative to Italy's *vongole*.)

You can add white wine or oregano to the soup before adding the clams, but I like the pristine flavors of the dish as prepared below. For a simpler version, and one that would make a delicious appetizer, simply substitute clams for the mussels in the Cozze alla Posillipo recipe on page 10. Clams will require a slightly longer—about 6- or 7-minute—cooking time.

Clams in a Savory Tomato-Vegetable Soup

Zuppa di Vongole

1 cup thin string beans (or thicker string beans halved lengthwise) or haricots verts, trimmed and cut into 1-inch lengths

1 cup fresh corn kernels

6 tablespoons extra-virgin olive oil, plus more for drizzling over the finished dish if you like

8 cloves garlic, crushed and peeled

One 14-ounce can Italian plum tomatoes (preferably San Marzano), with their liquid, coarsely crushed (about 1¾ cups)

1½ cups Vegetable Stock (see recipe, page 76) or water

Bring a medium saucepan of salted water to a boil over high heat. Add the string beans and cook 3 minutes. Stir in the corn and cook until the vegetables are tender but still firm, about 2 minutes. Drain, and rinse under cold water to cool.

Heat 3 tablespoons of the olive oil in a 3-quart saucepan over medium heat. Add 4 of the garlic cloves and cook, shaking the pan, until golden, 3 to 4 minutes. Carefully pour in the tomatoes and vegetable stock or water, sprinkle with the crushed red pepper, and season lightly with salt. Bring to a boil, then adjust the heat to simmering. Cook, partially covered, until the tomatoes are softened and the soup is slightly reduced, about 20 minutes.

Heat the remaining 3 tablespoons olive oil in a wide 4-quart casserole. Add the remaining 4 cloves garlic and cook, shaking the casserole, until the garlic is golden, 3 to 4 minutes. Slide the clams into the casserole, cover with a lid, and cook 2 minutes, shaking the pan several times. Pour the tomato-stock mixture into the casserole, stir in the string

½ teaspoon crushed hot red
   pepper, or to taste

Salt

4 dozen littleneck, Manila, or
   butter clams, cleaned as
   described on page 7,
   but not shucked

¼ cup chopped fresh Italian
   parsley

10 fresh basil leaves, shredded

Fried Bread "Clog" (page 11)
   or lightly toasted sliced
   country-style bread

Makes 6 servings

beans and corn, and bring to a vigorous boil. Cook, covered, until the clams open, about 4 minutes. Stir the clams once or twice so they cook evenly. Remove from the heat, discard any clams that haven't opened, and stir in the parsley and basil. Taste and season with salt if necessary. Divide the clams among warm soup bowls and, if you like, drizzle each bowl with a little extra-virgin olive oil. Pass a basket of the *zoccoli* or bread separately.

From Soup to *Minestra*

MINESTRA IS THE ITALIAN WORD for a soup that has been made heartier by the addition of either pasta or rice. If you'd like to turn any vegetable soup into a *minestra*, stir ¾ cup of long-grain rice or 1½ cups of ditalini (for every 10 cups of soup) into the simmering soup just before you serve it. (The rice will take about 10 minutes to cook, the pasta about 7 minutes.) Keep in mind that with the addition of either of these starches you may need to add hot water or stock to the soup as it cooks, in order to prevent it from becoming too dense. And remember to check the seasoning, especially the salt, after adding pasta or rice to your soup.

You may make the soup ahead of time, but don't stir in the rice or pasta until just before you serve it; otherwise the starch will overcook and become mush. Use this to your advantage: You can make the soup itself up to a few days before you serve it—it will even get better—and add the rice or pasta at the last minute. Or you can serve the soup as a first course one day and, with the addition of rice or pasta, as a heartier main-course *minestra* another day (or week, if you've frozen the soup base). To make life even simpler, you may cook the rice or pasta separately ahead of time and stir it into the hot soup just before serving. This comes in handy if you're entertaining or leaving some soup ready to go for the kids or a spouse, although I like the flavor and texture of soups that have the starch simmered right in them.

Pasta & Risotto

The Difference Between Good and Great Pasta

Cook pasta in abundant salted water at a full rolling boil. The recommendation I make throughout this chapter for cooking 1 pound of pasta is 6 quarts of salted water in an 8-quart pot. Salt is a matter of taste—I go with about 2 tablespoons for 6 quarts of water.

Bring the water to a full boil before you stir in the pasta, and get it back to a boil as soon as possible afterward. Covering the pot is the quickest way to get the water back to a boil, but a covered pot has a tendency to boil over. Try this trick: after adding the pasta to the water, put the top back on the pot, but prop it open slightly with a wooden spoon. That will bring the water back to a boil quickly but allow steam to escape, thereby preventing the water from boiling over.

A platter of antipasti

Clams Casino (foreground)
page 6

Stuffed Mushrooms (center)
Funghi Ripieni
page 18

Fried Banana Peppers (back)
Peperoni in Padella
page 50

Salt Cod, Potato, and String Bean Salad

Insalata di Baccalà, Patate, e Fagiolini

page 42

Fried Mozzarella
Sandwich Skewers
*Spiedini alla
Romana*
page 21

Lobster *fra Diavolo*
with Spaghettini
page 130

Linguine with Bacon and Onions

Linguine alla Carbonara

page 138

Italian-American Lasagna
page 156

Pizza Margherita Made with Fresh
Tomatoes and Sliced Mozzarella
Pizza alla Margherita Contemporanea
page 204

Veal Chops Stuffed with Taleggio and Broccoli

Costolette di Vitello Imbottiti

page 220

I don't know how the practice of adding oil to pasta-cooking water caught on, but I discourage it—with a few exceptions. If you add oil to pasta-cooking water, it reduces the starchiness on the pasta's surface. That comes in handy for keeping long or large shapes of pasta, like lasagna noodles or fresh pasta squares (see page 182), from sticking, but when pasta will be dressed with sauce, that surface stickiness will help the sauce adhere.

Recipes in this chapter call for cooking pasta "until done," which means until *al dente*. (More on this on page 106.) In a few cases—when pasta will be finished in the sauce, as I do with long, thin shapes like capellini, or when pasta will be recooked or baked, like the Baked Stuffed Shells on page 154, I may instruct you to undercook the pasta slightly.

Always combine pasta with the sauce and let the two cook together a minute or two before the final seasoning and serving. The pasta will absorb some of the sauce, and the sauce will intensify in flavor. I have a big restaurant stove at home—and big skillets to match—so I scoop the pasta out of the boiling water and right into the pan of sauce. You can do the same if you have a skillet or wide, deep braising pan large enough to hold the sauce and pasta. If not, simply drain the pasta, return it to the pot, add the sauce, and bring it to a simmer there. For pastas dressed with chunky sauces, I hold back some of the sauce to spoon on top. If the sauce is smooth, I combine all of it with the pasta in the pot.

Italians don't like their pasta swimming in sauce; there should be just enough sauce to let the pasta glide—not plop—into the plate. A dish of dressed pasta should be flowing, not sticky or soupy. And, of course, that last little touch of olive oil—either drizzled into the pasta and sauce as they simmer together, or drizzled over the pasta in the plate—makes a plate of pasta "smile."

Stir in grated cheeses like Parmigiano-Reggiano or Pecorino at the very end, after you remove the pasta and sauce from the heat and just before you plate it. Cheese breaks down—the fat separates from the protein, and the cheese becomes stringy—if it is heated too long or at too high a temperature.

I prefer shallow bowls to plates for serving pasta. If you pile the pasta in the bottom of the bowl—or, in the case of long shapes like spaghetti, make a little *nido* (nest)—the pasta will stay nice and hot. Pasta is one of the foods we Italians enjoy piping hot. For that reason, always warm up the soup bowls ahead, or the platter, if you plan to serve pasta family-style.

Vegetarian and Mostly Vegetarian

It doesn't get any simpler than this classic Italian dish that has found a permanent spot in the cuisine of the Italian-Americans.

Spaghettini with Oil and Garlic

Spaghettini Aglio e Olio

Salt

1 pound spaghettini or vermicelli

5 tablespoons extra-virgin olive oil

10 cloves garlic, peeled and sliced

½ teaspoon crushed hot red pepper, or more to taste

½ cup chopped fresh Italian parsley

1 cup freshly grated Parmigiano-Reggiano cheese or Pecorino Romano (optional)

Makes 6 servings

Spaghettini is very similar to vermicelli, and both are somewhere between capellini and spaghetti when it comes to thickness. Because they cook quickly, it's best to remove them from the boiling water when they are still undercooked, and to let them finish cooking in the sauce. I find this pasta very delicate but zesty and wouldn't serve it with cheese. But if you love cheese in your pasta, have it.

Bring 6 quarts of salted water to a boil in an 8-quart pot over high heat. Stir the spaghettini into the boiling water. Return to a boil, stirring frequently. Cook the pasta, semi-covered, stirring occasionally, until tender but still very firm, about 6 minutes. Meanwhile, heat 3 tablespoons of the olive oil in a large skillet over medium heat. Add the garlic and cook, shaking the skillet and stirring, until pale golden, about 2 minutes. Remove from the heat and add ½ teaspoon crushed red pepper.

Ladle about 1½ cups of the pasta-cooking water into the sauce. Add the parsley, the remaining 2 tablespoons olive oil, and salt to taste.

If the skillet is large enough to accommodate the sauce and pasta, fish the pasta out of the boiling water with a large wire skimmer and drop it directly into the sauce in the skillet. If not, drain the pasta, return it to the pot, and pour in the sauce. Bring the sauce and pasta to a simmer, tossing to coat with sauce. Cook until the pasta is coated with the sauce and done, about 1 minute. Remove the pot from the heat and toss in the grated cheese, if using. Check the seasoning, adding salt and crushed red pepper if necessary. Serve immediately in warm bowls.

I am sure you will love the flavor of this simple sauce, so don't limit it to this dish: use it to dress either Soft or Fried Polenta (page 346).

Spaghetti with Capers and Anchovies

Spaghetti con Capperi e Acciughe

Salt

1 pound spaghetti

1/3 cup extra-virgin olive oil

6 cloves garlic, peeled and sliced

1/4 pound salt-packed anchovies (see below), cleaned and coarsely chopped, or one 2-ounce can flat anchovy fillets

1/2 cup tiny capers in brine, washed and drained

1/3 cup chopped fresh Italian parsley

Makes 6 servings

Usually, pasta recipes contain something substantial such as sliced mushrooms, vegetables, seafood, or meat. This recipe, like the aglio e olio *on page 103, has a very simple sauce and will make 6 "Italian" portions. Simplicity goes a long way, especially with intense flavors such as anchovies and capers. If you'd like more substantial servings, increase the spaghetti to 1 1/2 pounds and the rest of the ingredients by one-half.*

Bring 6 quarts of salted water to a boil in an 8-quart pot over high heat. Stir the spaghetti into the boiling water. Return to a boil, stirring frequently. Cook the pasta, semi-covered, stirring occasionally, until done, about 8 minutes.

While the pasta is cooking, heat the olive oil in a large skillet over medium heat. Scatter the garlic over the oil and cook, shaking the pan, until golden, about 2 minutes. Add the anchovies and stir for a minute, until they begin to dissolve. Stir in the capers, then pour in 1/3 cup of the pasta-cooking water. Bring to a vigorous boil, then toss in the parsley. Remove the pan from the heat and stir the sauce to dissolve the anchovy fillets.

If the skillet is large enough to accommodate the sauce and pasta, fish the pasta out of the boiling water with a large wire skimmer and drop it directly into the sauce in the skillet. If not, drain the pasta, return it to the pot, and pour in the sauce. Bring the sauce and pasta to a boil, stirring to coat the pasta with sauce. Check the seasoning, adding salt if necessary. Serve immediately in warm bowls.

Spaghetti with Anchovies and Bread Crumbs

Prepare the sauce as described above, using or omitting the capers. After tossing the pasta and sauce together, sprinkle about $1/3$ cup toasted bread crumbs over the pasta and toss again. Serve immediately.

Anchovies

ANCHOVIES ADD AN UNMISTAKABLE or subtle flavor to all kinds of dishes, from hot to cold, raw to cooked, and simple to elaborate.

There are two main types of anchovies available. You are probably familiar with anchovy fillets that are packed flat in oil in little cans. If you can find anchovies packed in pure olive oil, stock up—they will have a richer flavor. Anchovies are also sold packed in salt, without oil, usually from huge cans kept on the counters of Italian, Greek, or Spanish specialty stores. Salt-packed anchovies have a firmer texture and a more pronounced flavor. They also need a little preparation before you eat them or cook with them. To clean anchovies packed in salt, wash them well under cool running water and pat them dry. On a cutting board, hold the anchovies by the tail and scrape off most of the skin from both sides with a paring knife. Separate the fish into fillets with the tip of the paring knife by prying the fillets apart through the stomach opening. Pull or scrape out the backbone, cut off the tail, and cut the anchovy fillets as described in the recipe.

Anchovies are best when used as soon after opening the container as possible, as they oxidize and taste stale when left to linger in the refrigerator (and if you're using anchovies in a tin, they pick up some of the metal flavor). If you'd like to keep anchovies for another use, remove them from the tin as soon as you open it and set them in the smallest glass container you have. Cover them with olive oil, seal tightly, and keep in the refrigerator. Nonetheless, use them as quickly as possible. Freezing is fine, but it will cause them to disintegrate quicker when thawed and used.

Salt-packed anchovies are wonderful in this simple salad: Clean the anchovies as described above, but leave the fillets whole. Toss the anchovy fillets in a bowl with sliced purple onions, cubes of warm cooked potatoes, and chopped Italian parsley. Dress the salad with extra-virgin olive oil and wine vinegar.

Al Dente

THE LITERAL TRANSLATION OF *al dente* is "to the tooth," but it means much more than that to an Italian. *Al dente* is a sensation of slight resistance, generated by the pressure of chewing, and it is a very important part of the overall enjoyment of food, especially pasta and rice.

Al dente is as hard to describe as it is easy to recognize. Pasta and rice cooked *al dente* will be tender and not at all raw-tasting, but with a firm texture and even a little "snap" at the center. It is easy to tell pasta or rice that has been cooked *al dente* by cutting through a piece of it crosswise and looking at it. In long pasta shapes, like spaghetti and linguine, there will be a dot of white at the center; in round pasta shapes, like ziti or penne, there will be a faint but clear ring of white that runs around the center of the pasta. (If you are going to simmer cooked pasta together with a sauce, as I do most of the time, then the pasta should be slightly less cooked than *al dente*. It will finish cooking in the sauce.) Rice for risotto that has been cooked *al dente* will have a pure white dot at the center.

The more we address all of our senses, the more we will enjoy food. Professional chefs pay keen attention to that fact. They know it is important that the food looks beautiful and is presented well. Aroma, and hence the last-minute addition of aromatic herbs and spices, is also very important. Our senses tell us a lot about what we are to eat, and prepare us in anticipation with the stimulation of saliva and gastric juices. Then, of course, the cavity of our mouth and throat is lined with papillae ready to give us the taste sensation.

Chewing our food not only starts the digestion process, but also generates a tactile sensation that gives another dimension to food enjoyment. Think of the crispness of a fresh stalk of celery, the movement of Jell-O on our tongue, or the crustiness of bread. These are all qualities in certain foods that we expect and anticipate before we even eat them; if they are not there we are disappointed, just as an Italian would be who has been served a mushy plate of pasta or risotto.

Spaghetti with Mushrooms, Garlic, and Parsley

Spaghetti ai Funghi

Salt

¼ cup extra-virgin olive oil

8 cloves garlic, chopped fine

1½ pounds assorted mushrooms, cleaned and sliced ¼ inch thick (about 6 cups)

Freshly ground black pepper

8 fresh sage leaves, chopped

1 pound spaghetti

1 cup Vegetable Stock (see recipe, page 76) or water

¼ cup chopped fresh Italian parsley

1 cup freshly grated Parmigiano-Reggiano cheese

Makes 6 servings

Bring 6 quarts of salted water to a boil in an 8-quart pot over high heat.

Heat the olive oil in a large skillet over medium heat. Scatter the garlic over the oil and cook, shaking the pan, until golden, about 2 minutes. Add as many of the mushrooms as will fit comfortably into the skillet. Season lightly with salt and pepper and toss in the sage. Add the remaining mushrooms as the mushrooms in the skillet wilt and make room. Cook, stirring and tossing frequently, until the mushrooms are sizzling and brown, about 10 minutes. (If the mushrooms have given off a lot of water during cooking, you'll have to wait for that liquid to boil off before the mushrooms begin to brown.)

Stir the spaghetti into the boiling water. Return to a boil, stirring frequently. Cook the pasta, semi-covered, stirring occasionally, until done, about 8 minutes.

Add the stock to the browned mushrooms, bring to a boil, and lower the heat so the sauce is at a lively simmer. Cook until the liquid is reduced by about half, about 5 minutes.

If the skillet is large enough to accommodate the sauce and pasta, fish the pasta out of the boiling water with a large wire skimmer and drop it directly into the sauce in the skillet. If not, drain the pasta, return it to the pot, and pour in the sauce. Toss in the parsley and bring the sauce and pasta to a boil, stirring gently to coat the pasta with sauce. Check the seasoning, adding salt and pepper if necessary. Remove the pot from the heat, stir in the cheese, and serve immediately in warm bowls.

This is more an American-Italian recipe than an Italian-American one. I found myself making this innovative dish, which always charmed our customers, quite a bit in the early 1970s.

Penne alla Vodka

Salt

One 35-ounce can Italian plum tomatoes (preferably San Marzano) with their liquid

1 pound penne

¼ cup extra-virgin olive oil

10 cloves garlic, peeled

Crushed hot red pepper

¼ cup vodka

½ cup heavy cream

2 tablespoons unsalted butter or olive oil for finishing the sauce, if you like

2 to 3 tablespoons chopped fresh Italian parsley

¾ cup freshly grated Parmigiano-Reggiano, plus more for passing if you like

Makes 6 servings

As simple a dish as this is, I have had requests for it in all my restaurants as far back as I can remember. I like the sauce a little feisty, so I'm generous with the crushed red pepper. You can add as much — or as little — as you like.

Often, restaurant chefs finish this dish by swirling butter into the sauce at the end. You can do the same, or use olive oil to finish the sauce. I prefer olive oil, but I probably don't have to tell you that by now.

Bring 6 quarts of salted water to a boil in an 8-quart pot over high heat.

Pour the tomatoes and their liquid into the work bowl of a food processor. Using quick on/off pulses, process the tomatoes just until they are finely chopped. (Longer processing will aerate the tomatoes, turning them pink.)

Stir the penne into the boiling water. Bring the water back to a boil, stirring frequently. Cook the pasta, semi-covered, stirring occasionally, until done, 8 to 10 minutes.

Meanwhile, heat the olive oil in a large skillet over medium heat. Whack the garlic cloves with the side of a knife and add them to the hot oil. Cook, shaking the skillet, until the garlic is lightly browned, about 3 minutes. Lower the work bowl with the tomatoes close to the skillet and carefully — they will splatter — slide the tomatoes into the pan. Bring to a boil, season lightly with salt and generously with crushed red pepper, and boil 2 minutes. Pour in the vodka, lower the heat so the sauce is at a lively simmer, and simmer until the pasta is ready.

Just before the pasta is done, fish the garlic cloves out of the sauce and pour in the cream. Add the 2 tablespoons butter or oil, if using, and swirl the skillet to incorporate into the sauce. If the skillet is large enough to accommodate the sauce and pasta, fish the pasta out of the boiling water with a large wire skimmer and drop it directly into the sauce in the skillet. If not, drain the pasta, return it to the pot, and pour in the sauce. Bring the sauce and pasta to a boil, stirring to coat the pasta with sauce. Check the seasoning, adding salt and red pepper if necessary. Sprinkle the parsley over the pasta and boil until the sauce is reduced enough to cling to the pasta.

Remove the pot from the heat, sprinkle ¾ cup of the cheese over the pasta, and toss to mix. Serve immediately, passing additional cheese if you like.

Mostaccioli with Fresh Basil and Mozzarella

Mostaccioli alla Caprese

Salt

3 tablespoons extra-virgin olive oil, plus more for drizzling over the finished pasta if you like

2 cloves garlic, peeled and sliced

One 35-ounce can Italian plum tomatoes (preferably San Marzano) with their liquid, seeded and crushed, or 3 cups peeled, seeded, and diced ripe plum tomatoes (see page 9)

½ teaspoon crushed hot red pepper

1 pound mostaccioli or penne pasta

1 pound bocconcini (bite-size fresh mozzarella), preferably *mozzarella di bufala* (see page 54), cut in half

1 cup freshly grated Parmigiano-Reggiano cheese

1 cup shredded fresh basil leaves

Makes 6 servings

Bocconcini, literally "little mouthfuls," are small rounds of fresh mozzarella that are often sold wherever larger rounds of fresh mozzarella are made. (If you can find bocconcini made from water buffalo's milk, they're even better for this pasta.) Bocconcini can vary in size from store to store. If yours are larger than the type called ciliege *(cherries), you may want to cut them into quarters, so they fit neatly on a spoon alongside the pasta. If you can't find bocconcini of any type, cut larger pieces of fresh mozzarella into 1-inch cubes.*

Bring 6 quarts of salted water to a boil in an 8-quart pot over high heat.

Heat the oil in a large skillet over medium heat. Scatter the garlic over the oil and cook, shaking the pan, until golden brown, about 2 minutes. Stir in the tomatoes and crushed red pepper. Season lightly with salt, bring to a boil, then lower the heat so the sauce is at a lively simmer. Cook, stirring occasionally, until the sauce is lightly reduced, about 10 minutes.

While the sauce is simmering, stir the penne into the boiling water. Return to a boil, stirring frequently. Cook the pasta, semi-covered, stirring occasionally, until done, 10 to 12 minutes.

If the skillet is large enough to accommodate the sauce and pasta, fish the pasta out of the boiling water with a large wire skimmer and drop it directly into the sauce in the skillet. If not, drain the pasta, return it to the pot, and pour in the sauce. Bring the sauce and pasta to a boil, stirring to coat the pasta with sauce. Check the seasoning, adding salt and crushed red pepper if necessary.

Remove the pot from the heat, and stir in the mozzarella, grated cheese, and basil. Serve immediately in warm bowls.

This uncooked version of the preceding recipe is excellent for those hot summer months when tomatoes are sweet and exploding with flavor.

Penne with Cherry Tomatoes, Basil, and Mozzarella

Penne alla Caprese in Crudo

1 pound ripe and juicy cherry tomatoes (the ones on the vine are the best), rinsed, dried, and cut in half

¼ cup extra-virgin olive oil, plus more for drizzling over the finished pasta if you like

1 teaspoon sea salt, preferably coarse

Pinch crushed hot red pepper

4 cloves garlic, peeled

1 pound penne

10 fresh basil leaves, shredded

½ pound bocconcini (bite-size fresh mozzarella; see preceding recipe), cut in half

Makes 6 servings

I like to eat the pasta hot with room-temperature sauce, but you could just as well serve it all cold. In that case, toss the tomatoes and pasta while still hot, then set them aside until you're ready to serve them. Finish the pasta by tossing in the basil and bocconcini and serve.

I can go on detailing recipes with minimal changes in the ingredient list or techniques, but what I want to leave with you is not only recipes but the understanding, and hence the liberty and confidence, to deviate from the recipe path and come up with a version of the plate that reflects your personal taste and local produce. When you reach this point, cooking is truly a joy.

Toss the tomatoes, oil, sea salt, and crushed red pepper together in a large bowl. Whack the garlic with the side of a knife and toss it into the bowl. Let marinate at room temperature, tossing once or twice, for 30 minutes.

While the tomatoes are marinating, bring 6 quarts of salted water to a boil in an 8-quart pot over high heat.

Stir the penne into the boiling water. Return to a boil, stirring frequently. Cook the pasta, semi-covered, stirring occasionally, until done, 10 to 12 minutes.

Remove the garlic from the marinated tomatoes and toss in the basil. Drain the pasta, add it to the bowl, and toss well to mix. Check the seasoning, adding salt and more crushed red pepper if necessary. Gently stir in the bocconcini and serve.

☞ Coarse Sea Salt: The melting of salt is a chemical reaction that draws the liquid from the tomatoes. The larger the salt crystal, the more liquid it will draw out. And that's exactly what we want—more juice to use as sauce for our pasta.

Bosco means "the woods," and I guess a mushroom forager might cook up a fancy meal with his harvest by adding sausage and ricotta—ingredients that are readily found in a country farmer's kitchen.

Rigatoni Woodsman-Style

Rigatoni alla Boscaiola

Salt

¼ cup extra-virgin olive oil

1 large onion, diced (about 1¼ cups)

½ pound sweet Italian sausages, preferably without fennel seeds

1 pound assorted mushrooms, trimmed, cleaned, sliced thin (about 5 cups)

1 cup peeled, seeded, and diced fresh tomatoes (see page 9), or 1 cup seeded and diced drained canned Italian plum tomatoes

1½ pounds fresh peas, shelled (about 1 cup), or 1 cup frozen peas, defrosted and drained

Freshly ground black pepper

1½ cups Chicken Stock (page 74), Vegetable Stock (page 76), or pasta-cooking water

½ cup heavy cream

1 cup fresh ricotta cheese or packaged whole-milk ricotta cheese

1 cup freshly grated Parmigiano-Reggiano cheese, plus more

Makes 6 servings

The "riga" in "rigatoni" means "stripe." It is those stripes and rigatoni's wide, hollow shape that make them perfect for a chunky sauce like this one. You can make the sauce a day or so in advance; just don't add the ricotta and grated cheese until the last minute.

Bring 6 quarts salted water to a boil in an 8-quart pot over high heat.

Heat the oil in a wide, heavy skillet over medium heat, toss in the onion, and cook, stirring, until wilted, about 4 minutes. Crumble the sausage into the skillet and stir, breaking up the sausage into small pieces as you do, until the sausage is lightly browned, about 5 minutes.

Stir about half the mushrooms into the sausage mixture. Add the remaining mushrooms as those in the pan wilt, making room for more. Cook, stirring occasionally, until all the mushrooms are lightly browned, about 5 minutes. If the mushrooms give off liquid, allow time for the juices to boil off before the mushrooms start to brown.

Pour the tomatoes into the skillet, stir in the peas, and bring to a boil. Lower the heat so the sauce is at a lively simmer, season lightly with salt and pepper, and cook a minute or two. Stir in the stock and bring to a boil. Cook until the sauce is lightly reduced and is perking like a little volcano, about 5 minutes. Pour in the cream and bring to a boil. Spoon the ricotta into the sauce and stir gently to mix.

If the skillet is large enough to accommodate the sauce and pasta, fish the pasta out of the boiling water with a large wire skimmer and drop it directly into the sauce in the skillet. If not, drain the pasta, return it to the pot, and pour in the sauce. Bring the sauce and pasta to a boil, stirring gently to coat the pasta with sauce. Remove from the heat and stir in 1 cup of grated cheese. Check the seasonings, adding salt and pepper if necessary. Spoon the rigatoni into warm bowls and serve immediately, passing additional cheese separately if you like.

Bucatini with Chanterelles, Spring Peas, and Prosciutto

Bucatini con Finferle e Prosciutto

1 cup shelled fresh peas or frozen peas, defrosted and drained

Salt

1 pound fresh chanterelle mushrooms

5 tablespoons extra-virgin olive oil

3 cloves garlic, peeled

2 ounces thinly sliced *prosciutto di Parma* or San Daniele prosciutto, chopped

Freshly ground black pepper

1 1/2 pounds ripe fresh plum tomatoes, peeled, seeded, and crushed (see page 9), or 2 cups canned Italian plum tomatoes (preferably San Marzano) with their liquid, seeded and crushed

1/4 cup chopped fresh Italian parsley

1 pound bucatini or perciatelli pasta

1/2 cup freshly grated Parmigiano-Reggiano cheese

Makes 6 servings

If using fresh peas, parboil them in a small saucepan of boiling salted water until softened, 3 to 5 minutes. Drain them and set aside. Trim the tough ends and wilted spots from the mushrooms. Wipe them clean with a damp paper towel, or wash them quickly and dry them well. Slice them thin and set aside.

Bring 6 quarts of salted water to a boil in an 8-quart pot over high heat.

Heat the olive oil in a large skillet over medium heat. Whack the garlic cloves with the flat side of a knife and add them along with the prosciutto to the oil. Cook, stirring, until lightly browned, about 4 minutes. Stir in the mushrooms, season them lightly with salt and pepper, and cook, stirring, until they are lightly browned and wilted, about 7 minutes. Pour in the tomatoes, season them lightly with salt and pepper, and bring the sauce to a boil. Lower the heat so the sauce is at a lively simmer and cook 5 minutes. Stir the peas and chopped parsley into the sauce and cook until the peas are tender, about 3 minutes.

While the sauce is simmering, stir the bucatini into the boiling water. Return to a boil, stirring frequently. Cook the pasta, semi-covered, stirring occasionally, until done, about 10 minutes.

Drain the pasta, return it to the pot, and pour in about three-quarters of the sauce. Bring the sauce and pasta to a boil, tossing to coat the pasta with sauce. Check the seasoning, adding salt and pepper if necessary. Remove the pot from the heat and stir in the grated cheese. Transfer the pasta to a warm platter, top with the remaining sauce, and serve immediately.

I use dried cavatelli— a sort of ridged, shell-shaped pasta—for this dish. There is also a type of cavatelli made with a ricotta-based dough that can be made fresh or bought frozen. Any of these will work fine with this recipe.

Cavatelli with Bread Crumbs, Pancetta, and Cauliflower

Cavatelli con Pancetta e Cavolfiore

Salt

¼ cup extra-virgin olive oil

Three ¼-inch slices pancetta (about 8 ounces), cut into 1 × ¼ × ¼–inch sticks (about 1½ cups; see note page 137)

1 pound dried cavatelli, cavatappi, or shells

2 medium onions, diced (½-inch) (about 2 cups)

½ head cauliflower, stalks removed, florets cut into ½-inch pieces (about 3 cups)

Crushed hot red pepper

1½ cups hot Chicken Stock (page 74) or canned reduced-sodium chicken broth

¼ cup fine, dry bread crumbs, or as needed

¼ cup chopped fresh Italian parsley

Makes 6 servings

The same principle I use to bring out the cauliflower's sweetness in this sauce—cooking raw cauliflower in olive oil—works well if you'd like to make cauliflower as a side dish. In that case, cut the cauliflower into individual florets rather than small pieces.

You might want to use a little fresh oregano here, but parsley fits right in.

Finishing this dish, like the Linguine with White Clam and Broccoli Sauce on page 122, is a bit of a balancing act. Bread crumbs will continue to thicken the sauce as it simmers, so be careful—it's easy to end up with a sauce that's too thick. On the other hand, if you don't add enough bread crumbs, the sauce will be too watery. If either of these is the case, remember, you're in control. Simply add a little hot stock or pasta-cooking water if the sauce is too thick. If it's not thick enough, add bread crumbs—a little at a time, because it takes a few seconds for them to do their thing.

Bring 6 quarts of salted water to a boil in an 8-quart pot over high heat.

Heat 2 tablespoons of the olive oil in a large skillet over medium heat. Add the pancetta and cook, stirring occasionally, until the pancetta has rendered some of its fat and is lightly browned but still soft in the center, about 4 minutes. Don't overcook the pancetta.

Stir the cavatelli into the boiling water. Return to a boil, stirring frequently. Cook the pasta, semi-covered, stirring occasionally, until done, about 10 minutes.

Stir the onions into the skillet and cook until barely wilted, about 2 minutes. Stir in the cauliflower and cook, stirring occasionally, until the cauliflower is wilted and begins to brown, about 4 minutes. Season lightly with salt and a little crushed red pepper.

Pour the chicken stock into the skillet, bring to a boil, and lower the heat so the sauce is at a lively simmer. Cook until the vegetables are tender and the liquid is reduced by about one-half, about 5 minutes.

If the skillet is large enough to accommodate the sauce and pasta, fish the pasta out of the boiling water with a large wire skimmer and drop it directly into the sauce in the skillet. If not, drain the pasta, return it to the pot, and pour in the sauce. Bring the sauce and pasta to a boil, tossing and stirring to coat the pasta. Check the seasoning, adding salt if necessary. Stir the bread crumbs, parsley, and remaining 2 tablespoons olive oil into the pot. Cook, stirring and tossing the pasta, until the sauce is lightly thickened. Serve at once.

Puttana is Italian for a lady who renders her services under cover of the night; *-esca* is a suffix that means "in the style of." This dish is quick to make, full of flavor, and, as the story goes, one that was often prepared by the ladies when they got hungry between their "appointments." The story could be true or it could be allegorical, but in either case, the name stuck.

This is a perfect illustration of how the flavor of a dish is the sum of its parts. Thirty years ago, when I opened my first restaurant in this country, the olives that were available to me were pimiento-stuffed green olives and watery canned black olives. We made do with what we had, but what a difference it made when we could get imported olives, San Marzano tomatoes, and great olive oil! Enjoy.

Fusilli as Made by Ladies of the Evening

Fusilli alla Puttanesca

Salt

One 35-ounce can Italian plum tomatoes (preferably San Marzano)

¾ cup Cerignola or other firm green olives

1 pound fusilli

5 to 6 tablespoons extra-virgin olive oil

6 cloves garlic, peeled

6 anchovy fillets

¾ cup oil-cured Gaeta or other black olives, pitted

½ teaspoon crushed hot red pepper

Some people dislike anchovies, but it would be a shame to leave them out of this dish. They add such wonderful flavor and, most likely, people won't even know they are there. They dissolve during the cooking and add complexity to the other assertive flavors in this dish.

I like to crush canned tomatoes with my hands, so I can feel when they are the right size and how tender or firm they are. That helps me to judge the cooking time better. If you prefer, you can mash them with a wire whisk or use a food processor. If you choose to process them, use just a few quick bursts — otherwise you'll chop them too fine and incorporate a lot of air into the tomatoes, and they will turn pink.

¼ cup tiny capers, rinsed and drained

¼ cup chopped fresh Italian parsley

½ cup grated Pecorino Romano cheese

Makes 6 servings

You can add basil to this sauce if you like, or stick to the traditional Italian-American accent of fresh parsley. I choose Pecorino Romano cheese for this dish. It is made from sheep's milk and is much sharper than Parmigiano-Reggiano, which is made from cow's milk. But if you prefer, you may use Parmigiano-Reggiano.

Bring 6 quarts of salted water to a boil in an 8-quart pot over high heat.

Pour the tomatoes and their liquid into a bowl. Mash them with your hands or a sturdy wire whisk until they are coarsely crushed. Whack the green olives with the flat side of a heavy knife or a small saucepan, remove the pits, and slice the olives coarsely. Set the tomatoes and olives aside.

Stir the fusilli into the boiling water. Return to a boil, stirring frequently. Cook the pasta, semi-covered, stirring occasionally, until done, about 10 minutes.

Meanwhile, heat 3 tablespoons of the olive oil in a large skillet over medium-high heat. Whack the garlic with the flat side of a knife, add it to the pan, and cook, shaking the pan, until lightly browned, about 2 minutes. Add the anchovies and press with the back of a spoon to break them up. Toss in the green and black olives and cook until sizzling, about 2 minutes. Pour in the tomatoes and their liquid and add the red pepper. Bring to a boil, adjust the heat to a lively simmer, and cook 5 minutes. Stir in the capers.

If your skillet is large enough to hold the sauce and pasta, scoop out the cooked pasta with a large wire skimmer and drop it directly into the sauce. If not, drain the pasta, return it to the pot, and add the sauce. Place over medium heat, and stir in the parsley and remaining olive oil. Remove from the heat and stir in the grated cheese. Check seasoning, and serve immediately in warmed bowls.

Pasta made out of all kinds of grains and nuts, including *farro* (spelt), *polenta* (corn), and *castagne* (chestnuts), is common in Italy. Pasta is also made from whole-wheat flour—that is, flour that is milled with the bran (outer skin of the kernel) intact. Whole-wheat flour has more fiber and a nuttier flavor than pasta made with regular flour.

Garden-Style Whole-Wheat Pasta

Pasta Integrale alla Giardiniera

Salt

2 small ("fancy") zucchini (about 6 ounces)

10 asparagus spears

¼ pound green beans, trimmed and cut into 1-inch lengths (about 1 cup)

1 cup broccoli florets, cut into ½-inch pieces

1 cup shelled fresh peas or frozen peas, defrosted and drained

⅓ cup extra-virgin olive oil

1 small onion, cut into thin strips (about ½ cup)

4 cloves garlic, peeled and minced

6 large mushroom caps, sliced thin (about 2 cups)

2 cups peeled, seeded, and sliced fresh plum tomatoes (see page 9) or canned Italian plum tomatoes (preferably San Marzano)

½ teaspoon crushed red pepper

Bring a large saucepan of salted water to a boil. Trim the ends from the zucchini and cut them in quarters lengthwise. With a paring knife, cut out and discard the seeds, leaving the green skin with about ½ inch of white attached. Cut the trimmed zucchini crosswise into 1½-inch lengths, then cut the pieces lengthwise into ¼-inch strips. Snap off the tough ends of the asparagus spears and cut the trimmed spears on the diagonal into ½-inch pieces. Parboil the vegetables as follows: Drop the green beans, broccoli, and fresh peas, if using, into the boiling water, and cook 2 minutes. Add the asparagus and frozen peas, if using, and cook 2 minutes. Drain the vegetables in a colander. Rinse them under cold water and drain again thoroughly.

Bring an additional 6 quarts of salted water to a boil in an 8-quart pot over high heat.

Heat the olive oil in a large, heavy skillet over medium-high heat. Add the onion and garlic and cook, stirring, until golden, about 6 minutes. Stir in the mushrooms and cook until wilted, about 3 minutes. Pour in the tomatoes, add the crushed red pepper, and season lightly with salt. Bring the sauce to a boil, then lower the heat so the sauce is at a lively simmer. Cook, stirring frequently, until the sauce is lightly thickened, about 10 minutes. Add the stock, the zucchini, and the parboiled green vegetables and cook, stirring occasionally, until all the vegetables are tender but not mushy, about 5 minutes. Stir in the basil, remove the sauce from the heat, and cover to keep warm.

½ cup hot Vegetable Stock
  (page 76), Chicken Stock
  (page 74), or canned
  reduced-sodium chicken
  broth
¼ cup chopped fresh basil
1 pound whole-wheat pasta,
  such as penne, spaghetti,
  or shells
1½ cups freshly grated
  Parmigiano-Reggiano
  cheese

Makes 6 servings

Stir the penne into the boiling water. Return to a boil, stirring frequently. Cook the pasta, semi-covered, stirring occasionally, until done, 8 to 10 minutes. Drain well and return the pasta to the pot. Add half the liquid portion of the sauce, leaving most of the vegetables behind, and bring the sauce and pasta to a boil, stirring well. Remove the pot from the heat and stir in half the grated cheese. Check the seasoning, adding salt if necessary. Spoon the pasta onto a warm platter or into warm bowls and spoon the remaining sauce and vegetables on top. Sprinkle with the remaining cheese and serve immediately.

My grandmother Rosa
with cousin Sonia in Pula,
Istria, c. 1970

Orecchiette with Braised Artichokes

Orecchiette con Carciofi

10 small fresh artichokes (about 1½ pounds)

Juice of 1 lemon

Salt

¼ cup extra-virgin olive oil, plus more for finishing the pasta if you like

6 cloves garlic, peeled and sliced

1 teaspoon crushed hot red pepper, or less to taste

1 to 1½ cups Chicken Stock (page 74) or canned reduced-sodium chicken broth

1 tablespoon chopped fresh mint

2 tablespoons chopped fresh Italian parsley

1 pound orecchiette pasta

1 cup freshly grated Pecorino Romano cheese

Makes 6 servings

Tiny artichokes—about 2 to 3 inches long—are ideal for this recipe. The larger an artichoke grows, the more developed the inedible choke becomes and the tougher the leaves that surround the choke. You can make this recipe with all artichokes, but the largest globe artichokes are the least desirable. Follow the directions on page 15 for stripping tough leaves and removing the choke from artichokes. Whatever type of artichokes you are using, the end result should be artichokes that almost "melt" into the sauce. That's why I have called for a variable amount of stock to be added while the sauce simmers.

Clean the artichokes as described for fully edible artichokes, page 15, putting the pieces in water acidulated with the lemon juice as you go. When all the artichokes are cleaned, drain them thoroughly and slice them very thin.

Bring 6 quarts of salted water to a boil in an 8-quart pot over high heat.

Meanwhile, heat the olive oil in a large skillet over medium-high heat. Scatter the garlic over the oil and cook, shaking the pan, until golden brown, about 2 minutes. Add the artichokes and crushed red pepper and season lightly with salt. Stir well to coat the artichokes with oil, and cook, stirring often, until the artichokes are softened, 5 to 10 minutes. Pour in 1 cup of the chicken stock, add the mint and parsley, and lower the heat so the sauce is at a lively simmer. Cook until the artichokes are very tender and the liquid is reduced by about half, about 10 minutes more. Add the remaining stock as necessary to keep the artichokes moist as they cook.

Stir the orecchiette into the boiling water. Return to a boil, stirring frequently. Cook the pasta, semi-covered, stirring occasionally, until done, 8 to 10 minutes.

If the skillet is large enough to accommodate the sauce and pasta, fish the pasta out of the boiling water with a large wire skimmer and drop it directly into the sauce in the skillet. If not, drain the pasta, return it to the pot, and pour in the sauce. Bring the sauce and pasta to a boil, stirring to coat the pasta with sauce. Check the seasoning, adding salt if necessary. Pour in a drizzle of olive oil, if you like. Remove the skillet from the heat, sprinkle the grated cheese over the pasta, and toss to mix. Serve immediately in warm bowls.

This recipe is loosely based on one for Pizzoccheri alla Valtellinese, a dish from the Valtellina region in the northeast of Piedmont that features pasta made with buckwheat cut into pappardelle. Although the pappardelle is silky, the dish is very hearty.

Whole-Wheat Pasta with Sausages, Leeks, and Shredded Fontina

Salt

¼ cup extra-virgin olive oil

3 links (about ¾ pound) Italian sausage, preferably without fennel seeds, removed from the casing and crumbled

2 small leeks, white parts only, trimmed, cleaned, and chopped (see page 80; about 2 cups)

4 cups shredded savoy cabbage

Freshly ground pepper

1 cup (or as needed) Chicken Stock (page 74) or canned reduced-sodium chicken broth

1 pound whole-wheat rigatoni or penne

1½ cups shredded imported Fontina cheese (about 5 ounces)

Makes 6 servings

Bring 6 quarts of salted water to a boil in an 8-quart pot over high heat.

Meanwhile, heat the olive oil in a large skillet over medium-high heat. Scatter the sausage over the oil and cook, stirring occasionally, until lightly browned, about 6 minutes. Stir in the leeks and cook until wilted, about 2 minutes. Scatter a handful of the cabbage over the sausage and cook, stirring until wilted. Repeat with the remaining cabbage. Season lightly with salt and pepper, and stir in about ½ cup of the stock. Bring to a boil, then reduce the heat so the sauce is simmering. Cook, adding more of the stock as necessary to keep the level of liquid more or less the same, until the vegetables are very tender, about 15 minutes. Remove from the heat and cover the pan to keep the sauce warm.

Stir the rigatoni or penne into the boiling water. Return to a boil, stirring frequently. Cook the pasta, semi-covered, stirring occasionally, until done, 8 to 10 minutes.

If the skillet is large enough to accommodate the sauce and pasta, fish the pasta out of the boiling water with a large wire skimmer and toss it directly into the sauce in the skillet. If not, drain the pasta, return it to the pot, and pour in the sauce. Bring the sauce and pasta to a boil, stirring to coat the pasta with sauce. Check the seasoning, adding salt if necessary.

Remove the pot from the heat, sprinkle the shredded Fontina over the pasta, and toss to mix. Serve immediately in warm bowls.

Seafood

This is a very popular dish at Felidia. Sometimes we substitute broccoli rabe for the regular broccoli, which is also delicious.

Linguine with White Clam and Broccoli Sauce

Salsa alle Vongole con Broccoli

Salt

3 cups broccoli florets

36 littleneck clams

1 pound linguine

½ cup extra-virgin olive oil

6 cloves garlic, peeled and sliced

½ teaspoon crushed hot red pepper

¼ cup chopped fresh Italian parsley

Makes 6 servings

You can chop the garlic if you like, but I prefer slices. They are mellower in flavor and become part of the texture of the dish. In most pasta dishes the idea is to make just enough sauce to coat the pasta lightly. When clam sauce is served with linguine, however, there should be a little extra broth.

Other hard-shelled clams, such as Manila or butter clams, make a good substitute, but I love littleneck clams for this sauce.

With this dish, as with many pasta dishes using long, thin pasta shapes, I prefer to cook the pasta very al dente *and finish it in the sauce. It's a balancing act—determining when the pasta is ready and the sauce is the right consistency—but you can always hold the pasta or the sauce for a minute or two, while the other one catches up.*

Cook the broccoli in a large saucepan of boiling salted water just until it is softened a little bit, about 2 minutes. Drain it well and cool under cold running water. Drain completely, then chop the broccoli coarsely.

Scrub and shuck the clams according to the directions on page 7, reserving the liquid. Strain the liquid, chop the clams, and combine them with the liquid.

Bring 6 quarts of salted water to a boil in an 8-quart pot over high heat. Stir the linguine into the boiling water. Return to a boil, stirring frequently. Cook the pasta, semi-covered, stirring occasionally, until not quite done *al dente,* about 6 minutes.

Meanwhile, heat ¼ cup of the olive oil in a large skillet over medium-high heat. Scatter the garlic over the oil and cook, shaking the pan, until golden, about 2 minutes. Add the blanched broccoli and crushed red pepper and cook until the broccoli is sizzling, about 2 minutes. Pour in the clams and their liquid and bring to a boil. Ladle about ½ cup of pasta-cooking water into the skillet. Bring to a boil, then lower the heat so the sauce is at a lively simmer. Cook until the broccoli is tender, about 4 minutes.

If the skillet is large enough to accommodate the sauce and pasta, fish the pasta out of the boiling water with a large wire skimmer and drop it directly into the sauce in the skillet. If not, drain the pasta, return it to the pot, and pour in the sauce. Bring the sauce and pasta to a boil, stir in the parsley, and check the seasoning, adding salt and crushed red pepper if necessary. Cook, stirring, until the pasta is done and there is enough sauce to coat the pasta generously but still form a small pool in the bottom of the pan, 1 to 2 minutes. Divide the pasta among warmed bowls, spooning some of the sauce from the pan and drizzling some of the remaining olive oil over each serving.

My grandmother Rosa
tying grape vines,
c. 1968

The preparation of the scungilli for this sauce is basically the same as it is for the salad on page 44, except they are slightly undercooked during the first simmering. They will finish cooking and become tender in the marinara sauce.

Scungilli in Marinara Sauce with Linguine

Scungilli alla Marinara con Linguine

For the Scungilli

1½ pounds frozen scungilli, or 20 pieces fresh scungilli in their shells

3 bay leaves

For the Marinara Sauce

¼ cup extra-virgin olive oil

6 cloves garlic, peeled and sliced

One 35-ounce can Italian plum tomatoes (preferably San Marzano) with their liquid, crushed

1 teaspoon crushed hot red pepper

2 bay leaves

1 teaspoon dried oregano, preferably the Sicilian or Greek type dried on the branch, crumbled

Salt

1 pound linguine

¼ cup chopped fresh Italian parsley

Makes 6 servings

Cook and clean the scungilli as described on page 44, cooking them until almost but not quite tender, about 25 minutes. Reserve 2 cups of the cooking liquid and slice the scungilli thin.

Make the sauce: Heat the olive oil in a large skillet over medium heat. Scatter the garlic over the oil and cook, shaking the skillet, until golden, about 2 minutes. Add the scungilli and cook, turning the pieces continuously, until light golden, about 4 minutes. Season lightly with salt.

Pour the tomatoes into the skillet, and add the crushed red pepper, 2 bay leaves, and oregano. Bring to a vigorous boil, season lightly with salt, and boil 10 minutes. Lower the heat so the sauce is at a lively simmer and cook until the scungilli are tender, about 30 minutes. Add the reserved scungilli-cooking liquid a little at a time to keep the consistency more or less the same as the sauce cooks. The finished sauce should not be too watery.

While the sauce is simmering, bring 6 quarts of salted water to a boil in an 8-quart pot.

When the scungilli are tender, reduce the heat under the skillet to very low. Stir the linguine into the boiling water. Return to a boil, stirring frequently. Cook the pasta, semi-covered, stirring occasionally, until very *al dente*, about 5 minutes.

Drain the pasta, return it to the pot, and ladle in about three-quarters of the sauce. Add the parsley and bring the sauce and pasta to a boil, stirring to coat the pasta with sauce. Simmer, tossing until the pasta is done, about 2 minutes. Check the seasoning, adding salt and crushed red pepper if necessary. Serve the pasta immediately in warm bowls, spooning the remaining sauce over the pasta.

Variation

Linguine con Frutta di Mare

Prepare the marinara sauce as above, omitting the scungilli and simmering the sauce for a total of 20 minutes. Heat an additional 3 tablespoons of olive oil in a large skillet over medium-high heat, add 2 cloves crushed garlic, and cook until lightly browned. Add $1/2$ pound sea scallops, each cut into two equal rounds and patted dry. Cook, stirring, until lightly browned, about 3 minutes. Remove the scallops with a slotted spoon and add $1/2$ pound of medium-size shelled shrimp, deveined and cut into $1/2$-inch pieces. Cook until the shrimp are bright pink on all sides. Stir the scallops and shrimp into the sauce, simmer 3 minutes, and proceed as above.

ALL DRY PASTAS ARE NOT THE SAME. The first thing you should look for is the phrase "100% durum semolina wheat" somewhere on the package. That indicates that only durum (hard) wheat was used and that the pasta will be easier to cook *al dente* and have a pleasant nutty flavor.

Here are a few more things to look for when buying dry pasta:

Color is important. Search out brands with a golden-yellow color. Dry pasta should have a translucent, not opaque, quality.

White spots on dry pasta are an indication that the pasta is old. Although dry pasta has a long shelf life, it is best if cooked and eaten sooner rather than later.

Blotchy, unevenly colored pasta may have been dried or stored improperly. Look for an even sheen.

Look for a slightly rough texture on the outside of the pasta. Sauces adhere better to rough-textured pasta than to pasta with a perfectly smooth surface.

What to Look For When Buying Dry Pasta

Shells with Fennel and Shrimp

Conchiglie con Finocchio e Gamberetti

Salt

1 medium fennel bulb

1/3 cup extra-virgin olive oil

4 cloves garlic, peeled

1 pound medium shrimp (about 30), shelled, deveined, and cut in half crosswise

1 pound pasta shells

2 tablespoons unsalted butter

Crushed hot red pepper

Makes 6 servings

Bring a medium saucepan of salted water to a boil over high heat. Pluck off and coarsely chop 3 tablespoons of the tender, fernlike center leaves from the fennel stalks and set the leaves aside. Trim the stalks from the fennel bulb. Cut the bulb into quarters through the core. Pull off and discard the tough outer layer from the fennel pieces. Plunge the fennel pieces into the boiling water, return to a boil, and cook 3 minutes. Reserve 1/2 cup of the cooking liquid, then drain the fennel and rinse under cold running water until cool enough to handle. Cut out the core section from each piece of fennel, then cut the fennel crosswise into 1/4-inch strips.

Bring 6 quarts of salted water to a boil in an 8-quart pot over high heat.

Meanwhile, heat the olive oil in a large skillet over medium heat. Whack the garlic cloves with the flat side of a knife, add them to the pan, and cook, shaking the pan, until golden brown, about 3 minutes. Increase the heat to high and immediately slide the shrimp into the pan. Cook, tossing constantly, just until the shrimp turn pink, about 2 minutes. Remove the shrimp to a small bowl with a slotted spoon and sprinkle them with salt. Remove the pan from the heat.

Stir the shells into the boiling water. Return to a boil, stirring frequently. Cook the pasta, semi-covered, stirring occasionally, until done, 8 to 10 minutes.

While the pasta is cooking, return the pan to medium heat. Add the butter, sliced fennel, and reserved fennel-cooking liquid to the skillet and bring to a boil. Season with salt and crushed red pepper. Lower the heat so the sauce is at a lively simmer and cook until the sauce is lightly thickened and the fennel is tender but not mushy, about 10 minutes. Stir in the fennel leaves and the reserved shrimp.

If the skillet is large enough to accommodate the sauce and pasta, fish the pasta out of the boiling water with a large wire skimmer and drop it directly into the sauce in the skillet. If not, drain the pasta, return it to the pot, and pour in the sauce. Bring the sauce and pasta to a boil, stirring to coat the pasta with sauce. Check the seasoning, adding salt and crushed red pepper if necessary. Serve immediately in warm bowls.

Capellini with Crabmeat

Capellini con Salsa di Granchio

1 pound "jumbo lump" crabmeat

Salt, preferably sea salt

6 tablespoons extra-virgin olive oil

1 salt-packed anchovy (see page 105), cleaned and chopped, or 2 canned anchovy fillets

1 small leek, white and light-green parts only, trimmed, cleaned, and sliced thin (about ½ cup) (see page 80)

½ cup chopped trimmed scallions

6 bottled cherry peppers, cored, seeded, and chopped (about ¼ cup)

2 cups Marinara Sauce (page 150)

1 pound capellini (angel-hair pasta)

Makes 6 servings

I prefer "jumbo lump" crabmeat picked from blue-claw crabs for this recipe. If you can't find that, substitute "lump" crabmeat—smaller pieces from the same species of crab—or chunks of king-crab meat. Avoid fine-textured crabmeat, like snow crab or spider crab.

Pick over the crabmeat, removing any pieces of shell or cartilage, but leaving the crab in as large pieces as possible. Bring 6 quarts of salted water to a boil in an 8-quart pot over high heat.

Heat 4 tablespoons of the olive oil in a large skillet over medium heat. Add the anchovy and stir until the anchovy dissolves, about 1 minute. Stir in the leek and cook, stirring, until wilted, about 2 minutes. Stir in the scallions and cherry peppers, and cook for 2 to 3 minutes. Ladle the marinara sauce into the skillet, bring to a boil, then lower the heat so the sauce is at a lively simmer.

Stir the capellini into the boiling water. Return to a boil, stirring frequently. Cook the pasta, semi-covered, stirring occasionally, until softened, but still quite firm, 2 to 3 minutes.

Stir the crabmeat into the sauce. Ladle off and reserve about 1 cup of the pasta-cooking water. If the skillet is large enough to accommodate the sauce and pasta, fish the pasta out of the boiling water with a large wire skimmer and drop it directly into the sauce in the skillet. If not, drain the pasta, return it to the pot, and pour in the sauce. Bring the sauce and pasta to a boil, stirring to coat the pasta. Drizzle in the remaining 2 tablespoons olive oil. Check the seasoning, adding salt if necessary. Pour in some of the reserved pasta-cooking water, if necessary, to make a light enough sauce to coat the pasta. Serve immediately in warm bowls.

Have some fun with the pasta shapes you choose. Long, springy fusilli may act like it has a mind of its own — but that's what makes it interesting and nice for a change of pace. The zucchini and spring onion (or scallion) are cut long and thin to match the shape of whichever pasta you choose for this dish.

Long Fusilli with Mussels, Saffron, and Zucchini

Fusilli Lunghi con Cozze al Zafferano

Salt

2 small ("fancy") zucchini (about 12 ounces)

1½ cups hot Chicken Stock (page 74) or canned reduced-sodium chicken broth

1 teaspoon saffron threads

5 tablespoons extra-virgin olive oil

5 cloves garlic, peeled

2 medium spring onions or scallions, white and light-green parts only, trimmed and cut into thin strips

2 tablespoons unsalted butter, cut into 4 pieces

2 pounds small mussels, preferably cultivated (about 40), scrubbed

1 pound long, curly fusilli, spaghetti, or linguine

3 tablespoons chopped fresh Italian parsley

Freshly ground black pepper

Makes 6 servings

Picking the mussels from their shells before you toss the pasta together with the sauce means less work for your guests, but feel free to skip that step. If you do skip it, put the pasta on to boil just before you start the sauce. Both will be done at about the same time.

Bring 6 quarts of salted water to a boil in an 8-quart pot over high heat.

Trim the ends from the zucchini and cut the zucchini lengthwise into quarters. With a paring knife, trim out the seeds from the zucchini quarters and discard them. Cut the rest of the zucchini into thin strips of about ¼ × ¼ × 2 inches. Pour the stock over the saffron in a small heatproof bowl and let steep while continuing with the sauce.

Heat 3 tablespoons of the olive oil in a large skillet over medium heat. Whack the garlic cloves with the flat side of a knife and toss them into the oil. Cook, shaking the pan, until golden, about 2 minutes. Scatter the zucchini and spring onions over the oil, then season them lightly with salt and stir until wilted, about 2 minutes. Toss the butter into the pan and lower the heat to medium-low. Continue cooking, stirring until the vegetables are tender, about 3 minutes. Remove the pan from the heat and set aside.

Pour the saffron and stock into the pan, increase the heat to high, and bring to a boil. Slide the mussels into the pan, cover and cook just until opened, about 4 minutes. Remove the pan from the heat and, with a slotted spoon, transfer about half the mussels to a heatproof bowl. Cover and set aside. Let the mussels remaining in the pan stand just until cool enough to handle.

Meanwhile, stir the fusilli into the boiling water. Bring the water back to a boil, stirring frequently. Cook the pasta, semi-covered, stirring occasionally, until done, 8 to 10 minutes.

When the mussels in the pan are cool enough to handle, pluck them from their shells and return the flesh to the sauce.

Drain the pasta and return it to the pot. Add the shelled mussels and their sauce and the parsley to the pasta. Bring to a boil over medium heat and stir until the sauce is lightly thickened and coats the pasta. Taste and season with pepper and, if necessary, salt. Transfer the pasta to a heated platter or serving bowls and top with the reserved mussels in their shells.

To: Lidia Bastianich
From: Lisa Towns
Subject:

> > > Lidia, you are one of the most intelligent and wonderful chefs I have ever had the pleasure to watch. Moreover, you sound like and you look like and you cook like all of the women I have loved most in my lifetime. I love the fact that you take familiar favorites and raise them to a more elegant level, while leaving the essence wholly intact. I love the way you emphasize the total sensory experience of cooking, eating, and, for that matter, simply being alive! Thank you ever so much, and God bless you and your family.< < <

Spotting *"fra diavolo,"* meaning, more or less, "caught up with the devil," on a menu is a sure sign that the dish it refers to is spicy. Used much more on Italian-American menus than on menus in Italy, a *fra diavolo* sauce is usually, but not always, a tomato-based one. *"Alla diavolo"* carries the same meaning.

Lobster *fra Diavolo* with Spaghettini

Three 1¼-pound live Maine lobsters

1½ cups vegetable oil, or as needed

Salt

All-purpose flour

¼ cup extra-virgin olive oil

8 cloves garlic

Two 35-ounce cans Italian plum tomatoes (preferably San Marzano) with their liquid, seeded and crushed

16 whole dried peperoncino or diavollilo hot red peppers, or 1½ teaspoons crushed hot red pepper

1 teaspoon dried oregano, preferably the Sicilian or Greek type dried on the branch, crumbled

1 teaspoon chopped fresh oregano

1 pound linguine

Makes 6 servings

Look for lobsters that are alive and kicking—the claws shouldn't hang limp—and ones that feel heavy for their size. Cutting and cleaning a live lobster may seem difficult, but it is very easy to get the hang of it. (Placing the lobsters in the freezer for half an hour beforehand makes it even easier.) The lobsters will give off a lot of liquid as you clean them; make cleanup easier by spreading a kitchen towel or two under the cutting board to absorb whatever liquid drips off the board.

I have stayed true to Italian-American cooking by seasoning this dish with dried oregano, but brought it into the present by adding a dose of fresh oregano as well. You may remember this as a very saucy dish, but I prefer to serve it Italian-style—not swimming in sauce, but condito, *tossed with just enough sauce to dress the pasta.*

Place the lobsters in the freezer about 30 minutes before beginning this recipe.

Bring 6 quarts of salted water to a boil in an 8-quart pot over high heat.

Cut off the lobster legs and claws from the body with a sturdy pair of kitchen shears. Divide the claw at the joint. Whack the claws with a meat mallet just hard enough to crack the shells. (If you wish, to make it easier to remove the meat from the shell after the lobster is cooked, cut along one side of each of the two joints that were attached to the claw.) Lay one of the lobsters on a cutting board with the tail stretched out. Cut the lobster body in half length-wise by taking firm hold of the tail and inserting a heavy, sharp knife where the tail meets the body section. Bring the knife down to the cutting board in a swift motion, cutting the body section cleanly in half. Turn the knife in the other direction and cut the tail in half in the same way. You now have two lobster halves, each of which consists of tail and body pieces. Do not separate the tail from the body. Cut off the antennae and eyes with the shears and scrape out the digestive sac located inside the shell, behind the eyes. Pull out the dark vein that runs along the tail, but leave the tomalley—the pale-green mass close to the tail—intact. (It adds wonderful flavor to the sauce.) Repeat with the remaining lobsters.

In a wide, heavy skillet, heat 1 cup of the vegetable oil over medium heat. Pat all the lobster pieces dry with paper towels. Dredge the meat side of the lobster halves lightly in flour and add as many of them, cut side down, as fit comfortably to the skillet. Cook until the lobster meat is lightly browned, about 5 minutes. Remove from the pan and repeat with the remaining lobster body pieces, adding more oil to the pan as needed. When all the lobster halves have been browned, add the claws and joints to the pan and cook, turning them with long-handled tongs, until the shells turn bright red on all sides, about 4 minutes. Turn the lobster pieces carefully—they are likely to splatter.

Heat the olive oil in a wide, deep braising pan large enough to hold all the lobster pieces over medium heat. Whack the garlic cloves with the side of a knife and add them along with the lobster legs to the oil. Cook, shaking the pan, until the garlic is lightly browned, about 3 minutes. Pour in the tomatoes, add the peppers and dried oregano, and season lightly with salt. Bring to a boil and adjust the heat to a lively simmer. Cook 10 minutes.

Stir in the fresh oregano and tuck all the lobster pieces into the sauce. Cook at a lively simmer just until the lobster meat is cooked through and juicy, about 5 minutes. If the sauce becomes too dense as it simmers, ladle a little of the pasta-cooking water into the pan. Keep the sauce and lobster warm over very low heat.

Meanwhile, stir the linguine into the boiling water. Cook, stirring frequently, until done, about 6 minutes. Drain the linguine and return it to the pot. Spoon the liquid portion of the lobster sauce over the pasta, leaving just enough sauce behind in the pan to keep the lobster pieces moist. Bring the sauce and pasta to a boil, stirring gently to coat the pasta with sauce. Check the seasoning, adding salt if necessary.

Divide the linguine among 6 pasta bowls. Top each with a lobster body and claw. Spoon some of the sauce remaining in the pan over each serving, and serve immediately.

Antonio Farina, chef and owner of Da Antonio in Castel Nuovo di Berardensa in Tuscany, showed me this unique way to cook pasta when I spent some time in his kitchen last summer. Antonio makes daily 2-hour trips from his exceptional seafood restaurant in the middle of Chianti country to Viareggio, on the Tyrrhenian Sea, to select the day's seafood. Antonio's simplicity of style and his attention to prime products exemplify a style of cooking that is, in my book, the only way to cook.

Capellini Cooked in Red-Mullet Stew

Capellini in Brodetto di Triglie

5 tablespoons extra-virgin olive oil

½ cup chopped shallots

1 small leek, white and light-green parts only, trimmed, cleaned, and sliced thin (about ½ cup) (see page 80)

⅓ cup finely chopped celery (with leaves)

1 pound skin-on red-mullet or red-snapper fillets

2 cups peeled, seeded, and chopped fresh tomatoes (from about 1¼ pounds) (see page 9)

2 whole dried peperoncini (hot red peppers)

1 quart hot water

1 pound capellini (angel-hair pasta)

⅓ cup shredded fresh basil

Salt

Makes 6 servings

Although this method for cooking capellini in a small amount of liquid is a little tricky—and somehow the opposite of everything I have told you about cooking pasta—the end result is a richly flavored pasta with a velvety texture. Be patient and thorough when you stir the capellini into the broth, making sure to separate the strands as they cook.

Heat 3 tablespoons of the olive oil in a wide 4-quart braising pan over medium heat. Stir in the shallots, leek, and celery and cook, stirring occasionally, until wilted, about 2 minutes. Push the vegetables to the sides of the pan to make enough room for the fillets. Slip the fillets into the pan, skin side down, and cook until the skin changes color, about 2 minutes. Flip the fillets over, cook 2 minutes, then stir in the tomatoes and peperoncini. Bring to a quick boil, stirring, and pour in 3 cups of the hot water.

Add the capellini to the pan gradually, stirring them constantly to separate them. (This will become easier as they soften and start to bend.) Don't worry if you break up the fillets as you stir the pasta. Add the remaining water a little at a time as the capellini begin to absorb the liquid in the pan. The goal is to end up with just enough sauce to coat the pasta generously—not a soupy dish—so be careful to add liquid very gradually. Cook, stirring almost constantly to keep the pasta from sticking together, until the pasta is done and glides easily in a creamy sauce, about 5 to 7 minutes. A minute or two before the end of cooking, stir in the basil and the remaining 2 tablespoons olive oil. Check the seasoning, adding salt if necessary. Remove the peperoncini peppers and serve the pasta immediately in warm bowls.

1

2

3

4

Cutting Up a Live Lobster

1. Divide the claw at the joint.

2. Cut the lobster body in half: Insert the knife where the body section meets the tail section and bring the knife down in a swift motion, then turn the lobster around and cut through the tail.

3. Cut off the antennae and eyes with the shears.

4. The lobster halves are ready to cook; note the dark mass of tomalley and roe in the body cavity.

Meat

I remember the *polpette* (meatballs) from my childhood as patties of meat about 1 inch wide and flat, like a crab cake. We pan-fried them and ate them with a side dish of vegetables or salad, or in a sandwich. The Neapolitan meatball is much smaller, fried, and used in between layers of lasagna without being cooked in sauce. The Italian-American method is another story, with the meatballs usually measuring 2 to 3 inches in diameter, cooked in tomato sauce. My version is somewhere in between.

Spaghetti and Meatballs

Spaghetti con Polpette di Carne

For the Sauce

Two 35-ounce cans Italian plum tomatoes (preferably San Marzano) with their liquid

¼ cup extra-virgin olive oil

1 medium onion, chopped (about 1 cup)

1 teaspoon crushed hot red pepper

2 bay leaves

Salt

Freshly ground black pepper

I like a mixture of beef and pork for meatballs, but you can use all of one or the other if you prefer. If you do use all beef, try this: moisten the bread crumbs in milk for a minute or two before adding them to the meatball mixture. It's not traditional, but it will help with the somewhat drier texture of beef. You can use a spoon or spatula to mix the meatballs, but I like to use my hands. I think it's the most efficient way, and I can feel the texture of what I'm mixing.

The mix of vegetable and olive oils gives you a higher smoking point for the oil with the benefit of the flavor of olive oil. The reason for flouring and browning the meatballs is to add flavor and to seal them so they hold together in the sauce, not to cook them all the way through — they will finish cooking in the sauce.

For the Meatballs

- ½ pound ground pork
- ½ pound ground beef
- 1 cup fine, dry bread crumbs
- ⅓ cup freshly grated Parmigiano-Reggiano cheese
- ¼ cup chopped fresh Italian parsley
- 2 cloves garlic, peeled and chopped fine
- 1 large egg
- 1 teaspoon salt
- ¼ teaspoon freshly ground black pepper
- All-purpose flour
- ¼ cup olive oil
- ¼ cup vegetable oil

- 1 pound spaghetti
- ⅔ cup freshly grated Parmigiano-Reggiano

Makes 6 servings

Pass the tomatoes and their liquid through a food mill fitted with the fine disc. Heat ¼ cup olive oil in a 4- to 5-quart pot over medium heat. Stir in the onion and cook, stirring, until wilted, about 4 minutes. Pour in the tomatoes, add the crushed red pepper and bay leaves, and season lightly with salt and pepper. Bring to a boil, then lower the heat so the sauce is at a lively simmer. Cook, stirring occasionally, 30 minutes.

Meanwhile, crumble the pork and beef into a mixing bowl. Sprinkle the bread crumbs, ⅓ cup grated cheese, the parsley, and garlic over the meat. Beat the egg with 1 teaspoon salt and ¼ teaspoon black pepper in a small bowl until blended. Pour over the meat mixture. Mix the ingredients with clean hands just until evenly blended. Don't overmix. Shape the meat mixture into 1½-inch balls.

Dredge the meatballs in the flour until lightly but evenly coated. Heat ¼ cup olive oil and the vegetable oil in a large, heavy skillet over medium-high heat. Slip as many meatballs into the skillet as will fit without crowding. Fry, turning as necessary, until golden brown on all sides, about 6 minutes. Adjust the heat as the meatballs cook to prevent them from overbrowning. Remove the meatballs, and repeat if necessary with the remaining meatballs.

Bring 6 quarts of salted water to a boil in an 8-quart pot over high heat.

Add the browned meatballs to the tomato sauce and cook, stirring gently with a wooden spoon, until no trace of pink remains at the center of the meatballs, about 30 minutes.

Stir the spaghetti into the boiling water. Return to a boil, stirring frequently. Cook the pasta, semi-covered, stirring occasionally, until done, about 8 minutes.

Drain the pasta and return it to the pot. Spoon in about 2 cups of the tomato sauce, tossing well until the pasta is coated with sauce. Remove from the heat and toss in ⅔ cup grated cheese. Check the seasoning, and add salt and pepper if necessary. Serve the pasta in warm bowls or piled high on a large warm platter. Spoon a little more of the sauce over the pasta, and pass the remaining sauce separately. Pass the meatballs family-style in a bowl, or top the bowls or platter of spaghetti with them.

Gemelli are twins in Italian, and that is what this short pasta shape with its intertwined strands resembles. If you can't find gemelli, I suggest another short, chunky shape, like penne or shells.

Gemelli with Sausage-Tomato Sauce

Gemelli con Sugo di Salsiccia

3 tablespoons extra-virgin olive oil

1 medium yellow onion, sliced (about 1 ½ cups)

Salt

1 pound (about 5 links) sweet Italian sausages, preferably without fennel seeds, casings removed

One 35-ounce can Italian plum tomatoes (preferably San Marzano) with their liquid, crushed

4 pickled cherry peppers, cored, seeded, and diced

½ teaspoon dried oregano, preferably the Sicilian or Greek type dried on the branch, crumbled

1 pound gemelli pasta

½ cup freshly grated Pecorino Romano cheese

Makes 6 servings

Heat the olive oil in a large skillet over medium heat. Stir in the onion, sprinkle lightly with salt, and cook, stirring, until wilted, about 3 minutes. Crumble the sausage into the skillet and stir until it is has rendered most of its fat and is golden brown, 5 to 7 minutes. (If the sausage has given off some water, allow time for the water to boil away before the sausage begins to brown.)

Drain the excess fat from the skillet. Add the tomatoes, cherry peppers, and oregano and bring to a boil. Lower the heat so the sauce is at a lively simmer and season the sauce lightly with salt. Cook, stirring occasionally, until the sauce is thickened, about 20 minutes.

Meanwhile, bring 6 quarts of salted water to a boil in an 8-quart pot over high heat. Stir the gemelli into the boiling water. Return to a boil, stirring frequently. Cook the pasta, semi-covered, stirring occasionally, until done, 8 to 10 minutes.

If the skillet is large enough to accommodate the sauce and pasta, fish the pasta out of the boiling water with a large wire skimmer and drop it directly into the sauce in the skillet. If not, drain the pasta, return it to the pot, and pour in the sauce. Bring the sauce and pasta to a boil, stirring the pasta gently to coat with sauce. Check the seasoning, adding salt if necessary. Remove from the heat and add half the grated cheese. Toss well, then transfer to a warm serving platter or individual bowls. Top with the remaining cheese, and serve immediately.

This dish is traditionally cooked with guanciale instead of pancetta. Pancetta is rolled and cured pork belly, while guanciale is cured pork cheeks—quite delicious but difficult to come by in stores. If you find guanciale, by all means use it here.

Bucatini with Pancetta, Tomato, and Onion

Bucatini all'Amatriciana

One 35-ounce can Italian plum tomatoes (preferably San Marzano)

Salt

5 tablespoons extra-virgin olive oil, or to taste

1 medium onion, sliced thin (about 2 cups)

Four ¼-inch slices pancetta (about 6 ounces), cut into 1½-inch julienne strips (about 1½ cups; see note below)

2 whole dried red peperoncino hot red peppers, or ½ teaspoon crushed hot red pepper flakes

1 pound bucatini or perciatelli pasta

1 cup grated Pecorino Romano cheese, plus more for passing

Makes 6 servings

Pass the tomatoes and their liquid through a food mill fitted with the fine disc. Set aside. Bring 6 quarts of salted water to a boil in an 8-quart pot.

In a large skillet, heat 2 tablespoons of the olive oil over medium heat. Add the onion and cook, stirring, until wilted, about 4 minutes. Stir in the pancetta and cook 2 minutes. Add the hot red peppers and the strained tomatoes and bring to a boil. Adjust the heat to a simmer, and season lightly with salt. Cook, stirring occasionally, until the sauce is thickened, about 20 minutes.

Meanwhile, stir the bucatini into the boiling water and cook, stirring occasionally, until done, about 12 minutes.

Check the seasoning of the sauce, adding salt if necessary (remember, the Pecorino is mildly salty).

Reserve about 1 cup of the pasta-cooking water. Drain the pasta, return it to the pot, and pour in half the sauce. Bring the sauce and pasta to a boil and drizzle in the remaining 3 tablespoons olive oil. Add some of the pasta-cooking water, if necessary, to make enough of the sauce to coat the pasta lightly. Check the seasoning, adding salt if necessary. Remove the pan from the heat, stir in 1 cup grated cheese, and transfer to a large, heated serving platter or bowl. Spoon the remaining sauce over the top and pass additional grated cheese separately, if you like.

☞ To cut the pancetta into julienne strips, first unroll each slice, and then cut the long strip crosswise into 1½-inch pieces. Cut the strips lengthwise into ¼-inch strips.

This dish is very typical of Roman pasta preparations, and although its origins are questionable, there seems to be some reference in the name to the charcoal makers who smoldered wood in the hills around Rome to make charcoal. In Ciociaria, the hills toward Abruzzo, pasta is traditionally dressed with bacon and eggs, products readily available at home. The traditional carbonara became popular in Rome after World War II—it was a time of meager existence. Basic food, such as bacon and powdered eggs, was distributed to needy families by the Allied forces in the aftermath of the war. It is unromantic to think that such a delicious dish was created under such stressful conditions, but it's a possibility. In the years following that war there was an influx of Italian immigrants to the United States. With them came carbonara, which was one of the main pasta preparations in Italian-American restaurants, and still is a favorite in Italian restaurants.

Linguine with Bacon and Onions

Linguine alla Carbonara

Salt

- 6 ounces slab bacon, in 1 piece
- 2 tablespoons extra-virgin olive oil, plus more if needed
- 2 large yellow onions, sliced ½ inch thick (about 3 cups)
- 1½ cups hot Chicken Stock (page 74) or canned reduced-sodium chicken broth, or as needed
- 1 pound linguine
- 3 egg yolks

I use slab bacon here because I like large pieces that are brown on the outside but still moist in the center. If you cannot find slab bacon, use the thickest-sliced supermarket bacon you can find. Just be sure not to overcook it. If you prefer, you can pour off all the bacon fat after browning the bacon and replace it with an equal amount of olive oil, but remember, the bacon fat has a much more pronounced flavor. If you don't have the stock called for in the recipe, just use water from the pasta pot.

Often you will see this dish prepared with cream. It's not the traditional style, but that's not to say it doesn't taste good. But I prefer my carbonara made this way, the sauce thickened lightly

1 cup freshly grated
Parmigiano-Reggiano
cheese
Coarsely ground black
pepper

Makes 6 servings

☞ The Importance of
Coarsely Ground Pepper:
Coarsely ground black
pepper is essential to this
dish. If your mill doesn't
grind pepper coarsely, try
the following trick: Place
the peppercorns on a flat
surface. Holding the rim
of a small, heavy saucepan
or skillet with one hand,
and pressing down on
the center of the pan
with the other, crush the
peppercorns until
coarsely ground.

with egg yolk. The heat of the pasta is enough to cook the egg yolks, but if you like, you may bring a small saucepan of boiling water to a simmer and, about a minute before draining the pasta, slip the yolks into a small sieve placed in the simmering water, to coddle them for a minute. Carefully lift the sieve from the water and add the coddled yolks to the pasta as described below.

Bring 6 quarts of salted water to the boil in an 8-quart pot over high heat.

Remove the rind, if necessary, from the bacon. Cut the bacon into $\frac{1}{4}$-inch slices, then cut the slices crosswise into $\frac{1}{4}$-inch strips. Heat the olive oil in a large, heavy skillet over medium heat. Add the bacon and cook, stirring, until the bacon is lightly browned but still soft in the center, about 6 minutes.

The amount of fat in the skillet will vary depending on the bacon. If there is more than 3 to 4 tablespoons of fat in the pan, pour off the excess. If there is less than 3 to 4 tablespoons, add enough olive oil to measure that amount. Add the onions and cook until wilted but still crunchy, about 4 to 5 minutes. Add the stock, bring to a boil, and adjust the heat to a lively simmer. Cook until the liquid is reduced by about half.

Meanwhile, stir the linguine into the boiling salted water. Return to a boil, stirring frequently. Cook the pasta, semi-covered, stirring occasionally, until done, about 8 minutes.

Ladle off about a cup of the pasta-cooking water. If the skillet is large enough to accommodate the sauce and pasta, fish the pasta out of the boiling water with a large wire skimmer and drop it directly into the sauce in the skillet. If not, drain the pasta, return it to the pot, and pour in the sauce. Bring the sauce and pasta to a boil, stirring to coat the pasta with sauce. Check the seasoning, adding salt if necessary. If necessary, add as much chicken stock or pasta-cooking water as needed to make enough sauce to coat the pasta generously. Remove the pan from the heat and add the egg yolks one at a time, tossing well after each. (A salad fork and spoon work well for this.) Add the grated cheese, then the black pepper, tossing well, and serve immediately in warmed bowls.

Perciatelli are long pasta, like spaghetti but hollow and a little thicker. They are a fun pasta to eat, though you may splash your clothes with the sauce while eating them—be prepared. They don't collect on your fork as easily as spaghetti, but, rather, flop around, snaking around to hit you right in the nose when you least expect it. As kids, we loved them—they almost seemed alive in the plate.

Perciatelli with Tomato and Prosciutto Sauce

Perciatelli al Filetto di Pomodoro

Salt

One 35-ounce can whole Italian plum tomatoes (preferably San Marzano)

1 pound perciatelli pasta

1/3 cup extra-virgin olive oil

1 large yellow onion, cut into 1/2-inch slices (about 1 1/2 cups)

2 bay leaves

4 ounces imported Italian prosciutto, sliced 1/8 inch thick and cut crosswise into 1/2-inch strips

1/2 teaspoon crushed hot red pepper

1 cup grated mild Pecorino Romano cheese

Makes 6 servings

This version of a classic Italian pasta dish is prepared with prosciutto, as was often done in Italian-American restaurants. For a more traditional version, substitute 6 ounces of guanciale (cured pork-cheek bacon) or regular bacon cut into $^1/_4$-inch strips for the prosciutto. Cook the guanciale or bacon in the skillet with the olive oil before adding the onion. Cook until lightly browned but still soft, about 4 minutes for the guanciale or 2 minutes for the bacon. Then add the onion and continue with the recipe as below.

Bring 6 quarts of salted water to a boil in an 8-quart pot over high heat.

Drain the tomatoes and reserve the juice. Cut the tomatoes in quarters lengthwise and scrape out the seeds and cores. Stir the perciatelli into the boiling water. Return to a boil, stirring frequently. Cook the pasta, semi-covered, stirring occasionally, until done, about 12 minutes.

Meanwhile, in a large, heavy skillet, heat 3 tablespoons of the olive oil over medium heat. Add the onion and bay leaves and cook until the onion is wilted but still crunchy, about 4 minutes. Add the prosciutto and stir 2 minutes. Add the tomatoes, about 1 cup of the reserved liquid, and the crushed red pepper. Bring to a boil, lower the heat so the sauce is at a lively simmer, and cook until the pasta is done.

Reserve about 1 cup of the pasta-cooking liquid, then drain the pasta and return it to the pot. Add half the sauce and the remaining olive oil. Stir until the sauce is bubbling and the pasta is coated. If necessary, add as much of the reserved pasta-cooking liquid as needed to make enough sauce to coat the pasta lightly but evenly. Remove the pot from the heat and stir in the grated cheese. Transfer the pasta to a heated platter or serving bowls and top with the remaining sauce.

☞ To open plastic packages of long pastas, like perciatelli, spaghetti, linguine, or vermicelli, hold them firmly around the center and give one end of the package a good whack on a firm surface.

Oxtail is exactly what it sounds like—the tail of an ox. The tail is a sequence of joints (almost like a spinal cord) that is wider the closer it is to the body and thins out as it lengthens. The flavor of oxtail is intense, and the meat is firm and gelatinous.

Braised Oxtail with Rigatoni

Coda di Bue Brasata con Rigatoni

2½ pounds oxtails (preferably all larger pieces, but probably one whole oxtail, cut between joints to pieces of varying size)

Salt

Freshly ground black pepper

6 tablespoons extra-virgin olive oil

2 medium yellow onions, chopped (about 2 cups)

2 medium carrots, peeled and shredded (about 1 cup)

1 cup chopped celery, with leaves

⅓ cup chopped fresh Italian parsley

3 cloves garlic, peeled and chopped

2 cups dry white wine

One 35-ounce can Italian plum tomatoes (preferably San Marzano) with their liquid, crushed

If possible, buy only the larger joints of the oxtail, since there is more meat on the bones and less work picking it off. But usually (and almost always in supermarkets) a single tail is cut and packaged together. If you're ordering oxtail through a butcher, ask him to remove as much of the outer fat as possible, and to cut the oxtail cleanly at the joints. If the tail is cut haphazardly, bone chips can occur, which are annoying and can be very dangerous. It's always a good idea to pick over the pieces of oxtail before you cook with them, to make sure there are no fine pieces of bone.

In the traditional Roman dish of coda alla vaccinara, *the cheeks of the oxen are braised along with the oxtails. Because this is a very rich and savory sauce, I do not use cheese to dress the pasta, but some people do. I'll leave it up to you. If you decide to dress the pasta with cheese, use grated Parmigiano-Reggiano.*

The braised oxtails, left on the bone, make an excellent cold-weather main course, served with polenta. If you're serving the oxtails as a main course, you might want to cut the vegetables larger, so they hold their shape during cooking.

3 to 4 cups Chicken Stock
(page 74) or canned
reduced-sodium chicken
broth

1 pound rigatoni

1 cup grated Parmigiano-
Reggiano cheese,
optional

Makes 6 servings

Soak the oxtails in cold water to cover for 30 minutes. Drain thoroughly and pat them dry. Season both sides of the oxtail pieces with salt and pepper.

Heat the olive oil in a wide, heavy pan or Dutch oven over medium heat. Add as many oxtail pieces as fit without crowding into the pan. Cook, turning as necessary, until golden brown on all sides, about 10 minutes. If necessary, remove the pieces as they brown to make room in the pan for remaining pieces. Remove all the oxtail pieces from the pan. Stir in the onions, carrots, celery, parsley, and garlic, season them lightly with salt and pepper, and cook, stirring, until the vegetables are wilted, about 4 minutes. Pour in the wine, bring to a vigorous boil, and cook until the wine is evaporated, about 10 minutes. Pour in the tomatoes and their liquid. Bring to a boil, lower the heat so the sauce is at a lively simmer, and season lightly with salt and pepper. Tuck the oxtails into the sauce and cook until they are very tender (the meat should be practically falling off the bone and the vegetables disintegrated into the sauce), about 3 hours. As the oxtails cook, add the chicken stock, about $1/2$ cup at a time, to keep the level of the liquid more or less steady during cooking. Cool the oxtails in the cooking liquid to room temperature. Skim the excess fat from the sauce.

Remove all meat from the bones, shred it coarsely, and return it to the sauce. (You may serve the oxtails whole, if you prefer.) The pasta sauce can be prepared and refrigerated up to 3 days in advance.

Bring 6 quarts of salted water to a boil in an 8-quart pot over high heat. Stir the rigatoni into the boiling water. Return to a boil, stirring frequently. Cook the pasta, semi-covered, stirring occasionally, until done, 10 to 11 minutes. While the pasta is cooking, return the oxtail sauce to the pan if necessary and bring to a simmer over medium-low heat.

Drain the pasta, return it to the pot, and pour in about half the sauce. Bring the sauce and pasta to a boil, stirring gently to coat the pasta with sauce. Remove the pot from the heat, toss in the cheese if using, and check the seasoning, adding salt and pepper if necessary. Spoon the pasta into warm bowls or a warm platter and ladle the remaining sauce over the top. Serve immediately.

Sauces

Italian-American Meat Sauce

Sugo di Carne

Two 35-ounce cans Italian plum tomatoes (preferably San Marzano)

¼ cup extra-virgin olive oil

2 medium yellow onions, diced (about 2 cups)

6 to 8 cloves garlic, peeled and chopped fine

5 to 6 meaty pork neck bones (about ¾ pound)

1 pound ground beef

1 pound ground pork

Salt

4 bay leaves

1½ teaspoons dried oregano, preferably the Sicilian or Greek type dried on the branch, crumbled

¾ cup dry white wine

⅓ cup tomato paste

3 to 4 cups hot water

Makes about 8 cups, enough to fill and sauce Italian-American Lasagna (page 156) or to dress about 2 pounds pasta

If you have trouble finding ground pork, or if you prefer to grind your own, it's really very easy. (And if you buy a piece of bone-in pork to grind, you'll have the bones you need for the sauce.) Remove all bones and gristle from the meat, but leave some of the fat. Cut the pork into 1-inch pieces, and chill them thoroughly. Grind about half at a time in a food processor fitted with the metal blade. Pulse, using quick on/off motions, until the meat is ground coarsely.

In my region of Italy, tomato paste is usually added along with the onions to caramelize a little bit. But around Naples, and the rest of southern Italy, tomato paste is stirred right into the sauce. That's how I do it here.

When the sauce is finished simmering, you can pull the meat from the bones and stir it into the sauce, or you can do what I do—nibble on it while the sauce perks away. This makes quite a bit of sauce—enough to feed a small crowd and have enough left over to freeze in small quantities for a quick pasta meal for one or two.

Pass the tomatoes and their liquid through a food mill fitted with the fine disc. Set aside.

Heat the olive oil in a heavy 4- to 5-quart pot over medium heat. Add the onions and cook, stirring occasionally, until golden, about 8 minutes. Make a little room in the center of the pot, dump in the garlic, and cook, stirring, until the garlic is lightly browned, about 2 minutes. Add the pork bones and cook, turning, until lightly browned on all sides, about 5 minutes. Add the ground beef and pork and season lightly with salt. Cook, stirring to break up the meat, until the meat changes color and the water it gives off is boiled away, about 10 minutes. Continue cooking until the meat is browned, about 5 minutes. Add the bay leaves and oregano, then pour in the wine. Bring to a boil and cook, scraping up the brown bits that cling to the pot, until the wine is almost completely evaporated. Pour in the tomatoes, then stir in the tomato paste until it is dissolved. Season lightly with salt. Bring to a boil, adjust the heat to a lively simmer, and cook, uncovered, stirring often, until the sauce takes on a deep, brick-red color, 2 to 3 hours. Add the hot water, about $1/2$ cup at a time, as necessary to maintain the level of liquid for the length of time the sauce cooks.

Skim off any fat floating on top and adjust the seasoning as necessary. The sauce can be prepared entirely in advance and refrigerated for up to 5 days, or frozen for up to 3 months.

Tomato Paste

TOMATO PASTE IS THE ESSENCE OF TOMATO in a concentrated form. I use tomato paste to bring an intense tomato flavor to a dish, or when I want the sweetness and mellow flavor of tomato without the acidity of fresh tomatoes. I also add tomato paste to soups, braised meat dishes, and slow-simmered tomato sauces for a rich color and complexity of flavor. The next time you make a roast, dilute a tablespoon of tomato paste in a cup of hot stock or water and add it to the pan. It will give the roast a bit of color and a lot of taste.

Traditionally, tomato paste is made by spreading very ripe tomatoes on a wooden board to dry in the sun. As they dry, the tomatoes are turned daily and spread out on the board, like plaster of Paris, until most of their water is evaporated. During the drying process, the tomatoes' acidity is greatly reduced and their flavor and sweetness are intensified. Today, tomato paste is dehydrated in commercial plants by boiling the tomatoes down, then drying them in a slow oven.

To give tomato paste a nuttier flavor, I like to caramelize it by cooking it in oil along with vegetables before the other ingredients are added to the pot. And, to get the most out it, I like to cook it longer than I would fresh or canned tomatoes.

Meat Sauce Bolognese

Sugo alla Bolognese

3 tablespoons extra-virgin olive oil

1 medium yellow onion, minced (about 1 cup)

1 medium carrot, peeled and finely shredded (about ½ cup)

½ cup minced celery, with leaves

Salt

1 pound ground beef

1 pound ground pork

½ cup dry red wine

1 tablespoon tomato paste

3 cups canned Italian plum tomatoes (preferably San Marzano) with their liquid, crushed

3 bay leaves

Freshly ground black pepper

4 cups hot water, or as needed

Makes 6 cups, enough to dress about 1½ pounds dried pasta

Bolognese is a very versatile sauce. Not only can it dress all shapes and sizes of pasta, like fresh tagliolini (page 180) or dried spaghetti or rigatoni, you can also use it instead of the Italian-American Meat Sauce (page 144) in the lasagna on page 156, or in a meaty version of the pasticciata on page 158.

This recipe makes enough sauce to dress 1½ pounds of dried pasta or one and a half recipes of tagliolini—good for feeding a hungry crowd. It also freezes well, if you'd like to enjoy it in smaller quantities. Warm the sauce while the pasta is cooking and toss it with the cooked pasta, adding a little of the pasta-cooking water if necessary to make a creamy sauce. Toss in some grated Parmigiano-Reggiano just before you serve it.

Heat the olive oil in a wide, 3- to 4-quart pan or Dutch oven over medium heat. Stir in the onion, carrot, and celery, season them lightly with salt, and cook, stirring, until the onion is translucent, about 4 minutes. Crumble in the ground beef and pork and continue cooking, stirring to break up the meat, until all the liquid the meat has given off is evaporated and the meat is lightly browned, about 10 minutes. Pour in the wine and cook, scraping the bottom of the pan, until the wine is evaporated, 3 to 4 minutes. Stir in the tomato paste and cook a few minutes. Pour in the tomatoes, toss in the bay leaves, and season lightly with salt and pepper.

Bring to a boil, then lower the heat so the sauce is at a lively simmer. Cook, stirring occasionally, until the sauce is dense but juicy and a rich, dark-red color. (Most likely, a noticeable layer of oil will float to the top toward the end of cooking.) This will take about 2 to 3 hours—the longer you cook it, the better it will become. While the sauce is cooking, add hot water as necessary to keep the meats and vegetables covered. The oil can be removed with a spoon or reincorporated in the sauce, which is what is done traditionally.

To serve 2: Boil 8 ounces of your choice of fresh or dried pasta until done. While the pasta is cooking, warm the sauce over medium heat. Fish the pasta out of the boiling water with a large wire skimmer and drop it directly into the sauce in the skillet. Bring the sauce and pasta to a boil, stirring to coat the pasta with sauce. Add some of the pasta-cooking water, if necessary, to make enough of sauce to coat the pasta lightly. Remove the pan from the heat and stir in grated Parmigiano-Reggiano cheese to taste. Check the seasoning, adding salt and pepper if necessary.

Pesto is the most popular and celebrated sauce of Liguria, the coastal region of which Genova is the capital. In its simplest and classic form, pesto consists of fresh basil leaves, garlic, olive oil, and salt. Liguria's neighbor in France, Provence, has its pistou, basically the same preparation with the addition of tomato.

The traditional way to make pesto is to work all the ingredients to a paste in a marble or wooden mortar with a pestle; a metal container or steel blade would render the basil black. Today, with stainless steel and the quick action of a food processor or blender, pesto can be made efficiently without a significant change in color.

Classic Pesto

4 cups loosely packed fresh basil leaves (about 60 small or 30 large fresh basil leaves), washed in cool water and dried

Pinch coarse sea salt

2 cloves garlic, peeled

3 tablespoons pine nuts, lightly toasted

2 tablespoons freshly and finely grated Pecorino Romano cheese

2 tablespoons freshly and finely grated Parmigiano-Reggiano cheese

3 to 4 tablespoons extra-virgin olive oil

Makes about ¾ cup, enough to dress 1 pound pasta

Pesto is at its best when used immediately after it is made. However, it can be refrigerated for up to a few weeks if it's spooned into a container, topped with olive oil, and sealed tight. If you find yourself with an abundance of basil in summer, make some pesto and store it in small portions in the freezer, where it will last for up to a few months. Frozen pesto gives great freshness of taste to hearty winter soups and pasta sauces.

Long pasta shapes, like fresh tagliatelle or dried spaghetti or linguine, pair well with pesto. When dressing pasta with pesto, remember these important points: Don't actually cook the pesto—you'll lose its fresh quality—but warm it together with the cooked pasta for a minute over low heat. There should be just enough pesto to coat the pasta lightly. If necessary, spoon in a little of the pasta-cooking water to help the pasta and pesto glide into a bowl.

Toasting Pine Nuts:

To make the pesto in a mortar: Place a few leaves of the basil in the bottom of a mortar and sprinkle the salt over them. Crush the leaves coarsely with the pestle, add a few more leaves, and continue crushing, adding new leaves each time those in the mortar are crushed, until all the leaves are coarsely ground. Toss in the garlic and pound until the mixture forms a smooth paste. Add the pine nuts and grind them to a paste. Stir in the cheese, then enough of the olive oil to give the pesto a creamy consistency.

To make the pesto in a food processor: Combine the basil, salt, and garlic in the work bowl, add 2 tablespoons of the oil, and blend at low speed, stopping frequently to press the basil down around the blades, until the basil forms a coarse paste. Toss in the pine nuts and pour in the remaining 2 tablespoons olive oil. Blend until the pine nuts are ground fine. Stir in the grated cheeses and enough additional olive oil to form a creamy paste.

To toast pine nuts, spread them out on a baking sheet and bake in a 325° F oven, shaking the pan once or twice as they bake, until lightly and evenly browned, about 6 minutes. Or toast the pine nuts in a small skillet over medium heat, shaking the pan continuously, until they turn golden brown, about 6 minutes.

To serve 2: Cook 8 ounces long (spaghetti or linguine, for example) dried pasta in a large pot of boiling salted water until done. Ladle out and reserve about 1 cup of the pasta-cooking liquid. Drain the pasta and return it to the pot off the heat. Add about 6 tablespoons of the pesto and enough pasta-cooking water to make the pesto fluid enough to coat the pasta lightly. Stir in grated Parmigiano-Reggiano to taste, if you like, and check the seasoning, adding salt and pepper if you like.

The difference between marinara sauce and tomato sauce (a recipe follows) is this: Marinara is a quick sauce, seasoned only with garlic, red pepper, and, if you like, basil or oregano. The pieces of tomato are left chunky, and the texture of the finished sauce is fairly loose. Tomato sauce, on the other hand, is a more complex affair, starting with pureed tomatoes and seasoned with onion, carrot, celery, and bay leaf, and left to simmer until thickened and rich in flavor.

Marinara Sauce

Salsa Marinara

¼ cup extra-virgin olive oil

8 cloves garlic, peeled

3 pounds ripe fresh plum tomatoes, peeled and seeded (see page 9), or one 35-ounce can peeled Italian plum tomatoes (preferably San Marzano), seeded and lightly crushed, with their liquid

Salt

Crushed hot red pepper

10 fresh basil leaves, torn into small pieces

Makes about 1 quart, enough to dress 6 servings of pasta

Make this sauce with fresh tomatoes only when the juiciest, most flavorful ripe tomatoes are available. (Increase the amount of olive oil a little if you make the sauce with fresh tomatoes.) Otherwise, canned plum tomatoes make a delicious marinara sauce.

Heat the oil in a 2- to 3-quart nonreactive saucepan over medium heat. Whack the garlic with the flat side of a knife, add it to the oil, and cook until lightly browned, about 2 minutes.

Carefully slide the tomatoes and their liquid into the oil. Bring to a boil and season lightly with salt and crushed red pepper. Lower the heat so the sauce is at a lively simmer and cook, breaking up the tomatoes with a whisk or spoon, until the sauce is chunky and thick, about 20 minutes. Stir in the basil about 5 minutes before the sauce is finished. Taste the sauce and season with salt and red pepper if necessary.

Tomato Sauce

Salsa di Pomodoro

3 pounds ripe fresh plum tomatoes, peeled and seeded (see page 9), or one 35-ounce can peeled Italian tomatoes, seeded and lightly crushed, with their liquid

¼ cup extra-virgin olive oil

1 small onion, chopped (about ½ cup)

¼ cup finely shredded peeled carrots

¼ cup finely chopped celery, including leaves

4 fresh bay leaves, or 2 dried bay leaves

Salt

Crushed hot red pepper

Makes about 3½ cups, enough to dress 6 servings of pasta

Pass the tomatoes through a food mill fitted with the fine disc. Heat the oil in a 2- to 3-quart nonreactive saucepan over medium heat. Stir in the onion and cook, stirring occasionally, until wilted, about 3 minutes. Add the carrots and celery and cook, stirring occasionally, until golden, about 10 minutes.

Add the food-milled tomatoes and the bay leaves and bring to a boil. Season lightly with salt and crushed red pepper. Bring to a boil, lower the heat so the sauce is at a lively simmer, and cook, stirring occasionally, until thickened, about 45 minutes. Remove the bay leaves. Taste and season with salt and red pepper if necessary.

In front of Buonavia, c. 1974

Baked Pasta

"Alla Norma" is the name for this Sicilian pasta dish, which always contains eggplant in one form or another. You can enjoy this pasta either right out of the pan—as we serve it at our restaurants, Becco in New York, and Lidia's in Kansas City and Pittsburgh—or topped with Fontina and baked as described below.

Ziti with Roasted Eggplant and Ricotta Cheese

Ziti alla Norma

2 large firm eggplants (each about 3 inches in diameter and 1¼ pounds)

2 tablespoons coarse salt, plus more for cooking the pasta and seasoning the sauce

6 tablespoons extra-virgin olive oil

2 cloves garlic, peeled and sliced

One 35-ounce can peeled Italian plum tomatoes (preferably San Marzano) with their liquid

1 teaspoon crushed hot red pepper

Salt

1 pound ziti

1 cup freshly grated Parmigiano-Reggiano cheese

To keep them both intact, add the little "pockets" of ricotta and the eggplant pieces just before serving the pasta or turning it into the baking dish. It is one of the nuances in cooking that make a difference. When you take a bite of the finished pasta, you'll get little bursts of different tastes, which you wouldn't enjoy if the eggplant pieces were broken apart and the ricotta was mixed in with the pasta.

If you choose to bake the pasta, make sure the pasta is well moistened when it goes into the baking dish—the heat of the oven will dry it out a little. You can toss little pieces of mozzarella or Fontina cheese in with the pasta before adding the ricotta and eggplant if you like. Just make sure the consistency of the pasta stays fluid and creamy.

Trim the stems from the eggplants. Remove strips of peel about 1 inch wide from the eggplants, leaving about half the peel intact. Cut the eggplant into 1-inch cubes. Toss in a large bowl with 2 tablespoons coarse salt. Dump into a colander and let drain for 1 hour.

1 cup fresh basil leaves, washed, dried, and shredded

½ pound (1 cup) fresh ricotta cheese or packaged whole-milk ricotta cheese

8 ounces imported Fontina cheese, sliced thin (if baking the pasta)

Makes 6 servings

Rinse the eggplant under cool running water, drain thoroughly, and pat dry.

Preheat the oven to 400° F. Brush a baking sheet with 3 tablespoons of the olive oil. Turn the eggplant cubes onto the baking sheet, toss to coat with oil, and spread them out in an even layer. Bake until the eggplant is very tender and browned, about 25 minutes. Turn and stir the eggplant cubes gently once or twice during baking so they cook evenly.

Bring 6 quarts of salted water to a boil in an 8-quart pot over high heat.

Heat the remaining 3 tablespoons olive oil in a large skillet over medium heat. Scatter the garlic over the oil and cook, shaking the pan, until golden, about 3 minutes. Pour in the crushed tomatoes, add the pepper flakes, and season lightly with salt. Bring to a boil, adjust the heat to simmering, and simmer for 10 minutes.

Stir the ziti into the boiling water. Return to a boil, stirring frequently. Cook the pasta, semi-covered, stirring occasionally, until done, about 10 minutes.

Drain the pasta and return it to the pot over low heat. Pour in all but about ¼ cup of the sauce, and toss lightly to coat the pasta with sauce. Remove the pot from the heat, and stir in ¾ cup of the Parmigiano-Reggiano and the basil. Gently stir in the eggplant. Add the ricotta by heaping teaspoonfuls, stirring it gently into the pasta; you want the ricotta to heat, but you do not want it to blend with the sauce completely. Either serve the pasta as is—right from the pot—sprinkled with the remaining ¼ cup grated cheese, or gently slide it into a 13 × 11–inch baking dish. Arrange the Fontina slices overlapping to cover the top of the pasta. Spoon the reserved sauce over the Fontina and sprinkle the top of the baking dish with the remaining ¼ cup grated cheese. Bake until the edges of the baking dish are bubbling and the cheese is lightly browned, about 20 to 30 minutes. Serve immediately.

Baked Stuffed Shells

Conchiglie Ripiene al Forno

1 ½ pounds fresh ricotta or packaged whole-milk ricotta

One 35-ounce can peeled Italian plum tomatoes (preferably San Marzano)

Salt

1 pound fresh mozzarella cheese

1 cup freshly grated Parmigiano-Reggiano cheese

⅓ cup chopped fresh Italian parsley

Freshly ground white pepper

1 large egg

¼ cup extra-virgin olive oil

6 cloves garlic, crushed

½ teaspoon crushed hot red pepper

10 fresh basil leaves

1 pound jumbo pasta shells

Makes 6 servings (about 5 stuffed shells for each serving)

A pound of "jumbo" pasta shells contains about thirty-six. This recipe makes enough filling for about thirty shells, so it's likely you'll have a few extra shells, which may come in handy, as some shells break in the box or during cooking. Be sure to cook the shells very al dente before filling them, or they will tear when you try to stuff them.

Individual servings of stuffed shells make an impressive presentation. If you have enough individual baking dishes, divide the shells and sauce among them, then top with cheese, keeping in mind that you might need a little more cheese to top individual servings than is called for in the recipe.

Place the ricotta in a cheesecloth-lined sieve and set the sieve over a bowl. Cover the ricotta with plastic wrap and place in the refrigerator for at least 8 hours or up to one day. Discard the liquid in the bowl.

Pass the tomatoes through a food mill fitted with the fine disc. (If you don't have a food mill, seed the tomatoes and place them in a food processor. Process the tomatoes, using quick on/off pulses, until they are finely ground. Don't overprocess, or you'll incorporate air into the tomatoes and change their texture and color.) Meanwhile, bring 6 quarts of salted water to a boil in an 8-quart pot over high heat.

Slice half the mozzarella thin and cut the remaining half into ¼-inch cubes. Turn the drained ricotta into a mixing bowl. Mix in the mozzarella cubes, grated cheese, and parsley. Season to taste with salt and white pepper. Beat the egg well and stir it into the ricotta mixture.

Heat the olive oil in a large skillet over medium heat. Scatter the garlic over the oil and cook, shaking the pan, until golden brown, about 2 minutes. Lower the tomatoes close to the skillet and carefully pour them into the skillet. Add the crushed red pepper and season lightly with salt. Bring the sauce to a quick boil, then adjust the heat to simmering. Cook until the sauce is lightly thickened, about 30 minutes. Stir the basil into the sauce a few minutes before it is done.

Meanwhile, stir the shells into the boiling water. Return to a boil, stirring frequently. Cook the pasta, semi-covered, stirring occasionally, until softened but still quite firm, about 7 minutes. Fish the shells out of the water with a large skimmer and carefully lower them into a bowl of cold water. Drain them carefully.

Preheat the oven to 425° F. Line the bottom of a 15 × 10–inch baking dish with about ¾ cup of the tomato sauce. Spoon about 2 tablespoons of the ricotta mixture into each shell. The shell should be filled to capacity but not overstuffed. Nestle the shells next to each other in the baking dish as you fill them. Spoon the remaining sauce over the shells, coating each one. Arrange the slices of mozzarella in an even layer over the shells. Bake until the mozzarella is browned and bubbling, about 25 minutes. Remove, and let stand 5 minutes before serving.

Italian-American Lasagna

2 pounds fresh or packaged whole-milk ricotta cheese

Italian-American Meat Sauce (page 144)

Salt

2 tablespoons olive oil

2 pounds lasagna noodles

2 large eggs

2½ cups freshly grated Parmigiano-Reggiano cheese

1 pound mozzarella cheese, preferably fresh, sliced thin

Makes 12 servings, plus leftovers

I am always telling you not to add oil to the water when you cook pasta, because it will reduce the adherence of sauce to the pasta. Cooking long, flat pasta — like these lasagna noodles — is the exception. They have a tendency to stick together when they cook; the oil will help prevent that. Inevitably, some noodles will break. Save the pieces; they will come in handy to patch the layers of lasagna.

You'll notice in the meat-sauce recipe that the final consistency of the sauce should be fairly dense. Following that pattern, I suggest you drain the ricotta first, to remove a lot of the moisture. Removing excess moisture from the ingredients will result in a finished lasagna that is more compact and intense in flavor.

You may assemble the lasagna completely up to a day before you serve it, but don't cook it until the day you plan to serve it. Lasagna tastes better and is easier to cut if it is allowed to stand about an hour after it is removed from the oven. It will retain enough heat to serve as is, or, if you prefer, pop it back in the oven for 10 to 15 minutes. My favorite way to serve lasagna is to bake it and let it stand 3 to 4 hours. Cut the lasagna into portions, then rewarm it in the oven.

Line a sieve with a double thickness of cheesecloth or a basket-type coffee filter. Place the ricotta over the cheesecloth and set the sieve over a bowl. Cover with plastic wrap and refrigerate overnight or up to 1 day. Discard the liquid that drains into the bowl. Make the meat sauce.

Bring 6 quarts of salted water and the olive oil to a boil in an 8-quart pot over high heat. Stir about one-third of the lasagna noodles into the boiling water. Return to a boil, stirring frequently. Cook the pasta, semi-covered, stirring occasionally, until *al dente,* 8 to 10 minutes.

While the pasta is cooking, set a large bowl of ice water next to the stove. When the lasagna noodles are *al dente,* remove them with a wire skimmer and transfer to the ice water. Let them stand until completely chilled. Repeat the cooking and cooling with the remaining two batches of lasagna noodles. When the cooked noodles are chilled, remove them from the ice bath and stack them on a baking sheet, separating each layer with a clean, damp kitchen towel.

While the noodles are cooking, beat the eggs with a pinch of salt in a mixing bowl until foamy. Add the ricotta and stir until thoroughly blended. Preheat oven to 375° F.

To assemble the lasagne, ladle about ¾ cup of the meat sauce over the bottom of a 15 × 10–inch baking dish. Arrange noodles lengthwise and side by side so as to cover the bottom of the baking dish and overhang the short ends of the dish by about 2 inches. (A little "cut and paste" might be necessary. Also, the noodles will most likely overlap in the center of the dish. That is fine.) Spoon enough meat sauce, about 2 cups, to cover the noodles in an even layer. Sprinkle the sauce with ½ cup of the grated cheese. Arrange a single layer of noodles crosswise over the cheese so they overhang the long sides of the baking dish by about 2 inches, trimming the noodles and overlapping them as necessary. Spread the ricotta mixture evenly over the noodles. Arrange a single layer of noodles lengthwise over the ricotta, trimming the noodles as necessary. Arrange the sliced mozzarella in an even layer over the noodles. Spread 1 cup of the meat sauce over the cheese and sprinkle 1 cup of grated cheese over the sauce. Cover with a layer of noodles, arranged lengthwise. Spoon enough meat sauce, about 2 cups, to cover the noodles in an even layer, and sprinkle the sauce with ½ cup grated cheese. Turn the noodles overhanging the sides and ends of the dish over the lasagna, leaving a rectangular uncovered space in the middle. Spread a thin layer of meat sauce over the top layer of noodles. Sprinkle with the remaining grated cheese. Cover loosely with aluminum foil and bake 45 minutes.

Uncover the lasagna and continue baking until the top is crusty around the edges, about 20 minutes. Let rest at least 30 minutes or up to 3 hours before cutting and serving. To rewarm a lasagna that has been standing, cover it loosely with foil and place in a 325° F oven until heated through, 15 to 45 minutes, depending on how long it has been standing.

Pasticcio is the Italian word for things that are put together in a messy fashion and in no particular order. In Italian cuisine, the same word is used to describe baked pasta dishes layered with different kinds of sauces and fillings. This *pasticciata* is made with layers of crepes and spinach-ricotta filling.

Crepe "Lasagna" Filled with Spinach and Herbs

Pasticciata alle Erbe con Spinaci

1 ½ pounds fresh ricotta cheese or packaged whole-milk ricotta cheese

Crepes (page 162)

2 pounds spinach or Swiss chard

Salt

3 tablespoons extra-virgin olive oil

3 leeks, white parts only, trimmed, cleaned, and chopped (about 3 cups) (see page 80)

1 bunch scallions, trimmed and chopped (about ½ cup)

2 large eggs

½ teaspoon freshly ground black pepper

½ pound mascarpone cheese

8 fresh sage leaves, chopped

20 fresh basil leaves, chopped

This pasticciata can be prepared entirely in advance and refrigerated for up to 1 day. Let the refrigerated pasticciata stand at room temperature for about an hour before baking.

Spoon the ricotta into a large, fine-mesh sieve or a colander lined with a double thickness of cheesecloth or a basket-type coffee filter. Place the sieve over a bowl and cover the ricotta well with plastic wrap. Let the ricotta drain in the refrigerator at least overnight, or up to 24 hours. Discard the liquid in the bottom of the bowl.

Make the crepes. (This can be done up to 24 hours in advance.)

Remove the stems from the spinach or chard. (Reserve chard stems for another use, if you like.) Wash and dry the leaves according to directions on page 67. Stir the greens into a large pot of boiling salted water and cook, stirring once or twice, until tender, about 2 minutes for the spinach or 5 to 6 minutes for the chard. Drain the greens in a colander and rinse them under cold water until cool enough to handle. With your hands, squeeze out as much water as you can from the greens. Chop coarsely.

Heat the olive oil in a large skillet over medium heat. Stir in the leeks and scallions and cook until wilted, about 4 minutes. Stir in the greens and cook, stirring, 2 minutes. Remove and cool.

Turn the drained ricotta into a clean bowl. Whisk the eggs together with 1 teaspoon salt and the pepper, then beat them into the ricotta. Stir in the mascarpone, herbs, and greens mixture until blended.

1 tablespoon chopped
fresh thyme

Béchamel Sauce (page 161)

2 tablespoons butter,
softened

3 cups freshly grated
Parmigiano-Reggiano
cheese

Makes 6 servings

Make the béchamel sauce, strain it, and keep it at room temperature with a piece of plastic wrap applied directly to the surface.

Using the softened butter, grease the bottom and sides of a 13 × 9–inch ceramic or glass baking dish. Arrange as many crepes as necessary, side by side and barely overlapping, so they cover the sides of the dish completely and overhang the sides of the dish by about 2 inches. Part of the bottom of the baking dish will be covered by the crepes; cover the exposed part with some of the remaining crepes. (You will need about ten crepes to cover and overhang the dish as described above.)

Preheat oven to 425° F. Reserve 1 cup of the béchamel sauce and 2 cups of the grated Parmigiano-Reggiano to dress the top of the pasticciata. Spread ⅓ cup of the béchamel in an even layer over the crepes lining the bottom of the dish. Spread 1½ cups of the ricotta filling over the béchamel and top that with another layer of ⅓ cup of the béchamel. Sprinkle about ⅓ cup of the Parmigiano-Reggiano over the béchamel. Cover this first layer of filling with a layer of crepes, folding the crepes as necessary to make a nice even layer. Make another filling layer using half the remaining ricotta mixture, béchamel, and grated cheese. Top with a layer of crepes. Make the last filling layer using the remaining ricotta mixture, béchamel, and grated cheese. Fold the overhanging edges of the crepes over the top layer of filling. Top any uncovered filling with additional crepes. Spread the reserved 1 cup of béchamel in an even layer over the pasticciata, then sprinkle the reserved 2 cups of Parmigiano-Reggiano over the béchamel.

Bake until the top of the pasticciata is well browned and the edges are crispy, about 30 minutes. Remove and let cool for 15 to 30 minutes. Cut the pasticciata into squares and serve.

Ricotta Cheeses

*R*ICOTTA, LITERALLY "RECOOKED," is a soft-curd fresh cheese made from the whey that is left over after hard cheeses are made. To make hard and semi-hard cheeses, rennet is added to warm milk, causing it to separate into curds (solids) and whey (the remaining liquid.) The curds are then drained and aged, resulting in all sorts of cheeses, depending on how they are handled. But there is another use for the whey, which still contains some milk proteins, called caseins. When some whole milk is added to the whey and the mixture brought to a boil or *ricotta*, a second round of curds forms. These ricotta curds, which contain less fat and are softer and wetter than the first round, are lifted from the whey and set in a basket to drain. Large curds, similar to the ones found in cottage cheese, are favored when it comes to ricotta cheese.

In Italy, ricotta is eaten "as is" on the same day it is made, without ever seeing the inside of the refrigerator. My grandmother made ricotta from goat's and sheep's milk—we ate it still warm, spread on a slice of country bread drizzled with honey as a morning or afternoon *merenda* (snack). Grandma fed the remaining whey to the hogs, completing the cycle of food in which nothing was wasted.

Most of the ricotta you buy today is made from cow's milk, but sheep's-milk, goat's-milk, and water-buffalo's-milk ricotta are slowly becoming more available. Each of these different sources yields a ricotta with a definitive flavor that is more intense than cow's-milk ricotta. Ricotta made from sheep's milk is quite intense, and, as in Pecorino, another sheep's-milk cheese, the sheep flavor is quite evident. Goat's-milk ricotta is less fatty but also very flavorful. Water-buffalo's-milk ricotta is richer than the cow's-milk variety, with a buttery and sweet flavor.

Think of this simple yet wonderful dessert the next time you find fresh, large-curd ricotta cheese: Spoon the cheese into a fine sieve or a colander lined with a basket-type coffee filter. Set the sieve over a bowl and let the ricotta drain in the refrigerator overnight. Spoon the drained cheese into a loaf pan lined with plastic wrap. Chill it until firm, then invert it onto a serving platter. Cut the loaf into $\frac{3}{4}$-inch slices, and drizzle them with honey.

Béchamel isn't the kind of sauce that you would make to serve with something. It is more a way to keep things — like the preceding pasticciata, or the cannelloni on page 166 — moist while baking. You should make *besciamella* just before you need it and keep it at room temperature, with a piece of plastic wrap pressed to the surface of the sauce, until you're ready to use it.

Béchamel Sauce

Salsa Besciamella

1 quart milk

Salt

Freshly ground pepper (preferably white)

Two large pinches nutmeg, preferably freshly grated

1 bay leaf

3 tablespoons unsalted butter

¼ cup all-purpose flour

⅓ cup freshly grated Parmigiano-Reggiano cheese

Makes about 1 quart

Stand by the pot as the sauce cooks — once it starts to thicken, it will stick to the bottom of the pan if you don't stir it constantly. And once the bottom scorches, the flavor will permeate the sauce. If the sauce does stick and burn, immediately transfer it to a clean pot without scraping the bottom. Check the sauce, make sure it doesn't taste scorched, then continue. Don't let these warnings scare you away from cooking the sauce enough, though; there is nothing worse than the taste of raw flour on your tongue.

Pour the milk into a medium saucepan, season lightly with salt and pepper, add the nutmeg, and toss in the bay leaf. Heat over medium-low heat until bubbles form around the edge. Remove and keep hot.

Melt the butter in a separate medium saucepan over medium heat. When it starts to foam, dump in the flour and whisk until smooth. Continue cooking, whisking constantly, until the flour mixture changes color, 3 to 4 minutes. Pour the seasoned hot milk into the flour mixture in a steady stream, whisking constantly. Cook the sauce, whisking constantly and paying special attention to the bottom and corners of the pan, until the sauce comes to the simmer. Adjust the heat to a slow boil and cook, whisking constantly, until the sauce is thickened, about 3 minutes. Remove from the heat and whisk in the grated cheese.

Strain the sauce through a fine sieve and into a clean bowl. The sauce will keep at room temperature for up to a few hours.

Crepes

Crespelle

2 large eggs

1 cup milk

1 cup water

½ cup club soda

1 tablespoon sugar

Grated zest of 1 lemon

¼ teaspoon salt

2½ cups all-purpose flour

6 tablespoons butter, melted

Vegetable oil, for frying

Makes about 32 crepes

The traditional crepe pan is made of steel and has short, sloping sides and a long handle. With use, the steel becomes seasoned—like cast iron—and needs only the lightest oiling. There are several other types of pans that work well for making crepes: pans with a nonstick surface are probably the easiest to work with, but any pan of the right size with a well-seasoned surface, including aluminum omelet pans, will do the job.

It is normal for the first few crepes of the batch to come out less than perfect. Once you find the right temperature for the pan and get the wrist action down, you'll see a noticeable improvement in the results. As you get the knack of making crepes, you'll be able to keep two pans going at once, cutting the time in half.

Whisk the eggs in a medium mixing bowl until blended. Pour in the milk, water, and club soda and stir together until blended. Add the sugar, lemon zest, and salt and blend well. Gradually sift the flour into the liquids, stirring constantly until the mixture is smooth. Stir in the melted butter. The batter will have the consistency of melted ice cream.

Heat about 1 tablespoon of vegetable oil in an 8-inch crepe pan over medium-high heat, swirl the pan to coat it evenly with the oil, then pour off the excess. Holding the pan at a 45-degree angle, pour 3 tablespoons of the batter into the pan, allowing it to run down from the highest point. The secret to making thin, even crepes is to flex your wrist, distributing the batter over the entire bottom of the pan as quickly as possible before the batter has a chance to set.

Return the pan to the heat, reduce the heat to moderate, and cook until the underside of the crepe is lacy and lightly browned, 30 to 40 seconds. Flip it over carefully with a spatula and cook the second side until it is lightly browned in spots, about 1 minute. Slide the crepe from the pan onto a large plate and repeat the process with the remaining batter, re-oiling the pan only as necessary and stacking the finished crepes one atop another. Crepes can be prepared up to a day in advance, covered tightly with plastic wrap, and stored in the refrigerator until needed.

My first encounter with "manicotti" was at the convent of the Canossiane nuns in Trieste, where, at the age of twelve, I helped in the kitchen to supplement my school tuition. Manicotti were white cloth "sleeves" about 1 foot long that looked like muffs with elastic on the top and at the wrist. The nuns slipped them onto each arm to cover the sleeves of their habits while they cooked in the kitchen. The similarity between the shape of the nuns' sleeve protectors and the pasta of the same name became clear to me when I first started cooking the Italian-American cuisine. Italian-American manicotti were made with fresh pasta cut into rectangles, filled, then rolled into tubes; I like a version made with *crespelle* (crepes), which yield very light manicotti. You can decide which you prefer.

Manicotti

1 pound fresh ricotta
   cheese or one
   15-ounce container
   whole-milk ricotta
   cheese

Tomato Sauce (page 151)

Crepes (page 162) or
   Cooked Pasta Squares
   (page 182)

2 large eggs

1 teaspoon salt

1½ cups cubed (¼-inch)
   fresh mozzarella
   (about 6 ounces)

1 cup freshly grated
   Parmigiano-Reggiano
   cheese

½ cup chopped fresh
   Italian parsley

¼ teaspoon freshly ground
   white pepper

ingredients continued
on next page

If you choose to make the manicotti with pasta squares, fill and roll them on a damp towel—it will make them easier to handle. For a lighter, thinner sauce, add a little stock to the tomato sauce or to the baking dish after you add the sauce, or don't cook the sauce quite so much when you make it. If you have some fresh basil in the kitchen, tear some leaves and scatter them over the manicotti in the dish right before you bake them.

Spoon the ricotta into a large, fine-mesh sieve or a colander lined with a double thickness of cheesecloth or a basket-type coffee filter. Set the sieve over a bowl and cover the ricotta well with plastic wrap. Let the ricotta drain in the refrigerator at least overnight, or up to 24 hours. Discard the liquid in the bottom of the bowl.

Make the tomato sauce and the crepes or pasta squares. (The crepes may be made up to one day in advance; the pasta squares up to several hours in advance.)

Whisk the eggs and salt together in a large bowl until foamy. Add the drained

continued on next page

Pinch ground nutmeg,
  preferably freshly
  grated

4 ounces fresh
  mozzarella cheese,
  grated (about 1 ¼
  cups), optional

**Makes 6 servings
(about 18 manicotti)**

ricotta, the mozzarella cubes, ½ cup of the Parmigiano-Reggiano, the parsley, pepper, and nutmeg. Stir well until blended.

Preheat the oven to 425° F. Coat the bottom of each of two 13 × 9–inch baking pans (or any two pans into which the manicotti will fit comfortably) with ½ cup of the sauce. Working with one crepe or pasta square at a time, spoon 3 full tablespoons of the ricotta filling about 1 inch from the edge closest to you. Roll loosely into a cylinder, smoothing out the filling along the length of the tube as you roll.

Arrange the manicotti, seam side down and side by side, over the sauce in the baking pans. Spoon the remaining sauce over the manicotti and sprinkle them with the remaining ½ cup of the Parmigiano-Reggiano. Cover the baking dishes loosely with aluminum foil and poke the foil several times with a fork.

Bake 20 minutes. Uncover the dishes, scatter the grated mozzarella, if using, over the top of the manicotti, and bake until the edges are bubbling and the cheese topping is golden brown, about 20 minutes.

To: Lidia Bastianich

From: Tom Colombo

Subject:

> > > Mom is always comparing your preparation to the cooking of her mother (my grandmother), who immigrated here from Italy in 1914.< < <

There are different strategies for preparing this dish ahead of time. You can make the filling up to 2 days in advance and prepare the pasta squares on the day you plan to serve the cannelloni. Or you can make the pasta dough, roll it, and cook the squares while the meat filling is cooking and cooling. Either way it can be completely assembled hours before you put it in the oven.

Meat and Spinach Cannelloni

Cannelloni Ripieni di Carne e Spinaci

I always roast meats by adding some liquid to the roasting pan first, then allowing it to cook away and the meat to brown. The aromatic steam penetrates the meat before the surface of the meat is seared by the heat. Then I add more liquid as the meat cooks, to make a delicious pan sauce.

Mortadella is one of those ingredients that give a tremendous amount of flavor to meat-based ravioli or cannelloni fillings. Think of mortadella as the Italian version of bologna, seasoned with Italian spices and studded, mosaiclike, with pistachios and cubes of seasoned pork fat. Thinly sliced mortadella is delicious as part of an antipasto assortment or in a sandwich. Add the mortadella to the meat and vegetables when they're fresh out of the oven: the steam coaxes the flavor out of the mortadella. To grind the meat-and-vegetable mixture, you can use a hand-cranked meat grinder or a grinder attachment for an electric mixer. In either case, choose a disc that is fine but not too fine. Although it isn't absolutely necessary, when I have besciamella handy, I like to stir a little into the meat filling. It helps to bind it and adds a smooth texture.

continued on next page

3 cups hot Chicken Stock or Mixed Meat Stock (pages 74, 75), or as needed

1 ounce (about 1 cup) dried porcini mushrooms

2 pounds fresh (not smoked) boneless pork butt or shoulder

2 large carrots, peeled and cut into thick slices (about 3 cups)

2 celery stalks, trimmed and cut into thick slices (about 2¼ cups)

1 onion, peeled and quartered

3 sprigs fresh rosemary, leaves removed from the branches

Salt

5 tablespoons extra-virgin olive oil

1 cup dry white wine

4 ounces mortadella, in 1 piece

4 cloves garlic, peeled

2 pounds spinach, stems removed, leaves washed and spun dry in a salad spinner, or two 10-ounce packages spinach

Freshly ground black pepper

Béchamel Sauce (page 161)

You can prepare this filling with a combination of beef, veal, and pork, or with leftover roasts, like turkey, pork, or beef. If you're making this filling with leftover meat, reheat it by simmering it with its own gravy and the porcini-soaking liquid, the soaked porcini, and some vegetables, like diced onions and celery and shredded carrots. When the meat is warmed through and moist and the vegetables are tender, season them, add the remaining ingredients, and grind as above.

Pour the hot stock over the porcini in a small heatproof bowl. Let stand until softened, about 20 minutes. Drain the porcini, reserving the liquid. Rinse the porcini to remove sand and grit, and strain the soaking liquid through a coffee filter or a double thickness of cheesecloth. Reserve the mushrooms and liquid separately.

Preheat the oven to 400° F. Cut the pork into 2-inch pieces and place them in a roasting pan large enough to hold them comfortably. Add the carrots, celery, onion, rosemary leaves, and the reserved porcini. Season lightly with salt, drizzle 3 tablespoons of the olive oil over all, and toss well. Pour in the wine. Roast until the wine has evaporated and the meat begins to brown, about 25 minutes. Continue roasting, adding ½ cup of the reserved mushroom-soaking liquid every 15 minutes or so, until the meat and vegetables are well browned and the meat is tender, about 2 hours. At the end of the roasting, there should be about 1½ cups of liquid in the roasting pan. Drain the meat and vegetables, reserving the liquid. Toss the mortadella in with the meats and vegetables and cool to room temperature.

Meanwhile, in a wide skillet, heat the remaining 2 tablespoons oil over medium heat. Whack the garlic with the flat side of a knife, add it to the oil, and cook until lightly browned, about 2 minutes. Add as much spinach as will fit comfortably into the pan. Continue cooking, stirring and adding the remaining spinach a large handful at a time when the spinach in the pan wilts enough to make room, until all the spinach is added. Season lightly with salt and pepper and cook until all the spinach is wilted and tender. Remove from the heat.

Make the béchamel sauce.

1 ¼ cups grated Parmigiano-
Reggiano, plus more
for serving if you like

Ground nutmeg, preferably
freshly grated

2 large eggs, beaten

Cooked Pasta Squares
(page 182)

**Makes 18 cannelloni
(6 generous servings)**

Pass the meat-and-vegetable mixture through a meat grinder fitted with a disc with holes about ¼ inch in diameter. Stir in ¼ cup of the grated cheese and ½ cup of the béchamel sauce, blending the filling well as you do. Season to taste with salt, pepper, and nutmeg. Beat the eggs until foamy, then stir them into the ground-meat mixture.

Preheat the oven to 375° F. Ladle about ¾ cup of the béchamel sauce in an even layer over the bottom of each of two 13 × 9–inch baking dishes. Spoon ⅓ cup of the filling in a more or less even mound along one edge of one of the pasta squares. Roll up into a tube, pressing and evening out the tube as you roll. Arrange the cannelloni into the prepared baking dish, side by side and seam side down. Divide the remaining béchamel evenly between the two baking dishes, smoothing it into an even layer over the cannelloni. Drizzle about three-quarters of the reserved meat-cooking liquid over the cannelloni, dividing it evenly. Sprinkle the tops with 1 cup of the grated cheese. Cover the dishes with aluminum foil and bake 20 minutes. Uncover the baking dishes and bake until the tops are golden brown and bubbling, about 20 minutes. If the tops are browning unevenly, rotate the baking dishes from side to side and shelf to shelf, then continue baking. Let stand 5 minutes before serving. Lift the cannelloni to warm plates with a spatula and spoon some of the sauce over each serving. Pass additional grated cheese if you like.

☞ Preparing Fresh Herbs: Remove rosemary (or other herb) leaves from the stem if the branches are tough and woody before adding them to a dish. The tannins in the tough stems can add bitterness to the finished dish.

Think of this dish as a quickly assembled individual lasagna. It takes its name from the little pasta squares, which resemble handkerchiefs.

"Little Handkerchiefs"

Fazzoletti

Cooked Pasta Squares
(page 182)

2 cups Meat Sauce
Bolognese (page 146)

1½ cups Béchamel Sauce
(page 161)

½ cup freshly grated
Parmigiano-Reggiano

Makes 4 servings

Prepare the pasta squares, but cut them into 4-inch squares instead of the 6-inch squares described in the recipe. Make the Bolognese and béchamel sauces.

Preheat the oven to 375° F. Choose a baking dish large enough to hold four pasta squares comfortably. Spread about 1 tablespoon of the Bolognese and 1 tablespoon of the béchamel sauce into a puddle roughly the size of a pasta square over one-fourth of the pan. Repeat in the other three-fourths of the pan. (The sauce helps prevent the *fazzoletti* from sticking to the pan as you build up the *fazzoletti*.) Center a pasta square over one of the puddles and spread an even layer of 2 tablespoons of the Bolognese and 1 tablespoon of the béchamel over it. Sprinkle 2 teaspoons of the grated cheese over the sauce, and top with another pasta square. Build three more layers like the first and top with a pasta square. Build three more stacks like the first, centering each over a puddle of sauce.

With the back of a spoon, make a shallow indentation in the center of each stack. Spread 1 tablespoon of the Bolognese and 1 tablespoon of the béchamel over the indentation. Sprinkle the remaining grated cheese over the tops of the stacks, and bake until the edges are crispy and the tops are lightly browned, about 20 minutes.

Gnocchi

Saucing Gnocchi

COOK FRESHLY MADE OR FROZEN GNOCCHI as described in the "Drooling" Gnocchi recipe (page 174). Reserve about a cup of the cooking liquid, drain the gnocchi gently, and return them to the pot over low heat. Dress with any of the following:

Add 3 to 4 cups Tomato Sauce (page 151) or Meat Sauce Bolognese (page 146) to the drained gnocchi in the pot. Bring to a simmer, adding as much of the cooking liquid as necessary to make a creamy sauce that evenly coats the gnocchi. Remove from the heat and stir in grated Parmigiano-Reggiano cheese to taste.

Add 3 or 4 new potatoes, boiled till tender and sliced thin, and $1^{1}/_{2}$ cups green beans, cut into 1-inch lengths and boiled till tender, to the drained gnocchi in the pot. Warm over low heat, adding cooking liquid as necessary to keep the gnocchi moist. Remove from the heat and stir in 1 recipe Classic Pesto (page 148). Taste and season with salt if necessary and grated Parmigiano-Reggiano if you like.

In Pula, posing in my sailor outfit a year before we left for Trieste

Potato Gnocchi

Gnocchi di Patate

4 large Idaho (russet) potatoes (about 2¼ pounds), unpeeled, washed

Salt

2 large eggs

Dash of freshly ground white pepper

3 cups unbleached all-purpose flour, or as needed

Makes 4 main-course or 8 appetizer servings

It isn't hard to make featherlight gnocchi. The main thing to keep in mind is this: the less flour you add and the less you handle the dough, the lighter the gnocchi will be. The less moisture there is in the potatoes before you start adding flour, the less flour you will need, so the following tips for making light gnocchi all have to do with removing as much moisture from the potatoes as possible:

Don't overcook the potatoes—their skins will pop open and the flesh will soak up water.

Rice the potatoes while they are still quite warm and steaming—rubber gloves help.

Spread the riced potatoes out in a thin layer so the steam rising from them has a chance to escape.

Once you form gnocchi, they must be cooked or frozen immediately or they turn to mush. To freeze them, pop the tray with the gnocchi on them right into the freezer. When they are solid, scrape them into a resealable plastic bag.

Put the potatoes in a large pot and pour in enough cold water to cover them by at least three fingers. Bring to a boil and cook until they are tender when pierced with a skewer, about 40 minutes. Lift them out of the water and let stand just until cool enough to handle. The hotter the potatoes are when you peel and rice them, the fluffier the riced potatoes will be. Scrape the peels off the potatoes and rice the potatoes. Spread the riced potatoes out in a thin layer to expose as much of their surface as possible to the air.

While the potatoes are cooling, bring 6 quarts of salted water to a boil in an 8-quart pot over high heat.

On a cool, preferably marble, work surface, gather the cold riced potatoes into a loose mound with a well in the center. Beat the eggs, 1 teaspoon salt, and the white pepper together in a small bowl until blended and pour into the well. Work the potatoes and egg together with both hands, gradually adding as much flour as necessary to form a firm but moist dough. Stop frequently as you mix to scrape up the dough that sticks to the work surface and reincorporate it into the dough. Forming the dough should take no longer than 10 minutes from start to end. The longer the dough is worked, the more flour it will require and the heavier the dough—and the finished gnocchi—will be. As you work, dust the dough, your hands, and the work surface lightly with flour as soon as the dough begins to feel sticky.

Cut the dough into six equal portions. Using the outstretched fingers and palms of both hands, roll each piece of dough into a rope about $^1\!/_2$ inch thick. Cut the rope crosswise into $^1\!/_2$-inch pieces. Sprinkle the pieces with flour, then roll each piece between your palms into a rough ball. Reflour your hands as necessary to prevent sticking. Hold a fork at an angle to your work surface. Dip the tip of your thumb in flour. Take a dough ball and, with the tip of your floured thumb, press it lightly but firmly against the tines of the fork while, at the same time, rolling it downward along the tines. The dough will wrap around the tip of your thumb, forming a dumpling with a deep indentation on one side and a ridged surface on the other. (You can use the nongrating side of a flat or curved cheese grater for a different effect.) Set the gnocchi on a baking sheet lined with a lightly floured kitchen towel as you form them. Repeat with the remaining five pieces of dough. At this point the gnocchi must be cooked or frozen immediately.

Forming Gnocchi

1. Work the dough with both hands.

2. Cut the dough in half (note the texture of the dough), and then cut each half into thirds.

3. Clean excess dough from your hands by rubbing them with some fresh flour.

4. After rolling each piece of dough into a rope, cut crosswise into ½-inch pieces.

5. Roll each piece into a rough ball with your floured hands.

6. Press a dough ball against the tines with your floured thumb, while rolling downward against the tines.

7. Or press the dough ball against the nongrating side of a cheese grater.

4

5

6

7

This rich and cheesy dish gets its name from the strands of cheese that "drool" back onto the plate when you lift the gnocchi with a fork.

"Drooling" Gnocchi

Gnocchi alla Bava

Potato Gnocchi (page 170)

Salt

½ cup Chicken Stock (page 74) or canned reduced-sodium chicken broth

6 tablespoons unsalted butter

¼ cup heavy cream

Freshly ground white pepper

1 cup freshly grated Parmigiano-Reggiano cheese

5 ounces Fontina Valdostana cheese, rind removed, shredded (about 1½ cups)

Makes 6 servings

Make the gnocchi.

Bring 6 quarts of salted water to a boil in an 8-quart pot over high heat. (If you plan to cook the gnocchi as soon as they are formed, put the water on to boil while the riced potatoes are cooling. If you are cooking previously frozen gnocchi, make sure the water is boiling before you remove the gnocchi from the freezer.)

Preheat the oven to 450° F. Bring the stock, butter, and cream to a boil in a large skillet over medium heat. Adjust the heat to simmering, season lightly with white pepper, and simmer until lightly thickened, 3 minutes. Remove from the heat.

Drop the gnocchi into the boiling water a few at a time, stirring gently and continuously with a wooden spoon. Cook just until they rise to the surface and roll over, 2 to 3 minutes. If the skillet is large enough to accommodate the sauce and gnocchi, gently scoop the gnocchi out of the boiling water with a large wire skimmer and add them directly to the sauce in the skillet. If not, drain the gnocchi gently, return them to the pot, and pour in the sauce. Bring the sauce and gnocchi to a boil, stirring gently to coat the gnocchi with sauce. Remove the pan from the heat and stir in the grated Parmigiano-Reggiano. Check the seasoning, adding salt if necessary, and gently spoon them into a large (about 15 × 10–inch) baking dish, or two smaller baking dishes into which they fit in a more or less single layer. Scatter the shredded Fontina over the gnocchi and bake until the sauce is bubbling and the top is golden brown, about 10 minutes. Serve immediately.

I love Gorgonzola cheese—eaten as is, or in a sauce for pasta or gnocchi. Gorgonzola comes in two grades: *dolce* (sweet) and *piccante* (piquant). Depending on your preference, either one can be used for this sauce

Gnocchi with Gorgonzola Sauce

Gnocchi alla Gorgonzola

Potato Gnocchi (page 170)

Salt

  ½ cup Chicken Stock (page 74) or canned reduced-sodium chicken broth

  ½ cup heavy cream

  4 tablespoons unsalted butter

Freshly ground black pepper

  4 ounces Gorgonzola

  1 cup freshly grated Parmigiano-Reggiano cheese

Makes 8 servings

Gorgonzola continues to age as it is stored in the refrigerator, intensifying in piquancy as it does. To slow this process down, wrap the cheese tightly in plastic wrap and store it in the coldest part of the refrigerator. This sauce is a good way to use leftover Gorgonzola cheese.

Make the gnocchi.

Bring 6 quarts of salted water to a boil in an 8-quart pot over high heat. (If you plan to cook the gnocchi as soon as they are formed, put the water on to boil while the riced potatoes are cooling. If you are cooking previously frozen gnocchi, make sure the water is boiling before you remove the gnocchi from the freezer.)

Bring the stock, cream, and butter to a boil in a large skillet over medium heat. Season lightly with salt and pepper and boil until the sauce is lightly reduced, about 3 minutes. Remove from the heat and stir in the Gorgonzola until dissolved.

Drop the gnocchi into the boiling water a few at a time, stirring gently and continuously with a wooden spoon. Cook just until they rise to the surface and roll over, 2 to 3 minutes. If the skillet is large enough to accommodate the sauce and gnocchi, gently scoop the gnocchi out of the boiling water with a large wire skimmer and add them directly to the sauce in the skillet. If not, drain the gnocchi gently, return them to the pot, and pour in the sauce. Bring the sauce and gnocchi to a boil, stirring gently to coat the gnocchi with sauce. Remove the pan from the heat and stir in the grated Parmigiano-Reggiano. Check the seasoning, adding salt if necessary. Serve immediately in warm bowls.

What's in a name? Sometimes the name of a dish reflects reality and sometimes it's pure romance. I'm not sure which contessa in what part of Italy enjoyed this dish, but from the ingredients and preparation, she lived somewhere in the north. Regardless, the flavors are excellent, and this was a big seller in my first restaurant, Buonavia, which we operated from 1971 to 1982.

Ricotta Gnocchi with Contessa Sauce

Gnocchi di Ricotta con Salsa "Contessa"

For the Gnocchi

1 ½ pounds fresh ricotta cheese or 3 cups packaged whole-milk ricotta cheese

1 ¾ teaspoons salt, plus more for the pasta water

2 large eggs

½ cup freshly grated Parmigiano-Reggiano cheese

½ teaspoon freshly ground white pepper

¼ teaspoon ground nutmeg, preferably freshly grated

2 cups all-purpose flour, or as needed, plus more for forming the gnocchi

For the Sauce

8 tablespoons (1 stick) unsalted butter

4 thin slices prosciutto (about 1 ounce), cut into ¼-inch strips

Make the gnocchi: Spoon the ricotta into a large, fine-mesh sieve or a colander lined with a double thickness of cheesecloth or a basket-type coffee filter. Set the sieve over a bowl and cover the ricotta well with plastic wrap. Let the ricotta drain in the refrigerator at least overnight, or up to 24 hours. Discard the liquid in the bottom of the bowl.

Bring 6 quarts of salted water to a boil in an 8-quart pot over high heat.

Turn the drained ricotta into a mixing bowl. Beat the eggs and 1 teaspoon salt in a separate bowl until foamy. Stir the eggs, ½ cup grated cheese, pepper, and nutmeg into the ricotta with a wooden spoon or spatula until thoroughly blended. Gradually add as much of the flour as necessary to form a soft and sticky dough. Ricotta-gnocchi dough is always soft and sticky—don't work in so much flour that you have a firm or smooth dough, or the gnocchi will be tough and heavy.

Divide the dough into six approximately equal pieces. Roll one of the dough pieces out with a back-and-forth movement of your palms and fingers to a rope about ½ inch wide. Flour your hands, the work surface, and the dough lightly, as necessary to prevent the dough from sticking. Cut the roll crosswise into ¼-inch lengths. Repeat with the remaining dough. Dust the cut gnocchi lightly with flour and toss them gently to separate. Let them stand while preparing the sauce.

Make the sauce: Melt the butter in a large skillet over medium heat. Add the prosciutto, basil, and pine nuts and cook, stirring, until the pine nuts are

10 fresh basil leaves, torn into quarters

¼ cup pine nuts

½ cup heavy cream

½ cup heavy cream, whipped

1 cup freshly grated Parmigiano-Reggiano cheese

Makes 6 servings

lightly browned, about 4 minutes. Pour in ½ cup heavy cream, bring to a boil, and boil until the sauce is lightly thickened, about 3 minutes. Remove from the heat while cooking the gnocchi.

Stir the gnocchi, a few at a time, into the boiling water, stirring gently but constantly. Return to a boil, stirring frequently. Cook, semi-covered, stirring occasionally, until they float to the top and are tender, about 5 minutes.

If the skillet is large enough to accommodate the sauce and gnocchi, fish the gnocchi out of the boiling water with a large wire skimmer and add them directly to the sauce in the skillet. If not, drain the gnocchi gently, return them to the pot, and pour in the sauce. Bring the sauce and pasta to a boil, stirring gently to coat the gnocchi with sauce. Stir in the whipped cream, remove from the heat, and stir in the grated cheese. Check the seasoning, adding salt if necessary, and serve immediately.

Fresh Pasta

Fresh Egg Pasta

Pasta all'Uovo

3 cups unbleached all-purpose flour, or as needed

4 large eggs

1 teaspoon extra-virgin olive oil

½ teaspoon salt

Warm water as needed

Makes enough pasta for 6 first-course or 3 to 4 main-course servings

Most countertops and work surfaces are built at a height that is comfortable for chopping and mixing. The best height for kneading any kind of dough is slightly lower—at about hip level, where you can really get your weight into the kneading process. If you have a convenient surface at such a height, use it to knead dough. If not, any countertop will do—just stand back a little from the table so you're pushing out, not down, on the dough. My grandmother's method for kneading dough is a little different from most—she taught me to dig my knuckles into the dough in between rounds of gathering and pushing the dough. I pass that method along to you here.

Even if you prepare the dough in a food processor, I suggest you finish kneading the dough by hand. Once you develop a feel for the right consistency of pasta dough, you'll never lose it. You'll be able to make adjustments to the kneading time or the amount of flour or water to work into a dough each time you make it.

Spoon 2⅔ cups of the flour into the work bowl of a large-capacity food processor fitted with the metal blade. Beat the eggs, olive oil, and salt together in a small bowl until blended. With the motor running, pour the egg mixture into the feed tube. Process until the ingredients form a rough and slightly sticky dough. If the mixture is too dry, drizzle a very small amount of warm water into the feed tube and continue processing. Scrape the dough out of the work bowl onto a lightly floured wooden or marble surface. (To mix the dough by hand, see below.)

Knead the dough by gathering it into a compact ball, then pushing the ball away from you with the heels of your hands. Repeat the gathering-and-pushing motion several times, then press into the dough, first with the knuckles of one hand, then with the other, several times. Alternate between kneading and "knuckling" the dough until it is smooth, silky, and elastic—it pulls back into shape when you stretch it. The process will require 5 to 10 minutes of constant kneading, slightly longer if you prepared the dough by hand. (Mixing the dough in a food processor gives the kneading process a little head start.) Flour the work surface and your hands lightly anytime the dough begins to stick while you're kneading.

Roll the dough into a smooth ball and place in a small bowl. Cover with plastic wrap. Let the dough rest at least 1 hour at room temperature, or up to 1 day in the refrigerator, before rolling and shaping the pasta. If the dough has been refrigerated, let it stand at room temperature for about an hour before rolling and shaping.

To mix the dough by hand: Pile 3 cups of flour in a mound on a marble or wooden surface. Make a well in the center of the mound, like a crater in a volcano, all the way to the work surface. Beat the eggs, olive oil, and salt together in a small bowl until the eggs are foamy. Pour them into the well. Beat the egg mixture with a fork while slowly incorporating the flour from the sides of the crater into the egg mixture. The more flour you incorporate, the thicker the egg mixture and the wider the well will become. Continue beating until the dough becomes too stiff to mix with a fork. If this happens before almost all of the flour is incorporated, drizzle a tiny amount of the warm water over the egg mixture and continue mixing. (It is possible you will not need any water at all.) Flour your hands well and knead the remaining flour into the dough until a rough and slightly sticky dough is formed. Shape the dough into a rough ball and set it aside. Sprinkle your hands generously with flour, rubbing them together to remove any remaining scraps of dough from your skin. Scrape any dough and flour from the kneading surface and pass all these scrapings through a sieve. Discard the scraps in the sieve and use the strained flour to continue kneading the dough. Make sure your hands are clean, and flour them lightly and knead the dough as described above.

continued on next page

Variation

Fresh Spinach Pasta

Wash 6 cups (lightly packed) stemmed fresh spinach in plenty of cool water, changing the water if necessary, to remove all traces of sand and grit. Drain the spinach well and transfer it, with just the water that clings to the leaves, to a large pot. Cover the pot and place it over medium heat. Cook, stirring the spinach once or twice, until tender, about 3 to 4 minutes after the water in the bottom of the pot begins steaming. Drain the spinach and let stand until cool enough to handle. Squeeze as much liquid from the spinach as possible with your hands. (The drier the spinach is, the less flour the pasta dough will absorb and the more tender the finished pasta will be.) Combine the eggs called for in the recipe and the squeezed spinach in the work bowl of a food processor fitted with the metal blade, and process until the spinach is finely chopped. Proceed as above, substituting the spinach-egg mixture for the eggs called for in the main recipe. It is likely the spinach-pasta dough will take a little more flour during mixing and kneading than egg-pasta dough, even if you have been very careful to squeeze out the water.

To Cut Fresh Pasta Dough

For fettuccine: If your pasta machine has cutter attachments approximately $\frac{1}{2}$ inch wide, use them to cut fettuccine. If not, cut them by hand as follows. Cut each sheet of pasta into 10-inch lengths. Brush the sheets lightly with flour, and roll them up lengthwise. Cut the rolls into $\frac{1}{2}$-inch strips. Unroll and set the strips and toss them lightly to separate them. Form little nests with the pasta strands, and keep them on a baking sheet lined with a lightly floured kitchen towel until you're ready to cook them.

For tagliolini (to use in the Paglia e Fieno recipe on page 183): If your pasta machine has cutter attachments approximately $\frac{1}{4}$ inch wide, use them to cut tagliolini. If not, flour and roll them as described above, and cut the rolls into $\frac{1}{4}$-inch strips.

For pappardelle: Cut sheets of hand-rolled pasta into 5-inch widths. (This won't be necessary if you've rolled out the pasta with a machine, as the width will be very close to 5 inches.) Cut the sheets into 12-inch lengths and stack several of them together. Cut the stack crosswise into $1\frac{1}{2}$-inch strips to make pappardelle.

Using a pasta machine: Cut the dough into six equal pieces, flour them lightly, and cover them with a kitchen towel. Working with one piece of the dough at a time, shape it into a rectangle about 5 × 3 inches. Set the rollers of the pasta machine to the widest setting and pass the pasta rectangle through the rollers with one of the short sides first. Fold the dough in half and pass the same piece of dough through the rollers a second time, short side first. Repeat with the remaining dough pieces. Flour the dough pieces very lightly as you work—just enough to keep them from sticking to the rollers. Continue rolling the pieces of dough in the same order (so they have a chance to rest a little between rollings), decreasing the width by one setting each time, until all the pieces of dough have been passed through the next-to-thinnest setting on the pasta machine. See illustration, page 190. Don't pull the dough sheets through the machine as they get longer or you will stretch the dough sheets out of shape, but support them lightly from underneath as they emerge from the rollers. Keep the pieces of dough that aren't being rolled covered with a towel. If you find the dough is very elastic, rest it 5 to 10 minutes, then continue. When all the pasta has been rolled into sheets, let them rest, completely covered with lightly floured towels, about 30 minutes before cutting them.

By hand: Cut the rested dough into four equal pieces and cover them with a clean kitchen towel. Working with one piece at a time, roll the pasta out on a lightly floured surface to a rectangle approximately 10 × 20 inches (if you plan to cut fettuccine or tagliolini; to make pasta squares for cannelloni or manicotti, see separate instructions below). Dust the work surface lightly with flour just often enough to keep the dough from sticking; too much flour will make the dough difficult to roll. If the dough springs back as you try to roll it, re-cover it with the kitchen towel and let it rest 10 to 15 minutes. Start rolling another piece of dough, and come back to the first one once it has had a chance to rest. Let the pasta sheets rest, separated by kitchen towels, at least 15 minutes before cutting them.

To Roll Fresh Pasta Dough

Cooked Pasta Squares

Fresh Egg Pasta (page 178)
or Fresh Spinach Pasta
(page 180)

Salt

2 tablespoons olive oil

**Makes 18 to 24 squares,
enough for either Manicotti
(page 163), Cannelloni
(page 165), or "Little
Handkerchiefs" (page 168)**

Prepare the pasta dough and let it rest.

To form the pasta squares by machine: Cut the dough into six equal pieces and roll them out, following the directions on page 181, to 6-inch-wide strips, each approximately 24 inches long. Cut each strip crosswise into 6-inch squares.

To form the pasta by hand: Cut the rested dough into four equal pieces. Following the directions on page 181, roll each piece about to a rectangle approximately 18 × 12 inches. Cut each rectangle lengthwise into two 6-inch-wide strips; cut each strip crosswise into three 6-inch squares.

Bring 6 quarts of salted water and the olive oil to a boil in an 8-quart pot over high heat. Set a large bowl of ice water next to the stove. Stir about half the pasta squares into the boiling water. Return to a boil, stirring gently. Cook the pasta, semi-covered, stirring occasionally, until the pasta squares float to the top, 1 to 2 minutes.

Remove the pasta squares with a wire skimmer and transfer them to the ice water. Let them stand until completely chilled. Repeat the cooking and cooling with the remaining pasta squares. When the cooked noodles are chilled, remove them from the ice bath and stack them on a baking sheet, separating the layers with clean, damp kitchen towels.

The colorful name of this dish comes from the strands of green spinach and golden egg fettuccine. Of course you can make it with all of one type or another of fresh pasta, or even dried pasta shapes like penne or shells.

"Straw and Hay"

Paglia e Fieno

½ recipe Fresh Egg Pasta (page 178)

½ recipe Fresh Spinach Pasta (page 180)

Salt

4 scallions

2 tablespoons extra-virgin olive oil

1 cup shelled fresh peas (see note) or frozen baby peas, defrosted

2 tablespoons unsalted butter

6 to 8 slices imported prosciutto, cut crosswise into ½-inch-thick ribbons

⅔ cup Chicken Stock (page 74) or canned reduced-sodium chicken broth

½ cup heavy cream

¾ cup freshly grated Parmigiano-Reggiano cheese

Makes 6 servings

Prepare the pasta, roll the dough, and cut into tagliolini as described on page 180.

Bring 6 quarts of salted water to a boil in an 8-quart pot over high heat. Trim the roots, tips, and any yellow or wilted leaves from the scallions. Cut them in half lengthwise, then crosswise into 3-inch lengths. Cut the scallion pieces lengthwise into thin strips. Heat the oil in a large, heavy skillet over medium heat. Add the scallions and cook until wilted, 1 to 2 minutes. Add the peas and butter and cook until softened, about 3 minutes. Add the prosciutto and toss until it changes color, 1 to 2 minutes. Add the chicken stock and heat to a boil. Reduce heat to simmering and cook until the liquid is reduced by half. Add the heavy cream and continue to simmer until the liquid is lightly thickened, 2 to 3 minutes. Shake the fettuccine in a colander to remove as much of the flour as possible. Stir the pasta into the boiling water. Return to a boil, stirring frequently. Cook the pasta, semi-covered, stirring occasionally, until done, about 2 minutes or less after the water returns to a boil. (When the pasta rises to the surface, it is done.)

If the skillet is large enough to accommodate the sauce and pasta, fish the pasta out of the boiling water with a large wire skimmer and add it directly to the sauce in the skillet. If not, drain the pasta, return it to the pot, and pour in the sauce. Bring the sauce and pasta to a boil, stirring to coat the pasta with sauce. Cook until the sauce is reduced enough to form a creamy, gliding sauce. Remove from the heat, toss in the grated cheese, and serve immediately in warm bowls.

☞ If using fresh peas, blanch them in boiling salted water until crisp-tender, 3 to 5 minutes depending on the peas. Drain them and rinse briefly under cold water.

Alfredo di Lelio, after whom this dish was named, was a restaurateur in Rome in the early 1900s. Alfredo prepared this pasta dish dressed simply with triple-rich cream, butter, and Parmigiano-Reggiano cheese as a restorative for his wife, who had recently given birth.

Mary Pickford and Douglas Fairbanks, on honeymoon in Rome, dined on this dish every night at Alfredo's restaurant. When they returned to the States, they shared their delightful experience at Alfredo's with the Hollywood set, and by the 1930s, restaurateurs in America were re-creating versions of Alfredo's fettuccine, compensating for the unavailable triple cream and Parmigiano-Reggiano by enriching American cream with egg yolks.

If you have good homemade fettuccine, farm-fresh triple cream, and young, milky Parmigiano-Reggiano, forget about the chicken stock and egg yolks and make this dish as Alfredo did.

Fettuccine Alfredo

1 recipe Fresh Egg Pasta (page 178), cut into fettuccine

Salt

4 tablespoons unsalted butter

⅔ cup heavy cream

½ cup Chicken Stock (page 74) or canned reduced-sodium chicken broth

Finely ground black pepper

2 large egg yolks

¼ cup freshly grated Parmigiano-Reggiano cheese

1 teaspoon coarsely ground black peppercorns (see note page 139)

Makes 6 servings

Prepare the fresh pasta and cut it into fettuccine.

Bring 6 quarts of salted water to a boil in an 8-quart pot over high heat.

Drop the butter into a large skillet and place over medium heat. Before the butter has a chance to melt fully and separate, pour in the heavy cream and chicken stock. Bring to a boil and season lightly with salt and finely ground pepper.

Shake the fettuccine in a colander to remove as much of the flour as possible. Stir the pasta into the boiling water. Return to a boil, stirring frequently. Cook the pasta, semi-covered, stirring occasionally, until done, about 2 minutes or less after the water returns to a boil. (When the pasta rises to the surface, it is done.)

If the skillet is large enough to accommodate the sauce and pasta, fish the pasta out of the boiling water with a large wire skimmer and add it directly to the sauce in the skillet. If not, drain the pasta, return it to the pot, and pour in the sauce. Bring the sauce and pasta to a boil, stirring to coat the pasta with sauce. Cook until the sauce is reduced enough to form a creamy, gliding sauce, then drop in the egg yolks, one at a time, stirring well after each. (If the sauce becomes too dense, thin it a little with more chicken stock or a little of the pasta-cooking water.) Remove from the heat, sprinkle the grated cheese and coarse black pepper over the pasta, toss well, and serve immediately in warm bowls.

☞ If you are at all concerned about the risks of eating eggs that are not fully cooked, I offer you the following suggestions: Poach egg yolks in a small sieve as described in the recipe for Linguine with Bacon and Onions (page 138), or search out pasteurized eggs or egg yolks, available in the dairy case of some supermarkets.

Grandpa Giovanni (right), taking a rest from work in the cement factory, Pula, c. 1922–23

Ravioli Stuffed with Ricotta and Spinach

Ravioli di Ricotta e Spinaci

For the Filling

1 ½ pounds fresh ricotta cheese, or 3 cups packaged whole-milk ricotta cheese

2 tablespoons extra-virgin olive oil

2 small leeks, white parts only, trimmed, cleaned, and chopped (about 1 cup) (see page 80)

½ cup minced scallions, including greens (about 6 scallions)

4 cups fresh spinach leaves, stemmed, washed, and dried (see page 67), chopped coarsely

Salt

Freshly ground black pepper

1 cup freshly grated Parmigiano-Reggiano cheese

2 tablespoons chopped fresh Italian parsley

1 large egg, beaten

Fresh Egg Pasta (page 178)

For Dressing the Ravioli

2 cups Tomato Sauce (page 151)

Spoon the ricotta into a large fine-mesh sieve or a colander lined with a double thickness of cheesecloth or a basket-type coffee filter. Set the sieve over a bowl and cover the ricotta well with plastic wrap. Let the ricotta drain in the refrigerator at least overnight or up to 24 hours. Discard the liquid in the bottom of the bowl.

In a wide braising pan or deep skillet, heat the oil over medium-low heat. Add the leeks and scallions and cook until softened, about 3 minutes. Stir in the chopped spinach and increase the heat to medium. Season lightly with salt and pepper and cook over moderate heat until the vegetables are tender and the liquid is evaporated, about 10 minutes. Set in a strainer and cool completely.

Stir the fresh ricotta, Parmigiano-Reggiano, parsley, and sautéed greens together in a bowl. Season to taste with salt and pepper and stir in the egg. Chill thoroughly.

While the filling is chilling, make the pasta dough and let rest.

Form and cut the ravioli according to directions on page 190. The ravioli should be cooked immediately or refrigerated up to 4 hours. (The ravioli may also be frozen: Place the sheets of ravioli onto a freezer shelf and freeze until solid to the touch. Carefully transfer the ravioli to resealable plastic bags or airtight plastic containers.)

Bring 6 quarts of salted water to a boil in an 8-quart pot over high heat. Slip the ravioli into the water a few at a time, stirring gently as you do. Cook until the edges of the pasta are tender but still firm to the bite and they rise to the surface, about 6 minutes after the water returns to a boil.

While the ravioli are cooking, divide the tomato sauce, olive oil, and basil between two large skillets and bring to a simmer over medium heat. Fish out the ravioli with a wire skimmer or large flat slotted spoon, drain them well over the pasta pot, and slide them into the pans of sauce, dividing them evenly. Simmer, stirring gently with a spoon until the sauce is lightly reduced and the ravioli are coated. Remove the pans from the heat, check the sea-

2 tablespoons extra-virgin olive oil

8 fresh basil leaves, washed and shredded

½ cup freshly grated Parmigiano-Reggiano cheese

Makes 6 servings (about 60 pieces)

soning, and add salt and pepper if necessary. Spoon the ravioli into warm bowls or onto a warm platter, sprinkle with the grated cheese, and serve immediately.

Variation

Butter-Sage Sauce
Conditi all Burro e Salvia

Melt one stick (8 tablespoons) unsalted butter in a large skillet over low heat. (The heat should be low enough to melt the butter slowly, without its separating or turning clear.) Add eight to ten whole sage leaves and remove the skillet from the heat. Ladle out about 1 cup of the ravioli-cooking water before you drain them. Either fish the ravioli out of the pot with a large wire skimmer or drain them gently. Add the ravioli to the skillet. Pour in enough of the cooking liquid to make a sufficient amount of creamy sauce to coat the ravioli generously. Bring to a quick boil, then remove from the heat. Stir in grated Parmigiano-Reggiano cheese, salt, and freshly ground black pepper to taste. Serve immediately.

```
To:       Lidia Bastianich
From:     JoAnna Destro
Subject:


> > > I enjoy the stories about your family the time
when you lived in Italy. Please don't ever stop cook-
ing for your fans. The meals you make are filled with
so much love.< < <
```

Ravioli with Meat Filling

Ravioli Ripieni di Carne

For the Filling

- 3 tablespoons extra-virgin olive oil
- 2 bone-in chicken thighs (about ½ pound)
- ½ pound Italian pork sausages (preferably without fennel seeds) in their casings
- ½ pound boneless veal, cut into 2-inch pieces
- ½ pound boneless pork butt, cut into 2-inch pieces
- 1 cup coarsely chopped onion
- 1 cup peeled and sliced carrot
- ½ cup diced celery
- 1 sprig fresh rosemary
- 2 sprigs fresh thyme
- 1½ cups (or as needed) Chicken Stock (page 74) or canned reduced-sodium chicken broth
- 3 ounces mortadella, cut into ½-inch dice (about ½ cup)
- ½ cup grated Parmigiano-Reggiano cheese
- 2 tablespoons bread crumbs
- 2 tablespoons chopped fresh Italian parsley

This meat filling is similar to the one for cannelloni on page 165. You can use them interchangeably.

Preheat the oven to 375° F. Heat the olive oil in a large wide pan or a heavy roasting pan over medium heat. Add the chicken, sausage, veal, and pork and cook, turning often, until the meats are evenly browned, about 10 minutes. Scatter the onion, carrot, celery, rosemary, and thyme over the meats and pour in enough chicken stock to cover the bottom of the pan by about 1 inch. Transfer the pan to the oven and cook until all the meats are very tender and well browned and the chicken is falling off the bone, about 2 hours. Check the meats occasionally as they cook, adding chicken stock as necessary to keep the level constant, and turning and basting the meats with the pan juices.

Remove the pan from the oven, toss in the mortadella, and let stand at room temperature until cool enough to handle. Pick the skin and bones from the chicken and remove the casing from the sausage. Drain the meat and vegetables and pour the drained cooking liquid into a small saucepan. Bring the cooking liquid to a boil and cook until reduced to about ½ cup. The liquid should be slightly syrupy and rich in flavor. Remove the saucepan from the heat and reserve.

Pass the meat-and-vegetable mixture through a meat grinder fitted with a disc with holes about ¼ inch in diameter. Stir ½ cup grated cheese, the bread crumbs, and parsley into the ground meats. Taste, and add salt and pepper as necessary. Pour in the eggs and blend well. Refrigerate until thoroughly chilled before filling the ravioli.

Make the pasta dough; form and cut the ravioli according to directions below. The ravioli should be cooked immediately or refrigerated up to 4 hours. (The ravioli may also be frozen: Place the sheets of ravioli on a freezer shelf and freeze until solid to the touch. Carefully transfer the ravioli to resealable plastic bags or airtight plastic containers.)

Bring 6 quarts of salted water to a boil in an 8-quart pot over high heat. Slip the ravioli into the boiling water a few at a time. Return to a boil, stirring fre-

Salt

Freshly ground black pepper

2 large eggs, beaten

Fresh Egg Pasta
(page 178)

To Serve

Tomato Sauce
(page 151, or
variation below)

1 cup freshly grated
Parmigiano-Reggiano
cheese

Makes 8 servings

quently. Cook, semi-covered, stirring occasionally, until the edges of the ravioli are tender, about 5 minutes after the water returns to the boil.

While the ravioli are cooking, bring the tomato sauce to a simmer in a medium saucepan over medium heat. Check the seasoning and add salt and pepper if necessary.

Drain the ravioli gently, return them to the pot, and pour in the tomato sauce and the reduced roasting liquid. Bring the sauce and pasta to a boil, stirring gently with a clean spoon to coat the ravioli with sauce. Remove the pot from the heat, stir in the cheese, and check the seasoning, adding salt and pepper as necessary. Spoon into warm serving bowls or onto a warm platter.

Variation

Try this simple sauce in place of tomato sauce: Melt 5 tablespoons of butter in a large skillet over medium heat. (If you do not have a skillet large enough to hold all the ravioli comfortably, divide the sauce ingredients between two skillets.) Before draining the ravioli, ladle about $\frac{1}{2}$ cup of the cooking water into the skillet. Gently transfer the ravioli into the skillet with a wire skimmer and bring the sauce to a boil. Cook, swirling the skillet to coat the ravioli with sauce, until the sauce is lightly thickened. Remove from the heat and sprinkle with 1 cup of Parmigiano-Reggiano. Spoon the ravioli onto a warm platter and drizzle with the hot reduced roasting liquid.

Making Ravioli

You can make ravioli with the meat filling on page 188 or the ricotta-spinach filling on page 186 using either hand-rolled or machine-rolled dough. Start by scooping scant tablespoonfuls of either filling onto a baking sheet. Refrigerate the filling mounds, then roll out and fill the pasta sheets as described below.

If you're rolling out the pasta sheets by hand, first divide the dough into three equal pieces. Roll each piece out as described on page 181 to sheets about 30 inches long by 11 inches wide. Keep two of the pasta sheets covered with kitchen towels and place the third on the work surface in front of you with one of the long edges toward you. Arrange twenty of the filling mounds in two rows of ten over the top half of the dough, starting them about $1\frac{1}{2}$ inches in from the sides of the dough rectangle and arranging them about $2\frac{1}{2}$ inches from each other. Pat the fillings into rough rectangles that measure about 2×1 inch. Dip the tip of your finger into cool water and moisten the edges of the top half of the dough and in between the mounds of filling. Fold the bottom of the dough over the mounds of filling, lining up the edges of the top and bottom halves as best you can. Press the top layer of dough to the bottom firmly, squeezing out any air pockets as you work. With a pastry wheel or knife, cut between the filling into rectangles approximately $2\frac{1}{2} \times 2$ inches. Pat lightly the tops of the ravioli to even out the filling. Pinch the edges of the ravioli to seal in the filling. Repeat with the remaining two pieces of dough.

To make ravioli with machine-rolled dough, first divide the pasta dough into six equal pieces. Working with one piece of dough at a time, and keeping the pieces of dough you are not rolling covered with a kitchen towel, roll each out, as described on page 181, to a $5\frac{1}{2} \times 30$–inch rectangle. Place the dough sheet on the work surface with one of the long edges toward you. Make a row of ten filling mounds along the length of the top half of the pasta sheet, starting about $1\frac{1}{4}$ inches from the sides and top edge of the pasta sheet. (The mounds should be about $2\frac{1}{2}$ inches from each other.) Dip the tip of your finger into cool water and moisten the edges of the top half of the dough and in between the mounds of filling. Fold the bottom of the dough over the mounds of filling, lining up the edges of the top and bottom halves as best you can. Press the top layer of dough to the bottom firmly, squeezing out any air pockets as you work. Cut between the filling into rectangles approximately $2\frac{1}{2} \times 2$ inches. Pinch the edges of the ravioli to seal in the filling. Repeat with the remaining five pieces of dough.

1. After passing the pasta dough through the rollers several times at progressively thinner settings, roll it through the next-to-last setting. The dough is now ready to be filled.

2. After you have spooned the filling onto the pasta dough, fold the bottom of the dough over the mounds of filling, lining up the edges of the top and bottom halves.

3. Trim the edges with a pastry wheel, and cut into rectangles between the fillings. Lightly pat the tops of the ravioli to even out the filling.

Agnolotti with Crabmeat and Shrimp in Clam Sauce

Agnolotti di Granchio e Gamberi

For the Filling

6 tablespoons unsalted butter, softened

1/3 cup minced fresh Italian parsley

1/2 teaspoon freshly ground black pepper

2/3 pound medium shrimp (about 20), shelled, deveined, and cut in thirds crosswise

Salt

1/2 pound jumbo lump crabmeat

Fresh Egg Pasta (page 178)

For the Sauce

2 cups peeled, seeded, and crushed tomatoes, either ripe fresh plum tomatoes (see page 9 for peeling and seeding directions) or canned Italian plum tomatoes (preferably San Marzano), or a mix of the 2

7 tablespoons extra-virgin olive oil

6 large cloves garlic, peeled

1 teaspoon crushed hot red pepper

If you have beautifully ripe fresh plum tomatoes, peel and seed them for the sauce. If it isn't tomato season, opt for canned tomatoes, but include a few fresh plum tomatoes to give the sauce a taste of freshness.

I like the sweetness of jumbo lump crabmeat in these agnolotti, but if that is not available, substitute any type of fresh, sweet crabmeat, or even fresh sea or bay scallops cut into 1/2-inch pieces.

Prepare the filling ingredients: Beat the butter, parsley, and black pepper together in a bowl until blended. Spoon the seasoned butter onto a square of plastic wrap and shape it into a rectangular loaf more or less the size of a stick of butter. Chill until completely firm, then cut into 1/4-inch cubes. While the butter is chilling, season shrimp pieces lightly with salt. Pick over the crabmeat, removing any pieces of shell or cartilage but leaving the pieces of crabmeat as large as possible. Refrigerate the butter cubes, shrimp, and crabmeat while you make the pasta dough.

Make the pasta dough and roll it into sheets by hand or machine, as described on page 181. Working with one sheet of dough at a time, cut out circles using a 3-inch round cutter. Brush the edges of the circles lightly with water. Place a piece of seasoned shrimp, a similar-size piece of crabmeat, and a seasoned butter cube in the center of each circle.

To form the agnolotti, fold each circle in half, enclosing the filling and pinching the edges to seal securely. Holding the half-moon shape with the rounded side up, wrap it around the tip of your index finger and pinch the two ends together firmly. Arrange the finished agnolotti in a single layer on baking sheets lined with lightly floured kitchen towels and cover them with additional towels. Repeat with the remaining dough, seafood, and butter. The agnolotti can be cooked immediately or refrigerated up to 4 hours. (To freeze the agnolotti, place them on the tray in the freezer until very firm to the

2 cups clam-shucking
liquor or bottled clam
juice

2 tablespoons chopped
fresh Italian parsley

**Makes 6 servings
(about 60 pieces)**

touch, then transfer them to resealable plastic bags or airtight plastic containers and freeze for up to 2 months.)

To make the sauce, pass the tomatoes through a food mill fitted with the fine disc. Heat 2 tablespoons of the olive oil in a large nonreactive skillet over medium heat. Whack the garlic cloves with the side of a knife and add them to the pan. Cook, shaking the pan, until lightly browned, about 3 minutes. Pour in the tomatoes, stir in the crushed red pepper, and bring to a boil. Adjust the heat to simmering and cook until lightly thickened, about 10 minutes. Pour in the clam juice and cook an additional 15 minutes.

While the sauce is cooking, bring 6 quarts of salted water to a boil in an 8-quart pot over high heat.

Slip the agnolotti into the boiling water a few at a time, stirring gently as you add them. Return to a boil, stirring frequently. Cook the pasta, semi-covered, stirring occasionally, until the edges are tender, about 4 minutes after the water returns to a boil.

If the skillet is large enough to accommodate the sauce and agnolotti, fish the agnolotti out of the boiling water with a large wire skimmer and add them directly to the sauce in the skillet. If not, drain the agnolotti gently and return them to the pot. Pour in the sauce and bring to a boil, stirring gently to coat the agnolotti with sauce. Drizzle the remaining 5 tablespoons olive oil over the pasta and sprinkle with 2 tablespoons chopped parsley. Check the seasoning, adding salt if necessary, and serve immediately.

☞ When you shuck clams, always reserve the juice and freeze it if you're not using it in the recipe. If you don't have fresh clam juice available, canned clam juice makes a fine substitute.

Risotto

Risotto is as Italian as pasta, but it took much longer to reach the American shores and be presented on the Italian-American table. Actually, serving it is a rather recent phenomenon—only in the last ten to fifteen years has risotto made its way onto menus in America and onto the stoves of American home kitchens.

Risotto—when made correctly—speaks of Italy. There are no two ways of making risotto; either you make it right, or it is not risotto. It was one of the first dishes that identified an Italian restaurant in America as authentically Italian. I know that risotto, along with polenta, gnocchi and other such dishes, set my first restaurant, Buonavia, apart from the other Italian restaurants of the time and led it to be labeled a "Northern Italian" restaurant.

Risotto does demand a lot of attention from the cook, because it needs to be stirred continuously. But it is well worth the effort. One of the questions I am asked most often is "Can risotto be cooked in advance?" The simple answer is no. Once the rice begins to release the starches and is wet, it will continue to break down until it becomes mush. There is one option that is acceptable, and that is to prepare the rice to the point where it is toasted and the wine has been added. But you must evaporate the wine completely and bring the rice back to a dry state. (See paragraph three of the Basic Risotto recipe, which follows.) Then you can wait a few hours before continuing with the recipe. Preparing the risotto through this step will save you about 5 to 7 minutes.

Think of this recipe as a master plan for making risotto, and the additions and variations that follow it as inspirations for your own creations. Just keep in mind, when adding ingredients, to time them so they are finished cooking at the same time as the rice. Once you've mastered the art of making a creamy risotto with each grain of rice cooked *al dente*, you'll never lose that skill. That is why I believe this is the only risotto recipe you'll ever need. For proper results, use only the traditional short-grain varieties of rice, like the Arborio or Carnaroli suggested below.

Basic Risotto

4½ cups hot Chicken Stock (page 74), Vegetable Stock (page 76), or canned reduced-sodium chicken broth

3 tablespoons extra-virgin olive oil

1 medium onion, minced (about ¾ cup)

1 medium leek, white parts only, trimmed, cleaned, and chopped (page 80; about 1 cup)

4 to 6 scallions, trimmed, white and green parts chopped separately

2 cups Arborio or Carnaroli rice

⅓ cup dry white wine

Salt

2 tablespoons unsalted butter, cut into 4 pieces

⅓ cup freshly grated Parmigiano-Reggiano cheese

Freshly ground black pepper

Makes 4 main-course or 8 first-course servings

Pour the stock into a 2-quart saucepan and keep it hot over low heat. (The texture of a properly cooked risotto is creamy, with each grain of rice separate and *al dente*. To achieve that, you are actually coaxing the starch gently out of the grains of rice. Adding cold stock to the risotto may cause the surfaces of the rice grains to "seize up" and seal in the starch, instead of releasing it into the liquid.)

Heat the olive oil in a wide 3- to 4-quart braising pan over medium heat. Stir in the onion and cook, stirring occasionally, until softened, about 4 minutes. Stir in the leek and the white parts of the scallions and cook, stirring, until the onion is golden, about 6 minutes. Adjust the heat under the pan as the onion browns so that it cooks slowly with gentle bubbling.

Stir in the rice and continue stirring until the grains are coated with oil and "toasted"—the edges become translucent—1 to 2 minutes. Pour in the wine and let it boil, stirring the rice, until evaporated. (Since the rice kernel is 98 percent starch, the acidity in the wine balances and imparts flavor to the rice kernel.)

Season the rice lightly with salt and ladle enough of the hot stock into the pan to barely cover the rice. Bring to a boil, then lower the heat so the stock is at a lively simmer. Cook, stirring constantly, until all the stock has been absorbed and you can see the bottom of the pan when you stir. Continue cooking, pouring in the remaining hot stock in small batches—each addition should be just enough to completely moisten the rice—and cook until each batch of stock has been absorbed. Stir constantly until the rice mixture is

continued on next page

creamy but *al dente;* this will take 16 to 20 minutes from the time the wine was added. When in doubt, undercook—risotto continues to cook, even after it is removed from the heat.

Adjust the level of heat throughout cooking so the rice is simmering very gently. The total amount of stock you use may vary for several reasons: the type of rice you are using, the shape and size of the pan, and the desired texture of the finished risotto which can be quite dense, or soft and runny, depending on your personal taste. If you like a creamier risotto—called *all'onda,* or "wavelike" in Italian—stir in a little more stock once the rice is *al dente,* but do not cook the rice any further. For a denser risotto, keep the rice over the heat and cook until the last addition of stock has been almost entirely absorbed by the rice. There is a general rule that risotto with seafood is looser and risotto prepared with meats, game, and mushrooms is more dense, but ultimately it depends on your taste and preference.

Remove the pan from the heat; stir in the butter and green parts of the scallion until the butter is completely melted. Stir in half the grated cheese, taste the risotto, and add salt, if necessary, and pepper. Always ladle risotto into warm, shallow bowls and serve immediately after finishing. Either top each serving with some of the remaining grated cheese or pass the cheese separately.

Variations

Tomato and Mozzarella Risotto

Heat 2 tablespoons extra-virgin olive oil in a wide skillet over medium heat. Add 2 cloves garlic, sliced, and shake the pan until the garlic is lightly browned. Slide in 2 cups halved cherry tomatoes and stir gently until they are juicy. Toss in a handful of shredded fresh basil, remove the pan from the heat, and set aside. Prepare the Basic Risotto, stirring in the sautéed cherry tomatoes halfway through the cooking. Remove the pan of risotto from the heat, and stir in $1^{1}/_{2}$ cups of cubed fresh mozzarella (preferably *mozzarella di bufala*) along with the grated cheese and butter.

Saffron and Clam Risotto

Add a generous pinch of saffron threads to the stock before placing it over the heat. Scrub 12 to 16 hard-shell clams—the smaller the better—such as

S TIR LEFTOVER COOKED VEGETABLES into the Basic Risotto during the last few minutes of cooking.

Leftover steamed clams or mussels, like the Mussels in Spicy Tomato Sauce (page 10) or the Clams in a Savory Tomato-Vegetable Soup (page 98), can be picked from their shells and added to the risotto at the very end of cooking. Substitute some of the liquid or sauce that the shellfish were cooked in for the stock called for in the above recipes. As a general rule, 1 cup of shellfish cooking liquid will flavor enough risotto for two.

If you find yourself with some leftover tripe after preparing the Tripe in Tomato, Carrot, and Celery Sauce, Roman-Style (page 228), it will be a great addition to risotto. One cup of tripe and sauce will flavor enough risotto for two. Cut the tripe into smaller pieces before adding it to the risotto about halfway through the cooking.

The same is true of leftover oxtails or short ribs (pages 142 and 218). Since the meat is already cooked, you can prepare the Basic Risotto as above, using some of the leftover sauce from the meat in place of the stock. Shred the meat finely and add it during the last few minutes of cooking.

Some Simple Additions to Basic Risotto

littlenecks, Manila, or butter clams, the smaller the better. Tuck the clams into the rice about 5 to 6 minutes after the first addition of stock, and continue as described in the Basic Risotto recipe.

Chicken and Mushroom Risotto

Pour one cup of the hot stock called for in the Basic Risotto recipe over $1/2$ cup dried porcini mushrooms in a small bowl. Let stand until the porcini are softened, about 20 minutes. Drain the porcini, straining the soaking liquid through a coffee filter or a sieve lined with a double thickness of cheesecloth. Pour the strained soaking liquid into the remaining stock. Rinse the soaked mushrooms thoroughly to remove any sand and grit. Drain the mushrooms well and chop them fine. Cut 12 ounces to 1 pound of boneless skinless chicken breasts into $1/2$-inch cubes and season them generously with salt and pepper. Heat 2 tablespoons extra-virgin olive oil in a wide skillet. Add the

continued on next page

chicken cubes and cook, stirring, until lightly browned on all sides, about 3 minutes. Scatter 3 cloves garlic, sliced, over the chicken and stir to mix. Add 3 cups sliced trimmed mushrooms (all one type or assorted) over the chicken and cook, stirring, until the mushrooms are wilted and lightly browned, about 4 minutes. Remove from the heat and set aside. Prepare the Basic Risotto, using the mushroom-enriched stock and adding the chopped dried porcini along with the onion. Stir in the chicken-mushroom mixture about two thirds of the way through the cooking.

Shrimp and Leek Risotto

Trim, wash, and slice one medium leek as described on page 80. Completely shell 1 pound medium shrimp and devein them. Cut them in half crosswise. Heat 2 tablespoons extra-virgin olive oil in a large skillet over medium heat. Scatter the leek over the oil and cook, stirring, until tender, about 4 minutes. Increase the heat under the pan to high, toss in the shrimp and cook, stirring constantly, until bright pink and seared on all sides, about 2 minutes. Remove from the heat and set aside. Prepare the Basic Risotto, stirring the leek and shrimp into the rice in the last 2 minutes of cooking.

Radicchio Risotto

Prepare the Basic Risotto, adding 4 cups shredded radicchio leaves (preferably *radicchio Trevisano*) to the pan after the wine has evaporated.

Pizza

Take a piece of bread dough, roll it out with a rolling pin, stretch it further with the tips of your fingers, top it with whatever comes to mind, dress it with oil or lard, cook it on a hearth, and you will know what pizza is. So wrote De Bourcard, in the middle of the eighteenth century. Although he was of French descent, he became Neapolitanized, and that means familiar with pizza and its delights and diversities.

Flat dough baked in a coal oven or on hot stones in one form or another belongs to every culture, but it is Italy's pizza that is universally known and enjoyed. Pizza, as we know it today, is a thin round dough to which tomato, cheese, and an infinite number of ingredients can be added before it is baked. Although most of the regions of Italy have some form of pizza—*focaccia* in Liguria and Tuscany, *pitta* in Calabria, *pinza* in the Veneto, and all kinds of *torte salate* found all over the peninsula—*pizza napoletana* is the epitome of pizza as we Americans know it. In its most common form—topped with tomato and cheese and dressed with olive oil—pizza seems to have appeared in and around Naples some time in the fourteenth century.

It was easy to transport the idea of pizza to the New World as the Italian immigrants—a large part of them from around Campagna—settled in this country. Since it was introduced to America at the turn of the last century, pizza has taken on a new life and has become more of an American phenomenon than an Italian one. From its simple beginnings, the pizza has, eventually, conquered America.

All sorts of people put all sorts of things into pizza dough. I want to give the recipe to you straight, as I had it in Naples—water, flour, yeast, and salt. This makes a soft but elastic dough that is easy to work with. Don't be afraid to stretch the dough when you're shaping it into pizza crusts; for something that feels so soft, it really is quite tough.

Pizza Dough

L'Impasto per la Pizza

1 teaspoon active dry
 yeast

1 cup warm water

3 cups all-purpose flour,
 and more as needed

1 ½ teaspoons salt

Olive oil

**Makes enough dough for four
12-inch Margherita pizzas, two
8-inch square Sicilian pizzas,
or fifteen 4-inch calzones**

Sprinkle the yeast over the warm water in a medium bowl and let stand until dissolved.

Toss the flour and salt together and stir into the dissolved yeast, using a wooden spoon or your fingers, until you have a stiff dough.

Turn the dough out onto a floured board and knead 5 to 10 minutes, adding flour as needed to prevent sticking, until the dough is smooth and elastic. Place the dough in a lightly oiled bowl, turn the dough to coat all sides with oil, and cover with a damp cloth. Set the bowl in a warm, draft-free spot until it doubles in volume, about 1 ½ hours.

Punch down the dough and, if necessary, divide into the number of portions called for in the recipe. Place the dough balls on a lightly oiled baking sheet and cover with a piece of plastic wrap pressed directly against the dough. Refrigerate until the dough is roughly doubled in bulk. This can take from 12 to 24 hours. Punch down the dough and continue with the recipe.

Traditional Pizza Margherita

Pizza alla Margherita

Pizza Dough (page 201)

3 tablespoons extra-virgin olive oil

Coarse cornmeal

1 cup Neapolitan Pizza Sauce (see following recipe)

½ pound fresh mozzarella, coarsely grated and drained in a sieve

20 fresh basil leaves, cut into very thin strips

Makes four 12-inch pizzas

If you want a really crispy, evenly baked crust, take the time to squeeze the tomatoes of excess liquid when you make the sauce (see following recipe) and drain the mozzarella briefly in a sieve before you put the pizzas together.

Prepare the pizza dough, dividing into four portions after the first rising.

When the dough has risen for the second time, place the oven rack in the lowest position, center a pizza stone over it, and preheat the oven to 475° F. (See below for notes on baking pizzas without a stone.)

Roll or stretch each of the dough balls out to a 12-inch circle about ¼ inch thick with a slightly thicker border around the edge. Brush each circle lightly with some of the olive oil. Working with one crust at a time, sprinkle a pizza peel or flat baking sheet generously with the cornmeal. Place the circle of dough on the cornmeal and spoon ¼ cup of the pizza sauce over the dough, leaving a thin border around the edge. Scatter one-fourth of the mozzarella over the tomato sauce. Sprinkle the pizza lightly with salt and scatter some of the basil over it. Drizzle a little of the remaining olive oil over the cheese.

To bake the pizzas on a pizza stone: Pull the oven rack out partially and slide the pizza onto the stone. The best way to do this is to bring the peel down to the stone and lift the peel until the pizza starts to slide. Once the crust makes contact with the stone, pull the peel quickly from the pizza. Make sure you center the peel and pizza over the stone so the pizza doesn't over-hang the stone when you remove the peel. Push the rack back in, close the oven, and bake until the pizza is golden brown underneath and the cheese is melted, about 8 minutes. (If you are using two stones, you may bake two piz-zas at a time. Position the stones on racks in the lowest and highest positions before heating the oven. Check the pizzas as they cook—they may brown dif-ferently from stone to stone.) Remove each pizza as it is done by nudging it onto the peel with a spatula or pair of tongs. Allow a few minutes for the stone to reheat before cooking another pizza on it.

To bake the pizzas without a pizza stone: Choose a heavy 12-inch skillet with a heatproof handle—cast iron is ideal. Lightly oil the bottom of the skillet, place the dough circle in the skillet, and arrange the toppings over the dough as described above. Set the skillet directly on the floor of the oven and cook until the underside is evenly deep golden brown, about 6 minutes. (If you have two such skillets, you may bake two pizzas at a time.) The pizzas may be baked on cornmeal-sprinkled cookie sheets as well. Arrange one rack in the lowest position and one in the upper third of the oven before preheating the oven. Slip one dough circle onto each cookie sheet, then top as described above. Bake two pizzas at a time, rotating the sheets from side to side and shelf to shelf once during baking. Pizzas baked on sheets will take from 10 to 12 minutes.

Neapolitan Pizza Sauce

Salsa per la Pizza Napoletana

One 14-ounce can Italian plum tomatoes (preferably San Marzano), drained

1 tablespoon extra-virgin olive oil

1 teaspoon salt

1 teaspoon dried oregano

¼ teaspoon crushed hot red pepper, or more to taste

Makes about 2 cups

Let as much liquid as possible drain from the tomatoes by cutting out the cores and allowing the juices and seeds inside to escape, and then squeezing them gently with your hands. If the tomatoes are too wet, the crust won't cook properly. Whether you choose a food mill or food processor to grind the tomatoes, make sure they stay a little chunky.

As with all the measurements for seasoning in this book, the amount of oregano I call for is a guideline. If you like a pronounced flavor of oregano, by all means add more.

Pass the tomatoes through a food mill fitted with the coarse disc into a mixing bowl. (Alternatively, you may pulse the tomatoes briefly, using quick on/off bursts, in the food processor.) Add the olive oil, salt, oregano, and crushed red pepper.

Pizza Margherita Made with Fresh Tomatoes and Sliced Mozzarella

Pizza alla Margherita Contemporanea

Pizza Dough (page 201)

3 tablespoons extra-virgin olive oil

Coarse cornmeal

2 large ripe tomatoes, cored and sliced ¼ inch thick

¾ pound fresh mozzarella, sliced ¼ inch thick

Salt

20 fresh basil leaves, cut into very thin strips

Makes four 12-inch pizzas

In the cantine or kitchens of Naples, you're likely to see, hanging from strings, clusters of pomodorini (cherry tomatoes) put there at summer's end to preserve their flavor for the cold winter months ahead. Because of their dry texture, these pomodorini are ideal for topping pizzas. If you'd like to approximate the texture and taste of cantina-dried pomodorini, cut ripe cherry tomatoes in half, arrange them, cut side down, on a baking sheet, and dry them overnight in the oven with only the pilot light lit. If you're using regular or plum tomatoes, be sure to slice them thin and not to cover them with slices of mozzarella, or else they won't dry and will make the crust soggy and undercooked.

Prepare the pizza dough, dividing into four portions after the first rising.

When the dough has risen for the second time, place the oven rack in the lowest position, center a pizza stone on it, and preheat the oven to 475° F. (See page 202 for notes on baking pizzas without a stone.)

Roll or stretch each dough ball out to a 12-inch circle about ¼ inch thick with a slightly thicker border around the edge. Brush each circle lightly with some of the olive oil. Working with one circle of dough at a time, sprinkle a pizza peel or flat baking sheet generously with the cornmeal. Place the dough on top and arrange alternating slices of tomato and mozzarella to cover the dough, leaving a thin border around the edge. Sprinkle the pizza lightly with salt and scatter some of the basil over it. Drizzle a little of the remaining olive oil over the cheese.

Bake the pizzas on a stone, in a skillet, or on cookie sheets, as described on page 202.

Sicilian-style pizzas are known for their thicker crusts and deep indentations in the dough, which absorb olive oil and the pizza sauce. This is a simple pizza, but don't be afraid to add whatever you like as a topping. Onion and olives are two of my favorites. If you've never worked with pizza dough before, this is a good place to start. You don't have to worry about stretching or rolling the dough out too thin, or getting an unbaked pizza onto (or off) a pizza peel.

Sicilian Pizza

Pizza Siciliana

Pizza Dough (page 201)

   3 tablespoons extra-virgin olive oil

   ½ cup Neapolitan Pizza Sauce (page 203)

Salt

   1 cup grated mozzarella cheese

   20 fresh basil leaves, cut into very thin strips

Makes two 8-inch square pizzas

Prepare the pizza dough, dividing the dough into two equal portions before the second rising.

Place the oven rack in the center position and preheat the oven to 475° F. Using a little of the olive oil, grease two 8-inch square baking pans.

Place a dough ball in each prepared pan. Stretch and push the dough out with your fingertips to a roughly even layer in the pan. Press firmly with your fingertips to leave deep indentations in the dough. Then brush with the remaining olive oil, allowing it to collect in the indentations. Spread the pizza sauce over the pizzas, dividing it evenly. Sprinkle the sauce with salt and scatter the cheese and basil over the sauce.

Bake the pizzas, rotating them so they cook evenly, until the underside is deep golden brown and crispy, about 20 minutes. Let stand a few minutes before removing from the pans and cutting into slices.

Calzoni ("big socks"), named for the shape, are found in all shapes and sizes, and with all different fillings, in and around Campania.

Calzones

1 pound fresh ricotta, or one 15-ounce container whole-milk ricotta

Pizza Dough (page 201)

2 medium leeks, white and light-green parts only, trimmed and cleaned (see page 80)

3 tablespoons extra-virgin olive oil, plus more for brushing the calzones

Salt

Freshly ground black pepper

1 pound fresh bunch spinach, stems removed, leaves washed and drained, or one 10-ounce bag spinach

12 ounces fresh mozzarella, cut into 1/2-inch cubes

Coarse cornmeal

**Makes about fifteen
4-inch calzones**

You may be used to the large, pizzeria-size version of calzones, but I'm offering you this more typical Neapolitan version. Once you have the knack of making and filling the dough, the rest is easy. You can put whatever you like inside. Just make sure the fillings are drained of most of their excess liquid — the way I drain the ricotta overnight or squeeze the excess moisture from the spinach.

Line a sieve with a double thickness of cheesecloth or a basket-type coffee filter. Dump the ricotta in and set the sieve over a bowl. Cover with plastic wrap and refrigerate overnight or up to 1 day. Discard the drained liquid.

Prepare the pizza dough. It isn't necessary to divide the dough before the second rising.

Slice the leeks crosswise, 1/2 inch thick. In a large, deep skillet or braising pan, heat 3 tablespoons olive oil over medium-high heat. Add the leeks, season lightly with salt and pepper, and cook until softened, about 4 minutes. Stir in the spinach a large handful at a time, waiting for each handful to wilt somewhat before adding the next. Continue cooking until the spinach is completely wilted and all the liquid is evaporated, about 4 minutes. Drain in a colander, pressing lightly to remove excess liquid. Stir the drained ricotta and mozzarella together in a bowl until blended. Season to taste with salt and pepper.

Place one oven rack in the lowest position and the second rack in the upper third of the oven. Center a baking stone, if using, over the lower rack. Preheat the oven to 450° F. If not using a baking stone, sprinkle two large baking sheets generously with coarse cornmeal.

Divide the dough in half. Working with one half at a time, roll the dough out on a lightly floured surface to about 1/4 inch thick. Cut the dough into 4-inch circles and reserve the unused dough. Spread 3 tablespoons of the cheese mixture in an even layer over half of each circle, leaving a 1/2-inch border around the edge. Top the cheese with about 1 tablespoon of the spinach and leeks. Brush the edges of the circles with water and fold the uncovered dough over the spinach-cheese filling. Seal the edges by pressing firmly with the tips of fork tines or by plaiting the edges. Poke holes into the top of each calzone several times with a fork. Brush the tops of the calzones with olive oil. Let stand until slightly puffed, about 15 minutes.

To bake the calzones on a baking stone: Sprinkle a pizza peel or perfectly flat baking sheet generously with cornmeal. Place three or four of the calzones on the prepared peel and slide them onto one side of the stone, leaving some space between them. Repeat with a second round of three or four calzones. Bake the calzones until lightly browned on the underside, about 8 minutes. Transfer the calzones directly to the upper rack and continue baking until deep golden brown, about 20 minutes. Start baking a second batch on the stone once you remove the first batch.

To bake the calzones on baking sheets: Transfer the calzones to lightly oiled baking sheets. Bake, rotating the pans side to side and shelf to shelf, halfway through cooking, until the calzones are golden brown, about 25 minutes.

Baked either way, let stand at least 10 minutes before serving. They are also delicious at room temperature.

My cousin Sonia and great-uncle
Menigo during the grape harvest
in Busoler, c. 1968

Entrees

The traditional Italian meal can include four or five courses and last for hours. The reason one feels satisfied and not stuffed at the end is that the entire meal is well balanced: from the antipasto through the pasta and on to the main course—always accompanied by vegetables—all the major food groups play a role. In an Italian meal, however, the main course, or *piatto forte* ("strong plate," as it is called), is quite different in its ratio of meat to vegetables from its American—and even its Italian-American—counterpart. Take, for example, the Italian-American "Sunday Sauce" on page 213. When cooked in and around Naples, that same sauce would call for one piece of pork to flavor the sauce *and* provide the protein for the meal. The Italian-American version, which I offer you, is filled with meatballs, sausages, and braciole.

In that recipe and others that follow, I use the New World portions of proteins. If you have a houseful of hungry teenagers, or if you like to eat like this, then by all means follow the guidelines I've set up for you. But keep in mind that, when served alongside two or more dishes from the *contorni* chapter, the recipes in this chapter that serve four can easily serve six.

The marvel of the Italian cuisine is that vegetables are an integral part of the majority of its dishes. Most pasta dishes contain vegetables as part of the sauce, starting with tomatoes and moving on to include mushrooms, broccoli rabe, and just about any kind of vegetable you can imagine. In meat and fish preparations, peppers, mushrooms, and tomatoes make a *pizzaiola* sauce; olives and capers are at the base of a *livornese;* a traditional tripe recipe has chunks of celery and carrot; a beefsteak *giambotta* has potatoes, peppers, and onions alongside cubes of tenderloin; sausages are simmered with crunchy bell peppers or bitter broccoli rabe, and so on.

Most of the recipes that follow contain some vegetables, or suggestions for which vegetables to serve alongside the meat or fish. I feel very strongly about the place of these side dishes in a meal. A meal without vegetables is a sorry meal indeed. And that doesn't apply to just Italian meals or the Italian-American menus I hope you create from this book. I'd like you to use this philosophy when you cook anything: how does a pan-seared hamburger with tomatoes, onions, and peppers cooked right alongside it sound to you?

Beef

This is a typical Italian-American Sunday meal if ever there was one. Serve the braciole as they are, or fish them out of the sauce, arrange them on a platter, and serve the sauce with rigatoni or gnocchi. Sausages and meatballs may also be added to the pot for an even more bountiful dinner. (See the recipe for "Sunday Sauce," which follows.)

Braised Beef Rolls

Braciole di Manzo

For the Braciole

1 ½ cups milk

2 cups cubed (½-inch) day-old Italian bread, crusts removed

2 hard-boiled eggs, peeled and coarsely chopped

¼ cup chopped fresh Italian parsley

¼ cup freshly grated Parmigiano-Reggiano cheese

¼ cup raisins

¼ cup toasted pine nuts (see page 149)

1 clove garlic, chopped fine

2 pounds beef bottom round, cut into 12 slices, each about ½ inch thick, or slice yourself following illustration on page 212

To make the stuffing: Pour the milk into a medium bowl, add the bread cubes, and let soak until the bread is very soft, 20 to 30 minutes. Drain the bread, squeeze out excess milk from the cubes with your hands, and return it to the bowl. Stir in the chopped eggs, parsley, Parmigiano-Reggiano, raisins, pine nuts, and garlic. Mix well and set aside.

Following the illustrations on page 212, with the toothed side of a heavy meat mallet, pound each slice of beef round to a thickness of about ¼ inch. Arrange one of the pounded meat slices in front of you with one of the short sides closest to you. Top with a slice of prosciutto, and tap the prosciutto with the back side of a knife so it adheres to the beef. Spread 2 tablespoons of the stuffing along the edge of the meat closest to you, leaving a ½-inch border. Place a stick of provolone over the stuffing. Fold the border over the provolone, then fold the side borders in to overlap the edges of the stuffing. Roll into a compact roll about 4 inches long. Secure the end flap with a toothpick. Repeat with the remaining beef and stuffing, then season the rolls with salt and pepper.

To brown the braciole and start the sauce: Heat 3 tablespoons olive oil in a large, heavy casserole over medium heat. Stir in the onions and garlic and cook until the onion is wilted, about 5 minutes. Add as many of the braciole as will fit in a single layer and cook, turning the braciole as necessary, until golden on all sides, about 7 minutes. If necessary, repeat with any remaining braciole. Adjust the heat under the pan as necessary to prevent the beef from scorching.

12 slices imported Italian prosciutto (about 6 ounces)

¼ pound imported provola or provolone cheese, cut into ¼ × ¼ × 2-inch sticks

Salt

Freshly ground black pepper

For the Sauce

3 tablespoons extra-virgin olive oil

2 small onions (about 8 ounces), chopped

2 cloves garlic, chopped fine

One 35-ounce can Italian plum tomatoes (preferably San Marzano)

½ cup dry red wine

3 tablespoons tomato paste

2 bay leaves

Water as needed

Salt

Crushed hot red pepper

Makes 6 servings

Meanwhile, empty the tomatoes into a bowl and squeeze them with your hands until coarsely crushed, removing the cores as you do.

If necessary, return all the braciole to the casserole. Pour the wine into the casserole, bring to a boil, and cook until most of the wine has evaporated. Stir in the tomatoes and bring to a boil. Add tomato paste and bay leaves and stir until the paste is dissolved. Season lightly with salt and crushed red pepper, adjust the heat to simmering, and cook, adding water as necessary to keep the braciole completely submerged, until the beef is tender, about 3 hours.

Remove the toothpicks before serving. The braciole can be prepared up to 2 days in advance, then reheated over low heat until heated through.

☞ The slices of beef should measure about 4 to 5 inches on each side before pounding. To obtain pieces of the right size, you want to cut—or ask your butcher to do it—six ½-inch-thick slices from the widest part of a bottom round, then cut those slices crosswise into two pieces.

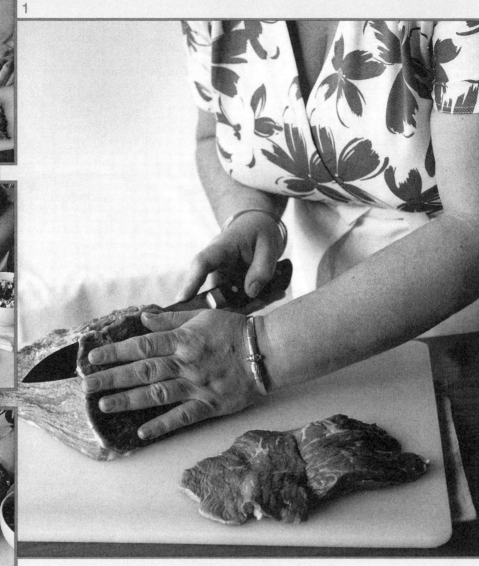

Preparing Braciole

1. Cut, against the grain, half-inch slices of beef, using your other hand pressed against the meat as a guide.

2. With the toothed side of a meat mallet, pound each slice of beef to a ¼-inch thickness.

3. After setting the filling in place, start folding the edge of the meat over the provolone.

4. Then fold the side borders in to overlap the edges of the stuffing.

5. Secure the end flap of the roll with a toothpick.

THIS SAUCE IS TRADITIONALLY SIMMERED for hours, until a finger's width of oil floats on top. Typically that oil was then reincorporated into the sauce. In true Italian family style, pass platters of the meat with some sauce spooned over them, and bowls of pasta dressed with the sauce around the table. *Buon appetito.*

Makes 12 servings

Prepare the braciole as described above, increasing the ingredients for the sauce to the following amounts: $1/3$ cup olive oil, 4 small onions, 4 cloves garlic, three 35-ounce cans tomatoes (crushed), 1 cup red wine, and 4 bay leaves.

After the braciole have been simmering in the sauce for about $1^1/2$ hours, add 2 pounds of hot or sweet Italian sausages (or a mixture of both), poked all over with a fork and browned. Prepare meatballs (page 135), brown them as directed, and add them to the pot after the braciole have been simmering for about 2 hours.

When the meats are cooked, transfer them to platters, spoon a little sauce over them, and cover with aluminum foil to keep warm. Cook 2 pounds rigatoni according to package directions, drain well, and return to the cooking pot. Add enough of the sauce to coat the rigatoni lightly, season with grated Parmigiano-Reggiano or Pecorino Romano cheese, and transfer the sauced pasta to a large platter. Pass any remaining sauce and some grated cheese separately.

Italian-American "Sunday Sauce"

To: Lidia Bastianich
From: Elisa Mezzacappa
Subject:

>>>Your show on making ragù was just wonderful. I remember so well waking up to the aromas of my mom's Sunday sauce and all the love, warmth, comfort, and security that it meant.<<<

Pan-Seared Steak with *Pizzaiola* Sauce

Bistecca alla Pizzaiola

1 small red and 1 small yellow bell pepper, cored, seeded, and cut into ½-inch slices (about 3 cups total)

Salt

4 strip or shell steaks, trimmed of most fat, each about 6 ounces and ¾ inch thick

5 tablespoons extra-virgin olive oil

6 cloves garlic, peeled

1½ cups sliced assorted mushrooms

Freshly ground black pepper

3 cups peeled, seeded, and crushed ripe plum tomatoes (see page 9), or one 35-ounce can Italian plum tomatoes (preferably San Marzano), seeded and crushed

1 teaspoon crushed hot red pepper

4 to 6 fresh basil leaves, shredded

Makes 4 servings

Stir the sliced peppers into a large pot of salted boiling water. Return to a boil, cook 2 minutes, and drain. Rinse with cold water and let cool.

Rub both sides of the steaks with 1 tablespoon of the olive oil and let them stand at room temperature while preparing the sauce. Place a large heavy skillet—cast iron is ideal—over low heat.

Heat the remaining 4 tablespoons olive oil in a separate large skillet over medium heat. Whack the garlic with the flat side of a knife, add to the oil, and cook, shaking the pan occasionally, until golden on all sides, about 3 minutes. Stir in the mushrooms, season them lightly with salt and pepper, and stir until wilted and caramelized, about 6 minutes. Pour in the tomatoes and stir in the crushed red pepper. Bring to a boil, adjust the heat to simmering, and cook 8 minutes. Stir in the sliced peppers and the basil. Simmer, stirring occasionally, until the peppers are crisp-tender, about 2 minutes. Remove the garlic cloves or, if you like, leave them in. Cover the skillet to keep the sauce warm.

Raise the heat under the empty skillet to medium-high. Add the steaks and cook until the underside is well browned, about 4 minutes. Turn the steaks and cook 3 minutes for a medium-rare steak, longer for more well-done steaks. Transfer the steaks to warm plates and spoon some of the *pizzaiola* sauce over each.

Meat-Stuffed Peppers

Peperoni Imbottiti

1/3 cup Arborio rice

Salt

8 cubanella or banana peppers or other long, thin-fleshed peppers, each about 6 inches long

3 tablespoons extra-virgin olive oil

1 medium yellow onion, chopped (about 1 cup)

8 ounces ground meat (see note below)

1 large egg

1/3 cup grated Parmigiano-Reggiano cheese

3 tablespoons chopped fresh Italian parsley

2 teaspoons chopped fresh oregano

3 cups (or as needed) Tomato Sauce (page 151) or sauce that accompanies Chicken Parmigiana, New-Style (page 266)

Makes 4 servings

Peppers with a slight kick to them, like the cubanellas or banana peppers suggested at left, are wonderful for this dish. If you can't find those, choose the long, thin-skinned peppers often sold as "Italian frying peppers" in supermarkets. You can serve the peppers alone or with a side of rigatoni, dressed with some of the sauce from the stuffed-pepper baking dish, grated Pecorino Romano cheese, and a drizzle of olive oil. This is a favorite dish at Becco, our restaurant in New York's Theater District.

Cook the Arborio rice in a large saucepan of boiling salted water until *al dente*—tender but firm—about 12 minutes. Drain and cool to room temperature.

While the rice is cooking, preheat the oven to 400° F, prepare the peppers, and start the filling: Cut the stems from the peppers and scrape out the seeds and membranes with a teaspoon. Heat 2 tablespoons of the olive oil in a small skillet over medium heat. Stir in the onion and cook, stirring, until wilted, about 4 minutes. Scrape the onion into a mixing bowl, add the ground meat, egg, grated cheese, parsley, oregano, and cooked rice, and stir together until evenly blended.

Divide the filling among the peppers, using about 1/4 cup to fill each pepper loosely. Rub the outside of the peppers lightly with the remaining tablespoon of olive oil, placing them in a 13 × 9–inch baking dish as you do so. Roast the peppers, turning once or twice with tongs, until softened and lightly browned in spots, about 20 minutes.

Pour in enough of the tomato sauce barely to cover the peppers. Cover the dish with aluminum foil and bake until the peppers are tender and the filling is cooked through, 30 to 40 minutes. Remove, and let stand 10 minutes before serving.

☞ A mix of ground beef, pork, and veal is best, but that might not be practical. Try at least to use a blend of ground pork and beef, but, failing that, all ground beef or pork will do.

This is sort of a quick version of the Giambotta on page 332, with the delicious addition of seared cubes of tender filet mignon. It makes an all-in-one meal that is a great way to deal with an end-of-the-season harvest from your kitchen garden.

Seared Filet Mignon with Braised Chunky Vegetables

Filetto di Bue con Giambotta di Verdure

2 medium Idaho potatoes (about 1 pound), peeled and cut into 1-inch cubes (about 3 cups)

Salt

½ cup vegetable oil

1½ pounds filet mignon, trimmed of excess fat and cut into 1-inch cubes

Freshly ground black pepper

½ cup extra-virgin olive oil

3 cloves garlic, peeled

2 small onions, peeled and cut into 1-inch chunks (about 2 cups)

2 small red bell peppers, cored, seeded, and cut into 1-inch cubes (about 2 cups)

2 small yellow bell peppers, cored, seeded, and cut into 1-inch cubes (about 2 cups)

Stir the potatoes into a large saucepan of boiling salted water. Return to a boil and cook just until the potatoes are tender when poked with the tip of a knife, about 4 minutes. The potatoes should still be quite firm. Drain the potatoes and spread them out on a baking sheet to cool.

Heat the vegetable oil in a small skillet over medium heat. Carefully slip half the potatoes into the oil and fry, turning them in the oil until golden and crisp on all sides, about 6 minutes. Remove them with a slotted spoon to a baking sheet lined with paper towels. Repeat with the remaining potatoes.

Season the beef with salt and pepper.

Heat ¼ cup of the olive oil in a large skillet over medium heat. Whack the garlic with the flat side of a knife and add to the oil. Cook, shaking the skillet, until golden, about 3 minutes. Scatter the onions into the skillet and cook, stirring occasionally, until softened, about 5 minutes. Add the red and yellow peppers, season lightly with salt and pepper, and cook, stirring, until the peppers are softened, about 5 minutes. Add the zucchini, season lightly with salt and pepper, and cook, stirring gently, until the vegetables are browned and tender, about 7 minutes. Add potatoes and toss.

After adding the zucchini, heat the remaining ¼ cup olive oil in a separate large skillet—preferably nonstick or well-seasoned cast iron—over medium-high heat. Pat the filet dry with paper towels and add half the cubes to the oil in the skillet. Cook, turning the meat in the oil, until seared on all sides but still quite pink in the center, about 4 minutes. Remove with a slotted spoon to a plate. Repeat with the remaining filet. (If the vegetables are ready before the meat is browned, remove them from the heat and cover to keep warm.)

2 small ("fancy") zucchini, ends trimmed, quartered lengthwise, and cut into 1-inch cubes (about 2 cups)

½ cup shredded fresh basil leaves

Makes 6 servings

When the second batch of filet is browned, leave it in the skillet, but tilt the skillet and spoon off excess fat. If you haven't already done so, remove the vegetables from the heat. Spoon half of the vegetable mixture into the skillet that still contains half the meat, and add the first batch of meat to the vegetables remaining in the skillet. (You now have two skilletfuls of a more or less even mix of seared filet and vegetables.) Place both skillets over low heat, divide the basil between them, and toss gently to mix. Taste, and season with salt and pepper if necessary. Serve immediately on warm plates.

Me with my son, Joseph, and daughter, Tanya, in Astoria, Queens, c. 1975

This is one of those dishes in which I combine the old with the new. The technique and seasonings in this dish are very close to a *guazetto*, a way of braising typical to the region of Italy in which I was born. But the use of short ribs and the way I reduce the wine before adding it to the stew bring it up to date and into America.

Beef Short Ribs Braised in Red Wine

Costolettine di Manzo Brasate

One 750-milliliter bottle dry
    red wine

  3 to 4 cups hot Chicken
    Stock (page 74) or
    canned reduced-sodium
    chicken broth

  ½ cup dried porcini
    mushrooms

  6 pounds beef short ribs,
    cut into 5- to 6-ounce
    pieces

Salt

Freshly ground black pepper

  ¼ cup vegetable oil

  2 large onions, chopped
    (about 3 cups)

  ¼ cup minced bacon or
    pancetta

1 ½ cups grated carrot

  2 sprigs fresh rosemary

  4 fresh or dried bay leaves

  6 whole cloves

  ⅓ cup tomato paste

  2 cups crushed Italian plum
    tomatoes (preferably San
    Marzano) and their liquid

Makes 6 servings

Bring the red wine to a boil in a medium saucepan. Lower the heat so the wine is boiling gently and cook until the wine is reduced to 1 cup. Set aside.

Pour 1 cup of the hot stock over the mushrooms in a small, heatproof bowl. Let stand until softened, about 20 minutes. Drain the mushrooms in a sieve lined with a double thickness of cheesecloth or a coffee filter; reserve the soaking liquid. Rinse the mushrooms briefly to remove any grit. Chop the mushrooms coarsely and set them aside.

Season the ribs generously with salt and pepper. Heat the oil in a wide, heavy braising pan over medium heat. Lay as many of the short rib pieces as will fit into the pan in a single layer. Cook, turning as necessary, until evenly and well browned on all sides. Remove them to a plate and repeat with the remaining ribs. Adjust the heat as the ribs cook, so that they brown without burning.

Pour off all but about 2 tablespoons of the fat from the pan. Stir in the onions and bacon and cook, stirring, until the onions are lightly browned, about 6 minutes. Stir in the carrot, rosemary, bay leaves, and cloves. Season lightly with salt and pepper, and cook until the carrot is wilted, about 3 minutes. Drop in the tomato paste and stir well until the vegetables are coated and the tomato paste begins to darken, 2 to 3 minutes. Pour in the reduced wine and the crushed tomatoes and tuck the browned short ribs into the pan. Pour in enough of the remaining chicken stock to barely cover the ribs. Bring to a boil, then lower the heat so the liquid is at a lively simmer. Cook, adding the remaining stock a little at a time as necessary to keep the ribs covered, until the ribs are tender and just about to fall off the bone, 2½ to 3 hours. Taste the cooking liquid from time to time as the ribs cook and add salt if necessary.

Pick out the ribs from the sauce, carefully so as to prevent the bone from falling out, and set them on a baking sheet. Ladle the cooking liquid into a sieve placed over a bowl and push the liquid through with the back of the ladle. Discard the solids in the sieve and return the strained liquid to the pan. Tuck the ribs back into the sauce. You may serve the ribs at this point, or cool them in the liquid and refrigerate them for up to three days. Bring them back to a simmer and cook until heated through before serving.

Garlic

GARLIC IS IMMEDIATELY ASSOCIATED with Italian cooking. Yes, we Italians use garlic abundantly in our cuisine, but it is in Italian-American cooking that garlic became so dominant and ever-present.

Garlic is used much more in the southern part of the Italian peninsula than in the north, where onions often form the base of a dish. A majority of the first Italian immigrants who came to America at the turn of the twentieth century were from the southern part of Italy. Cooking in the new land must have been a difficult adjustment, since most of the pungent and fresh herbs they cooked with—basil, oregano, thyme, bay leaves, and rosemary—were not available. Garlic, however, was available, and offered a lot of the intensity that the newcomers missed. So garlic was used with abandon.

Garlic's flavor is released when the cell walls are broken and the enzymes react with the flavor molecules. Therefore, the more you chop garlic, the more intense its aroma and flavor. There are different ways you can control the level of pungency when you cook with garlic.

For a milder garlic flavor, crush whole cloves of garlic by whacking them with the flat side of a knife before you add them to a dish. Cooking with crushed cloves of garlic, as I often do, has the added benefit of making the garlic easy to remove from the dish before serving, if that's what you choose to do.

Sliced garlic cloves will give you more flavor than crushed cloves, but can be selectively set aside, either by you before you serve the dish, or by your guests before they eat it. On the other hand, chopped garlic yields the most flavor, and most likely it will remain in the dish unless it is in a sauce that you can strain. As you can see in the recipes throughout the book, most of the garlic I use is either crushed whole cloves or sliced (because it is easy for people to spot and remove, if they choose). In the few instances in which I use finely chopped garlic in a recipe, I prefer to chop it with a knife rather than squeeze it through a press.

Cooking garlic gently and thoroughly mellows its pungency. Whole garlic cloves baked slowly while still in their skin, or peeled garlic cloves simmered till tender in milk, stock, or water, will give you a much milder garlic flavor and a more velvety texture than those that are lightly cooked, or not cooked at all.

Veal and Organ Meats

Taleggio is a cow's-milk cheese with a complex flavor and, when mature, a runny texture. If you can, prepare these chops with a younger, firmer Taleggio. If the Taleggio you're using for these chops is too soft to slice, simply stir the cheese and broccoli together to blend, then stuff the chops with this mixture.

Veal Chops Stuffed with Taleggio and Broccoli

Costolette di Vitello Imbottiti

1 scant cup broccoli florets, in pieces no larger than 1/2 inch

Salt

1 cup canned Italian plum tomatoes (preferably San Marzano)

5 ounces Taleggio cheese, sliced thin

4 thin slices (about 2 ounces) imported Italian prosciutto

4 bone-in veal rib chops, each about 10 ounces and 1 inch thick

Freshly ground black pepper

All-purpose flour

3 tablespoons extra-virgin olive oil

4 tablespoons unsalted butter

8 fresh sage leaves

Cook the broccoli florets in a medium saucepan of boiling salted water until tender but still bright green, about 4 minutes. Drain the broccoli and rinse under cold water until cool. Drain thoroughly.

Pass the tomatoes and their liquid through a food mill fitted with the fine disc, or blend them in a food processor or blender, using quick on/off pulses, just until smooth. (Overblending the tomatoes will incorporate air into them and turn them pink.)

Make 4 more or less even stacks with the cheese slices and cover each with a folded slice of prosciutto. Lay the broccoli florets along one edge of each stack, dividing the florets evenly. Roll the cheese and prosciutto around the broccoli into neat and compact rolls. Set the rolls aside.

Lay a veal chop flat on a cutting board. Following the illustrations on pages 222–3, make a horizontal cut through the meat all the way to the bone and open the chop up, butterflying it. With the smooth side of a meat mallet, gently pound each side until the veal is about 3/8 inch thick. Place a cheese roll over one side of the butterflied veal chop, close to the bone. Fold the other side of the chop over the filling to completely enclose the filling. Pound around the edges of the stuffed chop with the toothed side of the meat mallet to seal in the stuffing. For an extra measure of security, you may fasten the edges of the stuffed chop with a toothpick. Press the stuffed chops gently, to

⅔ cup dry white wine

1 ⅓ cups Chicken Stock (page 74) or canned reduced-sodium chicken broth

Makes 4 servings

flatten them slightly. Repeat with the remaining chops and cheese rolls. Season the stuffed chops with salt and pepper, then dredge them in flour to coat all sides lightly.

Heat the oil and 2 tablespoons of the butter in a large, heavy skillet over medium heat until the butter is light brown. Add the chops to the pan and cook until the underside is golden, about 4 minutes. (If your skillet isn't large enough to accommodate all four chops, divide the chops and sauce ingredients between two skillets.) Turn the chops, scatter the sage leaves around them and cook until the second side is golden, about 3 minutes. Remove the chops from the pan and drain the fat, reserving the sage leaves.

Return the chops to the pan, pour in the wine and add the remaining 2 tablespoons butter. Bring to a boil and cook until the liquid is reduced by half, about 5 minutes. Stir in the tomatoes, bring to a boil, then pour in the stock. Bring to a boil, lower the heat so the sauce is simmering and cook, covered, until no trace of pink remains near the bone and the sauce is syrupy, about 12 minutes. Turn the chops and baste them with the sauce several times as they simmer.

The chops can also be finished in the oven: Preheat oven to 375° F. After adding stock to the pan, set the uncovered pan in a hot oven and bake, basting periodically for 15 minutes.

Transfer the chops to warm plates and spoon some of the sauce over each. For a clearer sauce, strain it as you spoon it over the chops.

Variation

Veal Chops Stuffed with Asparagus and Fontina

Snap off the tough ends of four thin asparagus spears. Peel the stalk up to the tips and cut them into 1-inch lengths, leaving the tips intact. Cook the asparagus pieces in a small saucepan of boiling salted water until crisp-tender, about 3 minutes. Drain the asparagus and plunge it into a bowl of cold water. Let stand until chilled. Drain the asparagus thoroughly. Prepare the veal chops as described above, substituting Fontina for the Taleggio and the cooked asparagus for the broccoli.

Stuffing a Veal Chop

1. Make a horizontal cut through the meat all the way to the bone.

2. With the smooth side of a meat mallet, gently pound each side until the veal is about $\frac{3}{8}$ inch thick.

3. Place a cheese roll over one side of the butterflied chop, close to the bone.

4. Fold the other side of the chop over the filling.

5. Seal the edges by pounding with the toothed side of the mallet.

6. Fold the pounded side over the chop (you can secure the seal with a toothpick, if you wish).

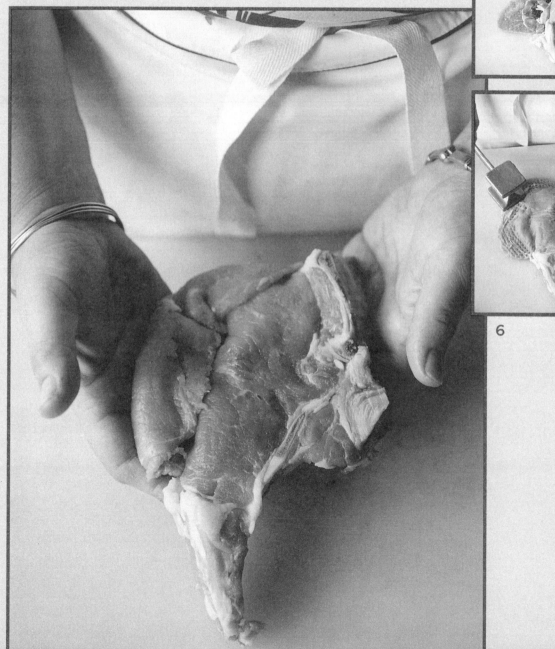

4

5

6

Stuffed Rolls of Veal

Involtini di Vitello

3 tablespoons extra-virgin olive oil

3 cloves garlic, peeled

½ cup fine, dry bread crumbs

1 tablespoon chopped fresh Italian parsley

Salt

Freshly ground black pepper

12 thin slices veal (1½ pounds)

6 ounces provola (young provolone), fresh mozzarella, or Fontina, cut into ¼ × 1½–inch sticks

3 plum tomatoes, peeled and seeded (see page 9), cut into ¼-inch strips

Thin lemon slices, optional

Makes 6 servings

Let the oil and garlic steep in a small bowl 30 minutes to 2 hours.

Toss the bread crumbs with half the infused oil and the parsley. Season to taste with salt and pepper.

Place two of the veal slices between two sheets of plastic wrap and, with the smooth side of a heavy meat mallet, pound each slice of veal into a rough rectangular shape about ¼ inch thick. Don't pound the veal too thin, or there is a possibility that the filling will leak during cooking. Repeat with the remaining veal. Divide the cheese and tomatoes evenly among the slices of veal, placing them along the center of one of the longer edges. Sprinkle half the seasoned bread crumbs over the tomatoes and cheese and drizzle on half the remaining infused oil. Roll the scallopine around the filling into compact rolls. Secure the flap with two toothpicks to keep the rolls intact while they cook.

Preheat the oven to 425° F. Lightly brush a baking pan into which the veal rolls fit comfortably with some of the remaining infused oil. Arrange the veal side by side and seam side down in the prepared dish. Scatter the remaining bread crumbs in an even layer over the veal and drizzle on the remaining infused oil. Bake until the bread crumbs are golden brown and the cheese in the filling is melted, about 20 minutes. Serve as is or with a slice of lemon.

Innards

INNARDS, ALSO CALLED "OFFAL" or "variety meats," are not very popular with Americans. Yet ask any European—or for that matter most chefs—about innards and they will get very excited. But what are innards? To a chef, innards are all the internal organs that can be cooked and eaten, and that means just about every organ.

Being raised as much by my maternal grandparents as by my parents, I was introduced firsthand to the importance of using every bit of food the land offered us. When it came to food, my grandparents were self-sufficient. They grew most of their vegetables; made wine and distilled grappa from the byproducts of winemaking; harvested olives and brought them to the mill to make oil; milled their own wheat for flour and their own corn for polenta. In the courtyard pens there were pigs, sheep, ducks, chickens, goats, and rabbits which were periodically slaughtered for food.

I remember the ritual of slaughter vividly, partly because I was a child who was perplexed by the reality of the food chain. But there truly is a harmony between the elements, and the fact is, we were dependent on these animals for nourishment. Our existence and coexistence with the world around us constitute a master plan that extends beyond our realm, which we have to live in harmony with and respect.

When an animal was slaughtered, every part was used. In comparison with today's perception of chicken—a boneless piece of breast in plastic wrap—my encounters with chicken were with the entire bird. After it was killed and plucked, the head, neck, gizzard, and feet were saved for soup. The liver, heart, and intestines (after being cut open with scissors and washed a dozen times) were made into a frittata with the unlaid eggs. These unlaid eggs, which ranged in size from a peppercorn to a blueberry to a cherry and to a full-grown yolk, were essentially yolks without shells. (Sometimes we would find a whole egg in a shell, soft and pliable because its shell hadn't yet hardened.) With some green onions and virgin olive oil, what a frittata those ingredients would make!

None of the lamb was wasted either. If the head wasn't roasted whole, the brain was sliced, breaded, and fried like veal cutlets and the tongue cooked and tossed in a salad with warm potatoes and red onions. The liver and lungs were sautéed *alla veneziana*—with onions and lots of freshly ground black pepper. The stomach was braised with onions and tomatoes into a great tripe dish, similar to the one on page 228. The sweetbreads, like those from the young calves, were either grilled or blanched, then sautéed with some wine or lemon. (There was an old saying that you rarely find sweetbreads at the butcher shop, and that is because they are so delicious that the butcher eats them himself.)

I do not recommend a daily diet of innards, because they are very caloric and rich, but treat yourself to them occasionally and you'll be surprised at how delicious they can be. With their uniquely diversified flavors, and extraordinary textures that range from the silkiness of liver to the velvety texture of brain and the resilient chewiness of tripe, I know I have to have my fix on a regular basis.

Seared Liver Steak with Onions

Fegato Scottato con Cipolle

5 tablespoons extra-virgin olive oil

2 large white onions, cut into ½-inch strips (about 3½ cups)

6 fresh or dried bay leaves

Salt

1 tablespoon white-wine vinegar

4 slices fresh calf's liver, each about 6 ounces and ¾ inch thick

1 teaspoon coarsely ground black pepper (see note page 139)

Makes 4 servings

When searing meats or fish, the size of the skillet is important. A roomy skillet will retain more heat after you add things to it, and will climb back to searing temperature much more quickly than a smaller skillet. Once you put the slices of liver in the pan, let them sit undisturbed, giving them a chance to form a caramelized crust. If you like your liver rare or medium-rare, as I do, the second side should always cook less than the first—about half the time. If you like more well-done meats, reduce the heat under the pan after you have flipped the meat over to prevent it from scorching, then cook it to your liking. Salt draws liquids and juices from meats, and that is why I season the liver after it is cooked.

Heat 2 tablespoons of the olive oil in a large skillet over medium-high heat. Add the onions and bay leaves, season generously with salt, and cook, stirring often, until golden but still firm, about 8 minutes. Sprinkle the vinegar over the pan, stir until evaporated, and continue cooking until the onions are deep golden brown, glossy, and crisp-tender, about 5 minutes.

Meanwhile, remove any skin and membranes from the liver. Pat the liver dry with paper towels, then toss the pieces gently in a bowl with 2 tablespoons of the remaining olive oil. Heat a heavy skillet wide enough to hold all the pieces of liver without touching over medium-high heat. (A well-seasoned cast-iron or nonstick skillet is ideal. If you don't have a skillet wide enough, cook the liver in two batches.) Lay the liver pieces in the pan and let them cook undisturbed until caramelized on the underside, 3 to 4 minutes. Flip the liver steaks over and cook about 2 minutes for rare liver, longer for more well-done liver. (If you're cooking the liver longer, lower the heat so the liver doesn't scorch.) Remove the pan from the heat, sprinkle the liver with salt, and transfer to warm plates. Toss the ground pepper and remaining 1 tablespoon olive oil with the browned onions. Pluck out the bay leaves and spoon the onions on top of the liver steaks.

Caramelization

CARAMELIZATION IS THE PROGRESSIVE BROWNING that occurs in food. Seemingly a simple process, it is actually a series of very complex chemical reactions. Also known as the Maillard reaction, caramelization requires high temperatures and dry heat.

The process begins at the point where sugars and proteins interact and form new molecules. These complex molecules undergo a series of changes that result in colors ranging from light golden brown to rich mahogany, depending on the length of time and at what temperature they are cooked. But be careful—caramelization is the step before scorching. When browning foods, you should stay close and stir or turn the foods as necessary to get maximum caramelization without any burnt or scorched surfaces, which will impart a bitter, unpleasant flavor to foods.

Caramelization adds much flavor and richness to all of your cooking, both by giving the food a delicious outer coating and by leaving behind little bits of caramelized food in the pan that can be "deglazed" and turned into a pan sauce. When chefs talk about deglazing, they mean adding a liquid—wine, stock, or even water—to dissolve all the browned bits that have stuck to the bottom of the cooking vessel, and scraping those caramelized bits into the sauce as the liquid simmers.

Be aware of that information when choosing a pan for browning. If you use a nonstick pan, although the surface of foods you cook in it caramelize nicely, there won't be much left behind to deglaze and turn into a pan sauce. That isn't so important if what you have browned is going to be simmered in liquid, like the Braised Pork Ribs with Rigatoni on page 245. Also, it's less important if the food you have browned is returned to the pan after you have deglazed it for a final, brief cooking with the pan sauce (as in most of the scallopine recipes). But if the browned food is not cooked at all with the sauce, as is the case with Sweetbreads with Lemon and Capers on page 230, the sauce you make in a nonstick pan will lack the flavor that comes from all those little bits stuck to the pan. So, in recipes like the one for sweetbreads, you're better off with an unlined or untreated pan. Don't worry, that doesn't mean more time spent cleaning your pan—deglazing removes all the flavorful bits that you would otherwise be scrubbing out at the sink.

Tripe in Tomato, Carrot, and Celery Sauce, Roman-Style

Trippa alla Romana

2 pounds honeycomb veal tripe

8 bay leaves

3 tablespoons extra-virgin olive oil

1 medium onion, chopped (about 1 cup)

2 medium carrots, peeled and chopped (about 1 cup)

2 stalks celery (with leaves), trimmed and chopped (about 1 cup)

Salt

1 cup dry white wine

1 teaspoon crushed hot red pepper

3 cups peeled, seeded, and crushed fresh plum tomatoes (see page 9) or one 35-ounce can Italian plum tomatoes (preferably San Marzano), seeded and crushed

2 cups hot water, or as needed

½ cup grated Parmigiano-Reggiano cheese

Makes 6 servings

Texture is a very important part of the gustatory pleasures of tripe. Tripe should be soft and yet resilient; you do not want it mushy. In this recipe, as I do when making many long-simmered sauces, I keep a pot of hot water near the tripe as it simmers. From time to time, I check the tripe, ladling in water if the sauce has cooked down and some of the tripe isn't covered. At the end of cooking, there should be enough sauce so the tripe is nice and juicy but not watery.

Trim any pieces of solid fat from the tripe and wash the tripe thoroughly under cold running water. Put it in a large pot and pour in enough cold water to cover by four to six fingers. Toss in four of the bay leaves and bring to a boil over high heat. Adjust the heat to a gentle boil and cook just until tender when poked with a fork. Don't overcook it to the point where it falls apart when poked.

Pick out the bay leaves, drain the tripe, and cool to room temperature.

When the tripe is cool, cut it into large pieces, removing all remaining pieces of fat that you uncover as you cut. (The most important part in the preparation of tripe is to remove all the fat.) Scrape both sides of the tripe with the back of a chef's knife to remove as many flecks of fat as you can. Clean all working surfaces of fat, and cut the tripe into strips about ½ inch wide and 2 inches long.

Heat the olive oil in a wide casserole over medium heat. Stir in the onion and cook, stirring, until wilted, about 4 minutes. Stir in the carrots and celery, season them lightly with salt, and cook, stirring occasionally, until softened, about 10 minutes. Add the remaining four bay leaves and the tripe and cook, stirring occasionally, until all the juices from the tripe have evaporated and the tripe has begun to caramelize and stick to the bottom of the pot, about 5 minutes. Pour in the wine and bring to a boil. Cook, stirring, until the wine is completely evaporated, about 6 minutes. Season lightly with salt, add the crushed red pepper, and pour in the tomatoes. Bring to a boil, then lower the heat so the sauce is simmering. Simmer until the tripe is tender but still resilient, about 1 hour. Add small amounts of the hot water from time to time while the tripe simmers, as necessary to keep the tripe covered with sauce.

Remove the bay leaves and taste, seasoning with salt and crushed red pepper as necessary. Serve the tripe in warm bowls, topping each helping with some of the grated Parmigiano.

Capers

CAPERS ARE THE BUDS OF A CRAWLING VINE, *Capparis spinosa*. The caper flower is a delicate white in color, with purple stigmas and a beautiful aroma. If you have traveled to southern Italy, specifically Sicily and the islands of Pantelleria and Lipari, you surely have encountered this plant crawling on old *murate* (walls). Although most of the Mediterranean Basin is home to the caper plant, some of the finest come from these islands.

The best capers are hand-picked when the bud is still small and tight. As the bud grows larger and comes closer to blooming, it becomes softer and loses the nutty intensity prized in smaller capers. Larger capers are less desirable and less expensive than tiny, or nonpareil, capers. But they are still very good—especially for sauces and stuffings.

Capers are preserved by dry-packing them in salt or by bottling them in brine. I prefer the ones in brine; if you choose salt-packed capers, make sure you wash them well and salt any dishes you're preparing with them lightly at first.

After the flower has bloomed, it matures into a caper berry, which looks like a gooseberry with a long stem. You can find them packed in a briny vinegar solution. They are crunchy, acidic, and flavorful—much like a pickle—with some hint of the caper's nuttiness. Caper berries are good served as part of an antipasto or tossed into salads, or used in a buttery pan sauce, as on the next page.

Sweetbreads with Lemon and Capers

Animelle con Capperi al Limone

2 whole veal sweetbreads (about 2 pounds)

Salt

Freshly ground black pepper

⅓ cup extra-virgin olive oil

All-purpose flour

4 tablespoons unsalted butter

1 lemon, sliced thin

¼ cup small capers in brine, drained

Juice of 1 lemon

¼ cup dry white wine

½ cup Chicken Stock (page 74) or canned reduced-sodium chicken broth

1 tablespoon chopped fresh Italian parsley

Makes 6 servings

Cleaning, rolling, poaching, and slicing the sweetbreads can be done in advance, but wait until the last minute to cook them and make the sauce. Two whole sweetbreads will serve six people — perfect if you're preparing this recipe for sweetbread lovers. If your circle of sweetbread fans is smaller, simply make this recipe with one sweetbread and cut the rest of the ingredients in half.

Veal sweetbreads are the thymus gland of young calves, which, when cooked, have a delicate flavor and a somewhat firm texture. Look for large, plump pairs of sweetbreads and trim off most of the outer membrane before you cook them, keeping enough intact to hold the sweetbreads together as they poach. (You can always trim more off after they cook.) My method of shaping and poaching the sweetbreads first, then pan-searing them just before serving, helps the sweetbreads keep their shape and reduces the amount of last-minute cooking.

Save any less-than-perfect slices and the trimmings from the end of the sweetbread "sausage" as a treat for the cook, or as a first course for another meal. (If you can't get to enjoy them right away, wrap them tightly and freeze them until you can.) Brown the sweetbread nuggets in a mix of butter and oil until crispy, remove them from the pan and drain them. Sauté some sliced mushrooms in the same pan, then toss the sweetbreads and mushrooms with a green salad dressed with lemon and oil.

Pour enough water into a 4- to 5-quart pot to fill halfway. Bring to a boil over medium heat. Trim the sweetbreads of all fat and peel off the outer membranes, working gently to keep the sweetbreads in one piece. Tear off two 20-inch lengths of plastic wrap and lay one out in front of you with one of the long sides closest to you. Center one of the sweetbreads over the edge of the plastic wrap closest to you and roll it up into a snug roll. Twist the two ends of the plastic wrap simultaneously to force the sweetbread into a neat and very compact large sausage shape. Tie the two ends of the plastic wrap together so the roll holds its shape. Repeat with the remaining sweetbread and plastic wrap. Lower the sweetbread rolls into the boiling water and cook 15 minutes.

Remove the sweetbreads from the water, drain, and cool to room temperature. Chill the sweetbreads on a plate in the refrigerator until cold and firm, at least 3 to 4 hours or up to 1 day.

Preheat the oven to 200° F. Unwrap the chilled sweetbreads, pat them dry, and cut them crosswise into $\frac{1}{2}$-inch slices. (You should have about ten perfect slices from each sweetbread roll.) Season the slices with salt and pepper. Heat the olive oil in a large skillet over medium heat. While the oil is heating, dredge the sweetbread slices in flour to coat both sides lightly, tap off excess flour, and add to the skillet as many slices as will fit without touching. Cook, turning once, until golden brown on both sides, about 3 minutes. Transfer to a baking sheet and keep warm in the oven. Continue with the remaining sweetbreads.

Pour off the oil from the skillet, return it to the heat, and add the butter. Heat until foaming, then scatter the lemon slices over the butter. Cook, stirring gently from time to time, until golden, 3 to 4 minutes. Remove the lemon to a plate, let the butter reheat a minute, then scatter the capers into the pan. Cook until they begin to sizzle, then pour in the lemon juice and wine. Bring to a vigorous boil, and boil until the liquid is reduced by about half, about 3 minutes. Pour in the stock, bring to a boil, and cook until the sauce is slightly syrupy, about 6 minutes. Stir in the parsley, taste the sauce, and season it with salt and pepper. Center the sweetbreads on hot plates, spoon some of the sauce over each serving, and arrange the lemon slices over or around the sweetbreads.

Pork and Lamb

Don't buy the super-expensive *tradizionale* balsamic vinegar to make this reduction. A good-quality supermarket brand is best. When it is reduced, you'll find the flavor of the balsamic as complex as really good chocolate—a little of the reduction goes a long way.

Oven-Braised Pork Chops with Red Onions and Pears

Costolette di Maiale Brasate in Forno con Pere e Cipolle

2 cups balsamic vinegar

3 tablespoons extra-virgin olive oil

6 cloves garlic, peeled

4 center-cut pork rib chops, each about 12 ounces and 1¼ inches thick

1 large red onion (about 12 ounces), cut through the core into 8 wedges

Salt

Freshly ground black pepper

2 ripe but firm Bosc pears, peeled, cored, and each cut into 8 wedges

¼ cup red-wine vinegar

2 tablespoons honey

Makes 4 servings

The sugar in the honey helps to caramelize the pork, onion, and pears as they oven-braise. It is a technique that works well with other roasted meats and birds as well. Just mix a little honey with the pan juices and baste or brush the roast with that during the last 10 minutes or so of roasting.

For some dishes, you want the onions cut fine, so they almost disappear. Here, I cut the onions large—and the pears, too—so they keep their shape and don't fall apart. Even when ripe, Bosc pears stay firmer than most, making them just right for this dish.

In a small saucepan, bring the balsamic vinegar to a boil over high heat. Adjust the heat to a gentle boil, and boil until the vinegar is syrupy and reduced to about ⅓ cup. Set aside.

Preheat the oven to 425° F. Heat the oil in a large, heavy skillet with a flame-proof handle over medium-high heat. Whack the garlic cloves with the flat side of a knife and scatter them over the oil. Cook, shaking the skillet, until brown, about 2 minutes. Lay the pork chops in and cook until the underside is browned, about 6 minutes. Remove and reserve the garlic cloves if they become more than deep golden brown before the chops are fully browned.

Turn the chops, tuck the onion wedges into the pan, and continue cooking until the second sides of the chops are browned, about 6 minutes. Season with salt and pepper. About halfway through browning the second side, tuck the pear wedges in between the chops.

Stir the red-wine vinegar and honey together in a small bowl, until the honey is dissolved. Pour the vinegar-honey mixture into the skillet and bring to a vigorous boil. Return the garlic cloves to the skillet if you have removed them. Place the skillet in the oven and roast until the onions and pears are tender and the juices from the pork are a rich, syrupy dark brown, about 30 minutes. Once or twice during roasting, turn the chops and redistribute the onions and pears. Handle the skillet carefully—it will be extremely hot.

Remove the skillet from the oven. Place a chop in the center of each warmed serving plate. Check the seasoning of the onion-pear mixture, adding salt and pepper if necessary. Spoon the pears, onion, and pan juices around the chops. Drizzle the balsamic-vinegar reduction around the edge of the plate.

My grandfather
Giovanni in
Busoler, c. 1971

Pork Chops Capricciosa

Costolette di Maiale alla Capricciosa

For the Pork Chops

2 loin pork chops, from the rib end of the loin, each about 8 ounces and ¾ inch thick

Salt

Freshly ground black pepper

All-purpose flour

1 cup fine, dry bread crumbs

1 large egg

¼ cup vegetable oil

2 tablespoons olive oil

For the Salad

4 cups arugula, washed and dried (preferably in a salad spinner) and torn into large pieces

1 ripe beefsteak tomato, or 3 ripe plum tomatoes, cored and cut into 1-inch chunks (about 1 cup)

½ small red onion, sliced thin (about 1 cup)

4 ounces fresh mozzarella cheese, cut into 1-inch cubes (about ⅔ cup), optional

¼ cup extra-virgin olive oil

1½ tablespoons red-wine vinegar, or to taste

Salt

Freshly ground black pepper

**Makes 2 servings
(can easily be doubled)**

"Frenching" the chops — cleaning up the bone — prevents the "eye" of the meat, which is pounded out, from overcooking before the meat next to the bone is cooked, and it does make the finished chops look pretty. It is something I do for guests in my restaurants, and it is easy enough for you to learn and do at home. You can, of course, prepare this recipe without Frenching the chops; just be careful that the meat next to the bones is fully cooked before you serve the chops.

You can prepare most of the ingredients — even bread the pork chops — in advance, but don't fry the pork, slice the onion, or toss the salad until the last minute.

Without the mozzarella in the salad, these chops are perfect for lunch or a light dinner. With the mozzarella, they are more substantial. You can use balsamic vinegar in place of all or part of the wine vinegar if you like. As always, dress the salad first with olive oil to coat the leaves, then sprinkle in vinegar to taste.

To French the chops, first cut away as much meat and fat as possible from the last 2 inches or so of the bone. Clean the exposed part of the bone further by scraping with the back of the knife. To get the Frenched part of the bone really clean, grab onto the remaining meat and fat with a kitchen towel and pull it from the bone, leaving the Frenched part of the bone completely stripped. (You can reserve the trimmed meat and fat to use in the *luganega* sausages on page 240.) Place the chops between two sheets of plastic wrap and pound the meat with the smooth side of a meat mallet to a thickness of about ⅓ inch. If you find the chops aren't thinning out, switch to the toothed side of the mallet for a few strokes, then back to the smooth side. Season the chops lightly with salt and pepper.

Preheat the oven to 400° F. Spread out the flour and bread crumbs on two separate plates or sheets of wax paper. Beat the egg in a wide, shallow bowl until thoroughly blended. Dredge the chops in flour to coat them lightly and tap off any excess flour. Dip in the beaten egg and hold them over the bowl, letting the excess egg drip back into the bowl. Move the chops to the bread crumbs and turn to coat completely, patting them gently to make sure the bread crumbs adhere.

Heat the vegetable oil and 2 tablespoons olive oil in a wide, heavy skillet over medium heat until a corner of one of the coated chops gives off a lively sizzle when dipped in the oil. Lay the chops in the oil and fry, turning once, until golden on both sides, about 6 minutes. Transfer to a baking sheet and bake until no trace of pink remains near the bone, about 6 minutes.

Meanwhile, prepare the salad: Toss the arugula, tomato, onion, and mozzarella, if using, together with $\frac{1}{4}$ cup olive oil in a large bowl until the vegetables are coated. Add vinegar, and salt and pepper to taste, and toss well.

Remove the chops from the oven. If they look a little oily, drain them briefly on paper towels. Arrange one chop in the center of each plate and mound half the salad over each chop. Serve immediately.

In Rome, where it is an honored tradition, making *porchetta* is a big event. First a whole suckling pig is boned, leaving just the meat attached to the skin. The meat is rubbed with an herb paste and then rolled up tight, skin side out, like a big jelly roll. After cooking on a spit for up to a day, it is rested for five to six hours before it is sliced and made into glorious sandwiches or served with some crusty bread and a sprinkle of salt. The best part for a Roman—or anyone, for that matter—is the crispy, crackling skin. *Porchetta* is sold in restaurants, in *trattorie*, and in the streets of Rome and the nearby country-side. The simplified version I offer here is a close runner-up to the Roman *porchetta* in flavor and can be done very easily at home.

Pot-Roasted Herb-Scented Pork Loin

Porchetta

½ cup fresh rosemary leaves, plus two fresh rosemary sprigs

6 tablespoons extra-virgin olive oil

10 cloves garlic

16 fresh sage leaves

2 teaspoons salt

3½ pounds boneless loin of pork roast (see note below)

1 bay leaf

Freshly ground black pepper

Makes 8 servings

Put ½ cup rosemary leaves, 3 tablespoons of the oil, five of the garlic cloves, eight of the sage leaves, and 1 teaspoon of the salt in the work bowl of a food processor or blender jar. Process or blend until you have a fairly smooth paste.

Following the illustrations on page 238, lay the loin on the work surface fat side down. Cut along the top side of the "tail" and into the eye of the roast. Continue your cut in a sawing motion, "unrolling" the loin into a rectangle of more or less even thickness. (The process is similar to that described in the recipe for Prosciutto-Stuffed Mozzarella on page 55). Spread the herb paste evenly over the entire top surface of the pork. Starting with the side of the pork opposite the tail, roll the roast into a compact roll with a spiral of the herb filling running through it. Tie the roast securely at 1-inch intervals with kitchen twine. Season the outside of the roast generously with salt and pepper.

Set the loin in a heavy flameproof casserole into which it fits snugly. (A round 5-quart casserole is ideal.) Add the rosemary sprigs, remaining 8 sage leaves, remaining 5 garlic cloves and the bay leaf. Pour in just enough water to cover the meat. Season the water lightly with salt and pepper. Bring to a boil over high heat, lower the heat so the water is simmering, and cook, occasionally turning the pork in the liquid, until almost all of the water has evaporated and the meat begins to stick to the casserole, about 2 hours. Skim the foam that rises to the surface regularly as the pork simmers.

Pour or spoon off the fat remaining in the braising pan, and pour in the remaining 3 tablespoons olive oil. Adjust the heat to very low. Cook, turning often, until the pork has a caramelized, golden-brown crust, 15 to 30 minutes.

To serve hot, as a main course, let the *porchetta* rest 20 minutes, then slice $\frac{1}{4}$ inch thick. *Porchetta* can also be served warm or at room temperature. Sliced leftover *porchetta* makes delicious sandwiches. If the *porchetta* has been refrigerated, be sure to dress the sandwiches well; chilling has a way of drying out the meat.

☞ When preparing a boneless loin of pork, butchers have a tendency to cut away the "tail"—that fatty, tapered strip that extends from the eye of the loin to the tip of the bone. Ask your butcher to leave the tail intact when boning pork for this recipe—it plays an important role in stuffing the roast and keeping the roast moist as it cooks.

My brother Franco, cousin Anci, and mother, Erminia, in Venice, 1956

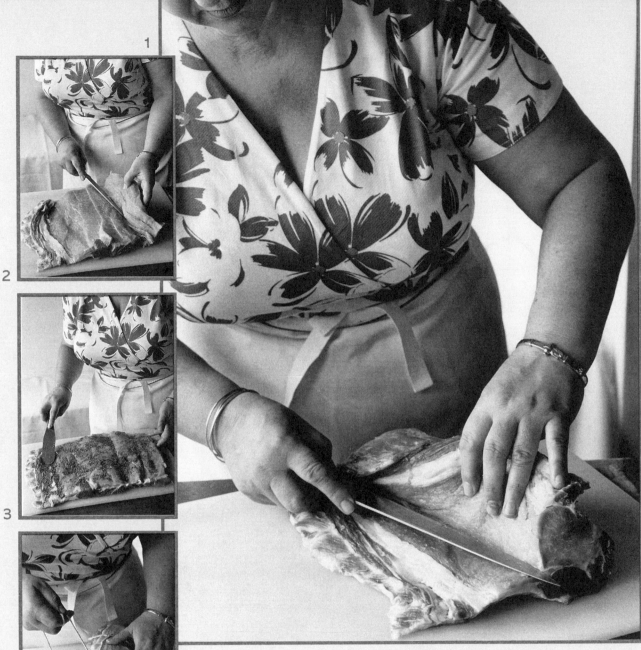

Unrolling and Stuffing *Porchetta*

1. Cut along the top side of the tail and into the eye of the roast.

2. Continue your cut with a sawing motion, unrolling the loin into a rectangle of more or less even thickness.

3. Spread the herb paste evenly over the entire top surface of the pork.

4. After rolling it up, tie the roast securely, at 1-inch intervals, with kitchen twine.

SAUSAGE-MAKING IS ONE OF the oldest methods of preserving meats. Although in Italy sausages are made mostly from pork meat, you can use beef, lamb, veal, chicken, horse, boar, or game. Basically, the technique is the same regardless of the type of meat or seasonings: Chop the meat, flavor it with spices and herbs, and stuff it into the casing. What is important is that sausages need a certain amount of fat to be moist; otherwise they will dry out during cooking.

I remember making the recipe for *luganega*, which follows, with my grandparents when the pig was slaughtered around November or December. When freshly made, the sausage was eaten grilled or pan-sautéed or else used to make *sugo*— sauce for polenta or pasta. But most of the sausage was wound into long double links and set to dry in the *cantina*, hanging from a cane or wooden pole. These dry sausages were delicious in frittatas or in sandwiches with Grandma's crusty bread. By February, Grandma would set the dried sausages in a tall can and cover them with rendered pork fat to keep them moist until they were used. (If they were left hanging, they would eventually become dry as a bone.) The sausages at our house were made only in the season when the pig was slaughtered, as was the prosciutto and pancetta. These foods were used judiciously so they would last until the new batch was made the following winter.

Some of the recipes in this book, such as the one for Rigatoni alla Boscaiola on page 112, call for taking the sausages out of their casing before cooking them. If you're preparing homemade sausage for recipes like that, do what we do in our restaurants — skip the step of stuffing the marinated meat into the casing. Just make the sausage stuffing, cover it with plastic wrap, and let it marinate in the refrigerator for 24 hours. You'll have the delicious flavor of homemade sausage without the effort of packing them into casings. You shouldn't keep the marinated sausage meat for more than two days in the refrigerator, but it can be frozen in smaller batches to be used periodically in pasta recipes.

Salsiccia

Sausages have always played a big role in Italian-American cuisine, mostly because they were an easy way for Italian immigrants to duplicate and recapture the flavors of home. In America they found plenty of meat, so sausages were (and are) made continuously—not only during slaughter time, as in the Old Country.

Homemade *Luganega* Sausages

Luganega

½ cup dry white wine

6 fresh or dried bay leaves

6 cloves garlic, peeled

6 pounds pork butt (see note), cut into 2-inch pieces

1½ tablespoons salt

1 teaspoon freshly cracked pepper

½ teaspoon ground allspice

Sausage casing (preferably ½-inch in diameter and all in one piece)

Makes 6 pounds (about 40 links; quantities can be cut in half)

If you intend to dry these sausages, make sure they are kept in a well-ventilated, cool (35- to 42-degree) place. They will be ready to eat about 2 months from the time you hang them.

You can vary the spices in this recipe to make different-tasting sausages. For example, in the north of Italy cinnamon is added, while in the south and here in the States, fennel seeds, crushed red pepper or pieces of dried tomatoes, and sometimes cubes of caciocavallo (semi-fresh cheese) flavor the sausages. As with all fillings, it is a good idea to cook a little bit of the meat mixture before stuffing the casings. Taste the cooked sample piece of sausage and adjust the seasoning to your liking if necessary.

Pour the wine over the bay leaves in a small bowl. Whack the garlic cloves with the side of a knife and toss them into the bowl. Let steep at room temperature for about 2 hours.

Grind the pork directly into a bowl, using a disc with holes about $\frac{3}{16}$ inch in diameter. Sprinkle the salt, pepper, and allspice over the meat. Fish the garlic and bay leaves out of the wine, wrap them in cheesecloth or a clean kitchen towel, and dunk the package in the wine. Squeeze the cheesecloth package over the meat in the bowl. Repeat until you have used up the remaining wine. The flavor of the garlic and bay leaves should permeate the meat. Toss everything together thoroughly. Cover the bowl and let rest in the refrigerator for 2 to 3 hours.

Meanwhile, push about 1 inch or so of one end of the casing over the spout of the faucet of your sink, making sure that the rest of the casing is in the sink. Run cold water slowly through the casing for a minute or two. Repeat if you are using more than one piece of casing.

Remove the casing from the spout and fill with marinated pork following the manufacturer's directions that come with your sausage stuffer. Twist the sausage into 3½-inch links as you go.

Variation

Italian-American Fennel Sausage

Choose wider sausage casings—about 1½ inches in diameter—for these sausages. Prepare the sausage mixture as above, omitting the allspice and adding 1 tablespoon fennel seeds and 1 teaspoon crushed red pepper (makes about 18 links).

☞ The pork you choose for sausage-making should have a ratio of fat to lean that is about 1:5. In other words, if you are making a full recipe of sausage, use about 1 pound of fat to 5 pounds of lean pork.

Those of you who have been to Italian-American street fairs in New York City will certainly be familiar with this dish, usually served as is or packed into a crusty hero roll. It is a great dish for a crowd, as part of a buffet or as the centerpiece of a dinner, served family-style.

Sausage and Peppers

Salsiccia con Peperoni

16 links sweet Italian sausages, with or without fennel seeds

¼ cup extra-virgin olive oil, or as needed

8 cloves garlic, peeled

1 pound white, shiitake, or cremini mushrooms (or a mix of them)

3 large yellow onions, cut into 1-inch wedges (about 5 cups)

6 pickled cherry peppers, stemmed and seeded, but left whole

2 medium yellow and 2 medium red bell peppers, cored, seeded, and cut into 1-inch strips (about 6 cups total)

Makes 8 servings (ingredients can easily be reduced by half to serve 4)

You may be surprised to see that there is no stock or wine in this dish. I prefer to let the sausages and vegetables simmer in their own juices. The flavors blend and mellow a little, but still stay intense. The key to making really wonderful sausage and peppers is to caramelize each ingredient separately, then to pile them into a baking dish and finish them in the oven.

Poke the sausages all over with a fork. Divide ¼ cup olive oil between two large, heavy skillets and heat them over medium heat. Divide the sausages between the skillets and cook, turning occasionally, until the sausages are well browned on all sides, about 8 minutes. About halfway through browning the sausages, whack the garlic with the flat side of a knife and toss half the cloves into each skillet. Transfer the browned sausages and garlic to a 13 × 9–inch baking dish, leaving the fat behind.

While the sausages are browning, prepare the mushrooms. Trim the stems from the shiitakes, if using. Trim the stems from the white and cremini mushrooms if you like. Cut any mushrooms with caps larger than 2 inches in half; leave smaller mushrooms whole.

Preheat the oven to 400° F. Scatter the onions and cherry peppers over the fat in one of the skillets, and the mushrooms over the fat in the other. Cook the onions, stirring often, until browned and wilted but still quite crunchy, about 8 minutes. Cook the mushrooms until they have absorbed the fat in the skillet and have begun to brown, about 6 minutes.

Slide the mushrooms into the baking dish. Spoon the onions into the baking dish, leaving behind some of the fat in the skillet. (If there is not enough fat left to coat the bottom of the skillet, pour in enough olive oil to do so.) Add the peppers to the skillet and cook, tossing frequently, just until wilted but still quite crunchy, about 6 minutes. Slide the peppers into the baking dish, toss all the ingredients together well, and place in the oven.

Bake uncovered, tossing occasionally, until the vegetables are tender but still firm and no trace of pink remains in the sausages, about 25 minutes. Serve hot.

Broccoli Rabe and Sausage

Broccoli di Rabe e Salsicce

2 pounds broccoli rabe

¼ cup extra-virgin olive oil

1 ½ pounds sweet Italian sausage (about 8 links) or *luganega* (see page 240), cut into 3-inch lengths

3 large cloves garlic, peeled

Salt

¼ teaspoon crushed hot red pepper

Makes 4 servings

Trim the coarse, tough ends from the broccoli rabe and remove any wilted or yellow leaves. Starting at the cut ends of the stems, pull off the tough outer coating of the stems with a paring knife or vegetable peeler. Cut any very thick stems in half lengthwise. Wash the broccoli rabe in plenty of cool water, then drain, leaving some of the water that clings to the leaves.

Heat 2 tablespoons of the oil over medium heat in a large deep, heavy skillet or casserole with a tight-fitting lid. Poke the sausages all over with a fork and lay them in the skillet. Cook, turning as necessary, until caramelized on all sides and no trace of pink remains in the center, about 8 minutes for thinner *luganega* or up to 12 minutes for thicker sausages. Adjust the heat as the sausages cook so they brown evenly without scorching. Remove the sausages to a plate and cover with aluminum foil to keep them warm. Drain the fat from the skillet without cleaning the pan. Pour in the remaining 2 tablespoons olive oil. Whack the garlic cloves with the flat side of a knife, scatter them over the oil, and cook until golden, about 3 minutes.

Add the broccoli rabe, and season lightly with salt and ¼ teaspoon crushed red pepper. Pour in ½ inch of water, bring to a boil, and cover the casserole. Steam, lifting the lid to stir occasionally, until the broccoli rabe is softened, about 5 minutes. Uncover and cook over medium heat until the liquid is evaporated and the broccoli rabe is tender, about 5 minutes.

Return the sausages to the skillet and turn them until warmed through. Serve the sausages on plates or a platter, flanked by the broccoli rabe.

Spare Ribs Roasted with Vinegar and Red Pepper

Costine di Maiale al Forno

1 rack (about 3½ pounds) pork spare ribs

Sea or kosher salt

Freshly ground black pepper

⅓ cup extra-virgin olive oil

12 cloves garlic, peeled

4 fresh or dried bay leaves

1 cup (or as needed) Mixed Meat Stock (page 75), Chicken Stock (page 74), or canned reduced-sodium chicken broth

1 cup dry white wine

½ cup red-wine vinegar

2 tablespoons honey

1 to 2 teaspoons crushed hot red pepper, pulverized or chopped fine

Makes 6 servings

Cut the rack of spare ribs between the bones into single ribs (or ask your butcher to do this for you). Preheat the oven to 425° F.

Pat the spare ribs dry and season them with salt and pepper. Toss them in a roasting pan into which they fit comfortably with the olive oil, garlic, and bay leaves. Pour in the stock and roast, turning occasionally, until the liquid is almost completely evaporated and the ribs are golden brown, 45 minutes to an hour.

Meanwhile, stir the wine, vinegar, honey, and crushed red pepper together in a small bowl until the honey is dissolved.

Brush all sides of the ribs with some of the vinegar glaze, then pour the remaining glaze into the roasting pan. Continue baking, turning every few minutes, until the glaze is syrupy and the ribs are mahogany brown and sticky to the touch, about 20 minutes.

Braised Pork Ribs with Rigatoni

Costine di Maiale Brasate con Rigatoni

One whole rack (about 4 pounds) pork spare ribs

Salt

Freshly ground black pepper

¼ cup extra-virgin olive oil

2 large yellow onions, sliced (about 3 cups)

8 cloves garlic, peeled

6 pickled cherry peppers, stemmed, seeded, and quartered

Two 35-ounce cans Italian plum tomatoes (preferably San Marzano) with their liquid, seeded and crushed

2 bay leaves

6 sprigs fresh thyme

2 to 3 cups hot water, or as needed

1 pound rigatoni

¼ cup chopped fresh Italian parsley

⅔ cup freshly grated Parmigiano-Reggiano cheese, plus more for passing if you like

Makes 6 servings

Cut the rack of spare ribs between the bones into single ribs (or ask your butcher to do this for you). Season the rib pieces with salt and pepper. Heat the olive oil in a large, heavy braising pan over medium heat. Add as many of the ribs as will fit without touching. Cook, turning occasionally, until browned on all sides, about 10 minutes. Remove the ribs and drain on a baking sheet lined with paper towels. Repeat with the remaining ribs. Adjust the temperature throughout the browning so the fat in the pan is sizzling but the pieces of pork that stick to the pan don't burn.

Pour off all but about 4 tablespoons of fat from the casserole. Add the onions, garlic, and cherry peppers and cook, stirring, until the onions are wilted and caramelized, about 4 minutes. Stir in the tomatoes, bay leaves, and thyme. Bring to a boil, scraping the pan to loosen the brown bits stuck to the bottom. Tuck the spare ribs into the tomato sauce, season lightly with salt and pepper, and bring to a boil. Adjust the heat to simmering and cook, turning the spare ribs in the sauce occasionally, until the ribs are fork-tender, about 2 hours. Ladle some of the hot water into the casserole from time to time as necessary to keep the ribs covered with liquid.

To serve: When the ribs are almost tender, heat 6 quarts of salted water to a boil in an 8-quart pot. Stir the rigatoni into the boiling water. Return to a boil, stirring frequently. Cook the pasta, semi-covered, stirring occasionally, until done, about 10 minutes. Drain the pasta, return it to the pot, and spoon in enough of the spare-rib sauce to coat the pasta generously. Toss in the parsley and bring the sauce and pasta to a boil, tossing to coat the pasta with sauce. Check the seasoning, adding salt and pepper if necessary. Remove the pot from the heat and stir in ⅔ cup grated cheese. Transfer the pasta to a warm platter or individual plates and top with the spare ribs. Spoon a little of the remaining sauce over the pasta and serve immediately, passing additional sauce and, if you like, grated cheese separately.

Lamb Shoulder

IF WHAT GUESTS ORDER IN MY RESTAURANTS is any indication, everyone loves lamb chops. But for me, some of the best-tasting—and challenging, from a chef's point of view—cuts of lamb are the shoulder and neck. (These cuts are also much less expensive than chops.) I like the neck for braising and making sauce to dress pasta, while for roasting I prefer the shoulder. Lamb shoulder has less meat than a leg of lamb, but has more cartilage and bones, which add a lot of flavor.

The shoulder is a difficult piece of meat to cut into roasting-size pieces. You might be better off asking your butcher to cut it on a bandsaw into 2-inch pieces. But if you'd like to try it at home, here's how to proceed: First, cut through the joints with a boning knife. Next, cut the large pieces of lamb into 2-inch cubes by cutting down to the bone with a knife, then cutting through the bones with a heavy meat cleaver, giving the bones a clean, strong whack.

Whether the lamb is cut by your butcher or you, it is probably a good idea to check for bone splinters before cooking.

Cooking with Wine

I AM ALWAYS ASKED WHICH WINE I use when cooking. Rule number one is, don't use anything labeled "cooking wine," which most likely contains salt and other ingredients you don't want in your sauce. Do use a good wine—remember, what you have left from wine after cooking is its flavor, and the better the wine, the better the flavor in your food. When cooking with wine, you want the alcohol to dissipate, so when you add wine to a pan, do not add any other liquid until the wine cooks for a few minutes and the alcohol has had a chance to evaporate, then proceed with the other ingredients.

Wine also adds acidity to dishes, which is one reason I rarely make a pasta sauce with wine. A wine high in acid will impart that to the food; on the other hand, sweet wine can be used well for sweet sauces and desserts. Wine also helps chemically to break down proteins. Therefore, marinating meats in wine, as well as adding wine to meats as they cook, will help to tenderize tougher cuts.

Rustic-Cut Roasted Lamb Shoulder

Spalla d'Agnello Arrosta

3 ½ pounds lamb shoulder (with bones), cut into 2-inch pieces (see opposite)

2 ribs celery, trimmed and chopped roughly (about 1 ½ cups)

2 large carrots, peeled, trimmed, and chopped roughly (about 1 ½ cups)

1 large onion, peeled and quartered

3 bay leaves

3 sprigs fresh rosemary

1 cup dry white wine

½ cup extra-virgin olive oil

¼ cup balsamic vinegar

Salt

Freshly ground black pepper

2 cups Chicken Stock (page 74) or canned reduced-sodium chicken broth

¼ cup dried porcini mushrooms

Makes 6 servings

Toss all ingredients except the stock and dried porcini together in a bowl large enough to hold them comfortably. Cover and refrigerate overnight, tossing several times. Let stand at room temperature 1 hour before roasting.

Bring the stock to a boil in a small saucepan. Remove from the heat, toss in the porcini, and let steep until softened, about 20 minutes. Scoop out the porcini and rinse them lightly to remove sand and grit. Strain the soaking liquid through a coffee filter, or carefully pour it off into a small bowl, leaving the sediment behind.

While the mushrooms are soaking, preheat the oven to 475° F. Turn the lamb and marinade ingredients into a roasting pan large enough to hold them in a single layer. (A 16 × 13–inch roasting pan works well.) Add the mushrooms and their soaking liquid. Cover with aluminum foil and roast 30 minutes.

Remove the foil, season lightly with salt and pepper, and roast until the meat is tender, about 1 hour. Turn the pieces of lamb and baste them several times as they cook.

Using a slotted spoon, transfer the meat to an ovenproof serving dish. Set the roasting pan over high heat, bring the liquid in the pan to a boil, and boil until the liquid is slightly syrupy, about 15 minutes. Strain the juices into a bowl, pressing on the vegetables to extract as much liquid from them as possible. Spoon off the fat from the surface of the juices and pour the remaining liquid over the meat. Return the lamb to the oven and roast, turning the meat frequently, until very tender and well browned all over, about 15 minutes.

Scallopine

Most likely, you'll recognize all or most of the dishes in this section from visits to your neighborhood Italian restaurant. Over the years, home cooks and restaurants have adapted these recipes, traditionally prepared in restaurants with veal scallopine, to include chicken, turkey, or pork, and that is how I offer them to you here. Any of the recipes in this section can be prepared with veal, chicken, turkey, or pork: simply prepare the scallopine of your choice as described below, then cook them as outlined in the individual recipes. One thing you will need is a meat mallet with both smooth and toothed sides. It doesn't have to be a large and heavy professional chef's model—a smaller "home version" will do.

Veal scallopine. Classically, veal scallopine are thin slices of veal cut across the grain from an individual muscle that has been completely trimmed of fat and connective tissue. Veal scallopine are cut about $1/4$ inch thick, then pounded to about $1/8$ inch. To serve four, start with twelve 2-ounce veal slices each about $1/4$ inch thick. Place the slices, two at a time, between two sheets of plastic wrap and pound them several times with the toothed side of a meat mallet. Switch to the smooth side of the mallet and pound the scallopine to a thickness of about $1/8$ inch. (If the plastic wrap starts to look tattered, replace it with two new sheets.) Proceed with the recipe.

Chicken scallopine. To serve four, start with four 6-ounce boneless and skinless chicken-breast halves. (If the chicken breasts you are working with have the "filet"—the long strip of meat that runs the length of the underside of the breast—do your best to keep it attached to the breast as you cut and pound them.) Cut each breast crosswise on the bias into two more or less equal pieces. Place the pieces, two at a time, between two sheets of plastic wrap and pound them with the smooth side of a meat mallet to a thickness of about $\frac{1}{4}$ inch. Proceed with the recipe.

Pork scallopine. To serve four, start with eight 3-ounce slices of boneless center-cut pork loin completely trimmed of fat. Place the slices, two at a time, between two sheets of plastic wrap and pound them several times with the toothed side of a meat mallet. Switch to the smooth side of the mallet and pound the scallopine to a thickness of about $\frac{1}{4}$ inch. (If the plastic wrap starts to look tattered, replace it with two new sheets.) Proceed with the recipe.

Turkey scallopine. To serve four, start with eight 3-ounce turkey cutlets. (Most turkey cutlets are sold precut in supermarket meat cases; come as close as you can to these weights.) Place the slices, two at a time, between two sheets of plastic wrap and pound them with the smooth side of a meat mallet to a thickness of about $\frac{1}{4}$ inch. Proceed with the recipe.

Scallopine Pointers

I<small>F YOU CHOOSE TO MAKE THESE RECIPES</small> with pork, turkey, or chicken, you'll be cooking eight 3-ounce scallopine to serve 4 people. If veal is your choice, you'll be cooking twelve 2-ounce scallopine for the same number of guests. The number of scallopine doesn't affect the amount of sauce or the cooking time, but it does alter the way you distribute toppings, like the eggplant on the Scaloppine alla Sorrentina on page 258. Simply divide the topping ingredients among the number of scallopine you have and continue with the recipe. (The shape of the scallopine, which might range from squarish to rectangular, doesn't affect the outcome of the recipe either.)

Flouring the scallopine—whatever kind you are using—serves two purposes: Flour helps to caramelize the outside of the scallopine before the inside becomes overcooked and tough. It also helps to thicken the sauce lightly and give it a velvety texture. Flour the scallopine just before browning them; flouring them ahead of time will result in a soggy coating.

Cook scallopine over medium heat to brown them gently without overcooking them. Adding butter to the oil helps the caramelization along.

Scallopine cook so quickly it is best to have your side dish ready to go before you put the pan on to heat for the scallopine.

If you read through the recipes, you'll notice that they all follow the same basic procedure: flour-coated scallopine are browned, then removed from the pan, and a sauce is made right in the same pan. Sometimes, as in the Scaloppine alla Marsala (page 252) or the Scaloppine alla Pizzaiola (page 256), other ingredients are cooked in the pan after the scallopine are removed and the sauce is made. Use this basic formula and these recipes as a jumping-off point for your own scallopine creations.

The traditional breaded cutlet is called a *milanese* in Italian—in other words, as they do it in Milano. This version is coated with bread crumbs and the addition of Parmigiano-Reggiano and doesn't come from any particular region. I first encountered this recipe in the United States in Italian-American restaurants in the 1970s. The cheese adds a lot of flavor and crunch to the meat. Just be careful not to overbrown the cheese-coated scallopine—the cheese will turn bitter if you do.

Pan-Fried Parmigiano-Reggiano—Coated Scallopine

Scaloppine Impanate al Parmigiano-Reggiano

4 portions Veal, Chicken, Turkey, or Pork Scallopine (page 248)

Salt

Freshly ground black pepper

2 large eggs

2 tablespoons milk

1 ½ cups fine, dry bread crumbs

1 cup freshly grated Parmigiano-Reggiano cheese

2 tablespoons chopped fresh Italian parsley

All-purpose flour

¼ cup extra-virgin olive oil

4 tablespoons unsalted butter

Lemon wedges

Makes 4 servings

Preheat the oven to 250° F. Season the scallopine with salt and pepper. Whisk the eggs and milk together in a wide bowl. Mix the bread crumbs, grated Parmigiano-Reggiano, and parsley together on a plate or sheet of wax paper. Spread the flour out on a separate plate or sheet of wax paper. Dredge the scallopine in flour and tap off excess. Dip the floured scallopine into the egg mixture, turning well to coat both sides evenly. Let excess egg drip back into the bowl, then lay the scallopine in the pan of bread crumbs. Turn to coat both sides well with bread crumbs, pressing with your hands until the bread crumbs adhere well to the scallopine.

Heat the olive oil and butter in a wide, heavy skillet until the butter foams, then subsides. Lay as many breaded scallopine into the pan as will fit without touching. Fry until the underside is golden, about 4 minutes. Flip the scallopine and fry until the second side is golden, about 3 minutes. As the scallopine fry, adjust the heat so they brown gently and slowly and the bits of coating that fall into the oil don't burn. There should be a steady bubbling around the scallopine, not a crackling and hissing. Transfer the scallopine to a paper-towel-lined baking sheet and keep warm in the oven. Remove as many browned bits from the pan with a slotted spoon as you can, and fry the remaining scallopine. Serve the scallopine immediately, garnished with wedges of lemon.

Scallopine with Mushrooms and Marsala Wine

Scaloppine alla Marsala

4 portions Veal, Chicken, Turkey, or Pork Scallopine (see page 248)

Salt

Freshly ground black pepper

All-purpose flour

3 tablespoons extra-virgin olive oil

8 tablespoons (1 stick) unsalted butter

2 tablespoons finely chopped shallots

3 cups thinly sliced trimmed mushrooms, such as shiitake, fresh porcini, or white

½ cup dry Marsala wine

1 cup Chicken Stock (page 74) or canned reduced-sodium chicken broth, or as needed

2 tablespoons chopped fresh Italian parsley

Makes 4 servings

Season both sides of the scallopine lightly with salt and pepper. Dredge the scallopine in flour to coat both sides lightly and tap off any excess flour.

Heat the olive oil and 2 tablespoons of the butter in a large, heavy skillet over medium heat until the butter is foaming. Add as many of the scallopine as fit without touching and cook until golden brown on the underside, about 3 minutes. Flip, and cook until the second side is lightly browned, about 2 minutes. Remove from the pan and repeat with the remaining scallopine, adding more oil to the pan if necessary. Remove all scallopine from the pan when browned and drain on paper towels.

Drain the fat from the skillet and return the pan to the heat. Add 2 tablespoons of the remaining butter, and when it is melted, stir in the shallots. Cook, stirring, until wilted, about 3 minutes. Scatter the mushrooms in the pan, season them lightly with salt and pepper, and cook until they are lightly browned, about 4 minutes. (If the mushrooms begin to give off liquid, you'll have to wait for that to evaporate before the mushrooms begin to brown.)

Pour in the Marsala, bring it to a boil, and cook until the Marsala is slightly syrupy, about 3 minutes.

Add the remaining 4 tablespoons butter and pour in 1 cup chicken stock. Bring to a vigorous boil and season lightly with salt and pepper. Boil until reduced by half, then return the scallopine to the pan, tucking them into the sauce. Cook, turning the scallopine in the sauce, until the scallopine are heated through and the sauce is lightly thickened. If necessary, add small amounts of chicken stock to make enough sauce to coat the scallopine generously. Swirl in the parsley and serve on hot plates, dividing the scallopine among the plates and spooning some of the sauce and mushrooms over each serving.

Saltimbocca literally means "jump in the mouth." This traditional Roman dish is so easy to prepare and appetizing, it almost jumps from the plate into the mouth.

Scallopine *Saltimbocca*, Roman-Style

Saltimbocca alla Romana

Sautéed Spinach (page 321)

4 portions Veal, Chicken, Turkey, or Pork Scallopine (page 248)

Salt

Freshly ground black pepper

4 slices (about 2 ounces) imported Italian prosciutto, cut in half crosswise (or in thirds crosswise, if preparing this recipe with veal scallopine)

8 to 12 large fresh sage leaves

All-purpose flour

3 tablespoons extra-virgin olive oil, or as needed

6 tablespoons unsalted butter

¼ cup dry white wine, see page 246 for guidance

1 cup Chicken Stock (page 74) or canned reduced-sodium chicken broth

Makes 4 servings

Prepare the spinach, remove it from the heat, and cover the pan to keep it warm. Season the scallopine lightly with salt and pepper, keeping in mind that the prosciutto is cured with salt. Cover each scallopine with a half-slice of the prosciutto. Tap the prosciutto with the back of a knife so it adheres well to the meat. Center a sage leaf over the prosciutto and fasten it in place with a toothpick, weaving the toothpick in and out as if you were taking a stitch. (Alternatively, you can place the sage leaf directly over the scallopine and cover it with the prosciutto.)

Dredge the scallopine in the flour to coat both sides lightly. Tap off excess flour. Heat 3 tablespoons olive oil and 2 tablespoons of the butter in a large, heavy skillet over medium heat until the butter is foaming. Slip as many of the scallopine, prosciutto side down, into the pan as fit without touching. Cook just until the prosciutto is light golden, about 2 minutes. (Overcooking will toughen the prosciutto.) Turn and cook until the second side is browned, about 2 minutes. Remove and drain on paper towels. Repeat with remaining scallopine, adding more oil if necessary.

Remove all the scallopine from the skillet and pour off the oil. Return the pan to the heat and pour in the wine. Add the remaining 4 tablespoons butter and cook until the wine is reduced by about half, about 3 minutes. Pour in the chicken stock and bring to a vigorous boil. Tuck the scallopine into the sauce. Simmer until the sauce is reduced and lightly thickened, about 3 to 4 minutes. Taste, and season with salt and pepper if necessary.

To serve, spoon the spinach in a mound in the center of each plate. Arrange the *saltimbocca* over the spinach. Spoon some of the pan sauce over the scallopine and serve immediately.

This dish is usually made with lemon, butter, and sometimes capers. I have given it a little twist by adding olives and lemon slices. Made with chicken and served over braised spinach, this dish is a favorite at our restaurants in Pittsburgh and Kansas City.

Scallopine in Lemon-Caper Sauce

Scaloppine Piccata

2 lemons

4 servings Veal, Chicken, Turkey, or Pork Scallopine (see page 248)

Salt

Freshly ground black pepper

All-purpose flour

6 tablespoons extra-virgin olive oil

6 tablespoons unsalted butter

2 cloves garlic, peeled

10 large green olives (preferably Cerignola), cut away from the pit in wide strips (about ½ cup)

¼ cup small capers in brine, drained

½ cup dry white wine, see page 246 for guidance

1 cup Chicken Stock (page 74) or canned reduced-sodium chicken broth

2 tablespoons chopped fresh Italian parsley

Makes 4 servings

Cerignolas are large green olives, each the size of a plump almond, with a very nutty, buttery flavor. They are usually kept in brine. If you cannot find them, other brined green olives will do. But use the ones with pits, which you will remove. They have more flavor.

Squeeze the juice from one and a half of the lemons and reserve. Lay the remaining half-lemon flat side down and cut into very thin slices with a paring knife. Remove the pits and set the lemon slices aside.

Season the scallopine with salt and pepper. Dredge in flour to coat both sides lightly and tap off excess flour. Heat 3 tablespoons of the olive oil and 2 tablespoons of the butter in a wide, heavy skillet over medium heat until the butter is foaming. Add as many of the scallopine as will fit without touching and cook until golden brown on the underside, about 3 minutes. Flip and cook until the second side is lightly browned, about 2 minutes. Remove and drain on paper towels. Repeat with remaining scallopine.

Remove all scallopine from the pan. Pour off the fat and carefully wipe out the skillet with a wad of paper towels. Pour in the remaining 3 tablespoons olive oil and add the remaining 4 tablespoons butter, the garlic, and lemon slices. Cook, scraping the bottom of the skillet, until the garlic is golden brown, about 3 minutes. Scoop out the lemon slices and set aside. Scatter the olives and capers into the skillet and cook, stirring gently, until they begin to sizzle, about 4 minutes. Pour in the wine, bring to a vigorous boil, and cook until the wine is reduced in volume by half. Pour in the chicken stock, bring to a boil, and cook until slightly syrupy, about 4 minutes. Return the scallopine to the skillet, turning the cutlets in the sauce until they are warmed through and coated with sauce. Swirl in the parsley and divide the scallopine among warm plates. Spoon the sauce over them, including some of the capers and olives in each spoonful. Decorate the tops of the scallopine with the reserved lemon slices.

Egg-Battered Scallopine with Lemon Sauce

Scaloppine alla Francese

2 large eggs

2 tablespoons milk

1 teaspoon salt, plus more for seasoning the sauce

½ teaspoon freshly ground black pepper, plus more for seasoning the sauce

4 portions Veal, Chicken, Turkey, or Pork Scallopine (page 248)

All-purpose flour

⅓ cup olive oil

⅓ cup vegetable oil

6 tablespoons unsalted butter

1 lemon, cut into very thin slices, pits removed

½ cup dry white wine, see page 246 for guidance

Juice of 1 lemon

2 cups Chicken Stock (page 74) or canned reduced-sodium chicken broth

2 tablespoons chopped fresh Italian parsley

Makes 4 servings

Whisk the eggs, milk, 1 teaspoon salt, and ½ teaspoon pepper together in a wide bowl until blended. Dredge the scallopine in flour to coat both sides lightly and tap off the excess flour. Heat the olive and vegetable oils in a large skillet over medium heat. Dip into the egg batter as many of the scallopine as will fit in the pan without touching. Let excess batter drip back into the bowl and place them into the skillet. Fry, turning once, until golden brown on both sides, about 4 minutes. Adjust the heat as the scallopine cook so they brown slowly and evenly, with a steady bubbling. (If the heat is too high, the egg coating will scorch and the bits of batter that stick to the pan will burn, turning the sauce bitter.) Drain the scallopine on a paper-towel-lined baking sheet and repeat with the remaining scallopine and egg coating.

Remove the pan from the heat and pour off the oil. Carefully wipe out the pan with a wad of paper towels and add half the butter. When the butter is melted, return the pan to the heat and scatter the lemon slices over the bottom of the pan. Cook, stirring gently occasionally, until the lemon slices are golden, about 3 minutes. Scoop the lemon slices out and set them aside. Add the remaining 3 tablespoons of the butter, the wine, and lemon juice and bring to a vigorous boil. Boil until the liquid is syrupy, 3 to 4 minutes. Pour in the stock, bring to a boil, and cook until reduced by about half, about 5 minutes. Tuck the scallopine into the sauce and simmer until the sauce is velvety and the scallopine are heated through, about 4 minutes. Sprinkle with the chopped parsley and divide the scallopine among warm serving plates. Spoon some of the sauce over each serving and decorate the tops with the reserved lemon slices.

Scallopine with Peppers, Mushrooms, and Tomato

Scaloppine alla Pizzaiola

½ cup extra-virgin olive oil

8 cloves garlic, peeled

1 medium red and 1 medium yellow bell pepper, cored, seeded, and sliced ½ inch thick (about 3 cups total)

2 cups trimmed and thinly sliced assorted mushrooms, such as shiitake, cremini, and/or button

Salt

Freshly ground black pepper

2 tablespoons unsalted butter

4 servings Veal, Chicken, Turkey, or Pork Scallopine (see page 248)

All-purpose flour

One 24-ounce can Italian plum tomatoes (preferably San Marzano), seeded and crushed (about 3 cups)

½ teaspoon crushed hot red pepper

6 fresh basil leaves, torn into quarters, plus basil sprigs for decorating the plates if you like

Makes 4 servings

Cooking is all about making decisions. Sometimes you have to decide if you are going to have great looks or great flavor. Of course, I try to have both, but if it is ever a question of giving up one or the other, I always go for the best flavor. In this dish, for example, lightly cooked peppers would look brighter, but I prefer the flavor of peppers that have simmered until they begin to break down. So I cook them longer, for better flavor. Choosing two different-color peppers helps make up for what little we lose in appearance by cooking the peppers fully.

Fresh herb sprigs serve as more than decoration. The heat from the dish releases the aroma and adds to the enjoyment.

Heat 3 tablespoons of the olive oil in a heavy, wide skillet over medium heat. Whack 3 of the garlic cloves with the flat side of a knife and toss them into the pan. Cook, shaking the pan, until golden, about 2 minutes. Stir in the peppers and mushrooms, season them lightly with salt and pepper, and cook, stirring, until the peppers are softened, about 8 minutes.

Meanwhile, heat 3 tablespoons of the remaining olive oil and the butter in a large, heavy skillet. Whack 3 of the remaining garlic cloves with the flat side of a knife and add them to the pan. Cook, shaking the pan, until golden, about 2 minutes. While the garlic is browning, dredge the scallopine in flour to coat both sides lightly, tap off the excess, and add as many scallopine to the pan as fit in a single layer. Cook until golden brown on the underside, about 3 minutes. Flip, and cook until the second side is lightly browned, about 2 minutes. Repeat with the remaining scallopine. Remove scallopine from pan.

Pour off the fat from the scallopine pan and pour in the remaining 2 tablespoons olive oil. Whack the remaining 2 garlic cloves with the flat side of a knife and toss them into the pan. Cook, shaking the pan, until golden, about 2 minutes. Stir in the tomatoes and crushed red pepper and season lightly with salt. Bring to a boil, then lower the heat so the sauce is simmering. Cook, stirring occasionally, until lightly thickened, about 10 minutes. Scrape the mushrooms and peppers into the tomato sauce and bring to a simmer. Cook until the peppers are tender but not mushy, about 3 minutes. Stir in the torn basil, then tuck the scallopine into the sauce. Simmer until the scallopine are heated through and the sauce is lightly thickened, about 2 minutes. Taste, and season with salt and additional crushed red pepper if you like. Divide the scallopine among warm plates, topping each serving with some of the sauce. Decorate the plates with basil sprigs, if you like.

Scallopine with Eggplant and Fontina Cheese

Scaloppine alla Sorrentina

1 medium eggplant (about 1¼ pounds)

Salt

6 tablespoons extra-virgin olive oil, or more as needed

8 to 12 fresh sage leaves, optional, plus more for decorating the plates

4 portions Veal, Chicken, Turkey, or Pork Scallopine (see page 248)

Freshly ground black pepper

4 slices (about 2 ounces) imported Italian prosciutto

5 tablespoons unsalted butter

All-purpose flour

6 cloves garlic, peeled

½ cup dry white wine, see page 246 for guidance

1 cup hot Chicken Stock (page 74) or canned reduced-sodium chicken broth, or as needed

¼ cup canned Italian plum tomatoes (preferably San Marzano), seeded and chopped

The title of this dish, alla sorrentina, means it comes from Sorrento, across the bay from Naples. You may have had this dish prepared with mozzarella cheese, which is the cheese of the area, but I am showing you an alternative way here, using Fontina. Use whichever you like, and whichever you can get. By the way, alla sorrentina is a good indicator that the dish you order will contain eggplant in some form or another. If you prepare this dish without the eggplant, you'll have scallopine alla bolognese.

You can add a little elegance to the dish by straining the sauce as you spoon it onto plates. That is something I do in my restaurants. But in my home—and most likely in yours—the sauce is just fine the way it comes out of the baking dish.

Trim the stem from the eggplant. Remove strips of peel about 1 inch wide from the eggplant, leaving about half the peel intact, and cut the eggplant into 1-inch slices. Sprinkle a baking sheet with salt. Arrange the eggplant slices over the salt and sprinkle the tops with salt. Let them stand until both sides are wet, about 30 minutes. Rinse the eggplant under cool running water, drain thoroughly, and pat dry.

Preheat the oven to 400° F. Wipe the baking sheet clean and oil it generously, using about 3 tablespoons of the oil. Arrange the eggplant slices on the baking sheet and turn to coat them with oil. Roast until tender and well browned, turning them and rotating them in the pan as necessary, about 20 minutes. Remove and cool. Increase the oven temperature to 450° F.

Lay one sage leaf, if using, over the center of each scallopine. Season the scallopine lightly with salt and pepper, keeping in mind that the prosciutto is cured with salt. Cover each scallopine with a piece of the prosciutto. and tap the prosciutto with the back of a knife so it adheres well to the meat.

5 ounces Italian Fontina cheese, cut into thin slices

2 tablespoons Tomato Sauce (page 151, or use another) or liquid from the canned tomatoes

Makes 4 servings

Heat 2 tablespoons of the remaining olive oil and 2 tablespoons of the butter in a heavy, wide skillet over medium heat. Dredge the scallopine in flour to coat both sides lightly. Tap off excess flour, and add as many scallopine to the skillet, prosciutto side down, as will fit without overlapping. Cook just until the prosciutto is light golden, about 2 minutes. (Overcooking will toughen the prosciutto.) Turn, and cook until the second side is browned, about 2 minutes. Remove and drain on paper towels. Repeat with remaining scallopine, adding more oil if necessary.

After removing the last scallopine, pour in the remaining tablespoon of oil and scatter the garlic in the skillet. Cook, turning, until golden brown, about 3 minutes. (Lower the heat, if necessary, so the bits of flour that stick to the pan don't burn while the garlic is browning.) Pour the wine into the skillet, bring to a boil, and boil until almost completely evaporated. Pour in the stock and drop in the remaining 3 tablespoons butter. Bring to a boil, stir in the chopped tomatoes, and boil until the sauce is lightly reduced and glossy, about 4 minutes.

Meanwhile, arrange the scallopine side by side in a baking dish. Cover each with eggplant, cutting or tearing the slices as necessary to cover all the scallopine more or less evenly. Top with the Fontina slices, dividing them evenly. Dot the top of each Fontina slice with a dab of tomato sauce. Pour the pan sauce around the scallopine.

Bake until the cheese is melted and lightly browned in places and the sauce is lightly thickened, about 10 minutes. Divide the scallopine among warm serving plates. Spoon the sauce—through a strainer, if you like—around the scallopine. Decorate the plates with sage leaves, if desired.

Poultry

Soft Polenta (page 346) is the perfect accompaniment to this juicy chicken dish. Otherwise, mashed potatoes or a loaf of crusty bread will do fine.

Chicken Cacciatore

Pollo alla Cacciatore

2 broiler chickens (about 2½ pounds each, preferably free-range)

Salt

Freshly ground black pepper

All-purpose flour

¼ cup vegetable oil

¼ cup olive oil

1 small yellow onion, cut into 1-inch cubes (about 1 cup)

½ cup dry white wine

One 28-ounce can Italian plum tomatoes (preferably San Marzano) with liquid, crushed

1 teaspoon dried oregano, preferably the Sicilian or Greek type dried on the branch, crumbled

2 cups sliced white or shiitake mushrooms (about 8 ounces)

The caccia in cacciatore means "hunt," so I guess this is chicken hunter's-style. Somewhere along the line—probably on its trip from Italy to America—the hunter's pheasant or guinea hen in this dish was replaced by chicken. If you don't want to cut up a whole chicken, you can buy pieces—get all legs and thighs, if that's what you like; they are very good in this dish. It can be made using only chicken breasts, if that's your preference, but to keep the chicken from drying out, you should cut the cooking time in half, and reduce the wine to ¼ cup and the tomatoes to 3 cups. Best of all, though, is to make this dish with an older hen. In that case, increase the cooking time by 20 minutes, adding more water or stock as needed to keep the hen pieces covered as they cook.

When you cut up chicken, or anything for that matter, your knife should glide along. If you're struggling, stop for a second and take a look at what you're cutting; you should be cutting between the bones at the joints, not actually cutting through the bones. If you're off target, just wiggle the blade of the knife to get a feel for where the joint is, then make another cut. With practice, you'll get a sense for where the joints lie.

1 red and 1 yellow
bell pepper, cored,
seeded, and cut into
½-inch strips (about
2 cups total)

Makes 6 servings

Cut each chicken into twelve pieces: With a sturdy knife or kitchen shears, remove the backbone by cutting along both sides. Remove the wingtips. Reserve the backbone, wingtips, and giblets — except for the liver — to make chicken stock. (See page 74. Or, if you like, cut the backbone in half crosswise and add it to this dish.) Place the chicken, breast side down, on a cutting board and cut the chicken into halves by cutting through the breastbone lengthwise. Cut off the wing at the joint that connects it to the breast, then cut each wing in half at the joint. Separate the leg from the breast. Cut the leg in half at the joint. Cut the breast in half crosswise, giving the knife a good whack when you get to the bone to separate the breast cleanly into halves. Repeat with the remaining chicken.

Season the chicken pieces generously with salt and pepper. Dredge the pieces in flour, coating them lightly and tapping off excess flour. In a wide (at least 12-inch) 5-quart braising pan, heat the vegetable oil with 2 tablespoons of the olive oil until a piece of chicken dipped in the oil gives off a very lively sizzle. Add as many pieces of chicken to the pan as will fit without touching. Do not crowd chicken; if skillet is not wide enough to fit all of the chicken, brown it in batches. Remove chicken pieces from the skillet as they brown, adding some of the remaining pieces of chicken to take their place. Remove all chicken from the skillet, add the onion to the fat remaining in the pan, and cook, stirring, 5 minutes.

Pour the wine into the pan, bring to a boil, and cook until reduced by half, about 3 minutes. Add the tomatoes and oregano, season lightly with salt and pepper, and bring to a boil. Tuck the chicken into the sauce, adjust the heat to a gentle boil, and cover the pan. Cook, stirring a few times, 20 minutes.

Meanwhile, in a large skillet, heat the remaining 2 tablespoons olive oil over medium-high heat. Add the mushrooms and peppers and toss until the peppers are wilted but still quite crunchy, about 8 minutes. Season the vegetables with salt.

Stir the peppers and mushrooms into the chicken pan. Cook, covered, until the chicken and vegetables are tender, 10 to 15 minutes. Check the level of the liquid as the chicken cooks. There should be enough liquid barely to cover the chicken. If necessary, add small amounts of water to maintain the level of liquid as the chicken cooks.

One story I've heard about the naming of *pollo scarpariello* is as follows: *Scarpa* means "shoe," and *scarpariello* means "shoemaker-style." When you eat chicken *scarpariello*, the small chicken bones protrude from your mouth as you are eating, reminiscent of a shoemaker as he holds nails between his lips while, with the other hand, he nails around the perimeter of the shoe.

There seems to be no Italian antecedent for this dish, although vinegar is used to cook chicken in Sicily. But this is an Italian-American dish with great appeal, and one you should really eat with your hands. Provide damp napkins for your guests, in addition to the regular kind, and a little plate for the bones. Pick up the first piece to make your guests comfortable with the idea.

Chicken *Scarpariello*

Pollo Scarpariello

2 small fryer chickens (about 2½ pounds each, preferably free-range)

Salt

Freshly ground black pepper

¼ cup olive oil, or as needed

½ pound sweet Italian sausage (preferably without fennel seeds), cut into 1-inch pieces

10 cloves garlic, peeled and chopped fine

4 pickled cherry peppers, cut in half and stemmed

¼ cup red-wine vinegar

Poussins — young chickens that weigh about 1 pound each — are great for this dish. Figure on one per person, and cut them into pieces at the joints; there's no need to cut them into smaller pieces across the bone. As good as poussins are, I made this dish using supermarket-bought fryer chickens, because I want to be sure you try this delicious recipe.

The secret to golden-brown chicken pieces is to leave them be as they cook. They will brown better if you're not constantly turning them or checking on their progress.

Cut each chicken into twelve pieces as described in preceding recipe. Wash and pat the chicken pieces dry, then season them generously with salt and pepper. Preheat oven to 475° F. Heat 2 tablespoons of the olive oil in a large skillet. Add to the skillet as many pieces of chicken — skin side down, and starting with the leg, thigh, and wing pieces — as fit without touching. Cook the chicken, turning as necessary, until golden brown on all sides, about 8

½ cup dry white wine

1 cup Chicken Stock (page 74) or canned reduced-sodium chicken broth

¼ cup chopped fresh Italian parsley

Makes 6 servings

minutes. Remove the chicken pieces as they brown, and drain them briefly on paper towels. Place the drained chicken pieces in a roasting pan large enough to hold all of them in a single layer. Repeat with the remaining chicken, adding more oil to the pan as necessary and adjusting the heat to prevent the bits that stick to the pan from overbrowning. As room becomes available in the skillet after all the chicken has been added, tuck in pieces of sausage and cook, turning until browned on all sides.

Remove all chicken and sausage from the pan, add the garlic, and cook until golden, being careful not to burn it. Scatter the cherry peppers in the skillet, season with salt and pepper, and stir for a minute. Pour in the vinegar and bring to a boil, scraping into the liquid the browned bits that stick to the skillet, and cook until the vinegar is reduced by half. Add the white wine, bring to a boil, and boil until reduced by half, about 3 minutes.

Pour in the stock and bring to a boil. Pour the sauce over the chicken in the roasting pan and stir to coat. Place the chicken in the oven and roast, stirring occasionally, until the sauce is thick and sticky, like molasses, about 10 minutes. If the sauce is still too thin, place the roasting pan directly over medium-high heat on the stovetop and cook, stirring, until it is reduced, about a minute or two. Once the sauce is thickened, toss in parsley and serve.

To: Lidia Bastianich
From: Mike Yurchak
Subject:

> > > One of the highlights of my weekend is your show on Sunday afternoon. It is special to me because you rekindle great memories of my mother and grandmother, both of whom passed on many years ago, when I watch you. < < <

Chicken Bites with Potato, Sausages, and Vinegar

Bocconcini di Pollo con Patate e Salsicce

2 frying chickens (about 3 pounds each, preferably free-range)

Salt

Freshly ground black pepper

¼ cup extra-virgin olive oil

½ pound sweet Italian sausage (see at right)

1 pound small red-bliss potatoes (about 12), washed and cut in half

6 cloves garlic, peeled

3 sprigs fresh rosemary

¼ cup red-wine vinegar

2 tablespoons chopped fresh Italian parsley

Makes 6 servings

For this dish I prefer luganega, *a thin (about ¹/₂-inch-wide) pork sausage seasoned only with salt and pepper and without fennel or other seeds. If that is unavailable, use the wider (about 1-inch-thick) sweet pork sausages, preferably made without aromatic seeds of any kind. Cut the smaller* luganega *into 1-inch lengths, and the wider sausages into ¹/₂-inch lengths.*

When I cook a whole chicken, or any chicken on the bone, I always salt it three times: in its raw state, when I first begin to cook it, and as it finishes cooking. It seems that the first two saltings are absorbed and somewhat dissipated, especially if you add more ingredients as the chicken cooks. The last salting should be to balance the whole act. Each time you salt, it should be done judiciously, to avoid oversalting and ruining the dish.

Cut each chicken into twelve pieces as described on page 261. Wash and pat the chicken pieces dry, then season them generously with salt and pepper. Preheat the oven to 450° F. Heat 2 tablespoons of the oil in a wide, heavy skillet over medium heat. Add the sausage and cook, stirring often, until lightly browned on all sides, about 3 minutes for thinner sausages or 5 minutes for wider sausages. Remove the sausage pieces with a slotted spoon and transfer them to a roasting pan or baking dish large enough to hold all the sausage, chicken, and potatoes comfortably while allowing room for stirring. (An 18 × 15–inch roasting pan is ideal.) Season the chicken generously with salt and pepper again. Increase the heat to medium-high and add to the skillet as many pieces, skin side down, as will fit in a single layer. Cook, turning once, until well browned on both sides, about 8 minutes. As the pieces are done, remove them to the roasting pan and add the remaining chicken pieces as room becomes available. When all the chicken has been browned and removed from the pan, add the potatoes, cut side down, and cook until browned, about 6 minutes. Transfer those to the roasting pan as well.

Whack the garlic cloves with the flat side of the knife and scatter them and the rosemary over the contents of the roasting pan. Drizzle with the remaining 2 tablespoons olive oil and roast 15 minutes, stirring gently occasionally. Sprinkle the chicken, sausage, and potatoes with the vinegar and continue roasting, stirring gently occasionally, until the chicken is cooked through and the potatoes are very tender, about 15 minutes.

Prop up one end of the roasting pan so the fat settles on one end and let rest 5 minutes. Spoon off the excess fat from the roasting pan, sprinkle the parsley over everything, and transfer to a warm serving platter. Serve immediately.

Chicken Parmigiana, New-Style

Pollo alla Parmigiana

4 boneless and skinless
chicken thighs or breast
halves (about 1 1/2
pounds)

Salt

Freshly ground black
pepper

All-purpose flour

3/4 cup fine, dry bread
crumbs or Seasoned
Bread Crumbs 2
(page 20)

2 large eggs

1 cup vegetable oil, or as
needed

3 ripe plum tomatoes,
cored and sliced thin

6 ounces fresh mozzarella
or Italian Fontina
cheese, sliced thin

For the Sauce

1/4 cup extra-virgin olive oil,
plus more for drizzling
over the finished dish

6 cloves garlic, peeled

8 ripe tomatoes or
12 ripe plum tomatoes,
peeled, seeded, and
chopped (see page 9)

1/4 cup shredded fresh
basil leaves

Makes 4 servings

This is a more contemporary version of one of the standbys of Italian-American cooking. Instead of coating a thin, breaded, and fried chicken cutlet with tomato sauce, I like to top a chicken thigh with sliced fresh tomatoes and slices of fresh mozzarella or Fontina cheese. A light sauce made with fresh tomatoes and basil finishes the plate.

Fontina is a mellow, lightly aged cow's-milk cheese that melts beautifully. Take the time to search out Italian Fontina — you'll appreciate the creamy difference.

You can prepare this dish using veal or pork cutlets as well (see variations below).

Cut off any fat, bone, and gristle remaining on the chicken thighs. Place two thighs between two sheets of plastic wrap. Pound them lightly with the toothed side of a meat mallet to a more or less even thickness. Don't over-pound the thighs or they will shred and be difficult to bread and cook. Repeat with the remaining thighs. Season the chicken thighs lightly with salt and pepper. Spread out the flour and bread crumbs on two separate plates. Beat the eggs in a wide, shallow bowl until thoroughly blended. Dredge the chicken in flour to coat lightly and tap off excess flour. Dip the thighs in the beaten egg and hold them over the bowl, letting the excess egg drip back into the bowl. Transfer the chicken, one piece at a time, to the plate of bread crumbs; turn it to coat with bread crumbs, patting gently and making sure that each thigh is well coated with bread crumbs.

Heat the vegetable oil in a wide, heavy skillet over medium-high heat until a corner of one of the coated thighs gives off a lively sizzle when dipped in the oil. Add to the oil as many of the chicken pieces as fit without touching. Fry, turning once, until golden on both sides and cooked through, about 8 minutes. Remove to a baking sheet lined with paper towels and drain well.

Remove the paper towels from the baking sheet. Top each chicken thigh with overlapping slices of tomato, dividing the tomato evenly. Drape the sliced cheese over the tomatoes to cover the chicken completely. (The chicken *parmigiana* can be prepared to this point up to several hours in advance. Keep refrigerated until ready to serve.)

Preheat the oven to 400° F.

Prepare the sauce: Heat 3 tablespoons of the olive oil in a wide, nonreactive skillet. Whack the garlic cloves with the side of a knife and drop them into the oil. Cook, shaking the pan, until golden brown, about 2 minutes. Carefully slide the chopped tomatoes into the skillet, season lightly with salt and pepper, and cook until lightly thickened, about 10 minutes. Remove from the heat and set aside.

Bake the chicken until the cheese is lightly browned, about 10 minutes. While the chicken is baking, reheat the tomato sauce to simmering, stir in the basil, and taste, seasoning with salt and pepper if necessary. Spoon the sauce onto a heated platter or plates, and place the chicken over the sauce. Drizzle the remaining 1 tablespoon olive oil over the sauce and serve immediately.

Variations

Pork or Veal Parmigiana

Pound four 5-ounce pork or veal cutlets with a meat mallet, one at a time, between two sheets of plastic wrap to a thickness of about ¼ inch. Bread, brown, and bake the cutlets as described above, and serve them with the same fresh tomato sauce.

N O DOUBT, MANY OF YOU LONG FOR the kind of chicken (or veal) parmigiana you enjoyed in your first visit to an Italian restaurant. Here's how to recreate that dish: Preheat the oven to 400° F. Bread and fry either chicken, pork, or veal cutlets as described above. Choose a shallow baking dish into which the cutlets fit in a single layer and pour in enough Tomato Sauce (page 151) to coat the bottom. Ladle enough sauce over the cutlets to coat them lightly, then top the cutlets with 6 ounces of grated or sliced fresh mozzarella or Fontina cheese. If you like, decorate the top of the cheese with dots or stripes of tomato sauce. Bake the parmigiana until the sauce is bubbling and the cheese is lightly browned, about 20 minutes.

Parmigiana, Old-Style

Roasted Cornish Hen with Balsamic Glaze

Galletto Glassato

2 Cornish hens (about 1¼ pounds each)

Salt

Freshly ground black pepper

5 fresh rosemary sprigs

10 sage leaves

2 fresh or dried bay leaves

¼ cup extra-virgin olive oil

2 bunches scallions, trimmed and cut into 2-inch lengths (about 2 cups)

1 cup peeled, trimmed, and thinly sliced carrots

½ cup thinly sliced celery

6 slices dried porcini mushrooms

2 cups Chicken Stock (page 74) or canned reduced-sodium chicken broth

3 tablespoons balsamic vinegar

1 tablespoon honey

Makes 4 servings

I like basting roasts with a mixture of pan juices, balsamic vinegar, and honey. It adds flavor and a wonderful mahogany color to all kinds of roasts, from poultry to pork to veal. I also like to serve roasted vegetables as a contorno *(side dish) with roasted meats. It makes sense: the oven is going, so you might as well make use of it. Sometimes I add more large-cut carrots and celery to the roasting pan with the meat and serve them alongside the carved roast. Or I put together a separate pan of other root vegetables—leeks, onions, parsnips, turnips, or even mushrooms—season them with salt, olive oil, some of the herbs I used to season the roast, and roast them on a separate shelf from the meat. While they roast, I add enough chicken stock to moisten them and stir them once in a while until they are caramelized and tender.*

Preheat the oven to 425° F. Remove all visible fat and the neck and giblets from the Cornish hens. Rinse the hens under cold water and pat them dry inside and out with paper towels. Season the birds generously with salt and pepper, inside and out. Place one rosemary sprig, 2 sage leaves, and 1 bay leaf in the body cavity of each bird.

Heat the oil in a heavy, flameproof roasting pan or very large ovenproof skillet over medium heat. Add the scallions, carrots, celery, porcini, and the remaining rosemary and sage leaves and cook, stirring, until the scallions are wilted, about 4 minutes. Smooth the vegetables into an even layer and nestle the prepared birds, breast side up, over them. Roast, basting frequently with enough of the chicken stock to keep the vegetables well moistened, until the vegetables and hens are golden brown—about 45 minutes.

Carefully tilt the pan and spoon off enough of the roasting juices to measure 1 cup, not including fat. Stir the balsamic vinegar and honey into the measured juices until the honey is dissolved. Return the birds to oven and roast, basting occasionally with the honey mixture, until the birds are a rich mahogany color and the leg joint moves easily when you wiggle it, about 15 minutes.

Remove the birds from the oven, transfer them to a platter or plates, and cover with a tent of aluminum foil to keep them warm. Strain the pan juices through a sieve into a small saucepan, pressing as much of the liquid from the vegetables as possible. Skim the fat from the surface of the sauce, and bring the sauce to a simmer while carving the birds. With a pair of kitchen shears, cut along both sides of the backbones to remove them. Cut the birds in half through the center breastbone. Cut each half into leg and breast portions. Arrange the pieces on a platter or plates, and spoon some of the roasting juices over them. Pass the remaining sauce separately.

My parents, Erminia and Vittorio, visiting friends in upstate New York, c. 1962

Breast of Chicken in a Light Lemon-Herb Sauce

Involtini di Pollo al Salmoriglio

6 boneless, skinless chicken-breast halves (about 5 ounces each)

½ cup fine, dry bread crumbs

¼ cup extra-virgin olive oil

3 tablespoons chopped fresh Italian parsley

1½ teaspoons dried oregano, preferably the Sicilian or Greek type dried on the branch, crumbled

Salt

1 cup dry white wine

½ cup Chicken Stock (page 74) or canned reduced-sodium chicken broth

¼ cup fresh lemon juice

1 teaspoon crushed hot red pepper

4 cloves garlic, peeled

Makes 4 servings

The finished sauce will be lightly thickened by the bread crumbs that fall into it as the chicken bakes. My favorite way to serve this is with simply steamed green beans: set the chicken on top of the beans and pour the tasty sauce around the chicken, not over it—you want the bread crumbs to stay crunchy.

Cut each chicken-breast half in half crosswise on a diagonal, to yield two pieces of roughly equal size. Place two pieces at a time between two sheets of plastic wrap. Pound gently with the flat side of a meat mallet or the bottom of a small, heavy saucepan to flatten them slightly, to about ½ inch thick.

Toss the bread crumbs, 1 tablespoon of the olive oil, 1 tablespoon of the chopped parsley, ½ teaspoon of the oregano, and salt to taste together in a bowl until blended. Spread 1 teaspoon of bread-crumb mixture over each piece of chicken, reserving the remaining crumbs. Roll each chicken piece into a compact shape with the bread crumbs running in a spiral through the center and fasten securely with a toothpick.

Preheat the oven to 475° F.

Arrange the filled chicken breasts side by side in a 13 × 9–inch, preferably flameproof baking dish. (There should be some space between the pieces of chicken.) Stir the wine, stock, lemon juice, hot pepper, the remaining 3 tablespoons olive oil, the remaining teaspoon of oregano, and salt to taste together in a small bowl. Pour into the baking dish. Whack the garlic cloves with the flat side of a knife and scatter them among the chicken pieces. Bake 10 minutes.

Top the chicken with the remaining bread-crumb mixture. Return to the oven and bake until the bread-crumb topping is golden brown, about 5 minutes.

If the roasting pan is flameproof, place it directly over medium-high heat, add the remaining 2 tablespoons parsley and bring the pan juices to a boil. Boil until lightly thickened, 1 to 2 minutes. (If the roasting pan is not flameproof, transfer the chicken rolls to a warm platter and pour the juices into a skillet before bringing them to a boil.) Remove the garlic cloves, or leave them in if you like. Gently transfer the chicken pieces to plates with a slotted spoon. Pull the toothpicks from the chicken without loosening the bread-crumb topping. Pour the sauce around, not over, the chicken pieces, and serve immediately.

Chicken Breast Valdostana with Braised Lentils

Petto di Pollo alla Valdostana con Lenticchie Brasate

Braised Lentils with Spinach
(page 351)

6 medium (about
7-ounce) boneless,
skinless chicken-breast
halves

6 thin slices imported
Italian prosciutto (see
note below)

All-purpose flour

4 tablespoons unsalted
butter

2 tablespoons extra-virgin
olive oil

⅓ cup dry white wine,
such as Pinot Grigio

½ cup Chicken Stock
(page 74) or canned
reduced-sodium chicken
broth

½ cup seeded and crushed
canned Italian tomatoes
(preferably San
Marzano)

Salt

Freshly ground black pepper

6 ounces Italian Fontina
cheese, sliced thin

2 tablespoons Tomato
Sauce (page 151, or
another) or additional
seeded and crushed
tomatoes

2 tablespoons freshly
grated Parmigiano-
Reggiano cheese

Makes 6 servings

I sometimes suggest some side dishes to go along with main courses and let you make up your mind which you prefer to serve. I love this combination so much, though, that I'm including the side dish as a part of the recipe. I hope you enjoy it as much as I do.

Prepare the braised lentils with spinach through step 1.

Preheat the oven to 375° F. Trim any excess fat, skin, and cartilage from the chicken pieces. Place a piece of prosciutto over each chicken breast, trimming and layering each so it covers the chicken breasts as neatly as possible. Using the back of a large knife, gently pound the prosciutto into the chicken so it adheres. Dredge the chicken breasts in flour to coat them lightly and tap off any excess flour.

Heat 2 tablespoons of the butter and the olive oil in a 12- to 14-inch skillet with an ovenproof handle until the butter is foaming. Place in the skillet as many of the chicken pieces, prosciutto side down, as will fit without touching. Cook just until they begin to brown, about 2 minutes. (Overcooking will toughen the prosciutto.) Turn the chicken and cook until the second side is golden brown, about 3 minutes. Repeat, if necessary, with the remaining chicken breasts, removing the browned chicken to make room. Adjust the heat as you work so the chicken doesn't burn or stick in places.

Pour the wine into the skillet and shake gently to dislodge any brown bits that stick to the pan. Boil until reduced by half. Pour the chicken stock into the skillet and distribute the crushed tomatoes and remaining 2 tablespoons butter in between the pieces of chicken. Season lightly with salt and pepper. Bring to a boil, then lower the heat so the sauce is simmering, tilting the skillet to mix the sauce. Drape the sliced Fontina over the chicken pieces to cover them completely. Dot the center of each chicken breast with a small circle of tomato sauce or a small mound of crushed tomatoes and sprinkle with the grated cheese.

continued on next page

Chicken Breast Valdostana with Braised Lentils *(continued)*

☞ Ask for the prosciutto sliced slightly thicker than paper-thin. You will need six slices if each slice is roughly the same size as a chicken breast. Buy more or fewer slices as necessary.

Place the pan in the oven and bake until the chicken is cooked through, the sauce is bubbling, and the cheese is lightly browned around the edges, about 10 minutes.

While the chicken is in the oven, finish the braised lentils.

Very carefully remove the pan to the stovetop and let stand a minute or two before serving.

Spoon a mound of lentils onto the center of a warm dinner plate. Top with a chicken breast and spoon some of the sauce around the lentils.

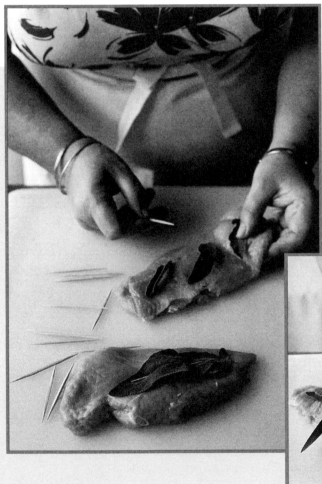

Attaching a Sage Leaf to Chicken

1. Lay two or three sage leaves on one side of each chicken breast and fasten them to the breast with toothpicks.

2. If you do not have toothpicks, tap the sage leaves with the dull edge of a knife to make sure the leaves adhere to the meat.

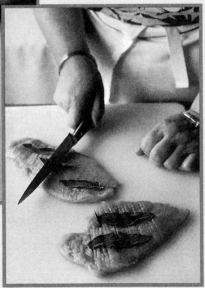

Lighter dishes, like these, became very popular at my first restaurant, Buonavia, when people became more health-conscious in the 1970s. Many of our customers began traveling to Italy at around the same time and developed a taste for these simpler, more authentically Italian dishes. This dish is as popular today at Becco in New York and Lidia's Kansas City and Pittsburgh as it was at Buonavia back then.

Seared Sage-Marinated Breast of Chicken

Petto di Pollo Marinato con Salvia

6 boneless, skinless chicken-breast halves (about 2 pounds)

12 fresh sage leaves

Salt

Freshly ground black pepper

½ cup extra-virgin olive oil

4 cloves garlic, peeled

Makes 6 servings

Here is a quick, tasty, and light dish that can also be done with veal scallopine or turkey-breast cutlets. Served with a tossed salad, it's all you need for a great summer meal. Leftovers, if there are any, make a tasty sandwich stuffer.

Place two chicken pieces between two sheets of plastic wrap and pound them lightly with the smooth side of a meat mallet or small, heavy skillet to a thickness of about ¼ inch. Repeat with the remaining chicken pieces.

Lay two or three sage leaves on one side of each breast and fasten them to the breast with a toothpick, weaving in and out as if you were taking a stitch (see opposite). The toothpicks should lie flat. (Or, if you don't have toothpicks, tap the sage leaves with the dull edge of a knife to make them adhere to the chicken.) Season the chicken generously with salt and pepper and lay them in a baking sheet into which they fit comfortably. Rub both sides of the chicken breasts with the oil. Whack the garlic cloves with the flat side of a knife and scatter them over the chicken. Cover the pan tightly with plastic wrap and refrigerate 1 hour.

Heat one or two large nonstick or well-seasoned cast-iron skillets over medium-high heat. Add as many of the chicken pieces, sage side down, as will fit in a single layer. Cook until well browned on the underside, about 2 minutes. Turn the chicken and cook until the second side is browned and no trace of pink remains in the center, 1 to 2 minutes. (If you don't have enough pans, or large enough pans, to cook the chicken in one batch, keep the first batch of chicken warm on a baking sheet in an oven turned to the lowest setting while cooking the remaining chicken.) Serve immediately.

Vegetables

Eggplant Parmigiana

Melanzana alla Parmigiana

3 medium eggplants, or
5 or 6 smaller
eggplants (about 2½ to
3 pounds total)

1 tablespoon coarse sea
or kosher salt

3 large eggs

1 teaspoon salt

All-purpose flour for
dredging

2 cups fine, dry bread
crumbs

½ cup vegetable oil, or as
needed

½ cup olive oil, or as
needed

Tomato Sauce (page 151)

2 cups grated
Parmigiano-Reggiano
cheese

12 fresh basil leaves

1 pound fresh mozzarella
cheese or Italian
Fontina cheese, cut into
slices ⅓ inch thick

Serves 6

When I bread and fry things like these slices of eggplant, I make a little assembly line that leads from the flour, to the eggs, on to the bread crumbs, and right into the pan of hot oil. Placing three rectangular cake pans side by side next to the stove works nicely — there is very little cleanup afterward — but any container wide enough to hold several slices of eggplant at a time will work just as well.

This dish can be made with roasted eggplant slices instead of breaded and fried eggplant. Although it will be good, it will not be as tasty, nor will it have the texture of the fried eggplant. The roasted version is very simple: Drain and rinse the eggplant as described above, but instead of coating the eggplant slices, toss them with a few tablespoons of olive oil. Brush a baking sheet with olive oil, and set the eggplant slices side by side on the baking sheet. Bake them in a 450° F preheated oven for 20 minutes, till they are golden brown. Let them cool, and proceed to layer and bake the ingredients as below.

Trim the stems and ends from the eggplants. Remove strips of peel about 1 inch wide from the eggplants, leaving about half the peel intact. Cut the eggplant lengthwise into ½-inch-thick slices and place them in a colander. Sprinkle with the coarse salt and let drain for 1 hour. Rinse the eggplant under cool running water, drain thoroughly, and pat dry.

Whisk the eggs and 1 teaspoon salt together in a 13 × 9–inch baking pan or wide, shallow bowl. Spread the flour and bread crumbs in an even layer in two separate wide, shallow bowls or over sheets of wax paper. Dredge the eggplant slices in flour, shaking off the excess. Dip the floured eggplant into the egg mixture, turning well to coat both sides evenly. Let excess egg drip back into the pan, then lay the eggplant in the pan of bread crumbs. Turn to coat both sides well with bread crumbs, pressing with your hands until the bread crumbs adhere well to the eggplant.

Pour ½ cup each of the olive and vegetable oils into a medium skillet. Heat over medium-high heat until a corner of one of the eggplant slices gives off a lively sizzle when dipped into the oil. Add as many of the eggplant slices as fit without touching and cook, turning once, until well browned on both sides, about 6 minutes. Remove the eggplant to a baking pan lined with paper towels and repeat with the remaining eggplant slices. Adjust the heat as the eggplant cooks to prevent the bits of coating that fall off the eggplant slices from burning. Add oil to the pan as necessary during cooking to keep the level more or less the same.

Preheat the oven to 375° F. Heat the tomato sauce to simmering, if necessary, in a small saucepan over medium heat. Ladle enough sauce into a 9 × 13–inch baking dish to cover the bottom. Sprinkle with an even layer of grated cheese and top with a layer of fried eggplant, pressing it down gently. Tear a few leaves of basil over the eggplant and ladle about ¾ cup of the sauce to coat the top evenly. Sprinkle an even layer of grated cheese over the sauce and top with a layer of mozzarella or Fontina, using about one-third of the cheese. Repeat the layering as described above two more times, ending with a top layer of sliced cheese that leaves a border of about 1 inch around the edges of the baking dish. Drizzle sauce around the border of the baking dish and sprinkle the top layer with the remaining grated cheese. Finish with a few decorative streaks or rounds of tomato sauce. Cover the baking dish loosely with aluminum foil and poke several holes in the foil with the tip of a knife. Bake 30 minutes.

Uncover, and continue baking until the top layer of cheese is golden in spots, about 15 minutes. Let rest 10 to 20 minutes, then cut into squares and serve.

Eggplant Rollatini

Rollatini di Melanzane

1½ pounds fresh ricotta cheese, or 3 cups packaged whole-milk ricotta

Tomato Sauce (page 151)

2 medium eggplants (each about 4 inches wide and about 1 pound)

Coarse salt

½ cup olive oil, or as needed

½ cup vegetable oil, or as needed

3 eggs

All-purpose flour

1 cup freshly grated Parmigiano-Reggiano cheese

3 tablespoons chopped fresh Italian parsley

Freshly ground black pepper

8 ounces fresh mozzarella cheese, cut into ¼ × ¼–inch sticks

8 fresh basil leaves (optional)

Makes 6 main-course servings or 12 first-course or buffet servings

I'm offering you the basic recipe for filling these eggplant rolls. You can take it in any direction you like, adding spinach, raisins, pine nuts, prosciutto, or whatever else sounds good to you. Eggplant rollatini are versatile in another way, too. Because the individual rolls are easy to serve, they are wonderful as a first course for a big crowd—like a family gathering—or as part of an Italian-American buffet. For a smaller crowd, this makes a substantial main course that needs only a first-course salad to make it a meal.

If you'd like to make these simple rolls even easier to fill, you can cut the sticks of mozzarella into little cubes and stir them right into the ricotta filling.

Spoon the ricotta into a large, fine-mesh sieve or a colander lined with a double thickness of cheesecloth or a basket-type coffee filter. Set the sieve over a bowl and cover the ricotta well with plastic wrap. Drain the ricotta in the refrigerator at least overnight, or up to 24 hours. Discard the liquid in the bottom of the bowl.

Make the tomato sauce.

Trim the stems and ends from the eggplants. Remove strips of peel about 1 inch wide from the eggplants, leaving about half the peel intact. Cut the eggplant lengthwise into ¼-inch-thick slices and place them in a colander. Sprinkle generously with the coarse salt, tossing to expose all slices, and let drain for 1 hour. Rinse the eggplant under cool running water, drain thoroughly, and pat dry.

Pour ½ cup each of the olive and vegetable oils into a medium skillet over medium-high heat. While the oil is heating, whisk 2 of the eggs and 1 teaspoon coarse salt together in a wide, shallow bowl. Spread flour in an even layer in a separate wide, shallow bowl or over a sheet of wax paper. Dredge the eggplant slices in flour, shaking the excess off. Dip the floured eggplant into the egg mixture, turning well to coat both sides evenly. Let excess egg drip back into the pan.

When a corner of a coated eggplant slice gives off a lively sizzle when dipped into the oil, it is ready for frying. Add as many of the coated eggplant slices as fit without touching and cook, turning once, until golden on both sides, about 4 minutes. Remove the eggplant to a baking pan lined with paper towels and repeat with the remaining eggplant slices. Adjust the heat as the eggplant cooks to prevent the egg coating from cooking too fast or overbrowning. Add oil to the pan as necessary during cooking to keep the level more or less the same; allow the oil to heat before adding more eggplant slices.

Preheat the oven to 375° F. Stir the drained ricotta, $1/2$ cup of the grated cheese, and the parsley together in a mixing bowl. Taste and season with salt and pepper. Beat the remaining egg in a separate small bowl and stir it into

continued on next page

Eggplant

EGGPLANTS CAN BE SMALL, large, or somewhere in between, with colors ranging from blackish purple to lilac to spotted. Regardless of the size or color, when buying eggplants look for those that are firm to the touch, with a shiny skin and a crisp, green stem. (If the stem and its cover are dry and brown, the eggplant is old. And an old eggplant is a bitter eggplant.)

The uses for eggplant in Italian and Italian-American cooking are endless. They can be simmered in a sweet-and-sour sauce for an appetizer (see Sweet and Sour Marinated Vegetables, page 52), roasted and tossed into pasta (see Ziti with Roasted Eggplant and Ricotta Cheese, page 152), or an integral part of such classics as the Scaloppine alla Sorrentina on page 258. (*Sorrentina* or *alla Norma* in a recipe title or on a menu is a tip-off that eggplant is included somewhere.) Breaded and fried, they are the center of a truly delicious sandwich or the heart of Eggplant Parmigiana (see page 274), a staple of the Italian-American table. Some people peel their eggplants completely, feeling the peel is tough and bitter. But, personally, I like the peel, so I remove only part of it, in strips. Generally speaking, when I am slicing eggplants for frying or roasting, I cut it lengthwise rather than into rounds. There are fewer slices to handle, making life a little easier.

the ricotta mixture. Pour 1 cup of the tomato sauce over the bottom of a 10 × 15–inch baking dish. (If you don't have a baking dish of that size, divide the sauce and rolls between two smaller dishes into which they fit comfortably.) Sprinkle lightly with 2 tablespoons of the remaining grated Parmigiano-Reggiano cheese.

Lay one of the fried eggplant slices in front of you with the short end toward you. Spoon about 2 tablespoons of the ricotta filling over the narrow end of the slice and top it with a mozzarella stick. Roll into a compact roll and place, seam side down, in the prepared baking dish. Repeat with the remaining eggplant slices and filling, placing the rolls side by side.

Ladle the remaining tomato sauce over the eggplant rolls to coat them evenly. Sprinkle the remaining grated Parmigiano-Reggiano cheese over the top of the eggplant and tear the basil leaves, if using, over the cheese.

Cover the dish loosely with aluminum foil and bake until the edges of the casserole are bubbling and the filling is heated through, about 30 minutes. Let rest 10 minutes before serving.

☞ Choosing Eggplants: When choosing eggplants for rollatini, pick staight-sided eggplants of even thickness. You will get more uniform, long slices from them than from eggplants that are fat at one end and thin at the other. If the eggplants in your market are curvy, you might want to buy an extra to make sure you'll end up with twenty-four slices.

Fried Potatoes and Eggs

Patate Fritte con Uova

1 medium Idaho potato
  (about 8 ounces)

½ cup extra-virgin olive oil

½ teaspoon fresh rosemary
  leaves

4 large eggs

Salt (preferably sea salt)

Freshly ground black pepper

Makes 2 servings

This recipe serves two, but it can easily be doubled or cut in half. Potatoes and eggs cooked like this are best when prepared from start to end in the same pan, so the potatoes stay crispy and hot. You might want to do one panful at a time the first time you try this recipe, but once you eat this, I guarantee it will become a favorite and soon you'll get the knack of working two pans at once. Serve for breakfast, or as lunch with a salad.

Peel the potato and cut it in half crosswise. Stand the halves cut side down and cut into ¼-inch slices, then cut the slices into ¼-inch strips. Divide the oil between two 8-inch nonstick or well-seasoned skillets and heat over medium-high heat. (If you don't have two such pans, cook the potatoes and eggs one serving at a time.) Divide the potatoes between the pans of oil and cook, shaking the pans and turning the potatoes as necessary, until they are golden on all sides, about 6 minutes. Hold the potatoes in place with a slotted spoon or wire skimmer while you pour off all but about 1 or 2 teaspoons of oil from each skillet. Return the skillets to the heat, sprinkle half the rosemary leaves over each, and toss well. Break two eggs into each pan. Season generously with salt and pepper, and mix the potatoes and eggs together with a fork until the egg is cooked to your liking. Serve hot.

Rice-Stuffed Tomatoes

Pomodori Imbottiti di Riso

Salt

¼ cup extra-virgin olive oil

2 bay leaves

½ cup Arborio rice

6 medium ripe but firm tomatoes (about 2½ pounds)

½ cup diced mozzarella, preferably fresh, or provola cheese

½ cup plus 1 tablespoon grated Parmigiano-Reggiano cheese

3 tablespoons chopped fresh basil

Pepper to taste

Makes 6 servings

Even though I call these "stuffed" tomatoes, don't actually stuff the rice filling into the tomatoes. Fill them loosely or they will be dense and dry after baking. You can put the tops back on the tomatoes flat or prop them up at an angle.

Rice cooked this way — with a little olive oil and bay leaves — is a good dish on its own. We used to feed it to children or adults when they were recovering from an upset stomach, but don't limit it to that. In addition to stirring the fresh basil into the filling, shred as much as you like and scatter it over the tomatoes after you put them on a plate. Basil and tomato is a union made in heaven, and who am I to question heaven?

In a 1-quart saucepan, heat 1½ cups salted water, 2 tablespoons of the oil, and the bay leaves to a boil. Stir in the rice and bring to a boil. Adjust the heat to a lively simmer and cook the rice, uncovered, until *al dente*, tender but firm, about 12 minutes. Most of the liquid should be absorbed, and the texture of the rice should be creamy. Drain any excess liquid from the rice and transfer the rice to a mixing bowl.

Meanwhile, preheat oven to 375° F. Cut a ½-inch slice from the top of each tomato and set aside. Scoop out the pulp and seeds with a teaspoon and drop into a strainer set over a bowl. Press on the pulp in the strainer to squeeze out as much liquid as possible. Reserve the liquid, and discard the pulp in the strainer.

Toss the rice, mozzarella, ½ cup of the Parmigiano-Reggiano, and the basil together in a small bowl. Taste, and season with salt and pepper.

Gently stuff the tomatoes with the rice mixture, dividing it evenly. Top each tomato with the reserved slices. Using some of the remaining oil, brush a baking dish into which the tomatoes fit comfortably. Set the stuffed tomatoes in the dish. Add the strained liquid from the tomatoes and, if necessary, pour in enough water to come about ¼ inch up the sides of the tomatoes. Drizzle the remaining oil over the tomatoes and sprinkle them with the remaining 1 tablespoon grated cheese. Cover the dish loosely with aluminum foil and bake 15 minutes.

Uncover the dish and bake until the tomatoes are very tender and the tops are lightly browned, about 10 minutes. Remove tomatoes from oven and let rest for a few minutes. Carefully transfer the tomatoes to a serving platter, or individual plates. Swirl the juices in the pan to incorporate the oil into the juices, and spoon the pan juices over and around the tomatoes. The tomatoes are best when served warm, with some of the pan juices drizzled over each serving.

This is a delicious dish that can be served hot or at room temperature. It can be included in an antipasto platter, served as a side dish, or as a main course. It is also an ideal family-style dish—just set it in the middle of the table so that all can help themselves.

Lightly Stuffed and Baked Zucchini

Zucchini Ripieni al Forno

1 cup cubed (1-inch) day-old bread, crusts removed

1 ½ cups milk

6 small ("fancy") zucchini about 3 inches long, or 4 medium zucchini about 5 inches long (about 1 ¼ pounds)

1 cup freshly grated Parmigiano-Reggiano cheese

¼ cup chopped fresh Italian parsley

2 tablespoons chopped fresh thyme leaves

Salt

Freshly ground black pepper

6 tablespoons extra-virgin olive oil

1 large egg, beaten

Makes 2 or 3 main-course servings or 6 appetizer or side-dish servings

Preheat the oven to 425° F.

Toss the bread and milk together in a small mixing bowl. Soak until the bread is completely saturated, about 20 minutes. Squeeze the bread between your hands to remove as much milk as possible and chop it very fine.

While the bread is soaking, wash the zucchini, trim both ends, and cut in half lengthwise. With a teaspoon, scrape out the seeds from the center, forming a groove down the length of the zucchini pieces.

Toss the chopped bread, grated cheese, parsley, and thyme together in a bowl until well mixed. Taste, and season with salt and pepper. Stir in 4 tablespoons of the olive oil and the egg. Fill the grooves in the zucchini and cover the halves evenly with stuffing. Brush a 9 × 13–inch baking dish, or other dish into which the zucchini will fit comfortably, with the remaining 2 tablespoons of olive oil. Arrange the zucchini in the dish side by side, stuffing side up. Cover it with aluminum foil, and bake 15 minutes.

Uncover the dish and continue baking until the top of the stuffing is crispy and the zucchini are tender, about 15 minutes. Let rest 10 minutes before serving.

Seafood

Whenever you cook any type of seafood, there is one undisputed prerequisite, regardless of the recipe: the fish must be fresh. Seafood is unforgiving in that way: it is one of the most sensitive ingredients in the kitchen. That's why it does make a difference in the finished dish if you are close to the source of your seafood. Maybe I am spoiled, but, having grown up in a seaside town, I like to see my fish still moving when they come to market, with bright shiny eyes, and flesh that is still stiff and firm.

New York, where I make my home now, is a great source for fresh fish. To supply our New York City restaurants—Felidia, Becco, and Esca—with fish, we shop every morning at the Fulton Street Fish Market. During local fishing season, we also go out to Long Island, a practice I started when I ran my first restaurant, Buonavia, in the Forest Hills section of Queens, from 1971 to 1980. We went regularly to Freeport, on the south shore of Long Island, where we bought from the fishermen—many of them Italian-American—seafood that wasn't in vogue at the time, and therefore not available from our regular suppliers: calamari, octopus, skate, monkfish, mackerel, blue-claw crabs, and black sea bass. I had a great time waiting for the fishing boats to pull into the dock, with swarms of seagulls hovering overhead waiting for an opportunity to snatch a fish from the decks.

It was all reminiscent of my childhood—the smells of the sea and the fresh fish, the sounds of the boats docking. And here I was, in another country, another time, carrying on my culinary heritage.

I recall from my childhood that seafood was pretty much served as it came from the sea—whole fish on the bone, with the skin and head left on, or crustaceans right in the shell. Some of my favorite parts of seafood are precisely the parts I have had trouble serving in my restaurants—sweet fish cheeks (however small), the eyes, the bit of fillet at the back of the fish's head (where it meets the body), the tail and skin of a crispy grilled fish, the cartilage of skate, the suction cups on an octopus, and the crunchy heads of fried calamari and whitebait. But things are changing; those delicacies, along with polipo, scungilli, baccalà, and seppie, which were a hard sell ten or fifteen years ago in Italian-American restaurants, are gaining in popularity daily.

Shrimp in a Chunky Marinara Sauce

Gamberi alla Marinara

6 tablespoons extra-virgin olive oil

6 cloves garlic, peeled and sliced

2½ pounds jumbo shrimp (about 30), peeled and deveined

Salt

One 35-ounce can Italian plum tomatoes (preferably San Marzano), cored and coarsely crushed

1 teaspoon crushed hot red pepper

8 fresh basil leaves, torn into quarters

2 tablespoons minced fresh Italian parsley

Makes 6 servings

This dish is excellent served as a main course or as a dressing for pasta. (Toss the pasta with the sauce and top the plates with shrimp.) It is also delicious spooned over hot Soft Polenta (page 346).

Heat 4 tablespoons of the olive oil in a large skillet over medium heat. Stir in the garlic and cook, shaking the pan, until golden, about 1 minute. Add as many shrimp as fit in a single layer with some space between each. (If you crowd the shrimp, they will steam in their own juices rather than get crunchy with a lightly browned exterior.) Cook, turning once, until lightly golden, about 3 minutes. Sprinkle with salt to taste.

With a slotted spoon, transfer the shrimp to a plate, leaving as much garlic as possible in the pan. Pour the remaining 2 tablespoons olive oil and the tomatoes into the skillet, season with salt and crushed red pepper, and bring to a vigorous boil. Lower the heat so the sauce is at a lively simmer, and cook until lightly thickened, about 10 minutes. Stir in the shrimp, basil, and parsley and cook until the shrimp are heated through, just a few seconds.

Fregola

FREGOLA, OR FREGULA IN SARDINIAN, consists of small balls of dry dough, like dry pasta but round. Fregola can range from the size of a grape pit to the size of a cherry pit. (The word *fregola* in Italian means "crumb," hence the name.) Today, fregola can be bought in specialty stores in plastic or cellophane bags like dry pasta and, like dry pasta, it keeps well for several months.

Fregola is a wonderful addition to fish soups or stews. Cook fregola as you would any pasta, in plenty of boiling salted water. (Or, for more flavor, cook it in stock.) Drain the fregola and dress it with sauce, or stir it into a saucy dish such as Savory Seafood Stew (Zuppa di Pesce, page 316). What makes fregola interesting is its texture.

Although you can buy fregola today, it is not very hard to make in the traditional way: Coat the bottom of a wide, round cake pan with some coarsely ground durum semolina flour. With your fingers, drizzle large drops of water all around the edge of the pan, then gently shake the pan until the water droplets have absorbed enough semolina to form small balls—which form the fregolas. Bounce the contents of the pan in a coarse sieve; all the fregolas will remain in the sieve and the semolina flour will pass through. Roll the fregolas onto a baking sheet and let set for 30 minutes.

While the fregolas are resting, heat the oven to 275° F. Dry the fregolas completely in the oven; it will take about 20 minutes. Let cool before cooking or storing in an airtight container in the cupboard.

Fregolas made with water and durum semolina flour are the traditional Sardinian version, but fregola can be made in the same way by dripping an egg beaten with some salt over all-purpose flour. Fregolas made that way will be smaller in size and have a richer taste, due to the egg. They will also need about half the time to toast in the oven. Fregolas made with egg are excellent in soups and served alongside braised meats.

Scampi (*Nephrops norvegicus*) are spiny, hard-shell crustaceans that resemble small lobsters more than shrimp, except that they are powder pink in color. They are much prized but not as abundant as they used to be in the Mediterranean. One of the most common ways to prepare them is to sauté them with garlic, onion, and white wine. The same method was used by chefs in Italian-American restaurants to prepare shrimp (*gamberi* in Italian), which were much more readily available. So they were called "shrimp scampi," and the name has stuck, meaning shrimp prepared in the style of the beloved scampi.

Shrimp Prepared in the Scampi Style

Scampi

2 tablespoons extra-virgin olive oil

3 large cloves garlic, minced

2 tablespoons finely chopped shallots

Salt

Freshly ground black pepper

½ cup dry white wine

2 tablespoons fresh lemon juice

8 tablespoons unsalted butter, softened

2 teaspoons minced fresh parsley

2 teaspoons minced fresh tarragon

36 "U-10" shrimp (about 3½ pounds) (see note)

6 to 8 sprigs fresh thyme

Makes 6 servings

Flavored butters—whether this one or a variation of it—are handy to have around. A little bit goes a long way to add flavor to quick dinners. Just slice the butter and use it to top broiled seafood or pan-seared chicken breast. If you need to speed things up a little, spoon the cooked garlic-shallot mixture into a small bowl, set that into a larger bowl of ice, and stir until it is completely chilled.

To make the flavored butter: Heat the olive oil in a small skillet over medium heat. Add the garlic and cook until pale golden, about 1 minute. Stir in the shallots, season generously with salt and pepper, and continue cooking, shaking the skillet, until the shallots are wilted, about 2 minutes. Add ¼ cup of the wine, bring to a boil, and cook until about half of the wine has evaporated. Stir in 1 tablespoon of the lemon juice and boil until almost all of the liquid has evaporated. Transfer to a small bowl and cool completely. Add the butter, parsley, and tarragon and beat until blended. To make the butter easier to handle, spoon it onto a 12-inch length of plastic wrap and roll it into a log shape, completely wrapped in plastic. Chill thoroughly. (The flavored butter can be made several hours, or up to a few days, in advance.)

continued on next page

Place the rack in the lowest position and preheat the oven to 475° F. Peel the shrimp, leaving the tail and last shell segment attached.

Devein the shrimp by making a shallow cut along the curved back of the shrimp and extracting the black or gray vein that runs the length of the shrimp. Lay the shrimp flat on the work surface and, starting at the thick end, make a horizontal cut along the center of the shrimp, extending it about three-quarters of the way down. Pat shrimp dry.

Using some of the flavored butter, lightly grease a shallow baking pan, such as a jelly-roll pan, or ovenproof sauté pan into which the shrimp fit comfortably without touching. Place each shrimp on the work surface with the underside of the tail facing up and away from you. With your fingers, roll each half of the slit part of the shrimp in toward and underneath the tail, forming a "6" on each side of the shrimp which will lift the tail up.

Arrange the shrimp, tails up, on the prepared sheet or sauté pan as you work, leaving some space between. Cut the remaining flavored butter into $1/2$-inch cubes and disperse the cubes among the shrimp. Mix the remaining $1/4$ cup wine and 1 tablespoon lemon juice and add to the pan. Scatter the thyme sprigs over and around the shrimp. Season with salt and pepper and place the pan on the oven rack. Roast until the shrimp are firm and crunchy and barely opaque in the center, about 5 minutes. Transfer the shrimp to a hot platter or divide among hot plates. Drain the pan juices into a small pan. Bring to a boil over high heat and boil until the sauce is lightly thickened, 1 to 2 minutes. Spoon the sauce over the shrimp as is, or strain it first for a more velvety texture. Serve immediately.

☞ When you are buying shrimp, the easiest way to determine the size is by using restaurant terminology. For example, "U-10" stands for "under 10," which means there are ten or fewer shrimp in a pound. "U-15" means fewer than 15 per pound; "21/25" means there are between twenty-one and twenty-five per pound, "16/20" between sixteen and twenty a pound, and so on. Retail terminology such as "large," "jumbo," or "medium" can be misleading.

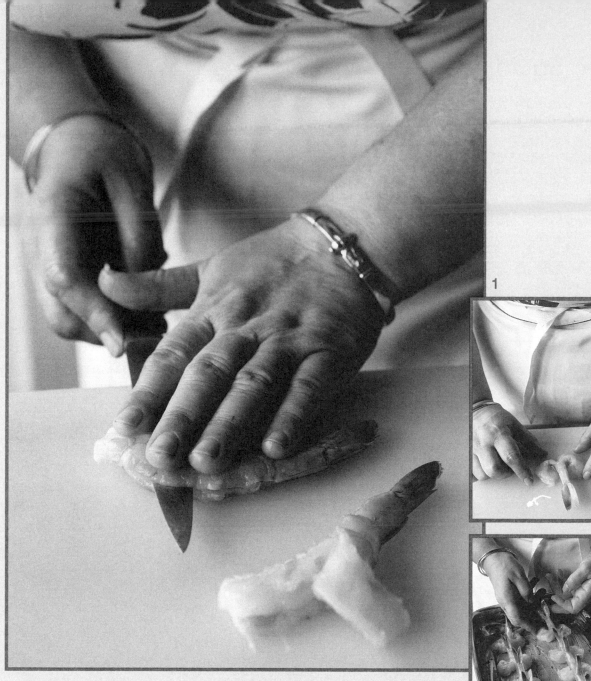

Preparing Shrimp Scampi Style

1. Make a horizontal cut along the center of the shrimp, extending it about three-fourths of the way down toward the tail.

2. Roll each half of the slit part of the shrimp in toward and underneath the tail, forming a 6 on each side of the shrimp, which will lift the tail up.

3. Arrange the shrimp, tails up, on the prepared pan.

Fried Squid

Calamari Fritti

8 medium squid or cuttlefish (about 3 pounds) (see opposite)

3 cups vegetable oil

2 cups all-purpose flour

½ teaspoon salt

Makes 4 servings

Clean calamari according to the directions on page 40. Detach the "wings" (fins) from the body and cut them in half from base to tip. Cut the body sac into ¼-inch rings. If the tentacles are larger than bite-size, cut them in two lengthwise. Drain all pieces well in a colander, pat them as dry as possible in a cloth towel, and divide into two batches.

Heat 1½ cups of the oil in a very large (12- to 14-inch) skillet over medium-high heat until it registers 375° F on a frying thermometer. (To cook the calamari without a thermometer, see next paragraph.) While the oil heats, dredge half the calamari in flour to coat all sides evenly. Bounce the calamari in a sieve to remove excess flour.

When the oil reaches temperature, or when one coated calamari ring gives off a lively sizzle when lowered into the oil, add the coated calamari a few pieces at a time. Fry, carefully tilting the skillet as necessary so the oil reaches all pieces, until golden on one side, about 2 minutes. Turn the calamari and fry until the second side is golden, about 2 minutes.

Remove the calamari with a skimmer or slotted spoon and drain them on a paper-towel-lined baking sheet. Discard the oil and repeat with the remaining oil and second batch of calamari. Sprinkle evenly with salt and serve immediately.

To prepare this dish using cuttlefish, clean and cut the cuttlefish as follows: Remove the tentacles and innards from the body as described in "To Clean Calamari" on page 40. Cut down one side of the cuttlefish body and cut out the blade-shaped "bone." Remove the skin and innards from the body and cut the body into strips roughly $1/3 \times 2^1/2$ inches. Cut off the tentacles just below the eyes, and cut each cluster of tentacles into two equal pieces. Rinse and dry the cuttlefish as described above, and proceed with the recipe.

If you are able to find cuttlefish and clean them for this recipe, you will have the ink from the sacs as a bonus to use for another dish—for instance, it could be added, along with strips of the cuttlefish, to the Basic Risotto on page 195.

To find and remove the ink sacs, look about halfway down the cluster of intestines for a grayish sac with black lines. The ink sacs can range in size from $1/2$ to 1 inch, and are about the width of a thin wooden skewer. Remove the ink sac by cutting on either side of it with a pair of kitchen shears or a paring knife. Don't cut through the sac itself, or the ink will leak. Store the ink sacs in a small bowl covered with olive oil for up to 2 days, until you are ready to use them. Press out all of the ink by cutting the end of the sac, and mix the ink in with the oil. Add all—including the sac—to the risotto about 8 minutes before it is done. One sac should color and flavor enough risotto for two.

Cuttlefish (Seppie)

Cooking Calamari: The Long and Short of It

If you want tender calamari, there are two ways to go about it: either cook them quickly—from 4 to 8 minutes, depending on the amount of calamari and how you cook them—or braise them slowly for 30 minutes or more. Anything in between and the calamari will remain tough.

The quick method of cooking calamari focuses more on the texture and fresh flavor of the sea and the calamari themselves. I recommend quick cooking if you want to enjoy the calamari as the prime ingredient, as in the Calamari Fritti on page 290, or as part of a Zuppa di Pesce–type dish (see page 316), where the texture of the fish is very important.

The long, braising method focuses more on the flavor of the sauce, by extracting the flavor of the calamari into the sauce, and is preferable if you want to make a calamari sauce to dress pasta, risotto, or polenta.

Grilled Calamari

Calamari alla Griglia

8 medium squid (about 3 pounds)

¼ cup extra-virgin olive oil, plus more for drizzling over the cooked squid if you like

6 cloves garlic, peeled and sliced

1 tablespoon fresh thyme leaves

½ teaspoon salt

½ teaspoon crushed hot red pepper

Chopped fresh Italian parsley

Makes 6 servings

This dish can be prepared on a charcoal grill or in a cast-iron pan or griddle. Just make sure, in either case, that the temperature is good and hot, so the calamari cook very quickly. For easy handling, especially on the grill, thread the calamari bodies onto a skewer—one or two per skewer, depending on the size. Thread the tentacles onto a separate skewer without crowding them, since they will need a few additional minutes to cook.

Clean calamari according to the directions on page 40, leaving the skin on if you like (as I do).

Toss the cleaned calamari bodies and tentacles, ¼ cup olive oil, the garlic, thyme, salt, and crushed red pepper together in a bowl until the calamari are coated. Cover the bowl, and marinate in refrigerator for 1 hour or up to overnight.

Prepare a charcoal grill well ahead, so you have hot, glowing coals. Or heat a wide cast-iron skillet or griddle over high heat until a drop of water bounces and sizzles. Lay the squid onto the grill or in the skillet. Set a heavy skillet on top of the calamari to weight them down so as much of them as possible makes contact with the hot grill or skillet. This makes it easier for the calamari to cook evenly and brown well. Cook, turning once, until golden on both sides, about 6 minutes. Transfer to a warm platter and drizzle with additional extra-virgin olive oil, if you like. Sprinkle with chopped Italian parsley and serve immediately.

Broccoli Rabe and Sausage

Broccoli di Rabe e Salsicce

page 243

Breast of Chicken in a Light
Lemon-Herb Sauce

Involtini di Pollo al Salmoriglio

page 270

Spare Ribs Roasted
with Vinegar and
Red Pepper

*Costine di Maiale
al Forno*

page 244

Scallopine in
Lemon-Caper Sauce
Scaloppine Piccata
page 254

Shrimp Prepared in
the Scampi Style

Scampi
page 287

Swordfish Skewers
Glazed with Sweet
and Sour Sauce

*Pesce Spada
allo Spiedo*

page 312

Savory Seafood Stew
Zuppa di Pesce
page 316

Lemon Delight (foreground)

Delizie al Limone

page 374

Coffee Granita (background)

Granita di Caffè

page 384

Calamari in the Luciana Style

Calamari alla Luciana

10 small (about 5-ounce) squid (about 3 pounds total)

6 tablespoons extra-virgin olive oil

6 cloves garlic, peeled and sliced

4 fresh thyme sprigs

Crushed hot red pepper

1 teaspoon red-wine vinegar

$\frac{1}{2}$ cup dry white wine

Salt

$\frac{1}{2}$ cup chopped fresh Italian parsley

Makes 6 servings

Traditionally, calamari are cooked with the skin on—it is the skin that gives a purple hue to the sauce. But if you want, you can peel it off.

Clean the calamari according to directions on page 40, leaving the skin intact if you prefer. Cut the bodies into $\frac{1}{2}$-inch rings and set them and the tentacles in a colander to drain well.

Heat the olive oil in a wide, heavy skillet over medium heat. Scatter the garlic over the oil and cook, shaking the pan, until golden, about 1 minute. Increase the heat to high, scatter the calamari in the skillet, and season with the thyme and lightly with crushed red pepper. Cook, stirring regularly, until the water from the calamari has evaporated and the calamari have begun to caramelize, 6 to 8 minutes.

Sprinkle the vinegar over the calamari and scrape up the browned bits from the pan. Pour in the wine and bring to a boil, continuing to scrape the skillet. Cook until the wine is evaporated and the calamari are golden, about 5 minutes. Season with salt and crushed red pepper to taste, stir in the parsley, and serve.

Oven-Baked Squid

Calamari al Forno

9 medium calamari (about 3½ pounds total)

6 tablespoons extra-virgin olive oil

8 cloves garlic, peeled and sliced

Salt

1 teaspoon crushed hot red pepper

¼ cup chopped fresh Italian parsley

Makes 6 servings

Roasting the calamari in a cast-iron skillet, or any pan or casserole that can go directly over open flame, makes life easier. If you don't have such a pan, roast the calamari in a regular baking dish, transfer them to a heated platter when they're done, and pour the pan juices into a small saucepan to boil them down. For this recipe, bake the tentacles together with the bodies and reposition the tentacles in the opening of the body before serving.

Preheat the oven to 450° F. Clean and rinse the squid according to the directions on page 40, but without removing the skin. Arrange the squid bodies and tentacles in a shallow cast-iron pan or other flameproof baking dish. Stir the olive oil, garlic, salt, and crushed red pepper together in a small bowl, pour over the squid, and turn them to coat with seasoned oil. Cover the dish with aluminum foil and roast 10 minutes.

Remove the foil and flip the pieces of squid. Continue baking, uncovered and turning occasionally, until the squid is tender when poked with a fork or skewer, about 10 minutes.

Transfer the pan to the stovetop and bring the liquid to a boil over high heat. Cook until the sauce is lightly syrupy, about 4 minutes. Toss in the parsley and transfer the squid to warm plates or a platter. Spoon the pan juices over the squid and serve immediately.

This dish is also delicious with fresh fava beans, when in season; lima beans are also good. The peas not only become part of the sauce and absorb the flavor of the calamari, they are also a built-in side dish.

Stuffed Calamari Braised with Fresh Peas

Calamari Ripieni Stufati con Piselli

Twelve 5- to 7-ounce calamari (about 4½ pounds total), cleaned according to directions on page 40, tentacles reserved

½ cup plus 2 tablespoons extra-virgin olive oil

4 cloves garlic, peeled and chopped

2 sprigs fresh thyme, leaves stripped and finely chopped

Crushed hot red pepper

Salt

¼ cup cognac

¼ cup fine, dry bread crumbs

¼ cup chopped fresh Italian parsley

3 tablespoons chopped onion

4 cups fresh shelled peas, or two 10-ounce packages frozen peas, defrosted and drained

ingredients continued on next page

Leave the calamari bodies whole and chop the tentacles into ¼-inch pieces.

To make the stuffing: Heat 4 tablespoons of the olive oil in a large skillet over medium heat. Add the chopped garlic and cook, shaking the pan, until golden, about 1 minute. Scatter the chopped tentacles over the oil, sprinkle the thyme over them, and season lightly with crushed red pepper and salt. Cook until the liquid given off by the tentacles is evaporated and the tentacles begin to brown, about 6 minutes. Stir in the cognac, bring to a boil, and cook until it is almost completely evaporated. Stir in the bread crumbs and cook until they begin to toast, about 5 minutes. Remove from the heat, stir in the parsley, and set aside until cool enough to handle.

Divide the stuffing evenly among the calamari, packing it lightly into the body cavities. An espresso spoon or small teaspoon is a good tool. (It will seem as though there is not enough stuffing, but the stuffing will expand and the calamari will shrink.) Seal the open end of the calamari with a toothpick.

Heat 4 tablespoons of the remaining olive oil in a large skillet over medium-high heat. Slip as many of the stuffed calamari into the skillet as fit in a single layer. Cook, turning as necessary, until caramelized on both sides, about 8 minutes. Slip more calamari into the oil as those in the pan shrink. Transfer the calamari to a plate as they are done, leaving behind as much oil as possible. Stir the onion into the oil remaining in the pan and cook, stirring, until wilted, about 4 minutes. Stir in the peas and season lightly with salt and crushed red pepper. Lower the heat to low and cover the pan. Cook, stirring occasionally, until the peas are tender, about 20 minutes for fresh peas or 10 minutes for frozen peas.

continued on next page

Stuffed Calamari Braised with Fresh Peas *(continued)*

1 bunch scallions,
trimmed and chopped
(about 1 cup)

1 ½ cups Vegetable Stock
(page 76), canned
reduced-sodium chicken
broth, or water

Makes 6 servings

Return the calamari to the pan. Sprinkle the scallions over them, pour in the stock, and season lightly with salt. Bring to a boil, then lower the heat so the sauce is simmering. Simmer, uncovered, until the calamari are tender and there is barely enough liquid to moisten the peas, about 20 minutes. Drizzle in the remaining 2 tablespoons oil. Transfer the calamari to warm plates or a platter and spoon the sauce and peas over and around them. Serve immediately.

Spring Peas and Other Seasonal Foods

THERE IS, AMONG SOME COOKS, a phobia about overcooking peas. To many people, peas must stay bright green and intact, little bullets running around the plate as you chase after them with a fork. Well, I love my fresh peas "smothered" until they are olive green in color—when their sweetness and flavors have really concentrated, and they begin to break down and cling together. I do not mean peas that are overcooked in lots of water, or steamed till they are gray-green, watery, and tasting of tobacco.

When I was growing up in Istria, we ate peas only in the springtime—when they were in season. There is much to be said for eating in season: it is truly the only way to be synchronized with what the land produces. Optimal flavors are always achieved when cooking with seasonal products; in a perfect world, it would be the only way to cook. You should make an effort to cook in rhythm with the seasons. When you do, I will venture to say that your food will taste noticeably better, even if you don't change anything else about the way you cook. This philosophy at the base of good cooking is simplicity and common sense.

Oh yes, those spring peas that my grandma cooked for us are still vivid in my mind. There would be no Easter dinner without braised peas, roasted baby goat seasoned with rosemary, and little spring potatoes roasted with their skins alongside the goat till the potatoes were golden brown and the goat would stick to your fingers.

Marinated Mackerel Fillets

Filetto di Sgombro in Savor

½ cup dry white wine

¼ cup raisins

½ cup extra-virgin olive oil

¼ cup vegetable oil

4 skin-on Spanish or other mackerel fillets, each about 5 to 6 ounces

Salt

Freshly ground black pepper

All-purpose flour

1 large yellow onion, sliced thin

1 sprig fresh rosemary

4 bay leaves

½ cup Chicken Stock (page 74), canned reduced-sodium chicken broth, or water

2 teaspoons white-wine vinegar

¼ cup toasted pine nuts (see page 149 for toasting instructions)

Makes 4 servings

Pour the wine over the raisins in a small bowl and let soak at room temperature while cooking the fish.

Heat ¼ cup of the olive oil and the vegetable oil in a large, nonreactive skillet over medium heat until rippling. Meanwhile, season the flesh side of the fillets with salt and pepper, and dredge them in flour to lightly coat both sides.

When the oil is ready, carefully slide the fillets into the pan. Fry, turning once, until lightly browned and cooked through, 4 to 5 minutes. Transfer to a paper towel–lined baking sheet to drain.

Pour off the oil from the skillet. Carefully wipe out the skillet with a wad of paper toweling. Pour in the remaining ¼ cup olive oil and return the pan to medium heat. Stir in the onion, season lightly with salt and pepper, and cook, stirring occasionally, until wilted, about 4 minutes. Toss the rosemary and bay leaves into the pan and continue cooking until the onion slices are light golden, about 5 minutes.

Pour in the wine and raisins, the stock, and the vinegar. Bring to a boil, then reduce the heat so the sauce is simmering. Simmer until the onion is translucent but not mushy, about 4 minutes. Stir in the pine nuts and simmer for 10 minutes.

Lay half the fillets in a baking or serving dish into which they will all fit comfortably. Spoon half the sauce over the fillets in the dish and cover with a second layer of fillets. Spoon the remaining sauce over the second layer of fillets. Let marinate at room temperature for at least 2 hours (up to 6 hours) before serving. Serve at room temperature, spooning some of the sauce over each serving.

This mackerel will keep well in the refrigerator for 4 to 5 days. Remove the mackerel and let come to room temperature 45 minutes before serving.

Marechiara means "sea light." When you see that name on a menu, it usually means a light tomato sauce, in most cases paired with fish. I season this marechiara sauce with green olives, but you can use black olives or capers if you like. When cooking baccalà, do not salt the dish until the very end. Then taste, and season with salt if you feel it necessary.

Salt Cod in the Style of Marechiara

Baccalà Marechiara

Four 8-ounce salt-cod fillets, or 1 whole side bone-in salt cod (about 3½ pounds)

One 14-ounce can peeled Italian plum tomatoes (preferably San Marzano)

½ cup extra-virgin olive oil, plus additional oil for the finished dish if you like

3 cloves garlic, peeled

8 large green olives, such as Cerignola, cut away from the pit in wide strips

1 tablespoon chopped fresh oregano

Freshly ground black pepper

Salt

Makes 4 servings

I prefer olives with the pits—I think they have better flavor. Adding the olives directly to the oil after the garlic has browned will give you a more pronounced flavor of olives. If you like a milder flavor, add them to the sauce once the tomatoes have come to a boil.

Baccalà has a tendency to curl up as it cooks. If yours does that, press on the fillets lightly with a metal spatula so they caramelize evenly. In order to keep the sauce light—as its name says—spoon in a little hot water from time to time as the sauce simmers.

Soak the cod according to directions below.

With your hands, remove the seeds from the tomatoes by squeezing them over a sieve, squeezing just enough to get the seeds out, then crush the tomatoes that you have in your hands coarsely and return them to the seedless liquid. Heat ¼ cup of the olive oil in a large, heavy skillet over medium-high heat. Whack the garlic with the flat side of a knife, scatter the cloves over the oil, and cook, shaking the pan, until lightly browned, about 2 minutes. Stir in the olives and cook until any liquid has evaporated and the olives begin to sizzle, about 1 minute. Add the tomatoes and oregano and bring to a boil. Lower the heat so the sauce is at a lively simmer and season lightly with pepper. Let simmer while you prepare the cod, spooning in a little hot water if the sauce begins to thicken.

Pat the salt-cod fillets dry with paper towels. Heat the remaining ¼ cup oil in a separate large skillet over medium heat. Add the fillets and cook, turning once, until lightly browned on both sides and opaque at the thickest point, about 10 minutes. Drain excess oil from the skillet and carefully pour in the tomato sauce. Bring to a quick boil, lower the heat so the sauce is simmering, and simmer 2 to 3 minutes, basting the fish with the sauce as it cooks. Taste the sauce and add salt and pepper, if necessary. Divide the sauce among four heated plates and top each pool of sauce with the fillets. Drizzle each fillet with additional olive oil, if you like.

Baccalà

THOUGH THE COD IS NOT NATIVE to the waters around Italy, it still plays an important part in Italian culture and cuisine — not as fresh fish, but in one of its preserved forms, baccalà.

Baccalà, fresh cod that has been salt-cured, is the type of cured cod most used in Italian cooking. Salting pulls moisture out of the fish and replaces it with salt, which acts as a preservative. The type of cure depends almost entirely on where the fish have been caught and/or salted. Gaspé, for example, is a very light salt cure that leaves the flesh a pale-yellow color and is popular in Mediterranean communities. A stronger cure, which leaves the cod saltier and drier, is favored among Caribbean peoples. Generally speaking, the firmer your salt-cod fillets, the more salt they will contain, and therefore the longer they will need to soak.

Baccalà is available as fillets and as "sides" — that is, half the fish, with bones and skin intact. Baccalà must be soaked in plenty of running cold water, both to restore its tender texture and to remove excess salt. To soak baccalà, put the side(s) or fillets in a container large enough to hold them comfortably. Place the container in a deep sink and fill it with cold water. Position the container under the faucet and allow the faucet to drip very slowly, continuously replenishing the salty water with fresh. Make sure the path to the drain is clear so the sink doesn't overflow. (If the baccalà container is too large to fit in the sink, you may soak it in a cool place, completely changing the water every few hours.) The cod will take at least 1 day of soaking, or up to 2 days, depending on the thickness of the baccalà and how heavily it has been salted. When fully soaked, the cod should be quite moist and pliable, and the water that is running over the fish will have little or no salt flavor. Once baccalà has been soaked, it must be cooked within 2 days.

Check for bones — even if you're working with "boneless" sides or fillets of salt cod — by running your fingers lightly over the whole surface of the fish. You'll feel the tips of any bones sticking out. Grab the tips of the bones with needle-nose pliers and pull them out. If you're working with a whole side of baccalà, cut off the tail, belly, and "collar" pieces, trimming the side into a neat rectangle. Cut the trimmed side into even portions. Save the trimmings for use in another dish. Use soaked baccalà in Baccalà Marechiara (opposite); Salt Cod, Potato, and String Bean Salad (page 42); or Salt Cod Fritters (page 24).

Salmoriglio is a traditional Italian sauce, usually served at room temperature with seafood. I like this more contemporary version, served warm next to a crunchy baked fillet of cod and an accent of simple dressed cherry tomatoes.

Fillet of Fresh Cod with Lemon-Parsley Sauce

Fileto di Merluzzo al Salmoriglio

8 cloves garlic, peeled

½ cup extra-virgin olive oil

1 cup dry, unseasoned bread crumbs

¼ cup chopped fresh Italian parsley

2 tablespoons plus 2 teaspoons chopped fresh thyme leaves

1 teaspoon finely chopped crushed hot red pepper

Six 1-inch-thick fresh cod fillets (about 2½ pounds)

Salt, preferably fine sea salt

4 cups yellow and red cherry tomatoes, stemmed, washed, and drained

3 tablespoons fresh lemon juice

Makes 6 servings

Cod is a very delicate fish — it will flake apart easily — so a nonstick baking pan is a great help. The seasoned bread crumbs I use as a topping for the cod are very versatile; if you don't care for cod, or if you can't find it, keep this preparation in mind for seasoning other baked fish.

Traditionally, salmoriglio is prepared with parsley, and that is how I present it here. But you can substitute other herbs, like thyme, that will marry well with the herbs you use to top the fish. If you have fresh basil, shred a few leaves and toss them in with the tomatoes.

Whack the garlic cloves with the side of a knife and stir them into the olive oil in a small glass bowl. Let steep at room temperature 30 minutes to 2 hours.

Preheat the oven to 475° F. Stir the bread crumbs, 2 tablespoons of the infused oil, 2 tablespoons of the parsley, 2 tablespoons of the thyme, and ½ teaspoon of the crushed red pepper together in a small bowl until blended.

Season the cod fillets with salt and brush both sides well with about 1 tablespoon of the infused oil. Set the cod on a lightly oiled or nonstick baking sheet. Distribute the seasoned bread crumbs over the tops of the fillets, patting them lightly to help them stick. Bake the cod until it is opaque white throughout and the crumbs are golden brown, 10 to 12 minutes.

While the cod is baking, make the tomato salad and prepare the sauce: Cut the tomatoes in quarters and toss them in a mixing bowl with salt to taste. Spoon in 2 tablespoons of the garlic oil and toss gently.

Strain the remaining infused oil into a medium skillet. Add the lemon juice, the remaining 2 teaspoons of thyme, and the remaining $\frac{1}{2}$ teaspoon crushed red pepper. Bring to a boil and cook until lightly thickened and emulsified. Stir the remaining 2 tablespoons parsley into the sauce and season to taste with salt.

Remove the fish and transfer to warm serving plates. Taste the tomatoes and their juice, adding more salt if necessary. Spoon the tomatoes and their juice in small mounds around the fish fillets. Spoon some of the sauce between the mounds of tomatoes and serve at once.

To: Lidia Bastianich
From: Mary Scott
Subject:

>>>I enjoy your show. You bring back a lot of memories. I watch a lot of the cooking shows, and I like yours because you get down to the basics. I'm a pretty good cook, but you made me realize that I need a little help.<<<

Sole meunière is of French, not Italian, origin, but it became extremely popular in Italian-American restaurants — probably because of the simplicity of its preparation and the availability of different kinds of sole. Whereas Italian cuisine was brought to this country by immigrants, French cuisine was introduced by professional chefs in fancy hotels all over the country, the most significant wave of which arrived for the 1939 World's Fair in New York. (Hence a notable difference in Italian restaurants versus French restaurants in the 1940s, '50s, and '60s.) While Italian restaurants were offering traditional fare in familial surroundings, the French were offering haute cuisine in chic settings.

I bring traditional dishes like this into my world with little touches like the whole lemon slices and finishing the sauce with olive oil. Pairing these delicate sole fillets with Spinach Sautéed with Bread Crumbs on page 321 makes a delicious and very quick meal.

Sole Meunière

Filetto di Sogliola al Limone

5 tablespoons extra-virgin olive oil, plus more for finishing the sauce if you like

6 tablespoons unsalted butter

6 gray or lemon sole fillets, approximately 2½ pounds

Salt

Freshly ground black pepper

All-purpose flour for dredging

12 thin lemon slices

5 cloves garlic, peeled

3 tablespoons tiny capers, drained

You know how much I love olive oil, but there is a time and place for everything. When sautéing foods that cook quickly, like these sole fillets, using some butter along with the oil helps the sole brown before they overcook. Thicker sole or flounder fillets are ideal for this dish, but if yours are thinner, you may find it easier to handle them if you cut them in half first.

Traditionally, the fillets are simmered in the sauce, but I like to cook the sauce separately and spoon it around the sole fillets — they stay crispier that way.

Preheat the oven to 250° F. Heat the 3 tablespoons of the olive oil and 4 tablespoons of the butter in a large, heavy skillet over medium-high heat until the butter is foaming. Meanwhile, season the fillets with salt and pepper and dredge them in the flour to coat both sides lightly. Gently lay as many of the

¼ cup fresh lemon juice

¼ cup dry white wine

½ cup Vegetable Stock
(page 76) or water

2 tablespoons chopped
fresh Italian parsley

Makes 4 servings

fillets into the pan as fit without touching. Cook just until the underside is lightly browned, about 4 minutes. Flip them gently with a wide metal spatula and cook until the second side is browned and the fish is opaque in the center, about 2 minutes. Transfer them with the spatula to a baking sheet and keep them warm in the oven. Repeat if necessary with the remaining fillets, adjusting the heat under the skillet to prevent the bits of flour in the pan from burning.

When all the sole fillets have been browned, carefully wipe out the skillet with a wad of paper towels. Add the remaining 2 tablespoons olive oil and the remaining 2 tablespoons butter and return to medium heat. When the butter is foaming, slide in the lemon slices and garlic and cook, stirring gently, until the lemon slices are sizzling and lightly browned. Remove the lemon slices and set them aside. Stir in the capers and heat until they are sizzling, about 1 minute. Pour in the lemon juice and wine, bring to a boil, and cook until reduced by about half. Pour in the vegetable stock, bring to a boil, and boil until the sauce is lightly thickened, about 2 minutes. If you like, drizzle in a tablespoon or two of olive oil to enrich the sauce. Sprinkle in the parsley and taste, seasoning with salt and pepper if you like.

Remove the sole from the oven and set 1 fillet in the center of each plate. Top each fillet with 2 of the lemon slices. Spoon the sauce around the fillets, dividing it evenly. Serve immediately.

Sole Oreganata

Sogliola Grattinata all'Oregano

For the Sole

   6 cloves garlic, crushed

   $1/2$ cup extra-virgin olive oil

   2 large Idaho potatoes
     (about $1 1/4$ pounds)

Salt

   1 cup fine, dry bread
     crumbs

   2 tablespoons chopped
     fresh Italian parsley

   1 teaspoon dried
     oregano, preferably the
     Sicilian or Greek type
     dried on the branch,
     crumbled

   1 teaspoon grated lemon
     zest

Freshly ground black
     pepper

   1 small Vidalia or other
     sweet onion, sliced very
     thin

   2 large tomatoes, cored
     and cut into 6 slices
     each

   6 large sole fillets (about
     $2 1/2$ pounds total)

For the Sauce

   $1/4$ cup extra-virgin olive oil

   3 tablespoons fresh
     lemon juice

   2 tablespoons chopped
     fresh Italian parsley

Salt

Freshly ground black
     pepper

Makes 6 servings

Let the garlic and olive oil steep at room temperature 30 minutes to 2 hours.

Meanwhile, cook the unpeeled potatoes in enough boiling salted water to cover them by three fingers until tender but not mushy when poked with a paring knife, about 35 minutes. Drain and let stand until cool enough to handle. Peel the potatoes and cut them into twelve slices each.

Make the seasoned bread crumbs: Toss the bread crumbs, 2 tablespoons parsley, the oregano, lemon zest, and $1 1/2$ tablespoons of the infused oil together in a small bowl until the crumbs are evenly moistened. Taste and add salt and pepper as necessary. Preheat the oven to 425° F. Brush a baking sheet large enough to hold all the sole fillets with some of the infused oil. (If you don't have a sheet large enough to hold all the fillets, use two smaller sheets.) Arrange one-sixth of the onion slices over the baking sheet in a shape roughly the same as one of the sole fillets. Top the onions with potato slices and tomato slices as follows: start with two potato slices, arrange a tomato slice overlapping those, then two potato slices overlapping the tomato, and finishing with a tomato slice. Repeat with the remaining onion, potato, and tomato slices. Season the vegetables generously with salt and pepper, drizzle them with half the remaining infused oil, and sprinkle them lightly with the seasoned bread crumbs. Season the fillets with salt and pepper and set one over each bed of vegetables. Brush the fillets lightly with infused oil, and top with the remaining seasoned bread crumbs, dividing them evenly over each fillet. Drizzle with the remaining oil. Bake until the onions are well browned, the sole is cooked through, and the bread-crumb topping is golden brown, about 25 minutes.

Make the sauce: Whisk $1/4$ cup olive oil, the lemon juice, and parsley together in a small bowl until well blended. Season with salt and pepper to taste.

Slide a long metal spatula under each set of vegetables and carefully slide a portion onto a hot plate. Drizzle some sauce around and serve immediately.

Variation

Scallops Oreganata

Arrange $2 1/2$ pounds of large, plump sea scallops over the prepared pan, leaving some space between them so they cook evenly. Top with an even layer of the seasoned bread crumbs and drizzle them with infused oil. Bake until the scallops are barely opaque at the center and the bread crumbs are well browned, 10 to 15 minutes depending on the size of the scallops. Serve hot.

Fillet of Sole with a Light Bread Crumb Stuffing

Involtini di Sogliola

6 cloves garlic, peeled

½ cup extra-virgin olive oil

1 cup bread crumbs

5 tablespoons chopped fresh Italian parsley

1 tablespoon chopped fresh thyme

2 teaspoons grated lemon zest

½ teaspoon crushed hot red pepper, lightly chopped

12 small sole fillets (about 4 ounces each)

Salt

1 large tomato, seeded and peeled (see page 9), cut into thin strips

2 tablespoons unsalted butter, cut into 8 pieces

½ cup dry white wine

½ cup Vegetable Stock (page 76) or water

¼ cup fresh lemon juice

Makes 6 servings

Whack the garlic cloves with the flat side of a knife and toss them into the olive oil. Let them steep together in a small bowl at room temperature from 30 minutes to 2 hours.

Toss the bread crumbs, 3 tablespoons of the parsley, the thyme, lemon zest, and ¼ teaspoon of the crushed red pepper together in a bowl. Spoon half the infused olive oil into the bowl and stir well to moisten the bread crumbs evenly.

Preheat the oven to 475° F. Spread the fillets out, skin side up, on the work surface. (The skin side will be smoother and darker than the other side.) Lightly season them with salt. Spread 1 tablespoon of the bread-crumb mixture over each fillet and set 5 or 6 strips of tomato over the thickest part of each fillet. Starting at the thickest end, roll the fish like a jelly roll, securing each roll with a toothpick. Prepare the remaining fillets in the same manner.

Brush a 13 × 9–inch or equivalent-size baking pan lightly with some of the remaining infused oil. Arrange the rolls side by side and seam side down in the pan, leaving some space between them. Drizzle about 2 tablespoons of the remaining infused oil over the fillets, and sprinkle the tops with the remaining seasoned bread crumbs. (Try to get most of the crumbs on top of the fillets, but don't worry if some of the crumbs fall into the dish; they will thicken the finished sauce.) Tuck the garlic cloves from the oil and the pieces of butter in between the rolls.

Pour the white wine, stock or water, lemon juice, and remaining infused oil into the pan. Crumble in the remaining crushed red pepper, and add 1 teaspoon salt to the baking dish. Bake until the bread crumbs are golden brown, 20 to 25 minutes.

Remove fillets gently from the pan to a warm platter and tent them with aluminum foil to keep them warm. Pour the pan juices into a small saucepan and bring sauce to a boil. Add remaining 2 tablespoons parsley and taste for seasoning. You should have 2 tablespoons of sauce per serving.

Spoon sauce on hot plates and set fillets on top of sauce.

This very simple and lively sauce is made in minutes, with only a few ingredients. You should never be afraid of simplicity when you cook; working with a few good-quality ingredients and handling them with respect is one of the keys to great cooking.

Bass Fillets with Olive-Caper Tomato Sauce

Branzino alla Livornese

6 sea-bass or striped-bass fillets, each about 8 ounces and at least 1 inch thick

Salt

Freshly ground black pepper

3 tablespoons extra-virgin olive oil, plus more for drizzling into the finished sauce

6 cloves garlic, peeled and sliced thin

2 small yellow onions, diced fine

1 cup Cerignola or other large, firm green olives, pitted and halved

¼ cup tiny capers, drained

3 cups canned Italian tomatoes (preferably San Marzano) with their liquid, seeded and crushed

¼ teaspoon crushed hot red pepper

Vegetable oil

All-purpose flour, optional

½ cup (or as needed) Vegetable Stock (page 76) or water

Makes 6 servings

Wild-caught striped bass are the best for this recipe, but you can use fillets from any firm-fleshed ocean fish. Whatever fish you choose, the shape and thickness of the fillets is important. Each fillet should be about 1½ inches thick and narrow enough so you can fit all six fillets in the pan with the sauce. If your pan isn't large enough to hold all the fillets, cook the sauce first, then divide between two skillets of fillets.

As with any dish, you can take this recipe in a lot of different directions. I sometimes prepare it using scallions in place of the onions, or black olives and capers in place of the green olives. Rather than add the olives and capers to the tomatoes, I like to cook them along with the onions for a minute or two to bring out their flavor. This "layering" of flavors is one of the little tricks we professional chefs use to get the most out of our ingredients.

Pat the bass fillets dry and season them with salt and pepper. Heat the olive oil in a large skillet over medium heat. Scatter the sliced garlic over the oil and cook until lightly browned, about 2 minutes. Add the onions and cook until wilted, about 4 minutes. Stir in the olives and capers and cook until they are sizzling and fragrant, about 2 minutes. Pour in the tomatoes, season them with crushed red pepper, and bring to a boil. Lower the heat so the sauce is simmering and cook until lightly thickened, about 5 minutes.

Pour enough vegetable oil into a separate large, heavy skillet to fill about ½ inch. Heat over medium-high heat until rippling. If the type of bass you're using is flaky, or if you like a delicate crust and a slightly thicker sauce, dredge the fillets in flour to coat them lightly. Add the bass fillets skin side up and cook until well browned. Turn the fillets and cook until the skin side is lightly browned, about 2 minutes. Spoon off excess oil from the skillet and add the *livornese* sauce to the skillet. Bring to a boil, adjust the heat to simmering, and cook until the fish is cooked through, about 5 to 10 minutes depending on the thickness and shape of the fish. Add vegetable stock or water, a small amount at a time, to keep the consistency of the sauce more or less the same. A minute or two before the fish is done, drizzle in some olive oil. Serve the fillets on warmed plates, spooning some of the sauce over each.

When fresh, anchovies are thin, silvery little fish about 2 inches long, with prominent round eyes. Their firm texture makes them perfect for this dish, but they are very hard to find at your fish market. Sardines, which are bigger—about 2½ to 3 inches long—with a shimmering, silvery-blue coloring, make a good substitute. This dish is so good and so easy that it is worth making whichever of the two you are able to get.

Baked Fresh Anchovies

Alici al Forno

1½ pounds fresh anchovies or sardines

6 tablespoons extra-virgin olive oil

12 bay leaves (preferably fresh)

1½ cups Seasoned Bread Crumbs 1 (page 20)

1 pound cherry tomatoes, cut in half

Salt

Freshly ground black pepper

Makes 6 servings

I love this prepared in individual baking dishes, as described in the note below. But I know most people don't have six such dishes, so I'm offering the recipe prepared in a single large baking dish— I don't want you to miss out on the wonderful flavor of fresh anchovies just because you don't have small baking dishes. If you serve the anchovies from a large round dish, cut them into wedges, like a cake. Don't be alarmed if the "slices" crumble a little; that is the nature of the dish.

You can easily prepare this recipe for two people: decrease the amount of anchovies by two-thirds to ½ pound, but cut the remaining ingredients in half.

Soak the anchovies briefly in cold water. Drain them and gently scrape the scales from the skin with the back of a paring knife. Remove the heads and innards as follows: Make a cut just behind the head, stopping about two-thirds of the way through to the stomach side. (Don't completely cut off the head.) Pull the head away from the body gently with the knife; most of the innards should follow. Open up the anchovies by running your thumb along the inside of the stomach cavity. Remove the entire skeleton and scrape away any remaining innards or bones with the back of a paring knife. Wipe gently with a paper towel if you feel there is still some debris attached to the fillets. (Sardines are cleaned in the same way.)

Preheat the oven to 375° F. Drizzle a little olive oil into the bottom of an 11-inch oval or 10-inch round baking dish or casserole. Scatter six of the bay leaves over the bottom, and top with a thin but even layer of bread crumbs. Arrange one-third of the anchovy (or sardine) fillets over the bread crumbs, spacing them evenly. Sprinkle with seasoned bread crumbs, then scatter one-third of the halved tomatoes over the anchovies. Top the tomatoes with an even layer of bread crumbs. Scatter the remaining six bay leaves over that layer, then repeat the anchovy/bread-crumb, tomato/bread-crumb sequence, layering two more times with the remaining ingredients. Press the layered ingredients down gently with a spatula, drizzle the top layer with olive oil, and bake until the topping is golden brown and the anchovies are cooked through, about 30 minutes. Serve hot.

☞ To prepare this recipe in individual dishes, choose six 4-inch round or 3 × 4–inch rectangular baking dishes. Layer the ingredients into the dishes as described above. Place the baking dishes on a baking sheet to make them easier to remove from the oven.

The firm texture of monkfish is ideal for grinding and rolling into fish "meatballs." Capers and parsley add a lot of flavor and stand up against the raisin–pine-nut sauce. Serving the monkfish meatballs over ziti tossed with the tomato sauce would be a fun way to take a break from the Italian-American standard—spaghetti and meatballs.

Monkfish Meatballs in Tomato Sauce

Polpette di Rospo in Sugo

1½ pounds monkfish fillets

2 cups cubed (1-inch) day-old Italian bread, crusts removed

1 large egg, beaten

⅓ cup chopped fresh Italian parsley

⅓ cup capers, drained and chopped

1 teaspoon salt, plus more for seasoning the sauce

¼ teaspoon freshly ground black pepper, plus more for seasoning the sauce

All-purpose flour

Vegetable oil

⅓ cup extra-virgin olive oil

1 medium yellow onion, chopped (about 1 cup)

One 28-ounce can Italian plum tomatoes (preferably San Marzano), seeded and crushed

2 bay leaves

½ cup raisins

½ cup pine nuts, toasted (see page 149)

Makes 6 servings

It is a good idea to roll up and fry one of these fish balls before forming the whole batch. You can check the seasoning and add a little salt and pepper if you like before you cook them all. Cooking a little sample is a good thing to keep in mind when you're making meatballs, too.

Trim any skin and the gray membrane from the monkfish fillets. Cut the fillets into 1-inch chunks and chill them thoroughly. Pass the fish through a meat grinder fitted with a disc with holes about ¼ inch in diameter. (Alternatively, you may grind the fish, half at a time, using quick on/off pulses in a food processor fitted with the metal blade. Either way, the fish should resemble ground beef after you grind it.)

Toss the bread into a mixing bowl and pour enough cold water over it to cover completely. Let soak until completely saturated. Drain the bread well and squeeze it between your hands to remove as much water as possible.

Crumble the bread into a mixing bowl and beat in the egg, parsley, capers, 1 teaspoon salt, and $\frac{1}{4}$ teaspoon pepper. Stir in the ground monkfish until incorporated. Using 1 tablespoon of the fish mixture for each, form balls by rolling the mixture between your palms. When you have formed all the balls, dredge them lightly in flour to coat all sides.

Heat the vegetable oil in a skillet or braising pan large enough to hold all the fish balls and sauce, until rippling. Add as many fish balls as will fit without touching. Fry, turning as necessary, until golden on all sides, about 5 minutes. Remove with a slotted spoon and drain on a paper-towel-lined baking sheet.

Pour off the oil from the pan, pour in the olive oil, and heat over medium heat. Stir in the onion and cook, stirring, until wilted, about 4 minutes. Stir in the tomatoes, bay leaves, and 1 cup of water. Season to taste with salt and pepper. Bring to a boil, then lower the heat so the sauce is at a simmer. Cook 15 minutes.

Stir in the raisins and pine nuts and nestle the fish balls into the sauce, shaking the pan gently till they are covered with sauce.

Simmer 20 minutes, shaking the pan occasionally. Let the fish balls rest in the sauce off the heat for 10 minutes, then serve.

This quick and tasty dish can be done on the grill in the summer or—it's almost as good this way—seared in a nonstick pan on top of the stove.

Swordfish Skewers Glazed with Sweet and Sour Sauce

Pesce Spada allo Spiedo

1 cup balsamic vinegar, preferably aged at least 6 years

18 red or white pearl onions

2 pounds skinless swordfish cut into 1-inch cubes (about 30 pieces)

4 teaspoons extra-virgin olive oil

Salt

Freshly ground black pepper

12 fresh bay leaves, sage leaves, or sprigs rosemary

Makes 6 servings

You can use 8-inch or longer metal or wooden skewers for this dish. If you use wooden skewers, soak them in water to cover for an hour or so before threading the ingredients onto them. That should help prevent the skewers from burning as they cook. If you are using fresh bay leaves or rosemary, you can use the thin branches from either herb as skewers, flavoring the ingredients even more. Because these branches will be shorter than store-bought skewers, you will probably need to make more and smaller skewers. Also, handle them carefully as they cook—herb branches aren't quite as sturdy as metal or wooden skewers.

Bring the balsamic vinegar to a boil in a small saucepan. Lower the heat to a gentle boil and cook until the vinegar is reduced to about $1/3$ cup. Set aside.

Drop the pearl onions into a medium saucepan of boiling water and cook until softened but still quite firm, about 4 minutes. Drain and let stand until cool enough to handle. Slip off the skins, leaving the root intact and the onion whole.

Toss the swordfish cubes, onions, and olive oil together in a bowl. Season lightly with salt and pepper and toss again.

Prepare a charcoal or gas grill.

Thread the fish, onions, and bay leaves onto long wooden or metal skewers, dividing the ingredients evenly among the skewers and alternating them as you like. Grill the skewers about 4 inches from the heat, about 1 minute on each side (for a total of 4 minutes). Serve with drizzles of balsamic reduction and pass remaining reduction separately.

☞ A cast-iron or other heavy griddle is ideal for preparing these swordfish skewers on the stovetop. Brush the griddle lightly with olive oil and heat over medium-high heat. Cook the skewers, turning them as necessary, until well browned on all sides, about 1 minute per side. Brush an even coat of the balsamic reduction over each side, then grill another minute, turning the skewers frequently—the balsamic reduction will burn if left too long on one side.

My grandma Rosa (left) with her brother Carlo and sister Anna in Istria, c. 1925

Oven-Roasted Whole Turbot

Rombo al Forno

One whole turbot or flounder, about 3 pounds

10 small Yukon Gold potatoes (about 1½ pounds)

2 medium yellow onions, peeled and quartered through the core

¼ cup extra-virgin olive oil, plus more for drizzling over the cooked turbot

Salt

Freshly ground black pepper

4 sprigs fresh rosemary

Makes 4 servings

In Italy, this dish would be prepared with rombo *(turbot), but flounder is certainly an excellent substitute. Flounder is a flakier fish and will cook quicker, so either cut the potatoes into slightly thinner wedges, or boil them a minute or two longer. The flounder you choose for this dish should be a thick one. The dark skin is removed while the white is left on the bottom so the fish does not fall apart when it is being served.*

Clean the turbot, cut off the head, and peel off the dark skin, but leave the tails, fins, and white skin intact. (Or ask your fishmonger to do this for you.)

Heat a large saucepan of salted water to the boil. Peel the potatoes, cut them in half, and cut the halves into 1-inch wedges. Cook the wedges in the boiling water until starting to soften, about 5 minutes. Drain the potatoes and toss them in a bowl with the onions and 2 tablespoons olive oil. Season with salt and pepper and toss again.

Preheat the oven to 425° F. Choose a wide roasting pan large enough to hold the whole turbot, potatoes, and onions in a single layer. Season the turbot generously with salt and pepper and brush the bottom of the roasting pan with the remaining olive oil. Place the turbot skin side down in the center of the pan, and arrange the potatoes and onions around the turbot. Distribute the rosemary evenly around the pan.

Roast until the fish is opaque at the thickest part and the potatoes are golden brown, about 30 minutes. To make sure the potatoes and onions cook and brown evenly, remove the pan from the oven and turn the potatoes and onions.

To serve, divide the fish into four fillets as follows: Run a small knife along the center of the top fillet down to the bone, following the dark line that runs along the center of the top of the fish. Wiggle the knife along the cut to separate the top half of the fish into two fillets. Slide a small metal spatula between the top fillets and the bone and transfer them to a warm platter. Check the fillets; they should be relatively bone-free. You are now left with the bottom fillet, entirely covered by the skeleton. You can remove most of the bones in one piece if you lift gently, starting at the tail end. Scrape any remaining bones from the fillets with a spoon, paying special attention to the bones around the edges. Divide the bottom half of the fish into two fillets, as you did the top half. Transfer them to the platter—with or without the skin—and flank all the fillets with the roasted potatoes and onions. Drizzle the fish and vegetables with extra-virgin olive oil and serve immediately.

```
To:      Lidia Bastianich
From:    Terry Frank
Subject:

>>>I am from an old, traditional Italian family.
Unfortunately they have all passed on, and I miss them—
the food, the atmosphere, and the tradition. Thank you
for bringing some of that back to me.<<<
```

Savory Seafood Stew

Zuppa di Pesce

For the Soup Base

  2 quarts water

One 35-ounce can Italian plum tomatoes (preferably San Marzano) and their liquid

  1 ½ cups dry white wine

  2 small leeks, white parts only, trimmed, cleaned, and cut into 3-inch lengths (about 2 cups) (page 80)

  2 medium carrots, trimmed and sliced thick

  1 large onion, cut into thick slices

  10 sprigs fresh thyme

Zest of ½ lemon, removed in wide strips with a vegetable peeler

  ½ teaspoon loosely packed saffron threads

  ¼ cup extra-virgin olive oil

Salt

To Prepare the Soup

  ¼ cup extra-virgin olive oil

  8 cloves garlic, peeled

  2 small leeks, white parts only, trimmed, cleaned, and sliced ½ inch thick (about 2 cups) (page 80)

  1 large onion, sliced thin

  4 medium calamari (about 1 ¼ pounds), cleaned according to directions on page 40, tentacles left whole, bodies cut crosswise into ½-inch rings

The traditional zuppa di pesce *that you most likely encountered in Italian-American restaurants was based on garlic and tomato sauce, which was simmered along with assorted fish to make a savory dish. Sometimes the sauce was used to dress pasta, and the shellfish and fin fish would be enjoyed as a second course. This version is more in a* brodetto *style, lighter and clearer than the traditional version, with saffron as a flavoring ingredient. This kind of preparation can be found with slight variations along the entire coast of Italy from Liguria to the Adriatic coast to the heel, Puglia, and the island of Sicily.*

I have given you the recipe with fish fillets, although traditionally zuppa di pesce *is made with slices of whole fish with bones and skin intact. But it is tricky to eat that way, even though the flavor is more complex.*

To make the soup base, combine the water, tomatoes, wine, leeks, carrots, onion, thyme, lemon zest, and saffron in a saucepan and bring to a boil. Lower the heat to a lively simmer and cook until reduced by about one-third, about 45 minutes. Stir in ¼ cup olive oil, season the mixture lightly with salt, and continue to simmer until the liquid portion of the soup base is reduced to about 8 cups, about 20 minutes. Strain the soup base into a 3-quart saucepan and keep it warm over low heat. Discard the solids. (The soup base may be prepared up to 3 days in advance and refrigerated.)

If you have prepared the soup base in advance, bring it to a simmer in a medium saucepan. Adjust the heat to very low and keep warm. Heat ¼ cup olive oil in a large (about 8-quart), heavy pot over medium heat. Add the garlic, leeks, and onion and cook, stirring, until the onion is wilted but still crunchy, about 4 minutes. Add the calamari and cook, stirring, until they turn opaque, about 2 minutes. Pour in all but 1 cup of the hot soup base

18 medium sea scallops
(about ½ pound)

8 ounces fresh firm-textured
fish fillets, such as salmon,
snapper, or swordfish, skin
removed, cut into 1-inch
pieces

2 cups Braised Cannellini
(page 349), optional

24 mussels, preferably
cultivated, cleaned

12 large shrimp, peeled
and deveined (about
½ pound)

¼ cup chopped fresh Italian
parsley

Salt

Freshly ground black pepper

Pan-Fried Garlic Bread (page
53) or crusty Italian bread

Makes 6 generous servings

and bring to a boil. Stir in the scallops, fish fillets, and beans, if using. Adjust the heat to simmering and cook until the seafood is barely opaque at the center, about 5 minutes.

Meanwhile, add the mussels to the soup base remaining in the saucepan. Increase the heat to high, cover the saucepan, and steam over medium heat, shaking the pan occasionally, until the mussels open, about 3 minutes.

Stir the shrimp, parsley, and steamed mussels into the large pot of soup. Simmer until the shrimp is cooked through, about 1 minute. Check the seasoning, adding salt, if necessary, and pepper. Ladle into warm soup bowls, passing a basket of the bread of your choice separately.

Mixed Fried Seafood

Fritto Misto

3 medium squid (about 1 ¼ pounds)

¾ pound thin, firm white fish fillets, such as whiting, ling, or flounder

½ pound sea scallops

½ pound whitebait, cleaned and heads removed or left on (according to preference) or cleaned fresh sardines (see page 308)

2 cups all-purpose flour

1 cup coarse cornmeal

3 cups vegetable oil

½ pound medium shrimp (about 16 shrimp), shelled and deveined

Salt

Lemon wedges

Makes 6 servings

The point of a fritto misto is to enjoy the flavors and textures of a variety of fish. You can vary the roster of fish according to what is in the market and increase or decrease the amount according to the number of guests you're cooking for.

Clean calamari according to the directions on page 40 and cut the bodies into ½-inch rings. Drain the pieces well in a colander. Slice the fish fillets on the bias 1 inch thick. Pinch the nubbins off the sides of the scallops, and cut the scallops in half widthwise if they are more than 1 inch thick. Clean the whitebait or sardines, leaving the heads on or taking them off according to preference. Leave the spines intact; they can be removed as the fish are eaten. Toss the flour and cornmeal together on a baking sheet.

Preheat the oven to 200° F. Heat oil in a very large (12- to 14-inch) skillet or wide braising pan over medium-high heat until it registers 375° F on a frying thermometer. While the oil heats, dredge the calamari in the flour-cornmeal mix to evenly coat all sides. Bounce the calamari in a sieve to remove excess flour.

When the oil reaches the correct temperature or when one coated calamari ring gives off a lively sizzle when lowered into the oil, slide the coated calamari into the oil. Fry, submerging the pieces of calamari with a wire skimmer or slotted spoon so they cook evenly, until golden on both sides, about 4 minutes. While the calamari are frying, dredge the shrimp in flour to coat.

Remove the calamari with a skimmer or slotted spoon and drain them on a paper-towel-lined baking sheet. Keep warm in the oven. Fry the shrimp as described above, until light golden and cooked through, about 4 minutes. Fish them out with the skimmer and set on the baking sheet with the calamari. Dredge, fry, and drain the fish fillets, sea scallops, and whitebait in the same way, transferring each to the baking sheet as it is done.

Pile the seafood onto a serving platter, season generously with salt, and serve immediately, passing lemon wedges separately.

Contorni (Side Dishes)

When I begin to cook, vegetables figure as prominently in the list of ingredients as do meat, fish, or poultry—if not more so. I personally love to cook with vegetables—and to eat them—but my practice goes beyond personal choice. It is the Italian culinary culture. Not only are vegetables used as *contorni*—side dishes—but one look at the antipasto, soup, or pasta chapter will show you they are a major consideration in those dishes as well. And as I have mentioned in the introduction to the section on main courses, vegetables are often cooked right into the principal dish as well.

This practice has held true in the Italian-American cuisine, too. However, Italian-American cuisine emphasizes New World vegetables, such as peppers, string beans, zucchini, and tomatoes, which were the most readily available produce the first Italian immigrants found when they came to these shores. Garlic, peppers, and onion—especially garlic—all of which they found in abundance here—are used much more in the Italian-American cuisine than in Italy.

It was most peculiar to me when I was running Buonavia in the 1970s that people requested, in most cases, spaghetti or pasta as a side dish. In Italy, although polenta can be a *contorno,* or occasionally rice—which is always served with *ossobucco alla milanese*—platters of braised, fried, steamed, sautéed, or baked vegetables are customary. That's not to say the Italian-American table was without its own favorite vegetable side dishes. Think of a visit to your favorite Italian restaurant in the 1970s that didn't include escarole (with or without white beans), broccoli with garlic and oil, string beans in tomato sauce, or *giambotta.* I have included all those recipes here for you, along with some less familiar ones and a whole section that will make it easy for you to enjoy the family of vegetable dishes cooked *all'aglio e olio*—with garlic and oil.

Sautéed Spinach

Spinaci Saltati

2 pounds bunch spinach, or two 10-ounce cellophane packages spinach

3 tablespoons extra virgin olive oil

5 cloves garlic, peeled

Salt

Freshly ground black pepper

Makes 6 servings

Wash the spinach according to the directions on page 323, but don't dry it completely. The water that clings to the leaves will steam the spinach as it cooks.

Heat the olive oil in a wide, heavy skillet over medium heat. Whack the garlic cloves with the side of a knife and toss them into the oil. Cook, shaking the pan, until golden, about 2 minutes. Scatter the spinach a large handful at a time into the pan, waiting until each batch wilts before adding another. Season lightly with salt and pepper and cover the pan. Cook until the spinach begins to release its liquid. Uncover the pan and cook, stirring, until the spinach is wilted and its water has evaporated, 1 to 3 minutes. Taste, and season with additional salt and pepper if you like. Serve hot.

Variation

Spinach Sautéed with Bread Crumbs

Adding a small amount of dry bread crumbs to the pan near the end of cooking is a traditional Istrian way to prepare spinach. Bread crumbs not only add flavor but also absorb some of the liquid that the spinach gives off, making the spinach neater if you're putting it on the same plate as something like the Sole Meunière on page 302. Prepare the sautéed spinach as described above, sprinkling 2 to 3 tablespoons of fine, dry bread crumbs over it just before removing it from the heat.

Leafy vegetables such as spinach, escarole, broccoli rabe, and Swiss chard have tender leaves that cook relatively quickly. The best way to cook them is to braise them—that is, cook them in oil over high heat, then simmer them with liquid, right in the same pan. You can embellish this simple technique by adding other flavors, like the bacon and onion in the Braised Kale recipe that follows.

Swiss Chard Braised with Oil and Garlic

Bietole Brasate

1 large bunch Swiss chard (about 2½ pounds)

3 tablespoons extra-virgin olive oil

4 cloves garlic, peeled

Salt

¼ teaspoon crushed hot red pepper, or to taste

Makes 4 servings

You can chop the chard stems coarsely and cook them in the oil and garlic for a minute or two before adding the chard leaves, or you can save them to serve as a side dish for a separate meal. In that case, trim them, cut them into 3-inch lengths, and cook them for a minute or two in boiling salted water. Drain them, press them gently to flatten them out, then either sauté them in a little olive oil, or coat them with flour, eggs, and bread crumbs and fry them. Either way they are delicious, with a flavor like cardi or cardoons—a very Italian vegetable with a flavor that is a cross between artichokes and celery.

Strip the stems from the chard and set them aside for another use. Chop the leaves coarsely and swish them around in a sinkful of cool water to remove all sand and grit. Fish them out of the water and let them drain in a colander for a minute or two.

Heat the olive oil in a wide, heavy skillet over medium heat. Whack the garlic cloves with the side of a knife and toss them into the pan. Cook, shaking the pan, until golden, about 2 minutes. Carefully stir in as many of the leaves—with the water that clings to them—as will fit comfortably into the pan. Cook, stirring, until the leaves begin to wilt. Continue adding more chard, a handful at a time, until all the chard is in the pan. Season lightly with salt and ¼ teaspoon crushed red pepper.

Lower the heat to medium-low, cover the skillet, and cook, stirring occasionally, until the chard is tender, about 8 minutes. If all the liquid in the pan evaporates and the greens begin to stick to the pan, sprinkle a tablespoon or two of water over them. Check the seasoning, add red pepper and salt if necessary, and serve immediately.

Variation

Other Braised Greens

Prepare any of these greens as described below and substitute them for the chard in the above recipe. Note that the longer a vegetable needs to cook to become tender, the more likely it is that the liquid in the pan will evaporate. Keep an eye on the greens; if they begin to stick, sprinkle a little water over them from time to time.

Spinach: If you like, leave the stems on tender, young, or flat-leaf spinach, but remove the stems from tougher, thick, curly spinach leaves. Wash the leaves in a sinkful of cold water, swishing them around to remove the sand and grit, then letting them float a minute or two to give the dirt a chance to settle to the bottom of the sink. Lift the leaves from the sink with your hands or a large wire skimmer into a colander to drain. Two 10-ounce cellophane bags of spinach, or three large bunches of leaf spinach, will yield about 1 pound spinach leaves when cleaned.

Savoy or White Cabbage: Cut a small (about 2-pound) head of white or savoy cabbage in half. Keep one half for another use, and cut out the core from the second half. Pull off any wilted or discolored leaves and cut the cabbage in 1 inch squares. Separate the layers of cabbage so they cook more evenly.

Broccoli Rabe: Clean the broccoli rabe as described in the recipe for Broccoli Rabe with Oil and Garlic on page 325. One hefty bunch of broccoli rabe will yield about 1 pound of stems and leaves.

Kale: Clean the kale as described in the recipe for Braised Kale with Bacon (below). Two medium bunches of kale will yield about 1 pound of leaves.

Escarole: Remove any wilted or discolored outer leaves from a small (about 1½-pound) head of escarole. Cut the head in half through the core, then cut out the core. Cut the leaves crosswise into 2-inch strips. Wash the escarole in plenty of cold water, swishing the leaves gently to remove all sand and grit, then drain in a colander. Proceed as in the above recipe.

Braised Kale with Bacon

Cavolo Nero Brasato

1 pound (approximately 2 medium heads) kale

3 tablespoons extra-virgin olive oil

6 cloves garlic, peeled

½ cup pancetta or bacon cut into ¼ × ¼ × 1–inch strips

Salt

¼ teaspoon crushed hot red pepper, or to taste

Makes 6 servings

Remove the outer leaves of kale if damaged or discolored. Cut off the bases of the stems, wash the leaves twice in abundant cold water, and drain. Cut the leaves crosswise into 1-inch strips.

Heat the olive oil in a wide, heavy skillet over medium heat. Whack the garlic cloves with the side of a knife and toss them into the oil. Stir in the bacon and cook, stirring, until the bacon and garlic are light golden, about 4 minutes.

Stir as many of the kale leaves into the skillet as will fit comfortably. Cook, stirring, until wilted enough to make room for more kale. Continue adding the kale, a handful at a time, until all the kale is in the skillet. Season lightly with salt and ¼ teaspoon crushed red pepper. Cover the skillet, lower the heat to low, and cook, stirring occasionally, until tender, about 10 minutes. If all the liquid in the pan evaporates and the greens begin to stick to the pan, sprinkle a tablespoon or two of water over them. Taste the greens and season with additional salt and red pepper if you like. Serve immediately.

Broccoli Rabe with Oil and Garlic

Broccoli di Rabe all'Aglio e Olio

1 pound broccoli rabe

3 tablespoons extra-virgin olive oil

2 cloves garlic, peeled and sliced

Salt

¼ teaspoon crushed hot red pepper, or to taste

¼ cup (or as needed) water

Makes 4 servings

Sometimes you see broccoli rabe cut into little pieces, but I like to serve the whole stems with the leaves attached. If you peel and trim them the way I describe below, the stalks will cook at about the same rate as the leaves. Broccoli rabe is a vegetable I like al dente. By that I don't mean really crunchy, but with some texture left to it.

To trim the broccoli rabe, first cut off any wilted or yellow leaves and the tough ends of the stems. Then, holding a stem with the florets in hand, nick a little piece of the end of the stem with a paring knife and pull the little piece of the skin toward you, peeling the stem partially. Continue working your way around the stem until it is peeled. As you peel the stem, some of the large, tough outer leaves will also be removed; discard those as well. Repeat with the remaining stems. Wash the trimmed broccoli rabe in a sinkful of cold water, swishing the stems gently to remove all dirt from between the leaves. Let the leaves sit a minute or two undisturbed, to allow the dirt to settle to the bottom of the sink, then lift the broccoli rabe from the water with your hands or a large skimmer. Drain in a colander.

Heat the olive oil in a large skillet over medium heat. Scatter the garlic over the oil and cook, shaking the pan, until golden brown, about 1 minute. Carefully lay the broccoli rabe into the oil and season lightly with salt and ¼ teaspoon crushed red pepper. Stir and toss to distribute the seasonings.

Pour ¼ cup water into the skillet and bring to a boil. Cover the skillet tightly and cook, lifting the lid to turn the stalks occasionally, until the broccoli rabe is tender, about 10 minutes. Taste, and season with additional salt and crushed red pepper if necessary. Serve hot.

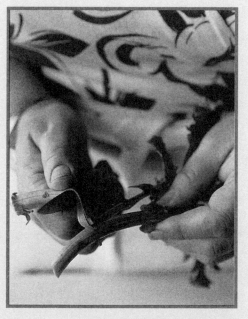

With a paring knife, pull the little piece of nicked skin toward you to partially peel the stem.

Steamed Broccoli with Oil and Garlic

Broccoli all'Aglio e Olio

4 heads broccoli (about
   1 ½ pounds)

Salt

3 tablespoons extra-virgin
   olive oil

4 cloves garlic, peeled

¼ teaspoon crushed hot
   red pepper, or to taste

¼ cup (or as needed)
   Chicken Stock (page
   74) or reserved broccoli
   cooking water

Makes 6 servings

If you're in the habit of throwing away broccoli stems, or even saving them for soup, I'd like you to try cooking broccoli this way. The stems are delicious, and if you peel them, they'll cook in the same time as the florets. Nothing could be simpler than this way of preparing broccoli—after a quick boiling, just plunk the pieces into the hot oil and let them go till they're tender.

You can skip the boiling step and add the raw broccoli directly to the oil and garlic, keeping more of the nutrients intact. In that case, add some water to the skillet along with the broccoli, and add more from time to time as they cook.

Cut the tough ends off the broccoli stalks. Peel the stalks with a vegetable peeler or paring knife up to the florets. Cut each head of broccoli lengthwise into two or three spears, depending on the thickness of the stalk. (The cut stalk should be no more than ½ inch thick at its widest point.)

Blanch the broccoli spears in a large pot of boiling salted water 3 minutes. Drain in a colander, reserving ½ cup of the cooking liquid if not using chicken stock.

Heat the olive oil in a wide skillet over medium heat. Whack the garlic cloves with the flat side of a knife and toss them into the oil. Cook, shaking the pan occasionally, until lightly browned, about 2 minutes. Add the broccoli and season lightly with salt and ¼ teaspoon crushed red pepper. Turn in the oil until coated. Pour in the stock or water, cover the skillet tightly, and cook until tender, about 8 minutes. Check the broccoli once or twice as it cooks, adding a tablespoon or two of stock if the liquid evaporates. Taste the broccoli, and season with additional salt and red pepper if you like. Serve immediately.

Other Steamed Stalk Vegetables

Cauliflower: Cut out the thick center stem and pull off the leaves. Cut the cauliflower into large florets, each with some of the stalk attached. Blanch the cauliflower florets in abundant boiling salted water 3 to 4 minutes, depending on the thickness of the stalk. Drain, reserve ½ cup of the cooking water if not using Chicken Stock, and proceed as in the above recipe.

Asparagus: Snap off the tough ends of the stems and peel the remaining part of the stalks. Blanch the asparagus in abundant boiling salted water 3 minutes. Drain, reserve ½ cup of the cooking water if not using Chicken Stock, and proceed as in the recipe.

Vegetables with Garlic and Oil

THE MOST COMMON WAY TO PREPARE VEGETABLES that immigrants from Italy brought to this country is to cook them *all'aglio e olio*, or with garlic and oil. It is a very simple flavor combination that you can think of in terms of composing music: three notes—garlic, oil, and a vegetable—combined in the right way, give you a perfect harmony. Food is much like music; we use ingredients like notes and blend them in different ways with different timings to give us certain end results.

There are several ways of cooking vegetables *all'aglio e olio*. The approach you take depends on the vegetable or vegetables you are cooking, and your preference. I have given you recipes that illustrate three of my favorite methods: braising greens (see Swiss Chard Braised with Oil and Garlic, page 322); blanching stalk vegetables, then steaming them (see Steamed Broccoli with Oil and Garlic, opposite), and potatoes cooked and mashed along with vegetables (see String Beans and Potatoes, page 342). Following each of these recipes are guidelines to help you adapt that technique to other vegetables, because, as I am always telling you, the recipes are only a guideline. Let your instincts and the freshest ingredients you can find serve as your inspiration.

There is the school of vegetable cooking that says vegetables should be served very *al dente*—still crunchy and bright green. If you like your vegetables like that, that's fine, just cook them less than I suggest. I like my vegetables still green, but cooked to the point where the vegetables are just beginning to be soft and release much more of their true vegetable flavor—not just a chlorophyll flavor.

Broccoli Rabe with Day-Old Bread

Broccoli Rabe con Crostino

1 bunch (about 1 pound) broccoli rabe

Salt

¼ cup extra-virgin olive oil

6 large cloves garlic, peeled

¼ teaspoon crushed hot red pepper, or to taste

2 cups cubed (1-inch) day-old country-style bread

Makes 6 servings

Trim and clean the broccoli rabe according to the directions on page 325.

Fill halfway with water a pot large enough to hold the broccoli rabe comfortably. Season generously with salt and bring to a boil. Stir the broccoli rabe into the water, cover the pot, and return to a boil. Uncover, and boil 3 minutes. Spoon off ½ cup of the cooking liquid and drain the broccoli rabe thoroughly.

Heat the olive oil in a wide, heavy skillet with a tight-fitting lid, whack the garlic cloves with the side of a knife, and toss them into the oil. Cook, shaking the pan, until golden, about 2 minutes. Lay the broccoli rabe in the skillet, season lightly with salt and ¼ teaspoon red pepper, and stir in the bread cubes. Lower the heat to medium-low, cover with the lid, and cook 5 minutes. Uncover, and cook, flipping the whole contents of the pan almost as you would a pancake about halfway through, until the bread is slightly browned, about 5 minutes. (Work the pieces of bread down to the bottom of the pan as the broccoli rabe cooks to ensure that the bread will brown.) There should be enough moisture from the broccoli rabe to keep it moist during cooking. If it becomes too dry, add some of the reserved vegetable water, a few tablespoons at a time. Taste, and season with additional salt and red pepper if you like. The broccoli rabe and bread should be juicy but not wet.

In Italy, celery is not used much as a side dish, but it is used a lot to flavor soups, sauces, and braised dishes. I enjoy this recipe, which pushes celery to center stage; it makes an unexpected side dish or appetizer when served with a selection of other grilled, marinated, or cooked vegetables, as is customarily done in Italy and Italian-American restaurants here in the States.

Celery Baked with Tomato and Parmigiano-Reggiano

Sedani alla Parmigiana

6 medium (about 8-inch) celery stalks

2 tablespoons extra-virgin olive oil

3 cloves garlic, peeled

1 cup canned Italian plum tomatoes (preferably San Marzano) with their liquid, crushed

½ cup water

Salt

Crushed hot red pepper

1 cup freshly grated Parmigiano-Reggiano cheese

Makes 4 servings

If you're starting with a whole head of celery, choose the right-size stalks for this dish: Use the larger, outer stalks and leaves for stock or soup, and the celery hearts as a snack or as part of an antipasto spread. Those medium-size stalks in between are ideal for baking.

What you're doing here is making a small amount of marinara sauce to bake the celery in. If you have on hand a little leftover marinara, you can certainly use it instead.

Trim the leaves and ends from the celery stalks and remove the strings, either by running a vegetable peeler over the surface of the stalk or by using a paring knife as follows: Hold the stalk in your hands and cut from the inside of the stalk to the outside without cutting all the way through. Just before finishing the cut, pull the knife toward you, and the strings should peel off down the length of the stalk. Cut the trimmed stalks in half crosswise and set them aside.

Preheat the oven to 400° F. Heat the olive oil in a small saucepan over medium heat. Whack the garlic cloves with the side of a knife and toss them into the pan. Cook, shaking the pan, until golden, about 2 minutes. Pour in the crushed tomatoes and their liquid and the water, and season lightly with salt and crushed red pepper. Bring to a boil, lower the heat so the sauce is simmering, and cook until the sauce is lightly thickened, about 10 minutes. Taste, and season with additional salt and red pepper if necessary.

continued on next page

Spoon half the sauce over the bottom of an 11-inch oval baking dish (or equivalent-size dish into which the celery pieces fit in a single layer). Lay the celery pieces, hollow side up and side by side, into the dish. Spoon the remaining sauce evenly over them and cover the dish with aluminum foil. Bake until the celery is tender but firm, 30 to 35 minutes.

Remove the aluminum foil, sprinkle the grated cheese in an even layer over the celery, and bake uncovered until the cheese is golden brown and the celery is tender, about 10 minutes. Let rest for 5 minutes and serve.

PARMIGIANO-REGGIANO is not the only cheese that goes extremely well with celery; Gorgonzola does as well. Take the smaller but tender ribs from a head of celery and fill the cavity with room-temperature sweet Gorgonzola. Serve as an appetizer or hors d'oeuvre.

Another marvelous way to enjoy the marriage of celery and Gorgonzola is to serve them together warm. Trim and cut the celery ribs as in the preceding recipe. Cook the cut stalks in lightly salted water for 10 minutes and drain them well. Press each one lightly with the side of a knife to flatten and set them side by side in a baking pan. Crumble Gorgonzola cheese over them and bake in a 425° F oven until the cheese is melted, about 5 minutes. These also make a great appetizer.

More
Celery

String Beans in Chunky Tomato Sauce

Fagiolini alla Marinara

3 tablespoons extra-virgin olive oil, plus more for finishing the dish if you like

6 cloves garlic, peeled

1 pound flat "Italian" string beans, regular string beans, or haricots verts, ends trimmed

Salt

Crushed hot red pepper

One 28-ounce can Italian plum tomatoes (preferably San Marzano) with their liquid

Makes 6 servings

I'm sure this dish will take you back, whether you make it with "Italian" string beans (those flat wide ones), regular string beans, or the more expensive, thinner haricots verts. It isn't necessary to start with a long-simmered tomato sauce for these beans; in fact, the flavor will be fresher with this quick-cooked marinara made right in the pan.

The acidity of the tomatoes will turn the string beans a sort of olive green. That doesn't bother me at all—it reminds me of the way my grandmother cooked vegetables. Maybe they weren't the brightest-green vegetables I've ever seen, but they certainly were the most delicious.

Heat the oil in a large, heavy skillet over medium heat. Whack the garlic cloves with the side of a knife and toss them into the pan. Cook, shaking the pan, until lightly browned, about 2 minutes. Scatter the string beans over the oil, season them lightly with salt and red pepper, and turn with tongs until they begin to wilt, about 3 minutes.

Meanwhile, crush the tomatoes coarsely with your hands. Add them to the string beans, cover the pan, and cook until the beans are tender, about 10 minutes. Taste the beans, and season with additional salt and red pepper if you like. Serve hot.

The secret to this dish is to cook each vegetable individually before combining them, and to not overcrowd the pans during the first stage of cooking. I have the luxury of a large commercial range, so I get three pans going at once. If you don't have that kind of space, work with two pans, as I describe below, and roast the potatoes and eggplant ahead of time to speed things along. (See the note below.)

Sautéed Summer Vegetables

Giambotta

3 cloves garlic, peeled

½ cup extra-virgin olive oil

1 small (about 8-ounce) eggplant, stem removed

Coarse sea salt or kosher salt

1 pound small new potatoes (about 12), scrubbed and cut in half

1 large yellow onion, cut into 1-inch chunks (about 2 cups)

2 medium red bell peppers, cored, seeded, and cut into 1-inch cubes (about 2 cups)

2 medium yellow bell peppers, cored, seeded, and cut into 1-inch cubes (about 2 cups)

2 cups zucchini, cut into 1-inch cubes

Whack the garlic cloves with the flat side of a knife, toss them into the olive oil, and let steep at room temperature 30 minutes to 2 hours.

Preheat the oven to 425° F. Remove strips of peel from the eggplant, leaving about half the skin intact. Cut the eggplant into 1-inch cubes. Toss the eggplant with 1 teaspoon salt in a large bowl, then transfer to a colander. Let stand about 30 minutes.

Meanwhile, toss the new potatoes with enough of the infused olive oil to coat them lightly. Season with salt. Arrange the potatoes, cut side down, on a baking sheet and roast until the underside is well browned and the potatoes are tender, about 25 minutes.

Rinse the eggplant under cool water and pat dry with paper towels. Toss the eggplant with enough of the infused olive oil to coat lightly. Spread out in a single layer on a baking sheet and roast until well browned and tender, about 20 minutes. It may be necessary to turn the eggplant once or twice during roasting to cook them evenly. (The eggplant and potatoes can be roasted and kept at room temperature up to several hours before starting the *giambotta*.)

Heat 2 tablespoons of the infused oil in a large skillet over medium-high heat. Fish out the garlic from the oil and add it to the skillet. Cook, shaking the pan, until the garlic is light brown, about 2 minutes. Scatter the onion over the oil. Season lightly with salt and cook, tossing or stirring often, until lightly browned, about 5 minutes.

One 1-pint basket ripe
cherry tomatoes
½ cup shredded fresh basil
Crushed hot red pepper

**Makes 6 appetizer or
side-dish servings**

In a second large skillet, heat 2 tablespoons of the infused oil over medium-high heat. Stir in the red and yellow peppers, season them lightly with salt, and cook, stirring or tossing often, until browned, about 5 minutes. Slide the peppers into the pan of onions and continue cooking, stirring frequently, as you continue.

Pour 2 tablespoons of the infused oil into the empty skillet and return to medium heat. Stir in the zucchini, season lightly with salt, and cook, tossing or stirring often, until browned, about 5 minutes. Slide the zucchini into the pan with the onion-pepper mixture. Add the cherry tomatoes to the empty skillet and cook, shaking the skillet until the skins pop, about 3 minutes. Slide them into the skillet with the other vegetables. Gently stir the potatoes and eggplant into the skillet. (Divide the vegetables between the two skillets if they don't fit comfortably into one.) Stir in the basil and cook until the potatoes and eggplants are heated through, 2 to 3 minutes. Taste, and season with salt and crushed red pepper if necessary.

☞ If you choose not to roast the eggplant and potatoes in advance, you may brown them in oil, as you did the other vegetables. If so, start with a few more tablespoons of olive oil in the infusion, parboil the potatoes before browning them in the skillet, and don't allow the other vegetables to overcook while you sauté the eggplant and potatoes.

Whether you choose to serve this salad at room temperature or chilled, you will find it a refreshing and welcome change.

Zucchini and Cherry Tomato Salad

Insalata di Zucchini e Pomodorini

Salt

4 small ("fancy") zucchini (about 1½ pounds), washed

1 pint ripe, juicy cherry tomatoes, rinsed and cut in half

16 fresh mint leaves, shredded

4 to 5 tablespoons extra-virgin olive oil

2 to 3 teaspoons balsamic vinegar

Freshly ground black pepper

Makes 8 servings

The secret to bringing out the flavor of the zucchini without making it soggy is to cook it whole for just long enough to soften it. If you don't have cherry tomatoes, cut regular tomatoes into chunks more or less the size of the sliced zucchini.

Bring a large saucepan or braising pan of salted water to a boil. Set a large bowl of ice water near the stove.

Slip the zucchini into the boiling water and cook just until softened and bright green, about 4 minutes. Transfer them to the ice water and let stand until cool. Drain well.

Trim the ends from the zucchini and cut the zucchini in half lengthwise, then crosswise into ½-inch slices. Toss the zucchini, tomatoes, mint, and enough olive oil to coat them lightly in a large serving bowl. Add salt, pepper, and vinegar to taste and toss again. Serve immediately or chill about 1 hour.

To: Lidia Bastianich
From: Linda Ager
Subject:

> > > Your cooking reminds me so much of the cooking that my mother and grandmother did. Your style of cooking is a culmination of food, love, and family. Thank you for reinventing this for us.< < <

This versatile dish of baked eggplant with a crunchy, zesty topping can be served warm or at room temperature as an appetizer, part of a buffet, or alongside grilled fish. I picked up this recipe while traveling through the inland portions of Campania—the region that surrounds Naples. In its simplicity, these baked eggplants have more complexity of flavor than a recipe with twenty ingredients thrown together by an overzealous cook. Simplicity reigns in my kitchen: do not be leery of a short list of ingredients in a recipe, just be sure when you buy those ingredients they are the best you can find.

Eggplant "of the Poor"

Melanzane Povere

4 small eggplants (about 1 ½ pounds; see note)

½ cup grated Pecorino Romano cheese

½ cup fine, dry bread crumbs

6 tablespoons extra-virgin olive oil

2 tablespoons chopped fresh Italian parsley

1 tablespoon capers, drained and chopped

1 teaspoon dried oregano, preferably the Sicilian or Greek type dried on the branch, crumbled

Salt

3 tablespoons red-wine vinegar

Freshly ground black pepper

Makes 6 servings

Preheat the oven to 400° F. Wash the eggplants, cut off the stems, then cut the eggplants in half lengthwise. Cut each half into two or three wedges, depending on size of eggplant. (The eggplant wedges should be no more than 1 inch at their widest.)

Toss the Pecorino, bread crumbs, 2 tablespoons of the olive oil, the parsley, capers, and oregano together in a small bowl until the crumbs are evenly moistened with the oil. Toss the eggplant wedges with the remaining 4 tablespoons olive oil in a separate bowl, season them with salt and pepper, and toss again. Lay the eggplant, cut side up, in a 15 × 11–inch baking dish (or other dish into which they fit comfortably in a single layer). Sprinkle the vinegar over the eggplant, cover the dish with aluminum foil, and bake until softened and lightly browned, about 25 minutes.

Remove the foil from the baking dish and bake the eggplant uncovered until it is tender and lightly browned, about 10 minutes.

Top the eggplant wedges with the seasoned bread crumbs, dividing them evenly. Bake until the eggplant is tender and topping is deep golden brown, about 25 minutes. Let it cool in the baking dish, and serve warm or at room temperature.

☞ If you cannot find eggplants of that size, substitute 2 larger (about ¾ pound each) eggplants. Cut off the stems and cut the eggplants in half crosswise before cutting them into 1-inch wedges.

The unbeatable flavor combination of eggplant, basil, and tomatoes brought together in this simple dish makes a great main course or appetizer when served hot. Baked in advance and served warm, the fans are a wonderful accompaniment to grilled foods.

Eggplant Fans

Ventaglio di Melanzane

2 small firm eggplants (about 10 ounces each)

Salt

¼ cup extra-virgin olive oil

12 ounces fresh mozzarella, cut into ½-inch slices

2 medium beefsteak tomatoes, cored and cut into 4 thick slices each

½ cup fine, dry bread crumbs

5 tablespoons freshly grated Parmigiano-Reggiano cheese

10 leaves fresh basil, torn into pieces

½ cup Tomato Sauce (page 151, or another) or canned reduced-sodium chicken broth

Makes 4 appetizer or side-dish servings

I always have tomato sauce in the kitchen, and that is what I would use to bake these eggplant fans. But if you don't have any on hand, or don't want to make it, just use homemade or canned chicken broth. The idea is to keep the eggplants moist as they bake.

Leave the eggplants untrimmed and cut them in half lengthwise through the stems. Lay the eggplant halves cut side down and, leaving the eggplants attached at the stem, make four evenly spaced cuts all the way down to the work surface that start just below the stem and run down to the tip of the eggplant. Sprinkle all the cut surfaces lightly with salt and rub them with 3 tablespoons of the olive oil. Lay the eggplant, cut side down and side by side, in a 13 × 9–inch baking dish (or equivalent-size dish into which the eggplants fit comfortably).

Cut the mozzarella and tomato slices in half. Tuck a half-slice of tomato and mozzarella in between the cuts in the eggplant. Season lightly with salt. Stir the bread crumbs and 3 tablespoons of the grated cheese together in a small bowl and sprinkle over the eggplants. Sprinkle the remaining 2 tablespoons grated cheese and the basil over the eggplants, and drizzle the remaining 1 tablespoon olive oil over them. Ladle the tomato sauce or broth between the eggplants and cover the dish with aluminum foil.

Bake 20 minutes, uncover the dish, and continue baking until the eggplants are tender and the bread-crumb topping is golden brown, about 10 minutes.

Open up the slits of the eggplant and fill with tomato and mozzarella.

Brussels Sprouts Braised with Vinegar

Cavolini Brasati con Aceto

1 ½ pounds Brussels sprouts

¼ cup extra-virgin olive oil, plus more for drizzling over the finished dish

6 cloves garlic, peeled

Salt

1 cup water, or as needed

½ cup red-wine vinegar

Freshly ground black pepper

Makes 6 servings

Trim the core even with the base of the sprouts. Remove the outer, discolored leaves and cut each sprout in half. Wash them thoroughly and drain well.

Heat ¼ cup olive oil in a 3-quart braising pot or wide, deep skillet. Whack the garlic cloves with the side of a knife and toss them into the oil. Cook, shaking the pan, until golden, about 2 minutes. Stir the sprouts into the oil, season them lightly with salt, and stir until they turn bright green, about 3 minutes. Pour in 1 cup of the water and the vinegar and bring to a boil. Lower the heat so the liquid is simmering. Cook, uncovered, until the sprouts are tender and almost falling apart and the liquid is almost completely evaporated, 20 to 25 minutes. If the liquid is evaporated before the sprouts are tender, add more water, about ¼ cup at a time, as necessary. Taste and season with pepper and, if necessary, salt.

Spoon the sprouts into a warm serving bowl, drizzle a little olive oil over them, and serve.

Variation

Savoy or White Cabbage Braised with Vinegar

Substitute one small (about 2-pound) head of Savoy or white cabbage for the Brussels sprouts. Peel off any discolored or wilted outer leaves and cut the head in quarters through the core. Remove the core and cut the cabbage into 1-inch-wide strips.

Fennel

1. After cutting off the stalks, trim the bottom of the fennel bulb.

2. Remove the tough outer layers.

3. Turn the bulbs cut side down and cut them into halves or quarters, trimming the top further if you like.

Braised Fennel

Finocchio Brasato

2 fennel bulbs

3 tablespoons unsalted butter

Salt

Freshly ground white pepper

⅔ cup Chicken Stock (page 74) or canned reduced-sodium chicken broth

Makes 4 servings

You can enjoy this dish slightly brothy, or lightly caramelized by continuing to simmer the fennel after it is tender, until all the stock evaporates. If you are serving the fennel with a grilled piece of fish or meat, keep it nice and juicy. On the other hand, if you are serving the fennel as a contorno *with a piece of meat or fish that has its own sauce, then cook off the liquid and serve the fennel dry.*

Trim the fennel following the illustrated directions opposite. Slice the pieces crosswise into ¾-inch strips.

Heat the butter in a medium skillet over medium heat until foaming. Scatter the fennel pieces over the butter, season them lightly with salt and pepper, and cook, tossing and stirring, until they begin to brown, about 6 minutes. Pour in the chicken stock and bring to a boil. Lower the heat so the stock is simmering. Cover the pan and cook until the fennel is tender, 15 to 20 minutes. During the last few minutes, remove the lid from pan so about half the liquid evaporates. If you'd like to serve the fennel "dry" and lightly caramelized, continue cooking until all the liquid has boiled off and the fennel is lightly browned, about 4 minutes. Taste, and add more salt and pepper if you like.

Cabbage salad is not something big in the Italian-American cuisine, but in the northern part of Italy, where I was born, it is a popular winter vegetable. Using it in a salad like this reflects the Middle European influence that seeped across the border into my corner of Italy. It is a different rendition of coleslaw.

Marinated Cabbage Salad

Insalata di Verza

1 small white cabbage (about 2 pounds; or ½ medium, 4-pound cabbage)

2 to 3 tablespoons kosher salt or coarse sea salt

3 tablespoons extra-virgin olive oil

2 tablespoons red-wine vinegar

Freshly ground black pepper

Makes 6 servings

If you are lucky, you own a mandoline (a professional chef's tool that makes slicing vegetables thin an easy chore) or even an old-fashioned coleslaw slicer. If not, shred the cabbage as thin as you can with a good sharp knife. The amount of salt you use depends on your taste and your cabbage. This makes a great winter salad, by itself or tossed together with salad greens.

Remove the tough and discolored outer leaves from the cabbage and cut the cabbage in half through the core. Cut out the core and shred the cabbage, with a mandoline or with a sharp knife, as thin as possible. You will have about 12 cups.

Toss the shredded cabbage well with 2 tablespoons of the salt in a large bowl. Let marinate in the refrigerator for about 1½ hours. Check the bottom of the bowl. There should be at least 2 tablespoons of water, and the cabbage should have lost some of its crunch. If not, toss in the remaining tablespoon of salt. In either case, return the cabbage to the refrigerator and marinate until wilted, about 1½ hours.

Drain the cabbage well and taste it. If it is a little salty for your taste, rinse it briefly under cold water. Using your hands, squeeze out as much water as possible from a handful of the cabbage at a time, transferring each handful to a serving bowl as you do. Pour the olive oil and vinegar over the cabbage, and toss and fluff it with a fork. Taste, and season with pepper.

Roasted Root Vegetables

Radici Invernali Arrostite

3 medium leeks

2 large parsnips (about 8 ounces), peeled and cut into 3-inch lengths (see note)

3 large carrots (about 8 ounces), peeled and cut into 3-inch lengths

2 large, outer celery stalks, trimmed and cut into 3-inch lengths

6 small red or white new potatoes (about ½ pound), cut in half

3 small yellow onions, peeled and cut in half through the core

20 large cloves garlic, peeled

3 tablespoons extra-virgin olive oil

2 sprigs fresh rosemary

Salt

Freshly ground black pepper

Makes 6 servings

Preheat the oven to 400° F. Following the illustrations on page 80, trim the dark-green leaves from leeks and cut the whites in half lengthwise. Trim the root ends of the leeks, leaving enough of the root core intact to hold the leek halves together. Rinse the leek halves under cold water, separating the layers to rinse out any grit from between them.

Toss all the vegetables together with the garlic, olive oil, and rosemary in a large bowl until the vegetables are coated with oil. Season generously with salt and pepper and toss again. Turn the vegetables into a 13 × 9–inch (or equivalent-size) roasting pan and roast until they are tender and well browned, about 1 hour. Remove the pan from the oven and stir the vegetables gently several times while they roast, so they cook and brown evenly.

☞ Parsnips can vary greatly in width from stem end to tapered end. If the tops of your parsnips are very wide, cut them in half lengthwise after cutting them into 3-inch lengths.

My mother, Erminia, at her first communion in Busoler, 1931

This dish is related to the other two *aglio e olio* "master recipes," Steamed Broccoli with Oil and Garlic on page 326 and Swiss Chard Braised with Oil and Garlic on page 322. And, like those two recipes, it is open to many possibilities, a few of which I've outlined for you below.

I remember as a child eating vegetables cooked with the addition of potatoes. Although I like the result very much—and those dishes are a part of my heritage—I imagine that the potatoes were added as much to bulk up the dish as for flavor.

String Beans and Potatoes

Fagiolini e Patate in Tegame

1 large Idaho or Yukon Gold potato (about 8 ounces)

1 pound fresh string beans, trimmed

¼ cup extra-virgin olive oil, plus more for drizzling over the cooked vegetables

4 cloves garlic, peeled and sliced

Salt

Freshly ground black pepper

Makes 4 servings

Peel the potato and cut crosswise into 1½-inch pieces. Pour enough cold water over the potato in a large saucepan to cover by 3 inches. Bring to a boil over high heat, lower the heat slightly to a gentle boil, and cook 8 minutes. Stir in the string beans and continue cooking until both vegetables are tender, 7 to 8 minutes.

Drain the vegetables well in a colander. Heat ¼ cup olive oil in a wide skillet over medium heat. Scatter the garlic over the oil. Cook, shaking the pan, until golden, about 1 minute. Slide the drained vegetables into the skillet, season with salt and pepper, and cook, stirring and mashing the potatoes to the desired consistency as you do. Drizzle additional olive oil into the vegetables and mix just before serving.

Variation

Other Potatoes and Other Vegetables

Think of the above recipe as a master recipe. You can use other types of potato in place of the Idaho or Yukon Gold, and a host of other "add-in" vegetables in place of the string beans. Whatever potato or add-in vegetable you choose, the technique is simple: Peel and cut the potatoes and put them on to cook. Then add the cleaned and cut add-in vegetable, timing it so both vegetables are cooked at the same time. (The proportions, generally speaking, should be around 60 percent vegetable and 40 percent potato, but you can vary that depending on preference or need.) The vegetables are then well drained and sautéed with garlic and olive oil, the vegetables mashed roughly as they're cooking. (Again, based on your preference, you can mash the vegetables smooth or not so smooth.)

The add-in vegetables that lend themselves best to this preparation are Swiss chard, Savoy cabbage, white cabbage, and spinach. Prepare any of these choices according to the directions that follow the Swiss Chard Braised with Oil and Garlic on page 322 and substitute them for the string beans.

Judge when to stir in the add-in vegetable based on the timing guidelines below. (If you find you misjudged the cooking time and one vegetable is tender before the other, simply fish the tender vegetable out of the pot, set it aside, and return it to the pot when the second vegetable is tender.)

New Potatoes: You can choose to peel or not peel new potatoes, depending on your preference. Choose small new potatoes, about $1^1\!/_2$ inches in diameter. Cut any potatoes larger than that in half. New potatoes of this size will take about 25 minutes of boiling to become tender.

Savoy Cabbage, Green Cabbage, Spinach, or Swiss Chard: See the directions for preparing these ingredients that follow the recipe for Swiss Chard Braised with Oil and Garlic on page 322. Add cabbage or chard to the pot about 5 minutes after the potato has been cooking, and the spinach about 10 minutes after the potato has been cooking.

Mashed Parsnips and Scallions

Purè di Pastinaca e Scalogno

1 pound parsnips, peeled and cut into 2-inch lengths

1 large Idaho potato (about 8 ounces), peeled and sliced 1½ inches thick

Salt

1 bunch scallions, including tender greens, trimmed, cleaned, and sliced thin (about 1 cup)

½ cup milk

4 tablespoons unsalted butter

1 teaspoon grated lemon zest

Freshly ground black pepper

Makes 4 servings

Pour enough cold water over the parsnips and potatoes in a 3- to 4-quart saucepan to cover them by three fingers. Season generously with salt and bring to a boil over high heat. Cook until tender, about 15 minutes. Add the scallions and cook 3 minutes.

Meanwhile, heat the milk and butter in a saucepan over low heat until the butter is melted. Drain the vegetables thoroughly and return them to the empty pot. Mash the vegetables with a potato masher, gradually adding the milk and butter, to a smooth texture. Stir in the lemon zest and season to taste with salt and pepper. Serve immediately.

My mother, Erminia, and her class
(she was a teacher) in Pula in 1956

Olive Oil Mashed Potatoes

Purè di Patate all'Olio

1 pound Idaho or Yukon
   Gold potatoes, scrubbed
   but unpeeled

Salt

¼ cup olive oil

Freshly ground pepper,
   preferably white

Makes 4 servings

Pour enough cold water over the potatoes in a large saucepan to cover them by three fingers. Season the water with salt and bring to a boil. Cook until the potatoes are tender but still hold their shape, 15 to 30 minutes, depending on the size and shape of the potatoes. Drain the potatoes and let stand until cool enough to handle.

Peel the potatoes, and pass them through a ricer or food mill fitted with the fine disk. Gently stir in the olive oil and season them to taste with salt and pepper. Serve hot.

Variations

Garlic Mashed Potatoes

Heat the olive oil in a small skillet over medium-low heat. Slice three peeled garlic cloves, scatter them over the oil and cook, shaking the pan, until light brown, about 2 minutes. Remove the pan from the heat and cool to room temperature before adding to the riced potatoes.

Anchovy Mashed Potatoes

Heat 2 tablespoons of the olive oil in a small skillet over medium-low heat. Add 2 anchovy fillets and cook, breaking them up, until they are dissolved. Remove from the heat, pour in the remaining 2 tablespoons olive oil and cool to room temperature. Beat the anchovy oil into the mashed potatoes.

Soft Polenta

Polenta Morbida

2 fresh or dried bay leaves

1 tablespoon coarse salt, or as needed

2 tablespoons extra-virgin olive oil

1 ½ cups "instant" polenta

4 tablespoons unsalted butter

½ cup freshly grated Parmigiano-Reggiano cheese

Makes 6 servings

Traditionally, we made polenta with coarse-grain cornmeal and cooked it for 40 minutes or even longer. Today, there is instant polenta, which cooks up nicely in about 15 minutes from start to end. I'm introducing you to polenta by cooking instant polenta; once you master the instant, you can move on to the traditional coarse polenta and you'll notice the difference in texture.

Polenta is unbelievably versatile. I could give you a thousand ways to enjoy it, because that's how many ways we ate it while we were growing up. It is delicious poured into a bowl and served as is, or allowed to chill and sliced, at which point you can grill or fry it for the next day's meal. You can even make a "mosaic" by folding diced cooked vegetables into the soft polenta, packing it into a loaf pan while it is still warm, then allowing it to chill. When you cut the chilled loaf into slices, the vegetables will form a mosaic and make an even prettier presentation when cooked.

Bring a kettle filled with about 4 cups of water to a boil, then lower the heat to very low and keep warm. Bring 4 cups water to a boil in a 3- to 4-quart heavy saucepan. Toss in the bay leaves and 1 tablespoon salt and stir in the olive oil.

Working with a small handful of the cornmeal at a time, let it fall through your fingers into the boiling seasoned water, while stirring constantly with a wooden spoon. (Pay special attention to the corners as you stir; it is there that the polenta will stick and scorch first.) It should take about 5 minutes to add all the cornmeal.

When all the cornmeal is added, the mixture should be smooth and thick and begin to perk like a little volcano. Lower the heat so the polenta continues to perk slowly, and cook, stirring constantly, until it is smooth and shiny, about 5 minutes. If at any point during the cooking the polenta becomes too thick to stir easily, add some of the water from the kettle — about $\frac{1}{2}$ cup — to loosen the consistency a little. It is possible that you will not need to add all the water in the kettle before the cornmeal is tender. The polenta is ready to serve at this point, or you can choose to cook it an extra minute or two, to intensify the flavor.

Remove the pan from the heat, stir in the butter and cheese, and pour into a ceramic serving bowl. Let the polenta stand for up to 10 minutes before serving. The longer the polenta stands, the firmer its texture will be.

My grandfather
Giovanni, c. 1920

Most people don't think of radishes as anything but a salad vegetable, but they make a wonderful side dish, with a little kick from the radish roots and a hint of bitterness from the greens.

Sautéed Whole Radishes

Ravanelli Saltati

2 bunches red or white radishes (about 16), each no more than 1 inch across, with bright, fresh greens

2 tablespoons extra-virgin olive oil

4 cloves garlic

¼ cup Chicken Stock (page 74), canned reduced-sodium chicken broth, or water

Salt

Freshly ground black pepper

Makes 4 servings

Make sure the radishes you choose are roughly the same size and have healthy-looking greens attached. If you find baby turnips in your supermarket or farmers' market, try them the same way. These radishes go very well with the Veal Chops Stuffed with Taleggio and Broccoli on page 220 or the Chicken Breast Valdostana on page 271.

Trim any wilted or discolored leaves from the radishes, but leave the healthy leaves attached. Wash the radishes in plenty of cold water, swishing them gently to remove all the sand and grit from between the leaves. Drain them in a colander. Trim the root tip and make a cut into the root end about halfway up to the leaves. Don't cut the radishes in half.

Heat the oil in a large skillet over medium heat. Whack the garlic cloves with the side of a knife and toss them into the oil. Cook, shaking the pan, until golden, about 2 minutes. Carefully add the radishes to the pan—they may splatter—and cook, turning, until the leaves are wilted, about 3 minutes. Pour in the stock, season lightly with salt and pepper, and cover the pan. Cook until the radishes are tender but firm, about 4 minutes. Remove the cover and boil until the liquid is almost completely evaporated, about 1 minute. Taste and season with additional salt and pepper if you like. Serve hot.

By being simmered slowly and allowed to absorb their cooking liquid gradually, these beans take on a creamy consistency and wonderful flavor. To reheat them, add a small amount of water and bring them to a simmer over low heat.

Braised Cannellini

Cannellini Stufati

½ pound (about 1¼ cups) dried cannellini or other small white beans, such as Great Northern or baby limas

4 sprigs fresh rosemary

2 tablespoons extra-virgin olive oil

Salt

Makes about 3 cups (4 servings)

Pour the beans into a deep bowl and pour in enough cold water to cover them by 4 inches. Let soak in a cool place or the refrigerator at least 8 hours or overnight.

Drain the beans and transfer them to a 2-quart saucepan. Pour in enough water to cover by two fingers and drop in two of the rosemary sprigs. Bring the water to a boil, then lower the heat so the water is at a bare simmer. Cook until the beans are tender but not mushy, with just enough liquid to cover them, 30 to 40 minutes. (If necessary, add more water a tablespoon at a time to keep the beans covered as they simmer.)

Remove the beans from the heat and gently stir in the oil, salt to taste, and the remaining 2 rosemary sprigs. Let stand to cool and absorb the cooking liquid. The end result should be tender beans with a creamy consistency in just enough liquid to coat them. Taste the beans occasionally as they cool and stir in more salt if necessary.

The juiciness of these beans, and the tinge of acidity they get from the vinegar, make them a great side dish for grilled or roasted meats.

White Beans with Rosemary and Vinegar

Cannellini Brasati al Rosmarino e Aceto

Braised Cannellini (see preceding recipe)

¼ cup extra-virgin olive oil

1 small yellow onion, sliced thin (about 1 cup)

Three ⅛-inch-thick slices Italian prosciutto, cut crosswise into ⅛-inch strips (about ½ cup)

2 sprigs fresh rosemary

¼ cup red-wine vinegar

Salt

Freshly ground black pepper

Makes 6 servings

Prepare the Braised Cannellini. (This can be done up to 2 days in advance. Refrigerate the beans in their liquid and bring them to a gentle simmer before continuing.)

Heat the oil in a 3-quart pot or braising pan over medium heat. Stir in the onion and cook, stirring occasionally, until translucent, about 3 minutes. Pour the beans into the pot and stir in the prosciutto, rosemary, and vinegar. Bring to a boil, then lower the heat so the beans are simmering. Season with salt and pepper and let simmer until the flavors have had a chance to blend, about 15 minutes. Remove the rosemary sprigs and serve.

Braised Lentils with Spinach

Lenticchie Brasate

2 cups brown lentils

2 small onions, diced (about 1½ cups)

2 medium carrots, peeled and diced (about 1 cup)

1 stalk celery, trimmed and diced (about ½ cup)

2 bay leaves

Salt

½ cup Chicken Stock (page 74) or canned reduced-sodium chicken broth

2 tablespoons extra-virgin olive oil

Freshly ground black pepper

4 cups finely shredded fresh spinach, thoroughly washed and drained

Makes 6 servings

Pour enough cold water over the lentils, onions, carrots, celery, and bay leaves in a 3-quart saucepan to cover by three fingers. Season with salt and bring to a boil over high heat. Adjust the heat so the water is at a gentle boil and cook, covered, until the lentils are tender, 20 to 25 minutes. Drain the lentils, discard the bay leaves, and transfer the lentils to a large skillet.

Pour in the chicken stock and olive oil and season lightly with salt and pepper. Bring to a boil and cook until the liquid is reduced enough to coat the lentils, about 3 minutes. Scatter the spinach over the lentils and toss just until the spinach is wilted, about 1 minute. Taste and add salt and pepper if necessary. Serve immediately.

```
To:      Lidia Bastianich
From:    Rosemary Fuchs
Subject:


> > > The way you explain the food and cooking methods
especially appeals to me. You treat your audience with
respect, always give an interesting, unhurried lesson,
and you don't clown around in the kitchen. And I love it
when you speak Italian!< < <
```

Rice Timbales

Timballi di Riso

4 cups water

3 tablespoons extra-virgin olive oil

2 teaspoons salt

2 bay leaves

2 cups long-grain rice

4 tablespoons unsalted butter, softened, plus more for the ramekins

¼ cup fine, dry bread crumbs

2 cups finely shredded fresh spinach

1 cup grated Parmigiano-Reggiano

2 tablespoons chopped fresh chives

Makes 6 timbales

I love the flavors of spinach and chives in these timbales when served with the Scampi on page 287. Vary the herbs and greens, or include other members of the onion family—sautéed leeks or onions, for example—if you are serving the timbales alongside other dishes.

You can make the timbales up to a couple of hours in advance and leave them at room temperature, but try to avoid refrigerating them. That will change the flavor, and not for the better.

Place the oven rack in the center position and preheat the oven to 375° F.

Bring the water, olive oil, salt, and bay leaves to a boil in a 2-quart saucepan over medium heat. Stir in the rice and bring the water back to a boil. Lower the heat so the water is simmering, cover the pan, and cook until the rice is *al dente* and the liquid is absorbed, about 15 minutes. (If there is still a little water left in the pan when the rice is cooked, remove the pan from the heat and let it stand, covered, a minute or two, until the liquid is absorbed.)

While the rice is cooking, butter six 8-ounce ramekins or custard cups and sprinkle the insides evenly with bread crumbs. Bring a kettle of water to a boil, then keep it hot over low heat.

Remove the rice from the heat and beat in 4 tablespoons butter, the spinach, grated cheese, and chives. Divide the rice mixture among the prepared ramekins and cover each with a small square of aluminum foil.

Set a baking pan large enough to hold the ramekins on the oven shelf. Set the ramekins in the pan, leaving some space between them, and pour in enough hot water from the kettle to come halfway up the sides of the ramekins. Bake 15 minutes.

Remove the aluminum foil and bake until the tops of the timbales are lightly browned and feel firm to the touch, about 15 minutes. Carefully remove the pan from the oven and remove the ramekins from the hot-water bath. Let stand 5 minutes.

Run a paring knife around the inside edge of the ramekins and, working one at a time, unmold the ramekins onto serving plates. If you have trouble freeing the timbales from one of the ramekins, leave the ramekin in place on top of the overturned timbale while unmolding another, then return to it.

Twice-Fried Istrian Potatoes

Patate Fritte Due Volte

6 cups vegetable oil

4 medium Idaho potatoes (about 8 ounces each), scrubbed but unpeeled

¼ cup extra-virgin olive oil

3 large cloves garlic, sliced thin

1½ tablespoons chopped fresh Italian parsley

Coarse sea salt or kosher salt

¼ teaspoon freshly ground black pepper

Makes 6 servings (quantities can easily be reduced to make fewer servings)

Thermometers — whether the instant-reading type used for meat, the large-dial models used to measure the temperature of oil for frying, or those used to test an oven's temperature — are key tools to have in the kitchen.

Why twice-fried potatoes? The first cooking, at a lower temperature, cooks the potato fully, and the second frying, at a higher temperature, makes a delicious crunchy crust. This comes in handy if you want to make the dish for company — the first frying can be done several hours in advance, and the second cooking takes only 5 minutes or so.

Heat the vegetable oil in a heavy 3-quart pot over medium heat until a deep-frying thermometer registers 300° F.

Meanwhile, pat the potatoes dry and cut each lengthwise into six even wedges. When the oil reaches temperature, carefully slip about one-third of the potato wedges into the oil. Fry until they are lightly browned and tender but firm when poked with a paring knife, about 10 minutes. Remove and drain. Repeat with the remaining potatoes. (Note: To prevent darkening, cut the potatoes as you fry them. I don't recommend putting cut potatoes in water to prevent darkening, as the water will splatter when you slip the potatoes into the oil.) These once-fried potatoes may be kept at room temperature for up to 8 hours.

Up to 2 hours in advance, mix together the olive oil, garlic, and parsley in a large bowl. Keep covered at room temperature until needed.

Just before serving, heat the vegetable oil in the pot to 375° F and preheat the oven to 300° F. Fry about one-third of the potatoes until golden brown and crispy, about 4 minutes. Transfer to paper towels to drain, then place on a baking sheet and keep hot in the oven. Repeat with the remaining potatoes.

Press both ends of each potato wedge till the center of the wedge "pops" but the wedge stays intact. Sprinkle the potatoes generously with salt and pepper and turn them gently in the seasoned olive oil until coated. Serve at once.

Warm Potato, Onion, and Caper Salad

Insalata Calda di Patate, Cipolla, e Capperi

1 pound Idaho or Yukon Gold potatoes, scrubbed but unpeeled

1 small red onion, sliced thin (about 1 cup)

⅓ cup chopped fresh Italian parsley

¼ to ⅓ cup tiny capers, drained

⅓ cup extra-virgin olive oil, or as needed

Salt (preferably sea salt)

Cracked black pepper (see note page 139)

Red-wine vinegar, optional

Makes 6 servings

Try this salad as it was made traditionally, without vinegar. If you feel the capers don't supply the necessary zing, sprinkle a little wine vinegar over the salad and toss it again. Warm salads like this take the chill out of a cold-cut lunch and go very well alongside grilled fish, chicken, or sausages.

Pour enough cold water over the potatoes in a medium saucepan to cover by three fingers. Bring to a boil over high heat, then lower the heat slightly to a gentle boil. Cook until the potatoes are tender when poked with a paring knife or skewer, 20 to 35 minutes, depending on the size and type of potato. Drain the potatoes and let them stand until cool enough to handle but still quite warm.

Cut the potatoes into ½-inch slices and set them in a serving bowl. Scatter the onion, parsley, and capers over the potatoes, drizzle ⅓ cup of the oil over them, and season with salt and pepper. Toss gently until all the ingredients are evenly distributed. There should be enough olive oil to make the vegetables glisten. If not, drizzle in a little more and toss gently. Taste, and season with additional salt and pepper and a drizzling of vinegar if you like. Serve immediately.

Potato croquettes were sure to appear on the table of Italian-American restaurants alongside platters of escarole sautéed in garlic and oil, string beans marinara, and fried zucchini. Fried vegetables—or, for that matter, fried fish or meats—have an honored place in both the Italian and Italian-American culinary repertoire.

Potato Croquettes

Crocchette di Patate

1 pound potatoes, preferably Yukon Gold

4 tablespoons unsalted butter

Salt

Freshly ground white pepper

Freshly grated nutmeg

3 large eggs

½ cup chopped Italian prosciutto

1 tablespoon chopped imported fresh Italian parsley

2 cups fine, dry bread crumbs, or as needed

All-purpose flour

2 cups vegetable oil

Makes about 24 croquettes (6 side-dish servings)

This is the side dish to make when you find yourself with leftover mashed potatoes. (If you are using leftover mashed potatoes, use your judgment about the ingredients you want to add, since the mashed potatoes may be flavored already.) It also makes a wonderful dish for entertaining—everyone loves them, and you can keep them warm in an oven up to 30 minutes after you make them.

Scrub the potatoes well, but don't peel them. Pour enough cold water over the potatoes in a medium saucepan to cover them by three fingers. Bring the water to a boil over high heat, then lower the heat slightly to a gentle boil. Cook until tender when poked with a wooden skewer or the tip of a paring knife, 20 to 35 minutes, depending on the size of the potatoes.

Drain the potatoes and let them stand until cool enough to handle. Scrape off the skins with a knife and pass the potatoes through a ricer or force them through a coarse sieve back into the empty pot. Stir in the butter, set the pot over medium heat, and stir until the puree is smooth. Remove from the heat and season with salt, white pepper, and a touch of nutmeg. Beat one of the eggs and stir it, along with the prosciutto and parsley, into the potato mixture until all the ingredients are evenly distributed. Cool to room temperature.

Using about 2 tablespoons of the potato mixture for each, form cylindrical croquettes about 2 inches long. Refrigerate the croquettes, uncovered, until firm, about 20 minutes. They can also be covered and refrigerated for up to 1 day before continuing with the recipe. *continued on next page*

Whisk the remaining two eggs well in a wide bowl. Spread the bread crumbs and flour out on separate plates or sheets of wax paper. Working with a few at a time, dredge the croquettes in flour to coat them lightly and tap off the excess. Dip the floured croquettes into the egg, turning well to coat all sides evenly. Let excess egg drip back into the bowl, then lay the croquettes in the pan of bread crumbs. Turn to coat all sides and ends well with bread crumbs, pressing very gently with your hands until the bread crumbs adhere well to the croquettes.

Heat the vegetable oil in a heavy, medium skillet over medium heat to 350° F.

When the oil reaches temperature, or when the edge of one of the croquettes gives off a lively sizzle when lowered into the oil, slip half the croquettes into the oil. Fry, carefully turning them as necessary, until golden on all sides, about 4 minutes. Adjust the heat under the pan as the croquettes cook so they cook evenly. Remove the croquettes with a slotted spoon and drain them on a paper-towel-lined baking sheet. Repeat with the remaining croquettes. Fried croquettes can be kept warm on a baking sheet in a 200° F oven for up to 20–30 minutes.

Nutmeg

NUTMEG IS ACTUALLY THE SHELLED SEED of an evergreen tree, *Myristica fragrans*, whose outer, lacy shell is mace—another spice used in sweet and savory dishes. Nutmeg is not indigenous to Italy, but it is used often in the Italian cuisine, especially in pasta fillings, gnocchi dough, and mashed potatoes. Use a light hand when seasoning with nutmeg. It is very aromatic, and its aroma becomes even more pronounced after cooking. A little goes a long way.

You can buy nutmeg whole or ground. But since you need small amounts at a time, I always recommend using the whole seed. Although there are special graters made just for nutmeg, the smallest teeth of a box grater or those new rasp-style graters work just fine. Grate only as much as you need at the time, and keep the rest of the nutmeg sealed tightly in plastic wrap in the freezer.

The *tarallo* is a traditional Neapolitan bread, the dough for which is shaped into rings, then boiled briefly before being well baked until crispy. You can think of a *tarallo* as a bread, roll, or cracker—sort of like a very crunchy Italian bagel. *Taralli* are enjoyed with a piece of cheese; they are nice to take along on a picnic or fishing trip; teething children love to nibble on them; and they are always present on the holiday table. They last for days without spoiling, and may be quickly "revived" by being dunked for a moment in soup or wine, or incorporated into a juicy tomato salad, as in the recipe that follows. There is also a richer version of *taralli*, made with lard and seasoned with crushed black pepper, which are topped with toasted almonds before baking.

Crunchy, Fennel-Scented Bread Rings

Taralli con Finocchietto

2½ teaspoons dried yeast

1 cup dry white wine, warmed to about 100° F

¼ cup extra-virgin olive oil

1 teaspoon salt

1½ teaspoons fennel seeds, cracked

3¾ cups unbleached all-purpose flour, or as needed

Vegetable oil for the rising bowl and baking sheets

Makes about 30 *taralli*

Stir the yeast and warmed wine together in a large warm bowl until the yeast is dissolved. Let stand until foaming a little, about 10 minutes. Stir in the olive oil, salt, and fennel seed. Add as much of the flour as necessary to make a rough dough, then turn it out onto a lightly floured work surface. Knead until the dough is smooth and elastic, about 5 to 7 minutes. You shouldn't need to add more flour, as the olive oil should prevent the dough from sticking, but if you find the dough is sticking to your hands or the work surface, dust them lightly with flour.

Set the dough in a lightly oiled bowl and turn it to coat lightly with oil. Cover the bowl with plastic wrap and place in a warm, draft-free area until the dough is puffy but not quite doubled in size, from 20 to 40 minutes, depending on the dough and the temperature.

Break off a piece of dough the size of a walnut and roll it between your palms and fingers to form a rope that is about as thin as a pencil. Set the dough rope aside and repeat with the remaining dough. Cut each rope into pieces about 4 inches long and shape them into rings about 2 inches in diameter. Press the ends together very firmly to keep them from separating during cooking.

continued on next page

Set the rings on lightly oiled baking sheets, cover them with a clean kitchen towel, and let rise until almost doubled, about 1 hour.

When the dough rings are almost ready, preheat the oven to 350° F, fill a wide braising pan or pot halfway with water, and bring to a boil.

Plunge as many of the risen *taralli* as will float freely into the boiling water. The *taralli* will sink or float, depending on the dough. If they sink, wait for them to rise to the surface, flip them over, and cook for a minute. If the *taralli* float, cook them 1 minute on each side. In either case, remove them with a slotted spoon, drain on paper-towel-lined baking sheets, and cool slightly.

Bake on lightly oiled baking sheets until deep golden brown and hard, 20 to 24 minutes.

Store the *taralli* in an airtight container at room temperature for up to 4 weeks.

☞ To crack the fennel seeds, roll a heavy rolling pin over them or press them with the bottom of a small, heavy saucepan.

Taralli make a great *panzanella,* a salad that is traditionally made with day-old bread, tomato, and basil.

Taralli and Marinated Tomato Salad

Panzanella con Taralli

8 *taralli,* each cut or broken into 4 pieces

1 pound ripe plum or beefsteak tomatoes at room temperature, cored, seeded, and cut into ½-inch cubes (about 3 cups)

1 small red onion, diced (about 1 cup)

12 fresh basil leaves, shredded

5 tablespoons extra-virgin olive oil

3 tablespoons red-wine vinegar

Salt

Freshly ground black pepper

Fresh basil sprigs

Makes 6 servings

Toss the *taralli,* tomatoes, onion, and shredded basil leaves together in a serving bowl. Drizzle the olive oil and vinegar over the salad and toss to mix thoroughly. Season to taste with salt and pepper and let stand 10 minutes before serving. Taste and season, if necessary, with additional salt and pepper. Decorate with sprigs of fresh basil.

Sardinian Old Bread and Tomato Casserole

Mazza Murru

3 pounds ripe fresh plum tomatoes, peeled and seeded (page 9), or one 28-ounce can Italian plum tomatoes (preferably San Marzano)

1 teaspoon sea salt, plus additional salt for water

1 pound day-old dry, crusty Italian bread, sliced (about sixteen ¾-inch slices)

¼ cup extra-virgin olive oil

1 large yellow onion, sliced (about 2 cups)

¼ cup chopped fresh oregano

2 cups grated Pecorino Romano cheese

Makes 6 servings

You know how I feel about wasting food; everything in my kitchen gets used, even old bread. I'd like you to try this dish, so, even if you don't find yourself with a leftover loaf of bread, buy a fresh one and let it dry overnight. Think of this side dish as a bread lasagna and serve it as a contorno *to fish or meat. For a different and delicious brunch dish, top each serving with a poached or fried egg.*

Pass the tomatoes through a food mill fitted with the fine disc and set aside. (Alternatively, process the tomatoes in a food processor, using quick on/off pulses until smooth. Don't overprocess the tomatoes or you will incorporate air into them and the sauce will look pink.)

Bring 2 quarts of salted water to boil in a saucepan. Dunk the bread slices, one by one, into the boiling water for a second or two—just long enough to wet them—and set them on a clean kitchen towel to drain. Press the moistened bread lightly to remove excess water.

Heat 3 tablespoons of the oil in a medium skillet over medium heat. Scatter the onion in the skillet and cook, stirring, until golden, about 8 minutes. Pour in the tomatoes and bring to a boil. Lower the heat so the sauce is simmering, and cook until the sauce is lightly thickened, about 20 minutes. Stir in the oregano and cook an additional 5 minutes.

Preheat the oven to 375° F. Oil an 11-inch oval baking dish (or equivalent-size baking dish) with the remaining 1 tablespoon oil. Spoon in enough of the tomato sauce to coat the bottom, and arrange half the bread slices over the sauce, tearing them and wedging them as necessary to make an even layer. Spoon half the remaining tomato sauce over the bread and sprinkle half the Pecorino over the sauce. Make another layer of bread slices, tomato sauce, and cheese.

Bake until the casserole is heated through and the cheese topping is browned, about 25 minutes.

Desserts & Coffee

Coffee and dessert certainly have a definitive place in the sequence of an Italian meal, but, in addition, there is a social ritual of enjoying dessert and coffee independent of mealtimes that's typically and distinctly Italian. As you travel through Italy, the essence of coffee that wafts through the streets will attest to the numerous cafés—*bar*s, as they are called in Italy—and the need to frequent them shared by Italians. Italians do not traditionally have a big breakfast—in most instances, they'll stop at their favorite café and have a *cornetto* (croissant) and cappuccino on their way to work. (Let me clear one thing up right now: Italians enjoy cappuccino only in the morning and/or with *dolci* in the afternoon [much rarer]. Never, never would they drink cappuccino after a meal.)

At the mid-morning break, between 10:00 and 11:00 a.m., the coffee bars are busy with housewives and mothers returning from their daily shopping or accompanying the children to school, the retired population meeting their friends, and business people taking a break or arranging quick meetings over a cup of espresso. A piece of *dolce crostata* (fruit tart) or a *tramezzino* (small white-bread sandwich) is enjoyed at this time, over significant conversation or just chitchat.

This ritual is so much a part of the Italian culture that it is repeated in the late afternoon, both by those who took a mid-morning break and by those who did not. The afternoon break is usually longer, because it becomes part of the afternoon siesta. Sitting outside under an umbrella enjoying a cup of coffee and *dolci* (sweets) or *gelato,* people watching and meeting with friends are part of what makes the Italian *dolce vita* so *dolce* (sweet).

Just as these bars, where one enjoys coffee, sweets, grappas, *amari,* or liquors, are gathering places, so are the *pasticcerie* (pastry shops) and *gelaterie* (ice-cream shops), which almost always offer the option of taking the sweets with you or enjoying them on-site with a good cup of espresso or cappuccino. Italians very rarely grab something and eat it while walking—they'll always take the opportunity to sit, relax, and socialize.

For not being big dessert eaters after a meal, the Italians have one of the largest dessert repertoires of any culture. I guess this diversity could be attributed to the strong regionality that still survives in

Italy. Like the Italian people themselves, Italian desserts have made their way to the States from all parts of Italy. You'll recognize many of the names and sweets I describe below from the dessert menu of Italian restaurants or from the shelves of your local Italian bakery.

In Piemonte the influence of French neighbors is very much reflected in desserts like *bonet* (hat)—a chocolate-amaretto custard—Monte Bianco (Mont Blanc), and *marrons glacés* (glazed chestnuts), all of which make use of the exceptionally large chestnuts that grow in Piedmont.

The *panettone*, bread (*pane*) embellished with raisins and candied fruit, exemplifies the businesslike, no-frills attitude of Milano, in the Lombardy region. *Gubana*, a roulade filled with dried fruit, nuts, chocolate, and grappa, and diversified strudels reflect the Middle European influence on Friuli-Venezia-Giulia—the most northeastern region of Italy, which now shares borders with Slovenia and Austria. Emilia-Romagna, the fertile plain of the Valle Padana, is rich in butter and fruits such as cherries, plums, and berries, and some of the best *crostate* (tarts) made from these fruits and jams come from there.

Tuscany's rustic cuisine has its *cantucci-biscotti*, twice-baked cookies that need a good glass of Vin Santo for dunking before they truly come alive.

In Campania, the region that claims Naples as its capital, desserts reflect the long years under French occupation. In Neapolitan *pasticcerie*, desserts are elaborate, creamy, soaked with liqueurs, glazed, decorated, stuffed, or made with lots of ricotta and candied citrus. And they are delicious, like the Delizie al Limone on page 374, which is also made *al cioccolato* (with chocolate), *alla fragola* (with strawberries), *alla nocciola* (with hazelnuts) or, at any given pastry shop, in a dozen different flavors. The mignon or petit-four versions — smaller than the standard — are always available. Sicily is known for its almonds, pistachios, and citrus fruit. Therefore, almond-paste marzipan, studded with some pistachio or candied citrus incorporated with sheep's-milk ricotta, is at the base of an extraordinary dessert tradition. And the long domination of the French, with their elaborate sweets and desserts, had its influence. Sicily's *pasticcerie* look as though they are always decorated for Christmas. Ice cream and granitas also seem to have had their origins in Sicily, stemming from the Arab influence there.

It is the dessert traditions of these last two regions — Campania and Sicily — that are mostly exemplified in Italian-American bakeries. (Mind you, in Italy, bread baking takes place in a *panetteria* and is completely separate from a *pasticceria,* where only sweets, desserts, cookies, chocolate, and candies are sold. The *gelatteria* or ice-cream shop is another completely separate entity.)

Many of these traditions were absorbed into Italian-American bakeries, such as the Pine Nut Cookies on page 393, the Sesame Cookies on page 394, or the *taralli* on page 357. Anise-flavored cookies, ricotta-stuffed cannoli, pistachio-almond torrone, baba au rhum, mignons, lemon *delizie* (page 374), and *pastiera* (page 372), are all associated with Italian pastry. As with the rest of Italian-American food, the strongest influence was from that first wave of southern-Italian immigrants, and most of the Italian-American bakeries still reflect the flavor and the culinary traditions of Campania and Sicily.

This is not a moist cake, but one with a dry, crumbly texture that makes it ideal for soaking with syrup, as you do in the following "English Soup" and the Lemon Delight on page 374. Even when wet, the cake will hold its shape without crumbling.

Sponge Cake

Torta di Spagna

Butter, at room temperature for greasing pan

7 large eggs, separated

1 1/3 cups sugar

2 tablespoons plus 1 1/2 teaspoons lemon juice

1 1/2 teaspoons grated lemon zest

1 1/2 teaspoons vanilla extract

1/2 teaspoon salt

1 1/2 cups sifted cake flour

Makes one 13 × 7–inch cake or two 11 × 15–inch cake layers

Lightly butter a 13 × 7-inch cake pan. Cut a piece of parchment paper or wax paper to fit the bottom of the pan. Fit the paper into the pan and lightly butter the paper. Preheat oven to 325° F.

In a medium bowl, beat the egg yolks and 2/3 cup sugar with a handheld electric mixer until they turn pale yellow and take on a ribbonlike texture. Beat the lemon juice, lemon zest, and vanilla into the yolks.

Clean the beaters well, or the egg whites will not whip properly. In a separate, large bowl, whip the egg whites with the salt until foamy. Continue beating, gradually adding the remaining sugar, until the whites form soft peaks when the beaters are lifted from them. With a large rubber spatula, scrape egg-yolk mixture over whites. Fold the yolks gently into egg whites by scraping along the bottom of the bowl and up through the center of the mixture. Fold until just a few streaks of white remain. Sift the flour over the egg mixture and fold it in gently.

Scrape the batter into the prepared pan. Bake until the top is golden brown and the cake begins to pull away from the sides of the pan, about 30 minutes. Remove, and cool in the pan on a wire rack 20 minutes. Invert the cake onto the rack, and cool completely before removing the paper.

The title of this dessert may sound funny, but there is a very good explanation for it. The *zuppa* part comes from *inzuppare*, which means "to soak," and refers to the way the layers of sponge cake are saturated with a liqueur-flavored syrup. The English part, I imagine, refers to the similarities between this creation and an English trifle.

"English Soup"

Zuppa Inglese

Sponge Cake (preceding recipe)

For the Pastry Cream

1 lemon

2½ cups milk

½ cup sugar

3 tablespoons cornstarch

Pinch salt

5 large egg yolks

1 teaspoon vanilla extract

½ cup finely diced candied fruit

To Assemble *Zuppa*

2½ cups heavy cream

½ cup sugar

½ cup simple syrup (see note below)

½ cup alchermes liqueur or rum

¼ cup Maraschino or other cherry brandy

Fruit for decoration

Makes 12 servings

In this recipe, I prepare the zuppa inglese *almost as you would a layer cake. Although the method is fairly easy, you may want to try the following more traditional and even easier way the first time you make it. Prepare all the components as described below, but assemble them thus: Line a 13 × 7–inch ceramic or glass serving dish with one layer of sponge cake, cut side up. Brush and fill the layers as described below, finishing with a layer of whipped cream over the top layer of cake. Chill and decorate as described below. To serve, spoon the* zuppa inglese *from the dish, passing any remaining whipped cream and pastry-cream sauce separately.*

Make the sponge cake.

Make the pastry cream: Remove the yellow zest from the lemon in long strips, using a vegetable peeler. (Avoid removing the white pith under the zest; it will add bitterness to the pastry cream.) Squeeze the juice from the lemon and set aside. Pour 2 cups of the milk into a heavy saucepan and toss in the lemon zest. Heat over medium heat just until bubbles form around the edge of the saucepan. Whisk the sugar, cornstarch, salt, and remaining ½ cup cold milk together in a small bowl until the cornstarch is dissolved. Ladle about half the hot milk into the cornstarch mixture, whisking constantly until the sugar is dissolved. Scrape the cornstarch mixture into the saucepan, increase the heat to medium, and cook, stirring constantly and paying special attention to the bottom and corners of the pan, until the mixture comes to a boil and thickens, about 3 minutes. Drop the yolks into the small bowl used above, and pour the hot-milk mixture slowly into the yolks, whisking constantly. Scrape the mixture back into the saucepan and cook, stirring constantly, until the pastry cream thickens further, 3 to 4 minutes. Strain the pastry cream into a bowl, whisk in the vanilla, and set aside to cool with a piece of plastic wrap pressed directly to its surface. Chill thoroughly.

Measure and set aside $1/2$ cup of the pastry cream. Place the candied fruit in a small bowl; strain the remaining pastry cream over the candied fruit. Cool both containers of pastry cream to room temperature with plastic wrap directly on the surface to prevent a skin from forming. Chill thoroughly.

In a medium bowl, beat 2 cups of the heavy cream and $1/2$ cup sugar at medium speed until the cream forms stiff peaks when the beaters are lifted from it. Set the whipped cream aside. Combine the simple syrup, alchermes, and Maraschino brandy.

With a long serrated knife, cut the sponge cake horizontally into three even layers. Place the top layer of the cake, cut side up, on a flat platter or plate at least 2 inches wider than the cake on all sides. Brush the cake layer generously with the syrup mixture. Spread one half of the fruited pastry cream evenly over the layer, then spread about 1 cup whipped cream over the pastry cream. Now place the middle layer over the whipped cream. Brush the surface with about half the remaining syrup, and repeat the layering with the remaining fruited pastry cream. Top with the final layer of cake, cut side down. Brush with the remaining syrup. Spread the remaining whipped cream in an even layer on the top and sides of the cake. Chill the *zuppa* at least 2 hours or up to 1 day.

To finish decorating and serve the *zuppa inglese:* Combine the reserved $1/2$ cup pastry cream and the remaining $1/2$ cup heavy cream in a small bowl and whisk gently to blend. Strain into a small pitcher. Decorate the top of the *zuppa inglese* with the remaining $1/2$ cup whipped cream and the fruit. Cut the *zuppa* into squares, place on chilled serving plates, and pour a little of the pastry-cream sauce around each serving.

☞ To make simple syrup, stir $1/2$ cup sugar into $1/2$ cup water in a small saucepan. Bring to a boil, stirring, over low heat. Boil 1 minute and remove from the heat. Cool before using.

San Martino Pear and Chocolate Tart

Torta di Pere San Martino al Cioccolato

For the Caramel
⅔ cup sugar

2 tablespoons water

For the *Torta*
16 amaretti cookies, crushed

½ cup unsweetened cocoa powder

¼ cup sugar

⅓ cup milk

2 large eggs, plus 1 large egg yolk

1 tablespoon rum

½ teaspoon baking powder

¾ cup plus 2 tablespoons heavy cream

3 ripe Bosc pears, peeled, cored, and cut into very thin slices

Makes 12 servings

The texture of the chocolate-amaretto custard is very delicate, so be sure to slice the pears very thin, so you can eat the dessert with a spoon.

Stir the sugar and water together in a medium skillet. Set over medium heat and cook, stirring occasionally, until the sugar is melted and the syrup is boiling. Don't stir the syrup after it comes to a boil, as this will most likely form crystals in the syrup. Cook, swirling the pan occasionally to prevent the syrup from hardening on the sides of the pan, until the syrup begins to turn a very pale golden brown. You will be able to tell when the syrup is about to change color—the bubbles will be larger and will move a little more slowly. When the syrup begins to change color, reduce the heat to low and continue cooking and swirling until the syrup is a medium-amber color (about 340° F on a candy thermometer). If the caramel begins to color too quickly, dip the bottom of the skillet or saucepan in a basin of cool water for a second or two. Pour the caramel immediately into a 10-inch round heatproof pie dish or shallow casserole and tilt to coat the entire bottom with caramel.

Preheat the oven to 325° F. Choose a roasting pan large enough to fit the pie plate and place it on the center rack of the oven. Heat a kettle of water to boiling.

Pour the crumbled cookies into a blender jar and blend, using on/off motions, until finely ground. Pour in the cocoa and sugar and pulse to mix with the cookies. Pour in the milk, eggs and yolk, rum, and baking powder and blend at low speed, stopping occasionally to scrape down the sides of the jar, until smooth. Pour in the heavy cream, and blend just enough to incorporate the cream. Scrape into a mixing bowl and stir in the pears.

Pour the chocolate-pear mixture into the prepared dish and set the dish in the roasting pan. Pour in enough of the boiling water from the kettle to come halfway up the mold. Bake until firm in the center and lightly browned on top, about 40 minutes.

Remove carefully from the water bath and place on a wire rack. Cool completely to room temperature, then chill thoroughly. To serve, run a thin knife around the edges of the custard to loosen them. Invert a plate large enough to hold comfortably over the tart, then, in one quick motion, flip the tart over and set the plate down. The tart may take several seconds to work itself loose from the dish. After it does so, gently lift off the dish and serve the tart.

Variation

Caramel-Pear Sauce for the Tart

If you'd like to take this dessert one step further, prepare this simple sauce that echoes the caramel-pear flavors for the tart. Peel and slice thin an extra pear and double the amount of caramel called for in the recipe. When the caramel is done, pour half of it into the dish and immediately scatter the extra sliced pear over the caramel remaining in the pan. Shake the pan off the heat until the liquid given off by the pears begins to loosen the caramel. Stir in 2 tablespoons of rum and stir until all the caramel is dissolved. If necessary, return the pan to low heat to dissolve the last bits of caramel. Serve the sauce at room temperature, or rewarmed over very low heat, spooned around individual servings of the tart.

Baked Peaches with Amaretti Filling

Pesche al Forno con Amaretti

12 amaretti cookies, coarsely crumbled

8 tablespoons unsalted butter, softened

½ cup sugar, plus more for dipping the peaches

⅓ cup amaretto liqueur or Malvasia or other sweet dessert wine

¼ cup coarsely chopped toasted almonds

½ teaspoon unsweetened cocoa powder

3 large ripe but firm peaches

1 lemon, cut in half

½ cup water

Vanilla ice cream, optional

Makes 6 servings

Preheat the oven to 375° F. Process the amaretti cookies in the work bowl of a food processor fitted with a metal blade, using on/off pulses, until ground coarsely. Add 4 tablespoons of the butter, 2 tablespoons of the sugar, 2 tablespoons of the amaretto liqueur, the almonds, and cocoa, and process until ground fine.

Cut the peaches in half and remove the stones. Brush the cut surfaces of the peaches with a lemon half and dip them in sugar. Combine the water and the remaining 6 tablespoons sugar in an oval 11-inch casserole or 9-inch glass pie plate, and stir to dissolve the sugar. Squeeze in the juice from the lemon halves and add the remaining amaretto.

Divide the amaretti stuffing among the peach halves, packing it lightly into the cavity and forming a thin, even layer over the cut side of the peach. Arrange the peaches, stuffed side up, side by side in the prepared baking dish. Dot the top of each with about a teaspoon of the remaining butter. Cut the remaining butter into 4 pieces and add to the liquid in the baking dish. Cover the dish with aluminum foil and bake 15 minutes. Uncover, and continue baking until the filling is lightly browned and the juices in the pan are bubbling and lightly thickened, about 20 minutes. Remove, and cool at least 10 minutes before serving. The peaches can be served hot or at room temperature, with vanilla ice cream if you like. Spoon some of the juices in the baking dish over the peaches and, if serving, the ice cream.

Cakes made with ricotta cheese—like this one and the *pastiera*, a traditional Easter dessert from Campania (recipe follows)—are very typical of Italian desserts. This cheesecake is both dry and wet at the same time.

Ricotta Cheesecake

Torta di Ricotta

3½ cups fresh or packaged whole-milk ricotta cheese

½ cup raisins

3 tablespoons dark rum

Butter, at room temperature for greasing pan

¼ cup fine, dry bread crumbs, or as needed

5 large eggs, separated

¾ cup sugar

Pinch salt

Grated zest of 1 large lemon

Grated zest of 1 large orange

½ cup heavy cream

½ cup pine nuts

Makes 8 servings

Spoon the ricotta into a large fine-mesh sieve or a colander lined with a double thickness of cheesecloth or basket-type coffee filter. Set the sieve over a bowl and cover the ricotta well with plastic wrap. Drain in the refrigerator at least overnight, or up to 24 hours. Discard the liquid in the bottom of the bowl.

Soak the raisins in rum in a small bowl, tossing occasionally, until the raisins are softened and have absorbed most of the rum, 1 to 2 hours.

Smear an 8-inch springform pan with enough softened butter to coat lightly. Sprinkle the bread crumbs over the butter to coat generously. Shake out the excess crumbs. Preheat the oven to 375° F.

Beat the egg yolks, sugar, and salt with a whisk in a large bowl until pale yellow. Add the drained ricotta and lemon and orange zest, and beat until blended thoroughly. Beat in the heavy cream. Fold in the pine nuts and the raisins and rum with a rubber spatula. Beat the egg whites in a separate bowl with a handheld electric mixer or wire whisk until they form firm peaks when the beater is lifted from them. Fold about one-fourth of the egg whites into the ricotta mixture to lighten it. Use a large rubber spatula to scrape the batter from the bottom of the bowl up and over the whites. Fold in the remaining egg whites in the same way. Pour the ricotta mixture into the prepared pan, and bake until the cake is golden brown on top and set in the center, about 1 hour and 10 minutes.

Cool the cake completely before removing the sides of the pan. Serve the cake at room temperature or chilled.

Grain and Ricotta Pie

Pastiera Napoletana

4 cups fresh or packaged whole-milk ricotta

For the *Pasta Frolla* Dough

2 cups granulated sugar

4 large egg yolks

Grated zest of 1 lemon

2 cups (1 pound) unsalted butter or shortening, cut into 1-inch pieces, at room temperature

4 cups all-purpose flour

For the Filling

2 cups hulled wheat kernels

4 cups milk

2½ cups granulated sugar

3 large eggs

2 large egg yolks

2 teaspoons orange water (see note below)

½ teaspoon ground cinnamon

½ cup candied lemon or orange peel, cut into ¼-inch dice

Confectioners' sugar

Makes 16 servings

If you can't find hulled whole-wheat kernels (sometimes sold as "pastry wheat"), substitute barley, skip the soaking, and cook it as described below, but for only about 30 minutes. Whole-wheat kernels—grano, in Italian—are used for this traditional Neapolitan dessert that became a mainstay in Italian-American restaurants and bakeries. In Italy, cooked whole-wheat kernels can be found in cans; if you spot some, it will make this recipe a little simpler.

This pastiera *and the preceding Ricotta Cheesecake were sometimes confused with each other, especially in the 1950s and '60s, when Americans were being introduced to these specialties—and they still are today. But in reality, they are quite different in taste and texture.*

Spoon the ricotta into a large fine-mesh sieve or a colander lined with a double thickness of cheesecloth or a basket-type coffee filter. Set the sieve over a bowl and cover the ricotta well with plastic wrap. Drain in the refrigerator at least overnight, or up to 24 hours. Discard the liquid in the bottom of the bowl.

Make the dough: Process 2 cups granulated sugar, 4 egg yolks, and the lemon zest in the work bowl of a food processor fitted with a metal blade until all ingredients are blended. Add the butter and process, using quick on/off pulses, just until incorporated. Scrape out the dough into a mixing bowl and stir in the flour just until you have a smooth dough. Wrap the dough in plastic wrap and chill for at least an hour, or up to 1 day.

Make the filling: Soak the wheat kernels in a bowl with enough water to cover by three fingers until softened, 3 to 4 hours. Drain well.

Bring the milk to a simmer in a medium saucepan. Stir in the drained wheat and ¼ cup of the granulated sugar. Return to a gentle simmer and cook, stirring occasionally, until the wheat kernels are tender but still have some bite, about 45 minutes. (Most of the milk will have been absorbed.) Drain, and cool to room temperature.

Preheat the oven to 350° F. Butter a 12-inch springform pan. Roll out two-thirds of the dough into a 16-inch circle about $^1/_4$ inch thick. Lift the dough circle into the pan, pressing it gently against the bottom and sides and into the corners of the pan. Most likely the dough will tear. Don't be alarmed, simply press the torn edges together after fitting the dough into the pan. Roll out the remaining dough on a lightly floured surface to a 12-inch circle, and slide onto a baking sheet. Refrigerate the lined pan and rolled dough until needed.

Process the remaining $2^1/_4$ cups granulated sugar, the eggs, and egg yolks in the work bowl of a food processor fitted with the metal blade until pale yellow. Spoon in the drained ricotta and add the orange water and cinnamon. Mix, using quick on/off pulses, just until blended. Scrape the ricotta mixture into the bowl with the grain, scatter the candied fruit peel over all, and fold together with a rubber spatula until blended. Scrape the filling into the prepared pastry shell.

Cut the 12-inch pastry circle into $^1/_2$-inch strips. Make a lattice top by laying strips of the dough in alternating directions over the filling. Press the strips of dough gently to join them to the dough along the sides of the pan, and pinch off any overhanging dough.

Bake until pastry is golden brown and the center feels springy when poked with a finger, about $1^1/_2$ hours. Remove, and cool completely before serving. The cake will keep, refrigerated, for up to a week. It will be better a day or two after baking. Sprinkle with confectioners' sugar before serving.

Variation

A version of this *pastiera* that I made in my first restaurants was a bit creamier and lighter. To make that version, which is quite common in Campania, substitute 1 cup pastry cream (see page 366) for $^1/_2$ cup of the ricotta, 1 egg, and $^1/_2$ cup granulated sugar. Add the pastry cream to the filling along with the ricotta mixture.

☞ Orange-flower water is made by distilling orange oil. It is available in specialty food stores and Middle Eastern groceries.

Lemon Delight

Delizie al Limone

Butter

Flour

Sponge Cake batter
  (page 365)

For the Pastry Cream

  2 small lemons

  2 cups milk

  ½ cup granulated sugar

  ¼ cup cornstarch

  ½ teaspoon salt

  4 large egg yolks

  1 large egg

For the Lemon Syrup

  ½ cup water

  ½ cup granulated sugar

  ½ cup Limoncello (Italian
    lemon liqueur)

For Limoncello Sauce

  2 lemons

  1 cup Limoncello

  1 cup fruity white wine

  ½ cup granulated sugar

  2 tablespoons potato
    starch or cornstarch

  1 tablespoon water

  1 cup heavy cream

For the Simple Fondant

3½ cups confectioners'
  sugar

  5 tablespoons water

  1 tablespoon corn syrup

Makes 8 servings

The part of the sponge cake that is left behind after the rounds are cut for the delizie *makes a nice snack. Although these are traditionally served robed in plain white, you could crumble the leftover cake into crumbs and sprinkle them over the fondant before it has a chance to harden.*

Make the sponge cake circles: Arrange one rack in the upper third of the oven and the other in the lower third. Preheat the oven to 325° F. Lightly butter two 15 × 11–inch baking pans, cut parchment or wax paper to fit over the bottoms, and butter the parchment paper. Sprinkle flour over the parchment and tap it around to cover the butter evenly. Tap out any excess flour. Prepare the Sponge Cake batter as described on page 365. Divide the batter between the two pans, spreading it into an even layer that reaches into the corners of the pans. Bake until the cake is light golden and the center springs back when poked lightly with a finger, about 20 minutes. Remove and cool in pans on wire racks 15 minutes. Invert the cake pans onto the racks. Carefully lift the pans and peel off the parchment paper. Cut eight 3-inch circles from each cake with a biscuit cutter or glass. Set the cake circles aside.

Make the pastry cream: Remove the yellow zest from the lemons in long strips with a vegetable peeler. (Avoid removing the white pith under the zest; it will make the pastry cream bitter.) Squeeze the juice from the lemons and set aside. Pour 1½ cups of the milk into a heavy saucepan and toss in the lemon zest. Heat over medium heat just until bubbles form around the edge of the saucepan. Whisk granulated sugar, cornstarch, salt, and remaining ½ cup cold milk together in a small bowl until the cornstarch is dissolved. Ladle about half the hot milk into the cornstarch mixture, whisking constantly until the sugar is dissolved. Scrape the cornstarch mixture into the saucepan, increase the heat to medium, and cook, stirring constantly and paying special attention to the bottom and corners of the pan, just until the mixture comes to a boil and thickens, about 3 minutes. Remove the pan from the heat, drop the yolks and egg into the same small bowl used above, then pour about half the thickened milk mixture slowly into the yolks, whisking constantly. Scrape the mixture into the saucepan and return pan to the heat.

Stir constantly, until the pastry cream thickens further, 3 to 4 minutes. Strain the pastry cream into a bowl and beat until smooth and creamy. Set aside to cool, with a piece of plastic wrap pressed directly to the surface of the pastry cream. Beat in the lemon juice. Chill thoroughly.

Make the lemon syrup: Stir water and granulated sugar together in a small saucepan over medium heat until the sugar is dissolved and the syrup comes to a boil. Pour into a heatproof bowl and stir in $1/2$ cup Limoncello.

Make the Limoncello sauce: Remove the zest from the lemons in wide strips with a vegetable peeler. Pour the Limoncello, white wine, and granulated sugar into a small saucepan. Toss in the lemon zest and bring to a boil, stirring to dissolve the sugar. Stir the potato starch and the water together in a small bowl until the starch is dissolved, then stir into the boiling liquid. The sauce will thicken immediately. Lower the heat so the sauce is simmering, and cook, stirring, until the sauce is thickened further, about 5 minutes. Strain the sauce into a small bowl and cool to room temperature.

Assemble the *delizie*: Whip the heavy cream in a chilled bowl until it forms stiff peaks. Fold the whipped cream into the chilled pastry cream with a rubber spatula. Pour the lemon syrup into a wide, shallow bowl. Dip eight of the sponge-cake circles in the syrup for a second or two. Arrange the circles, dipped side up, on a wire rack set over a baking sheet. Spread $1/4$ cup of the pastry cream over each cake circle. Dip the remaining cake circles in the remaining syrup, and center them, dipped side up, over the pastry cream. Top with the remaining pastry cream, dividing it evenly and spreading the cream into a dome. Place the baking sheet in the refrigerator and chill thoroughly. The *delizie* can be prepared to this point up to 1 day in advance. Cover them securely with plastic wrap.

While the cakes are chilling, make the simple fondant: Stir the confectioners' sugar, water, and corn syrup together in a small saucepan. Stir over the lowest heat possible until the mixture is smooth and an instant-reading thermometer registers 95° F. (Alternatively, you can dip the bottom of the saucepan in very hot water until the fondant reaches the desired temperature.) Pour or drizzle the fondant over the chilled cakes slowly, to enrobe them completely. The coated cakes can be refrigerated for up to 1 day, but after that the fondant will begin to melt. Serve chilled, spooning some of the Limoncello sauce around each one.

Zeppole di San Giuseppe can still be found in New York's Italian bakeries on St. Joseph's Day—March 19—and the aroma of frying *zeppole* can be smelled for blocks around most of the city's street fairs. The *zeppole* hail from Naples, where frying is a large part of the traditional cuisine. If you visit Naples, you'll be tempted by the wafting smells of fried foods as you walk the streets. You may satisfy your craving at the *frigitteria* (frying shop), where you'll find just about anything breaded or enveloped in a dough. That said, these *zeppole* can be baked instead of fried, a version I prefer.

Traditional St. Joseph's Ricotta Cream Puffs

Zeppole di San Giuseppe

For the Filling

3 cups fresh ricotta (preferably water buffalo) or packaged whole-milk ricotta

½ cup confectioners' sugar

3 tablespoons Grand Marnier or other orange-flavored liqueur

¼ cup finely diced candied orange peel

¼ cup finely diced candied lemon peel

¼ cup small chocolate chips, or bittersweet chocolate chopped into small pieces

For the *Zeppole*

1 cup water

4 tablespoons unsalted butter

1 tablespoon granulated sugar

A day before preparing the filling: Spoon the ricotta into a large, fine-mesh sieve or a colander lined with a double thickness of cheesecloth or basket-type coffee filter. Set the sieve over a bowl, and cover the ricotta well with plastic wrap. Drain in the refrigerator at least overnight, or up to 24 hours. Discard the liquid in the bottom of the bowl.

Process the drained ricotta and ½ cup confectioners' sugar in the work bowl of a food processor fitted with the metal blade until creamy. Pour in the Grand Marnier and process until incorporated. Scrape the ricotta mixture into a bowl and stir in the candied fruits and chocolate chips. Store in the refrigerator, covered, until needed, up to 2 days.

Make the *zeppole*: Bring the water, butter, granulated sugar, and salt to a boil in a large, heavy saucepan. Add the flour all at once, and beat vigorously with a wooden spoon over medium heat until the dough leaves the sides of the pan and forms a ball around the spoon. Remove from heat, and quickly beat in one egg at a time, beating until the batter is smooth after each addition. Add the orange and lemon zest, and continue beating until mixture is smooth and glossy.

For the fried version: Heat the vegetable oil in a heavy 3-quart pot until a deep-frying thermometer registers 350° F. Carefully drop rounded tablespoonfuls of the batter into the oil, about six at a time. (There should be enough room in the pot for the *zeppole* to float freely.) Fry, turning the *zeppole* as necessary, until golden brown on all sides, about 6 minutes. Adjust the

½ teaspoon salt

1 cup unbleached, unsifted flour

4 large eggs

1 teaspoon grated orange zest

1 teaspoon grated lemon zest

6 cups vegetable oil (if frying the *zeppole*)

Confectioners' sugar

Makes 12 *zeppole*

heat under the pot to maintain the temperature of the oil as the *zeppole* fry. Remove with a skimmer and drain on paper towels. Repeat with the remaining batter, allowing the oil to return to 350° F before continuing, if necessary.

For the baked version: Preheat the oven to 425° F. Drop the batter by rounded tablespoonfuls onto a lightly greased or nonstick baking pan. Bake until evenly and lightly golden brown, about 20 minutes. Reduce the oven temperature to 350° F, and continue baking until medium golden brown and a *zeppola* feels very light when picked up from the baking sheet, about 15 minutes. Transfer to a rack and cool completely.

Cut the *zeppole* in half, leaving them attached on one side. Spoon the filling into the *zeppole*, dividing evenly. Dust the tops of the *zeppole* with confectioners' sugar and serve at room temperature or, if you prefer, chilled.

My parents surrounded by family and friends at their wedding, 1940

Italian-American cooking is a story of adaptation and evolution. But here is one dish that made it intact from the old country to the new.

Honey Balls

Struffoli

For the Dough

4 cups all-purpose flour

1 tablespoon sugar

Grated zest of ½ lemon

Grated zest of ½ orange

Pinch salt

4 large eggs

1 tablespoon unsalted butter

1 teaspoon grappa, rum, or vanilla

3 cups vegetable oil for frying

For the Honey Syrup

2 cups honey

½ cup sugar

⅓ cup water

¼ cup tiny round colored candy sprinkles

Makes 10 servings

You may have seen struffoli *jazzed up with pine nuts, candied fruit, or slivered almonds. Sometimes they are piled into one big mound, sometimes shaped into several smaller mounds, or, especially around the holidays, formed into a wreath. Once you have the basics down, you can go off in any direction.*

Stir the flour, sugar, lemon and orange zest, and salt together in a bowl and turn it out onto a clean work surface. Make a well in the center of the dry ingredients and add the eggs, butter, and grappa to it. With your fingertips, work the eggs, butter, and grappa together until more or less blended, then begin working in the dry ingredients. Continue working the dough until it is smooth and evenly blended. Gather the dough together into a ball, wipe the dough from your hands, and add it to the dough ball. Clean your hands and the work surface, flour both lightly, and knead the dough until smooth, 3 to 4 minutes. Wrap the dough in plastic wrap, and let stand at room temperature 1 hour.

Pull off a plum-size piece of the dough and roll it out with your palms and fingers to a rope about ⅓ inch in diameter. Repeat with the remaining dough. Cut the dough ropes crosswise into ⅓-inch lengths.

Pour the oil into a wide, deep skillet or braising pan and heat over medium heat until a deep-frying thermometer registers 350° F or a piece of dough gives off a lively sizzle when slipped into the oil. Carefully slide about one-fourth of the pieces of dough into the oil and fry, turning and immersing them with a wire skimmer or slotted spoon, until golden brown on all sides, about 4 minutes. Adjust the heat under the pan as necessary while the *struffoli* are frying to maintain an even temperature. Transfer them with the skimmer to a paper-towel-lined baking sheet to drain, first allowing any excess oil to drip back into the pan. Repeat with the remaining dough, allowing the oil to return to the correct temperature, if necessary, before frying the next batch.

Have a bowl of cold water and a serving plate large enough to hold the finished *struffoli* (about 12 inches in diameter) close by. Stir the honey, sugar, and water together in a heavy, wide pot, large enough to hold all the dough balls, over low heat until the sugar is dissolved. Increase the heat to high and bring the syrup to a boil. The syrup will foam up dramatically when it comes to a boil. Continue cooking until the foam dies down and the mixture becomes just a shade darker, about 4 minutes. Remove from the heat, and immediately add all the fried dough balls. Toss them in the syrup with a wire skimmer or slotted spoon until they are coated. Remove the dough balls from the syrup with the skimmer, allowing excess syrup to drip back into the pan first, and mound them on the serving plate like a pyramid, helping yourself with your hands from time to time after dipping them into the cold water to protect them.

Scatter the sprinkles over the mound of *struffoli* until they are colorful enough for you. You may serve them the same day, or keep them for several days covered loosely with plastic wrap.

Cannoli are a traditional Sicilian dessert. I am sure you've had the crunchy, fried, tube-shaped dough filled with sweetened ricotta cheese, chocolate, and candied orange peel. To prepare these pastries in the traditional way, you need cannoli-shell forms, around which the dough is rolled and fried. This version requires no special equipment and has a contemporary, layered look while maintaining a traditional flavor and texture. (See below for a more traditional version.)

Felidia's Stacked Cannoli

Cannoli Rivisitati

1½ cups fresh or packaged whole-milk ricotta cheese

For the Pastry

1½ cups all-purpose flour

2 tablespoons granulated sugar

¼ teaspoon salt

2 tablespoons olive oil

1 teaspoon white vinegar

⅓ cup dry red wine, or as needed

For the Filling

¾ cup confectioners' sugar, plus more for decoration

3 tablespoons chopped bittersweet chocolate

1½ tablespoons finely chopped candied orange rind

Spoon the ricotta into a large, fine-mesh sieve or a colander lined with a double thickness of cheesecloth or basket-type coffee filter. Set the sieve over a bowl and cover the ricotta well with plastic wrap. Drain the ricotta in the refrigerator at least overnight, or up to 24 hours. Discard the liquid in the bottom of the bowl.

Make the pastry: Pour the flour, granulated sugar, and salt into the work bowl of a food processor fitted with the metal blade. Add the oil, vinegar, and ⅓ cup wine. Process the dough, adding more red wine a few drops at a time if necessary, until you have a smooth, supple dough. Wrap the dough in plastic wrap, and refrigerate from 2 hours to overnight.

Make the filling: Beat the drained ricotta and ¾ cup confectioners' sugar in a mixing bowl with a handheld electric mixer until the mixture is light and fluffy, about 2 minutes. Fold in the chocolate, orange rind, and pistachios. Store in the refrigerator until needed.

Roll half the dough out 1/16 inch thick (about the thickness of a dime) on a lightly floured surface. Cut the dough into 3-inch rounds, setting them on a lightly floured kitchen towel as you do. Repeat with the other half of the dough. Gather the scraps together and reroll them, cutting as many rounds as possible. You should have at least eighteen rounds. Let the dough rest at least 15 minutes before continuing, or the finished pastry layers will be tough.

Pour enough of the vegetable oil into a large, heavy skillet to fill about ½ inch. Heat over medium heat until the oil appears rippling and an edge of one of the dough rounds gives off a slow sizzle when dipped in the oil. Carefully slide as many of the rounds into the oil as will fit without touching. Fry, turning once, until both sides are golden brown, about 2 minutes. The dough

1 ½ tablespoons chopped
toasted pistachios
(see note below),
plus more for serving

Vegetable oil for frying
Honey

Makes 6 servings

☞ To make chopped toasted pistachios, blanch the shelled nuts in vigorously boiling unsalted water until they turn bright green and the skins are loosened, about 20 seconds. Drain the nuts and immediately run them under cold water. Slip off the skins and drain them briefly on paper towels. Toast the nuts on a baking sheet in a 350° F oven until lightly browned, about 10 minutes. Remove, and cool completely before chopping.

circles will bubble and take on an irregular shape as they fry; make sure the oil is deep enough to cook and brown all the surfaces of the dough as they fry. Adjust the heat during cooking to maintain a lively sizzle and to give the dough a chance to cook through to the center. Don't allow the oil to get too hot: the dough colors quickly and can burn before the center is sufficiently cooked. Transfer the cooked pastry rounds to paper towels to drain, and fry the remaining rounds, adding more oil to the pan and waiting for the oil to reheat as necessary. Cool the circles completely before continuing.

To assemble the cannoli: Place a circle of the fried dough in the center of a serving plate and top with a rounded 2 tablespoons of the ricotta filling. Repeat with another dough circle and more filling, and top with a dough circle. Make five more stacked cannoli in the same way. Drizzle honey over each and sprinkle with powdered sugar. Sprinkle some of the chopped toasted pistachios around the cannoli.

Variation

Classic Cannoli

To prepare classic, tube-shaped cannoli, you will need metal cannoli tubes about 1 inch in diameter, available in specialty cookware shops. Prepare the filling as described above. (The above amount will fill about eight traditional cannoli.) Prepare and roll out the dough as described above, and beat an additional egg with a few drops of water until foamy.

Wrap one of the dough circles around a cannoli tube; you will see that the edges overlap. Lift the top edge and dab the lower edge with a few drops of the beaten egg. Press the two edges together to seal them tightly. Let the dough tubes stand a minute or two so the egg will dry. Repeat with the remaining dough and tubes. If you don't have enough cannoli tubes to accommodate all the dough circles, work in batches.

Pour enough vegetable oil into a deep, heavy braising pan to fill 3 inches. Heat over medium heat until a deep-frying thermometer registers 350° F. Carefully slide a few of the shells and tubes into the hot oil. Fry, turning as necessary, until the shells are golden brown and blistered evenly on all sides, 3 to 4 minutes. Remove them carefully with a wire skimmer or slotted spoon and drain them on paper towels. As soon as the tubes are cool enough to handle, slide the shells off the tubes. Cool completely before filling. Fill the cannoli shells with a teaspoon just before serving, or they will become soggy. However, the fried shells can be stored at room temperature for several hours before filling.

Zabaglione

6 egg yolks, at room
   temperature

¼ cup dry Marsala wine

¼ cup sugar

**Makes about 2 cups
(3 or 4 dessert servings, or
 6 servings as a sauce for fruit)**

Whisk the egg yolks, Marsala, and sugar together in the top of a double boiler or a wide heatproof bowl until smooth. Place over, not in, barely simmering water, and continue beating (switching to a handheld electric mixer at medium speed, if you like) until the mixture is pale yellow and frothy and falls back on itself in thick ribbons when the whisk or beaters are lifted, about 8 minutes. Immediately scrape the zabaglione into serving glasses and serve warm.

Variation

Chocolate Zabaglione

Melt 3 ounces chopped semisweet chocolate, stirring often, in the top of a double boiler or in a heatproof bowl set over a pan of barely simmering water. Remove the pan from the heat, but leave the bowl of chocolate over the water to keep it warm. Make the zabaglione as described above, then fold in the warm melted chocolate with a rubber spatula. Serve immediately.

Roasted Pears and Grapes

Pere e Uva al Forno

2 cups seedless red
   grapes

1 cup sugar

⅔ cup Moscato or other
   fruity white wine

Juice of 2 lemons

2 tablespoons apricot jam

½ vanilla bean, split
   lengthwise

3 ripe but firm Bosc pears

Makes 6 servings

Preheat the oven to 375° F. Place the grapes in an 11 × 7–inch baking dish. Stir the sugar, Moscato, lemon juice, apricot jam, and vanilla bean together in a bowl until blended. Pour over the grapes. Cut the pears in half through the core and remove the stems, cores, and seeds. Nestle the pear halves, cut side up, into the grapes.

Bake, uncovered, until the pears are tender and the liquid around the grapes is thick and syrupy, about 50 minutes to 1 hour. Remove the pears and let stand until the pan syrup thickens, about 10 minutes. Serve the pears hot or warm, with some of the grapes and their pan syrup spooned around them.

This is an old recipe from the Convent of Dimess in Udine, Italy. It is served on Christmas Eve.

Chocolate Soup

Zuppa al Cioccolato

5 cups milk

3 tablespoons all-purpose flour

4 ounces semisweet chocolate, grated or chopped fine

2 tablespoons sugar

1 tablespoon unsalted butter

Ground cinnamon

Brioche or panettone, torn into pieces, or hard buttery cookies

Makes 6 servings

Stir $^1/_2$ cup of the milk and the flour together in a small bowl until smooth. Bring the remaining $4^1/_2$ cups milk just to the simmer in a medium saucepan over medium heat. Ladle 1 cup of the simmering milk over the chocolate in a heatproof bowl, let sit a minute, then whisk to dissolve the chocolate. Stir the chocolate mixture into the simmering milk. Strain the flour mixture into the saucepan, then stir in the sugar, butter, and cinnamon. Return to a simmer and cook, stirring, until thickened and smooth, about 5 minutes. Remove from the heat and let stand a minute or two. Ladle the soup into warm bowls. Pass the brioche, panettone, or cookies for dunking separately.

To: Lidia Bastianich
From: Phyllis Bergantini
Subject:

> > > You put the "Italian" back in Italian kitchen with your warmth and easy-to-watch style. Thank you for so many memories of my Italian background. Please keep up the wonderful work.< < <

The name *granita* comes from the Italian *grano* (kernel) and describes the grainy texture of this super-simple Italian dessert. Granita is loved by Italians, inasmuch as Italians do not eat much dessert after a meal but, rather, dedicate a special time of the day to have just that—coffee and dessert. This usually happens in the morning, around ten to eleven, and/or in the afternoon, around four to five. The Italians, being very social and gregarious people, need continual human contact. The dinner table, of course, is the main gathering place, but these other little social rituals are very important to an Italian. They contribute to the quality of life that Italians are known and envied for.

So let's get back to that coffee granita. In one of the many beautiful Italian piazzas, with the Mediterranean sunshine caressing us, the chiming bells of a nearby church tower marking the time, watching elegantly dressed ladies pass by, we sat with a *coppa* of coffee granita crowned by a dollop of unsweetened semi-whipped cream. You might not be able to re-create that piazza, but you certainly can re-create the flavor of that *granita di caffè*.

Coffee Granita

Granita di Caffè

4 cups brewed espresso
½ cup sugar, or to taste
½ teaspoon fresh lemon juice
1 cup heavy cream

Makes 10 servings

If you don't have the means to make espresso at home, use American-style coffee. (This is also a very good way to use leftover brewed American coffee.) To make up for the lack of coffee punch that you'll find in an espresso granita, sample your coffee and stir in instant coffee or espresso to taste.

Keep in mind that the technique used to make coffee granita can be applied to juices, teas, herbs, or any flavored and sweetened liquid of your choice. Liquids that contain alcohol don't work well for granita, since alcohol does not freeze at the temperatures that household freezers reach.

Brew the espresso and, while it is still hot, stir in ½ cup sugar and the lemon juice until the sugar is dissolved. Taste, and add more sugar if you like. Cool to room temperature.

Pour the coffee mixture into a 13 × 9-inch baking pan and set it on a level shelf in the freezer. When ice crystals begin to form around the edges—from 30 minutes to an hour, depending on your freezer—remove the pan from the freezer and stir the crystals into the liquid. Return the pan to the freezer and repeat every time crystals form. The more of the liquid that turns to ice, the quicker the remaining liquid will freeze after the pan is returned to the freezer. Continue until all the liquid has turned to crystals. The granita is now ready to serve and should be served within a few hours.

Whip the heavy cream until it holds soft peaks. Run a fork through the granita to break up any large crystals, and spoon the granita into tall glasses. Top with a dollop of whipped cream. Serve immediately.

Variation

Blender Granita

Pour the coffee mixture into ice-cube trays and freeze until solid. Grind the cubes in an ice crusher or blender. This method will give you more of a coffee slush than a true granita.

Lemon Ice

Granita al Limone

3 cups water

¾ to 1 cup sugar

Grated zest of 1 lemon

1 cup fresh lemon juice

Fresh mint sprigs and/or
whipped heavy cream

Makes 6 servings

Granita is nothing more than a flavored liquid (in this case lemon) sweetened with sugar and frozen until crystallized. Understanding this makes it very easy to make any flavor granita that you desire.

You can also use orange juice for granita; simply freeze it as is. Should you choose to flavor your granita with alcohol, don't add it to the syrup — it will inhibit the freezing process. Instead, pour it over the granita just before you serve it. It will get slushy, but a good slush on a hot summer day might be just the right thing.

Pour the water into a heavy medium saucepan. Stir in between ¾ and 1 cup of sugar, depending on your preference. Bring to a boil, stirring to dissolve the sugar, over medium heat. Lower the heat so the syrup is simmering, and cook 5 minutes.

Pour the syrup into a heatproof bowl and cool to room temperature. (If you'd like to speed up the process, place the bowl of syrup into a larger bowl half full of ice, and stir the syrup until cool.)

When cool, stir in the lemon zest and juice. Pour the lemon mixture into a 13 × 9–inch baking pan and set on a level shelf in the freezer. When ice crystals begin to form around the edges—from 30 minutes to an hour, depending on your freezer—remove the pan from the freezer and stir the crystals into the liquid. Return the pan to the freezer and repeat, every time crystals form. The more of the liquid that turns to ice, the quicker the remaining liquid will freeze after the pan is returned to the freezer. Continue until all the liquid has turned to crystals. The granita is now ready to serve and should be served within a few hours.

Whip the heavy cream, if using, until it holds soft peaks. Run a fork through the granita to break up any large crystals, and spoon the granita into tall glasses. Top with a dollop of whipped cream and/or a mint sprig. Serve immediately.

Schiuma (*spiuma* in my dialect) in Italian means "froth." I guess the presence of whipped cream in this ice-cream preparation gave it the name. Some spumoni features three flavors of ice cream—vanilla, chocolate, and strawberry—but I have chosen to include just two.

Spumoni

For the Vanilla Ice Cream

2 cups milk

¾ cup sugar

5 large egg yolks

1 vanilla bean, cut in half, or 1½ teaspoons vanilla extract

For the Chocolate Ice Cream

2 cups milk

¾ cup sugar

5 large egg yolks

½ cup cocoa powder

For the Whipped Cream

1 cup heavy cream

¼ cup sugar

12 *amarene* cherries, cut in half (see note below)

3 tablespoons toasted pistachio nuts, cut in small pieces (see note on page 381)

1 tablespoon candied orange peel, chopped very fine

Makes 12 servings

A simple way to make spumoni in the shape you remember is to use tall 10-ounce paper cups, like the ones you get when you order a soda. You can make the layering process simpler by spooning in a level layer of vanilla ice cream, then chocolate ice cream, then flavored whipped cream.

If you'd prefer to serve one large spumoni instead of individual ones, prepare the spumoni in a 6-cup soufflé dish, layering it into the dishes as described below. Let the frozen large spumoni stand at room temperature 10 to 15 minutes before inverting it onto a serving plate. Cut it into wedges to serve.

Prepare the vanilla and chocolate ice-cream bases: Whisk 2 cups milk, ¾ cup sugar, and 5 egg yolks together in a heavy 2-quart saucepan until blended. Drop in the vanilla bean, and set the saucepan over very low heat. Switch to a wooden spoon and cook, stirring constantly, until the mixture is thick, about 10 minutes. (If you have an instant-reading thermometer, check the temperature from time to time. The base will thicken shortly after the temperature reaches 180° F.) Strain the mixture into a small bowl, and cool to room temperature with a piece of plastic wrap pressed directly to the surface. Clean the saucepan. Whisk 2 cups milk, ¾ cup sugar, 5 egg yolks, and the cocoa together in the saucepan until blended. Cook and stir as described above until thickened. Strain the chocolate mixture into a separate small bowl and cool as above. The bases can be refrigerated for up to 1 day before continuing.

If you have an ice-cream maker, freeze the ice-cream bases separately, according to manufacturer's directions, and set the finished ice creams in the freezer as you finish. If you don't have an ice-cream maker, place the bowls of

continued on next page

☞ *Amarene* are pitted wild cherries preserved in syrup. Fabbri is a very good brand. If you can't find them, substitute four canned black cherries, drained and chopped coarsely, or six very good candied cherries, chopped fine.

ice-cream base in the freezer and freeze, stirring occasionally, until the mixture is frozen but soft enough to be spooned out easily.

Whip the cream and ¼ cup sugar in a chilled bowl until it holds stiff peaks. Gently fold the cherries, nuts, and candied peel into the whipped cream. Refrigerate the whipped cream.

Line up six 10-ounce paper soft-drink cups on your work surface. Remove the vanilla ice cream from the freezer. (If it has become too hard to scoop easily, let it stand at room temperature 5 to 10 minutes.) Working quickly, scoop one-sixth of the ice cream into one of the cups and spread it into an even layer that comes about 3 inches up the sides of the cup and is about ¼ inch thick, leaving enough room in the center for a layer of chocolate ice cream and the whipped-cream filling. Place the cup in the freezer immediately and repeat with the remaining ice cream and cups. Freeze until the vanilla ice cream is solid, 15 to 30 minutes.

Check the consistency of the chocolate ice cream. If it is too solid to spoon easily, let it stand at room temperature 5 to 10 minutes. Tear off six squares of plastic wrap or wax paper large enough to cover the tops of the ice-cream molds, and set them close by. Take the flavored whipped cream out of the refrigerator and have it close by. Take one of the cups out of the freezer and spoon a layer of the chocolate ice cream inside the vanilla ice cream, making that layer even with the top of the vanilla ice cream and leaving enough space in the center for the whipped-cream filling. (You may not need a full sixth of the chocolate ice cream to do this.) Drop a little of the whipped cream into the center of the mold and tap the surface of the cup to settle the whipped cream into the indentation. Add the whipped cream little by little, tapping the cup after each addition, until the whipped cream is even with the ice-cream layers. Cover with a piece of plastic wrap or wax paper pressed directly to the surface, and return immediately to the freezer. Repeat with the remaining cups. Freeze for at least 2 hours or up to one day before serving.

To serve, remove wax paper or plastic wrap. With a sharp, serrated knife, cut the cup in half lengthwise from the top, straight through the ice cream. Working carefully, peel the cup from the spumoni halves and serve on chilled plates.

The name says it all: these crunchy, nutty cookies may not be much to look at, but they certainly are delicious.

"Ugly but Good" Nut Cookies

Brutti ma Buoni

Butter, softened, for the pans, if using

8 large egg whites

Pinch salt

2 cups confectioners' sugar, sifted

2 cups shelled hazelnuts, toasted, skins removed, and chopped fine

Makes about 48 cookies

Preheat the oven to 275° F. Lightly grease two baking sheets, or line them with parchment paper.

Beat the egg whites and salt in a bowl with a handheld electric mixer until foamy. As you continue beating, add the sugar gradually, until it is all incorporated and the egg whites hold soft and shiny peaks. Scrape the beaten whites into a wide, heavy saucepan and set over medium-low heat. Stir in the hazelnuts and cook, stirring, until the batter is light golden brown, about 20 minutes. (The batter will deflate quite a bit as it cooks.)

Remove the pan from the heat. Drop the batter by rounded teaspoonfuls onto the prepared baking sheets, leaving about 1 inch between them. Bake until golden brown and firm to the touch, about 30 minutes. Remove, and cool completely before serving. Store at room temperature in an airtight container for up to 1 week.

Hazelnut-Chocolate Ice Cream Truffle

Tartufo al Cioccolato e Nocciola

1 quart milk

1½ cups cocoa powder, sifted

5 large egg yolks

2 cups sugar

2 cups shelled hazelnuts, toasted

12 ounces bittersweet chocolate, chopped fine

¾ cup heavy cream

Makes about 12 "truffles"

Tartufi made with homemade chocolate ice cream are delicious. You can make your life simpler by substituting store-bought ice cream and proceeding to form and coat the tartufi as described below.

Whisk the milk and cocoa powder together in a small heavy saucepan until blended. Set over low heat and cook, stirring constantly, until the cocoa is completely dissolved.

Whisk the egg yolks and sugar together in a second small heavy saucepan until thick and lemon-colored. Ladle the hot cocoa mixture a little at a time into the egg mixture, whisking constantly until well blended. Set the saucepan over low heat and cook, stirring constantly, until dense and creamy, about 3 minutes. Strain into a bowl and cool to room temperature, covered with plastic wrap pressed directly to the surface.

If you have an ice-cream maker, freeze the chocolate mixture in it according to manufacturer's directions. If not, set the bowl on the freezer shelf and let it sit, stirring occasionally, until frozen but still soft and moldable, from 2 to 3 hours. (You can "still-freeze" the ice cream like this up to a day in advance. Let it sit at room temperature until softened, about 10 minutes, before continuing.)

To form the "truffles": Using a 4-ounce ice-cream scoop, scoop up a ball of the chocolate ice cream and poke a hazelnut into the center while the ice cream is still in the scoop. Drop the truffles onto a wax-paper-lined baking sheet. Repeat with the remaining ice cream and hazelnuts, setting the formed truffles and the ice cream in the freezer if they begin to melt. Set the truffles on a level freezer shelf and freeze until firm, about 30 minutes.

Meanwhile, chop the remaining hazelnuts to the size of the chopped chocolate. Toss the chopped hazelnuts and the chocolate together on a separate baking sheet.

Take the truffles out of the freezer and roll them one at a time in the chopped chocolate and hazelnuts until they are lightly coated. Return to the wax-paper-lined tray, and when all are coated, return the tray to the freezer. (Depending on the temperature and how quickly the truffles start to melt, you may have to do them in batches.) Freeze at least 2 hours or up to 2 days. If keeping the truffles more than a few hours, transfer them to a covered container once they are frozen solid.

To serve, let the truffles stand at room temperature until softened, about 5 minutes, before serving. Meanwhile, whip the heavy cream in a chilled bowl until it holds stiff peaks. Divide the whipped cream among chilled plates, mounding it in the center. Top with truffles and serve immediately.

Biscotti, like pizza, have become part of the American culinary scene and have seen endless variations, from white-chocolate-dipped to macadamia-ginger and just about anything else you can imagine. These are the classic twice-baked and crispy cookies, perfect for snacking or dunking.

Biscotti

6 cups cake or all-purpose flour

¼ cup cornmeal

1 tablespoon baking powder

1 teaspoon salt

6 tablespoons unsalted butter, softened

2½ cups sugar

4 large eggs

¼ cup anisette

2 cups peeled and toasted whole almonds or hazelnuts

Makes 48 cookies

If you don't have a baking sheet large enough to hold the two loaves of dough side by side with a little room between them, use two sheets. Position the oven racks in the lower and upper thirds of the oven before preheating it, and rotate the pans from shelf to shelf and front to back about halfway through baking.

Preheat the oven to 350° F. Line a 15 × 11–inch jelly-roll pan with parchment paper. Stir the flour, cornmeal, baking powder, and salt together in a bowl. Beat the butter with a handheld electric mixer until creamy. As you continue beating, add the sugar gradually, until light and fluffy. Beat in the eggs one at a time, beating well after each addition. Stir in the anisette. Pour the dry ingredients and almonds into the bowl, switch to a wooden spoon, and stir until the dough is smooth.

Divide the mixture into two equal portions. Shape each into a loaf 12 inches long by 3 inches wide, making the sides and top even and smooth. Place the loaves side by side on the parchment-lined jelly-roll pan, leaving at least 2 inches between them and 1 inch between each loaf and the side of the pan. Bake until loaves are golden and the tops spring back when lightly poked with a finger, about 30 minutes. Remove the baking sheet from the oven and reduce the oven temperature to 300° F. Cool the loaves until barely warm but still soft enough to cut, about 30 minutes.

Slice the loaves crosswise into ½-inch-wide cookies. Lay the cookies on their side and bake until evenly golden brown and very firm, about 10 minutes. Cool completely. Biscotti can be stored in a covered container for up to 2 weeks.

Pine Nut Cookies

Amaretti con Pignoli

Butter, softened for the pans,
if using
1 pound canned almond
paste
1½ cups sugar
3 large egg whites
1½ cups pine nuts

Makes 36 cookies

Arrange one rack in the upper third of the oven and the other in the lower third. Preheat the oven to 350° F. Line two baking sheets with parchment paper, or grease them lightly.

Crumble the almond paste into a mixing bowl. Beat with a handheld electric mixer till crumbled fine. Sprinkle the sugar over the almond paste while continuing to beat, until the sugar is incorporated. Beat in the egg whites, one at a time, and continue beating until the dough is smooth. (The batter can be formed into cookies and baked at this point, or wrapped in plastic wrap and refrigerated for up to 1 day.)

Spread the pine nuts out on a plate. Roll 1 tablespoon of the dough into a ball between your palms. Drop the dough ball onto the plate of pine nuts. When you have formed several dough balls, roll them in the pine nuts to coat lightly on all sides. Transfer them to the prepared baking sheets and press them lightly, to flatten them slightly and help the pine nuts adhere to the cookies. Repeat with the remaining batter and pine nuts.

Bake the cookies until lightly browned and soft and springy, about 15 minutes. Remove, and cool completely on wire racks before serving. The cookies can be stored in a covered container at room temperature for up to a week.

Variation

If you cannot find almond paste, try the following variation, which will yield equally delicious cookies with a slightly grainier consistency than those made with store-bought almond paste. Grind 1 pound blanched slivered almonds and 1½ cups sugar to as fine a paste as possible in a food processor, stopping several times to scrape down the sides of the workbowl. Add 3 large egg whites and continue mixing until the whites are thoroughly incorporated and the batter is smooth. Continue to roll, coat, and bake the cookies as described above.

Sesame Cookies

Biscotti ai Semi di Sesamo

¾ cup sesame seeds

½ cup (1 stick) unsalted butter, cut into 8 pieces, at room temperature, plus more for the baking sheets

1 cup all-purpose flour

1 cup semolina flour

1½ teaspoons baking powder

Pinch grated nutmeg

2 large eggs

½ teaspoon salt

1 teaspoon vanilla extract

⅔ cup sugar

Makes about 60 cookies

Arrange one oven rack in the upper third of the oven and the other in the lower third. Preheat the oven to 350° F. Spread the sesame seeds out on a baking sheet and bake them on the lower rack until toasted to golden brown, about 10 minutes. Shake the pan once or twice as they bake so they toast evenly. While the sesame seeds are toasting, lightly grease two baking sheets with some of the softened butter. (This isn't necessary if you're using non-stick baking sheets.)

Stir the all-purpose flour, semolina flour, baking powder, and nutmeg together in a mixing bowl until blended. Beat the eggs and salt together in a separate mixing bowl with a handheld electric mixer until blended, then beat in the vanilla. Continue beating, adding the sugar gradually, until smooth. Drop the eight pieces of butter into the bowl and beat until almost smooth. Pour the dry ingredients into the egg mixture and beat at low speed just until incorporated. Wrap the dough in plastic wrap, and chill at least 1 hour or up to 1 day before forming and baking the cookies.

Pinch off a nectarine-size piece of the dough and roll it out with the palm and fingers of your hands, using light pressure, to a rope about ½ inch in diameter. Cut the rope into 2-inch lengths, and roll them in the sesame seeds to coat completely. Transfer the coated cookies to the prepared baking sheets, and repeat with the remaining dough and seeds.

Bake the cookies until deep golden brown, about 20 minutes. Rotate the baking sheets from rack to rack and side to side at least once during baking, so the cookies bake and brown evenly. Remove, and cool completely before serving.

These cookies, which feature the crunch of cornmeal, were and are favorites at Italian-American bakeries.

Cornmeal Cookies

Crumiri

2 sticks (8 ounces) unsalted butter, at room temperature, cut into 16 pieces, plus more for the baking sheets

2 cups very fine yellow cornmeal

1 cup all-purpose flour, plus more for the baking sheets

2 large eggs

2 large egg yolks

1 teaspoon vanilla extract

¾ cup sugar

Makes about 48 cookies

If you don't have a pastry bag, you can still enjoy these delicious and crunchy cookies in their traditional shape: Chill the cookie dough for about 1 hour; then divide it into fourths. Roll each piece out with the palms of your hands to a rope about ¹/₂ inch thick. Cut the rope into 4-inch lengths and lay them on the prepared baking sheets, shaping them into crescents and leaving about ³/₄ inch between them. Lightly drag the tines of a fork over the crescents to create ridges. Bake and cool them as described below.

Arrange the racks in the upper and lower third of the oven and preheat the oven to 400° F. Lightly butter and flour two baking sheets. (This isn't necessary if using nonstick pans.)

Stir the cornmeal and 1 cup flour together in a small bowl. Beat the eggs, egg yolks, and vanilla together in a separate bowl with a handheld electric mixer until foamy. As you continue beating, pour in the sugar gradually, until smooth. Spoon in the dry ingredients and beat at low speed just until incorporated. (The dough can be formed into cookies and baked at this point, or wrapped in plastic and refrigerated up to 1 day.)

Divide the dough into three pieces. Working with one at a time, roll it into a thick log and slide it into a pastry bag fitted with a large star tip. Squeeze the dough out of the pastry bag and onto the prepared baking sheet, cutting it into 4-inch lengths and leaving ³/₄ inch between them as you do. Shape the strips of dough into crescents. Bake until golden, about 20 minutes.

Cool the cookies completely before serving. The cookies can be stored in an airtight container at room temperature for up to a week.

I don't know the true origins of these cute "*pesche*," but I remember them being served at very special occasions. They were always made for weddings.

Desserts are always very abundant at an Istrian wedding—a sign of how special an event it is. Wedding gifts were always things for the couple's new home, but with every gift there were sweets made by the donor. *Pan di Spagna* (bread from Spain) was always one of those sweets. It was usually a very light but unfilled round sponge cake, left natural, with lacelike decorations made in white icing on top. The bride would get a multitude of them, and they would all be displayed along with the *pesche* and other cookies for the guests to enjoy as they came to offer their best wishes to the newly married couple during the week that followed the wedding. The *pesche* were a favorite at these occasions. They are tasty, a perfect mouthful, look good, and keep well for a whole week.

Peach Petits Fours

Pesche

For the Cakes

1 large egg

1 teaspoon vanilla extract

1 cup sugar

1 cup vegetable oil, plus more for the baking sheets

½ cup milk

1 ½ teaspoons rum

Grated zest of 1 lemon

3 ½ cups all-purpose flour, or as needed

1 ½ teaspoons baking powder

Lightly grease two baking sheets with vegetable oil. Preheat the oven to 350° F. Beat the egg and vanilla in a large bowl until foamy. As you continue beating, gradually pour in the sugar, until the mixture is smooth. Beat in the oil, then the milk, rum, and lemon zest. Stir 3½ cups flour and the baking powder together in a separate bowl, add it to the liquids, and stir until you have a smooth dough. If necessary, add enough additional flour to make a smooth but moldable dough.

Roll 1 level tablespoonful of the batter into a ball between the palms of your hands and set it on a lightly greased baking sheet. Fill the two prepared baking sheets with the dough balls, leaving about 1 inch between them. Bake until golden and firm to the touch, about 18 minutes. Remove, and set on wire racks just until cool enough to handle. While the cookies are cooling, form and bake the remaining batter.

While they are still warm, scoop out and reserve the flat side of each cookie with a small spoon, leaving a hollow shell that will be stuffed with the filling. Be careful not to break through the shell.

For the Filling

- 6 ounces semisweet chocolate, chopped into small pieces (about 1 cup)
- 1 cup slivered almonds, toasted and chopped fine
- 4 tablespoons unsalted butter, melted
- 2 tablespoons dark rum
- 2 tablespoons peach schnapps

- 1 cup milk, or as needed
- Strawberry or cherry Jell-O or other brand of flavored gelatin powder
- Lemon Jell-O or other brand of flavored gelatin powder
- Fresh mint leaves

Makes about 36 petits fours

Make the filling: Mix the chocolate, almonds, butter, rum, schnapps, and the reserved cookie pieces together in a bowl until evenly blended. Spoon the filling into the hollowed-out cookie shells, overstuffing each just a bit. Press the stuffing sides of two cookies together, forming a "peach." Repeat with the remaining cookies and filling.

Hold each "peach" between your fingers and dunk for just a second in milk. Place on a wire rack for a minute, until barely damp to the touch. (Until you get the knack, you may want to work with only six or so of the peaches at a time.) Roll the peaches in red, then yellow gelatin powder, to coat them lightly but completely. Return to the wire rack and let dry completely. Garnish the top of each peach with a mint leaf.

My mother,
Erminia, 1938

This recice was given to me by Giovanna Ruizzo, the *pasticciera* (pastry chef) of La Caveja, a charming trattoria in Pietravariano, a small town near Caserta, in the inland of Campania.

By traveling through Campania, and researching the cuisine of the region where so many immigrants came from, I felt I could better understand the Italian-American cuisine. My friend and traveling companion was Mario Picozzi—a dentist from Trieste whose only reason to be a dentist is to keep the chewing apparatus of his clients in ideal condition so they can enjoy good food—who took me to visit his friend Bernardino, who ran La Caveja. Mario loves good food and wine, making him the ideal person to travel with.

La Caveja was indeed a true Neapolitan restaurant, serving traditional regional food, made only with seasonal local products and without fuss or pretense. I spent a few days in the kitchen of La Caveja with Bernardino and Giovanna. She did not give me the exact name for this simple dessert—she just said it was a *delizia napoletana.* And that it is.

Neapolitan Delight

Delizia Napoletana

For the *Pasta Frolla*

2 cups sifted all-purpose flour

1 cup granulated sugar

Pinch salt

½ cup (1 stick) unsalted butter, at room temperature, plus more for the baking sheets if using

2 large eggs

Grated zest of 1 lemon

Make the *pasta frolla:* Sift the flour, granulated sugar, and salt onto a clean, dry work surface. Make a well in the center of the dry ingredients and add the butter, eggs, and lemon zest to the well. Work the butter and eggs together with your fingertips, then gradually begin to incorporate the flour into the egg mixture. Continue working the dough with your fingertips until smooth. Gather the dough into a ball, wrap it in plastic wrap, and refrigerate at least 30 minutes or up to 1 day.

Meanwhile, make the filling: Cut the dried figs into quarters, dropping them into a small bowl as you do. Pour the Marsala over the figs and soak, tossing from time to time, 30 minutes.

Scrape the figs and Marsala into the work bowl of a food processor fitted with the metal blade. Process the figs and wine to a smooth paste. Scrape the paste

For the Filling

1 cup dried figs (about 10)

⅓ cup dry Marsala wine

1 cup raisins

¼ cup honey

1 cup chopped walnuts

1 cup chopped almonds

Grated zest of 1 lemon

Grated zest of 1 orange

Confectioners' sugar, optional

Makes 8 servings

into a medium bowl, and stir in the raisins, honey, walnuts, almonds, and lemon and orange zest.

Lightly grease two baking sheets with butter. (This is not necessary if you're using nonstick baking sheets.) Cut the *pasta frolla* into quarters. Roll each into an 8 × 8–inch square. Spread one-fourth of the filling evenly over the square and roll it up like a jelly roll. Cut the roll crosswise into ¾-inch slices. Lay the slices flat on the prepared baking sheets and bake until the underside is deep golden brown, about 20 minutes. Remove to a wire rack to cool completely. Serve at room temperature, plain or sprinkled with powdered sugar.

Meringue Drops

Baci Bianchi

1 large egg white, at room
temperature

2 tablespoons sugar

¼ cup heavy cream

Makes about 16 drops

*These little "white kisses" are very light and not too sweet. The key
to success is to refrigerate them for the right amount of time. After
about an hour in the refrigerator, the whipped cream will have
softened the center of the meringues, but not the outsides, so you'll
have a crunchy-chewy kiss. If you leave them much longer, the
meringues will turn sticky.*

Preheat the oven to 150° F, or the lowest setting possible. Line two baking
sheets with parchment paper.

Beat the egg white in a small bowl with a wire whisk until foamy. As you continue beating, add the sugar gradually, until the meringue holds stiff and
glossy peaks when the whisk is lifted from them. Spoon the meringue into a
pastry bag fitted with a star tip and pipe onto the prepared baking sheet to
form ¾-inch rounds. (If you don't have a pastry bag, drop the beaten whites
by the slightly rounded teaspoonful, keeping the little mounds as high as
possible.) Bake until the meringues are completely dry and very light, about
2½ hours. Cool completely.

Pour the cream into a small, chilled bowl. Beat with a wire whisk or an electric mixer until the cream holds stiff peaks. Spoon about 1 teaspoon of the
whipped cream onto the flat side of one of the meringues. Press the flat side
of a second meringue gently onto the cream to make a meringue sandwich.
Repeat with the remaining meringues and cream. Chill the meringue drops
on a serving plate in the refrigerator 1 hour before serving.

Fruit Jam Tartlet Cookies

Crostata

1 ½ cups all-purpose flour, plus more as needed

¼ cup sugar

½ teaspoon baking powder

8 tablespoons (1 stick) cold unsalted butter, cut into 12 pieces, plus more for the baking sheet

1 large egg yolk

¼ cup ice water, or as needed

1 ½ cups chunky apricot, cherry, peach, or plum preserves

Makes 36 cookies

Stir 1 ½ cups flour, sugar, and baking powder together in a mixing bowl. Drop in the butter and toss to coat with the flour mixture. Using the tips of your fingers, rub the butter into the flour until the pieces of butter resemble small corn flakes. (Work quickly, to keep the butter as firm as possible.) Beat the egg yolk and ¼ cup ice water in a separate, small bowl until blended. Drizzle over the flour-butter mixture and toss just until you have a rough dough. Don't overmix. If there are some pieces of unmoistened dough, drizzle more ice water, about 1 teaspoon at a time, over the dough, and toss lightly to mix. Turn out onto a work surface and knead lightly a few times, just to gather the dough into a ball. Wrap the dough tightly in plastic wrap, and refrigerate at least 1 hour or up to 1 day.

Lightly butter a 9 × 13–inch baking sheet. Preheat the oven to 350° F. Cut off and set aside one-third of the dough. Roll out the remaining two-thirds of the dough on a lightly floured surface to a 10 × 14–inch rectangle. (Don't worry if it's not perfectly shaped—you'll have a chance to patch the dough.) Flour the surface lightly, as necessary to keep the dough from sticking. Transfer the dough to the prepared pan, covering the bottom completely and pressing the dough along the sides. Trim any overhanging dough, and use the pieces to patch any holes and gaps. Spoon the preserves in an even layer over the dough. Roll out the remaining dough to a circle about 10 inches in diameter. Cut the dough into ½-inch strips. Form a lattice pattern over the preserves with the strips of dough by arranging half of them diagonally, then laying the second half of the dough strips perpendicular to the first. Bake until the dough is golden brown, about 25 minutes. Remove, and cool completely before cutting into squares. *Crostate* can be stored in an airtight container at room temperature for up to 3 days.

The Ritual of Coffee

Il Rito del Caffè

COFFEE HAS BEEN A SOCIAL DRINK FOR SOME TIME. It originated in Ethiopia, East Africa, and spread east in the thirteenth century. During its westward march it was first roasted and drunk as an infusion, as we know it today.

The very first coffeehouse was established in Constantinople in 1554. The Venetians, who are thought to have established the first European coffeehouse, *Bottega del Coffe* (coffee store), brought coffee to Italy in the 1580s; coffee and Italy have been inseparable ever since.

The success of coffee was immediate. Coffee spread throughout Italy and Europe and became known as the drink *dello spirito* or "of the soul." Soon coffeehouses became meeting places for politicians, literary figures, and businessmen; coffee became the drink of intellectuals.

It is impossible today to walk in an Italian city and not be lured by the wafting aroma of *caffè*. Italians drink it in small, concentrated doses often; in fact it is quite normal for an Italian to take a break and have coffee three to four times daily. The art of coffeemaking is a true culture in Italy today.

It is said in Italy that in order to make a good cup of espresso, you need to master the four "M's":

1. *Macchina*   Each coffeemaker yields a slightly different taste
2. *Miscela*   The right blend and roast of coffee beans
3. *Macinadosatore* The right grind of coffee in the maker
4. *Mano*   The human element; that special touch

Espresso Coffeemakers

When it comes to espresso coffeemakers, there are three principal types:

The Napoletana is a three-part pot, made up of two containers—one with a spout—and a basket insert. Fill the plain container with water and top with the basket insert packed with ground coffee and seal. Screw the spouted container onto the top of the filter basket. At this point, the spout is pointing downward. Place the entire unit over high heat. When the water boils, invert and remove from heat. Let drip and pour.

The Moka is another three-part pot, with a top, bottom, and filter basket. Fill the base with water, insert the basket packed with ground coffee, and screw on the top tightly. When the water boils, steam is funneled upward through the grounds to condense as coffee in the top compartment of the pot. Be sure to lower the flame as soon as the steam starts rising.

The espresso machine was invented by Italians. Water is literally "pressed" through the coffee grounds under high pressure. This allows for the freshest coffee, prepared in individual servings, using fresh grounds for each cup. A characteristic of coffee made with an espresso machine is the dense foam on the top of the coffee as a result of the strong pressure produced by the machine.

Tips for Making a Good Cup of Coffee

1. Choose a good espresso coffee mix (*miscela*). Store beans in a well-sealed glass or opaque container. When choosing beans, it is often recommended to select those that are *veste di frate*—the color of a monk's robe. Avoid very dark colored beans and those that are excessively shiny. The best blends come from such reputable makers as Illy Caffe, Lavazza, and Crem Caffe—the blending and roasting of varietal beans is what makes each brand unique.
2. Grind the beans very fine just before using them.
3. If your tap water has too much calcium or other minerals, use bottled water.
4. Use a coffeemaker that will make only the number of cups needed.
5. Water temperature should reach just below the boiling point—200°F.
6. Use 1 tablespoon (¼ to ½ ounce) of coffee per cup.
7. Warm pot before beginning, and serve coffee in warmed cups. Serve immediately. Drink hot. Do not reheat espresso.

Creamy Espresso—Without an Espresso Machine

Whether you are making espresso in a Napoletana, where the boiling water is poured over the espresso grounds and the coffee slowly drips into the bottom of a container, or a Moka, where the water boils up from the bottom and seeps through the coffee into a top receptacle, you can produce a good cup of espresso. However, they will not give you the foam (*crema*) that an espresso machine creates.

There is a very simple way to achieve that special, creamy espresso flavor without an actual espresso machine.

To augment the creaminess, place $1\frac{1}{2}$ teaspoons of sugar per cup of coffee and $\frac{1}{4}$ teaspoon of the first drips of coffee in a small bowl (for example, 6 teaspoons of sugar and 1 teaspoon of the first drips of coffee). While the remainder of the coffee is dripping, whisk vigorously with a fork to form a creamy, frothy caramel-colored type of zabaglione. When you serve the coffee, set $1\frac{1}{2}$ teaspoons of this mixture in each cup, then pour in the coffee, and let the guests stir and enjoy; a nice froth should rise to the top of the cup. Obviously this can be done only for guests who take sugar in their coffee.

Italy's most famous coffee is deep, dark espresso—served in thimble-sized portions and packing a wallop of satisfying flavor. However, there are a number of variations on simple espresso that are worth trying when you find them on a menu:

Caffè Ristretto	*Espresso, more concentrated—less water*
Caffè Lungo	*"Long" coffee—extended with more water*
Caffè Macchiato	*With just a touch of steamed milk*
Caffè Latte	*Scalded milk with coffee, usually served in the morning*
Cappuccino	*Coffee topped with the foam of steamed milk; usually served mid-morning—not after dinner.*
Caffè Corretto	*Coffee "corrected" with a bit of grappa, cognac, or other spirit*

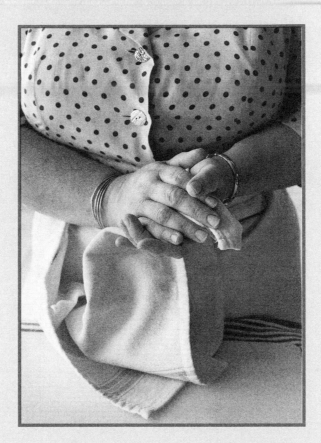

Tutti a tavola a mangiare.

Let's all go to the table and eat.

Index

cheese (*cont.*)

pizza Margherita made with fresh tomatoes and sliced mozzarella, 204

prosciutto-stuffed mozzarella, 55

ravioli stuffed with ricotta and spinach, 186–7

ricotta cheesecake, 371

ricotta frittata, 36

ricotta gnocchi with contessa sauce, 176–7

salad of dandelion greens with almond vinaigrette and dried ricotta, 64

scallopine with eggplant and Fontina cheese, 258–9

tomato and mozzarella risotto, 196

traditional St. Joseph's ricotta cream puffs, 376–7

veal chops stuffed with asparagus and Fontina, 221

veal chops stuffed with Taleggio and broccoli, 220–1

side dishes for, 348

whole-wheat pasta with sausages, leeks, and shredded Fontina, 121

ziti with roasted eggplant and ricotta cheese, 152–3

cheesecake, ricotta, 371

cherries, *amarene*, 388

chicken

breast of chicken in a light lemon-herb sauce, 270

chicken and mushroom risotto, 197–8

chicken and rice soup, 75

chicken bites with potato, sausages, and vinegar, 264–5

chicken breast Valdostana with braised lentils, 271–2

side dishes for, 348

chicken cacciatore, 260–1

chicken *parmigiana*, new-style, 266–7

chicken *parmigiana*, old-style, 267

chicken *scarpariello*, 262–3

side dishes for, 56

chicken stock, 74

recipes using, 16, 18–19, 21–2, 26–8, 72, 77, 78–9, 81, 112, 114, 118–19, 120, 121, 128, 138, 142–3, 165–7, 174, 175, 183, 184–5, 195–6, 218–19, 220–1, 230–1, 244, 247, 252, 253, 254, 255, 258–9, 262–3, 268–9, 270, 271–2, 326, 348, 351

entrees, 260–73

ravioli with meat filling, 188–9

"reinforced" soup, 78–9

rice salad with chicken and vegetables, 66

roasted Cornish hen with balsamic glaze, 268–9

sage leaves attached to, 272

seared sage-marinated breast of chicken, 273

see also scallopine

chickpeas

chickpea and tuna salad, 46

chickpea and white-bean soup, 88–9

chocolate

chocolate soup, 383

chocolate zabaglione, 382

hazelnut-chocolate ice cream truffle, 390–1

San Martino pear and chocolate tart, 368–9

clam juice, 193

clams

agnolotti with crabmeat and shrimp in clam sauce, 192–3

baked clams oreganata, 8

escarole

escarole and white-bean soup, 86–7

side dishes for, 53

escarole braised with oil and garlic, 323

espresso, *see* coffee

F

fazzoletti, 168

fennel

braised fennel, 339

cracking fennel seeds, 358

crunchy, fennel-scented bread rings, 357–8

cutting technique, 338

Italian-American fennel sausage, 241

shells with fennel and shrimp, 126

fettuccine

cutting fresh dough, 180

fettuccine Alfredo, 184–5

Fontina cheese, 266

fried Fontina and prosciutto-wrapped asparagus, 29–30

scallopine with eggplant and Fontina cheese, 258–9

veal chops stuffed with asparagus and Fontina, 221

whole-wheat pasta with sausages, leeks, and shredded Fontina, 121

fra diavolo sauce, 130–1

fregola, 286

Frenching technique, 234

frittatas

artichoke and bread frittata, 36

potato and pepper frittata, 35–6

ricotta frittata, 36

fritters, salt cod, 24–5

fruit

baked peaches with amaretti filling, 370

breast of chicken in a light lemon-herb sauce, 270

caramel-pear sauce, 369

egg-battered scallopine with lemon sauce, 255

fillet of fresh cod with lemon-parsley sauce, 300–1

fruit jam tartlet cookies, 401

lemon delight, 374–5

lemon ice, 386

oven-braised pork chops with red onions and pears, 232–3

roasted pears and grapes, 382

San Martino pear and chocolate tart, 368–9

scallopine in lemon-caper sauce, 254

sweetbreads with lemon and capers, 230–1

frying techniques, 28

fusilli

fusilli as made by ladies of the evening, 116–17

long fusilli with mussels, saffron, and zucchini, 128–9

G

garlic

broccoli rabe with oil and garlic, 325

garlic-infused oil, 17

recipes using, 12, 16

garlic mashed potatoes, 345

pan-fried garlic bread, 53

dishes for serving with, 317

roasted root vegetables, 341

sautéed summer vegetables, 332–3

R

radicchio
  radicchio risotto, 198
  radicchio zuccherino salad, 62
  tri-color salad, 57
radishes, sautéed whole, 348
ragù, 26–7
ravioli
  making ravioli, 190–1
  ravioli stuffed with ricotta and
    spinach, 186–7
  ravioli with meat filling, 188–9
red-mullet stew, capellini cooked
    in, 132
"reinforced" soup, 78–9
ribollita, 94–5
rice
  chicken and rice soup, 75
  rice and spring pea soup, 77
  rice salad Caprese, 65–6
  rice salad with chicken and veg-
    etables, 66
  rice salad with seafood and
    capers, 67
  rice-stuffed tomatoes, 280–1
  rice timbales, 352
  stuffed rice balls, 26–8
  see also risotto
ricotta cheese
  baked stuffed shells, 154–5
  calzones, 206–7
  crepe "lasagna" filled with
    spinach and herbs, 158–9
  facts about, 160
  Felidia's stacked cannoli, 380–1
  grain and ricotta pie, 372–3
  Italian-American lasagna, 156–7
  manicotti, 163–4
  ravioli stuffed with ricotta and
    spinach, 186–7
  ricotta cheesecake, 371

ricotta frittata, 36
ricotta gnocchi with contessa
    sauce, 176–7
salad of dandelion greens with
    almond vinaigrette and dried
    ricotta, 64
traditional St. Joseph's ricotta
    cream puffs, 376–7
ziti with roasted eggplant and
    ricotta cheese, 152–3
rigatoni
  braised oxtail with rigatoni, 142–3
  braised pork ribs with rigatoni,
    245
  rigatoni woodsman-style, 112
risotto, 194
  basic risotto, 195–6
    simple additions to, 197
  chicken and mushroom risotto,
    197–8
  radicchio risotto, 198
  saffron and clam risotto, 196–7
  shrimp and leek risotto, 198
  tomato and mozzarella risotto,
    196
romaine lettuce
  Caesar salad, 58–9
rosemary and vinegar, white beans
    with, 350

S

saffron
  long fusilli with mussels, saffron,
    and zucchini, 128–9
  saffron and clam risotto, 196–7
sage
  butter-sage sauce, 187
  seared sage-marinated breast of
    chicken, 273
sage leaves attached to chicken,
    272

A Note on the Type

The text of this book was set in a typeface called Didot, designed by the celebrated typographer Adrian Frutiger for Linotype in 1992. Didot is a revival of the typefaces of the eminent Parisian printer, publisher, and typefounder Firmin Didot (1764–1836). A contemporary of Giambattista Bodoni, Didot cut what many consider to be the first typeface of the Modern genus, a neoclassical form of letter characterized by horizontal stress, flat unbracketed serifs, and substantial stems flowing into extremely thin hairlines.

Composed by
North Market Street Graphics, Lancaster, Pennsylvania

Printed and bound by
R. R. Donnelley and Sons, Crawfordsville, Indiana

Designed by
Ralph L. Fowler